Black and Ethnic Leaderships in Britain

In the struggle for cultural autonomy and political influence, ethnic and black activists play a primary, and yet little analysed, role. *Black and Ethnic Leaderships in Britain* is the first book to compare different forms of leadership in Britain's black and ethnic minority communities, which mainly originate from the Caribbean and South Asia. The essays in this book create an unusual blend of current anthropological, sociological and historical theory with analyses of specific social situations and richly documented case studies. These studies highlight the rhetoric leaders use and the conflicts in which ethnic groups are embroiled. They demonstrate that culture and ideology are constituted in practice, and that political discourse must be understood as sited communication. The leaders described in this book form a vanguard in diverse urban movements, all seeking local – as well as national – group autonomy and influence in relation to the state and local state. Many are fighting to establish the validity of a 'black' experience of racism that transcends ethnic boundaries. Yet, at the same time, the need to forge broader alliances is equally compelling. So too is the authenticity of specific cultural, religious or class claims which underlie the complex nature of ethnic organisation, and the dilemmas and choices leaders face.

This is a highly topical work: it examines central debates in today's multi-ethnic and multi-racial societies. While it focuses on Britain, the experiences and processes it documents are general and worldwide. *Black and Ethnic Leaderships in Britain* thus addresses central questions in urban and political anthropology and sociology. It will be invaluable to anyone interested in the relationship between culture, agency and political action.

Pnina Werbner and Muhammad Anwar have both written extensively on migration and ethnicity in Britain and bring their respective expertise to bear on the present theme. Pnina Werbner is a Research Associate in the Department of Sociology at Manchester University, and Muhammad Anwar is the Director of the Centre for Research in Ethnic Relations at the University of Warwick.

Black and Ethnic Leaderships in Britain

The cultural dimensions of political action

Edited by

Pnina Werbner

and

Muhammad Anwar

London and New York

First published 1991
by Routledge
11 New Fetter Lane, London EC4P 4EE

Simultaneously published in the USA and Canada
by Routledge
a division of Routledge, Chapman and Hall, Inc.
29 West 35th Street, New York, NY 10001

Typeset by NWL Editorial Services, Langport, Somerset

**Printed and bound in Great Britain by
Billings & Sons Limited, Worcester**

British Library Cataloguing in Publication Data
Black and ethnic leaderships in Britain.
  1. Great Britain. Coloured persons. Political aspects
  I. Werbner, Pnina *1944–*   II. Anwar, Muhammad
  305.800941

Library of Congress Cataloging in Publication Data
Black and ethnic leaderships in Britain: the cultural dimensions
  of political action/ edited by Pnina Werbner and Muhammad
  Anwar.
  p.   cm.   Includes bibliographical references.
  1.   Blacks – Great Britain – Politics and government.
  2.   Minorities – Great Britain – Political activity.   3. Political
  leadership – Great Britain.   4. Great Britain – Politics and
  government – 1979.   5. Politics and culture – Great Britain
  I.   Werbner, Pnina   II. Anwar, Muhammad
  DA125.N4B52   1990   90-8530
  323.1'196041 – dc20   CIP

ISBN 0-415-04166-X

Contents

DA
125
.N4
B52
1990

209109

List of contributors   vii

**Introduction I   The context of leadership: migration,
settlement and racial discrimination**   1
Muhammad Anwar

**Introduction II   Black and ethnic leaderships in
Britain: a theoretical overview**   15
Pnina Werbner

Part one   Community, Party Politics, and the Black Experience

1   **Ethnic minorities' representation: voting and electoral
politics in Britain, and the role of leaders**   41
Muhammad Anwar

2   **Black Sections in the Labour Party: the end of ethnicity
and 'godfather' politics?**   63
Sydney Jeffers

3   **The political construction of class and community:
Bangladeshi political leadership in Tower Hamlets,
East London**   84
John Eade

Part two   Culture Politicised: Protest and Autonomy

4   **The fiction of unity in ethnic politics: apects of
representation and the state among British Pakistanis**   113
Pnina Werbner

5   **Red Star over Leicester: racism, the politics of
identity, and black youth in Britain**   146
Sallie Westwood

v

Contents

6 **Drama and politics in the development of a
London Carnival** 170
Abner Cohen

7 **Striking a bargain: political radicalism in a
middle-class London borough** 203
Iris Kalka

8 **Competing to give, competing to get: Gujarati Jains
in Britain** 226
Marcus Banks

Part three   Community Associations and the National Context

9 **Organisational splits and political ideology in
the Indian Workers Associations** 253
Sasha Josephides

10 **The churches, leadership, and ethnic minorities** 277
Mark R.D. Johnson

11 **The offence of the West Indian: political leadership
and the communal option** 296
Harry Goulbourne

Name Index 323

Subject index 328

Contributors

Muhammad Anwar is Director of the Centre for Research in Ethnic Relations at the University of Warwick, United Kingdom. He has written extensively on ethnic and race relations. His publications include *Between Two Cultures* (Community Relations Commission, 1976), *The Myth of Return* (Heinemann, 1979), *Ethnic Minority Broadcasting* (Commission for Racial Equality, 1983), and *Race and Politics* (Tavistock, 1986). Dr Anwar's research interests include political participation of ethnic minorities, young people and the media.

Marcus Banks gained his doctorate in anthropology at the University of Cambridge in 1985 and went on to train at the National Film and Television School. He has conducted fieldwork and made films in England and India, and, more recently, in Hungary. He has published various articles on the Jains of India and England in academic journals, and is currently preparing a book on the ethnography of Jain religious organisation. He teaches anthropology at the University of Oxford.

Abner Cohen, Emeritus Professor of Anthropology in the University of London, carried out field studies in West Africa, the Near East and Britain, with particular focus on the relations between cultural forms and political formations. He authored *Arab Border Villages in Israel* (1965), *Custom and Politics in Urban Africa* (1969), *Two-Dimensional Man* (1974), *The Politics of Elite Culture* (1981), and edited and introduced *Urban Ethnicity* (1974).

John Eade is a Senior Lecturer in Social Anthropology at the Roehampton Institute, London. He followed research on the educated Bengali Muslim middle class in Calcutta with a study of the politics of Bangladeshi Community Representation in Tower Hamlets. He has authored *The Politics of Community* (Gower, 1989), co-edited, with the late Michael Sallnow, *Contesting the Sacred: The*

Anthropology of Christian Pilgrimage (Routledge, 1991), and has written several academic articles.

Harry Goulbourne is a Senior Research Fellow at the Centre for Research in Ethnic Relations, University of Warwick. For over ten years he lectured in politics at the University of Dar es Salaam (Tanzania) and the University of the West Indies (Jamaica), and has published extensively on the politics of these regions. He has also taught at the University of Warwick. His main publications include *Politics and State in the Third World* (Macmillan, 1979), *Teachers, Education and Politics in Britain* (Macmillan, 1988) and *Black Politics in Britain* (Gower, 1990). Whilst continuing to publish on African and Caribbean politics Gouldbourne's immediate research interests are in ethnicity and politics in Britain. His *Nationalism and Ethnicity in Post-Imperial Britain* is currently being published.

Sydney Jeffers is 33 years old, lives in Clapton, supports the Arsenal, and works as a Research Fellow at the School for Advanced Urban Studies University of Bristol. His current research includes an examination of multi-racial community involvement initiatives for the Home Office. He is also looking at attempts to construct a new black social policy lobby.

Sasha Josephides is a Social Anthropologist whose doctoral dissertation was based on fieldwork in Papua New Guinea. For the past eight years she has been studying ethnic organisation in Britain, and the present paper is based on research carried out between 1985 and 1989, while she was a research fellow at the Centre for Research in Ethnic Relations at the University of Warwick. Her recent publications include several chapters on Greek Cypriot and Indian organisations in Britain, and she is currently completing a book on the Indian Workers Association. She currently lives in Toronto, Canada.

Mark Johnson is a Senior Research Fellow in the Centre for Research in Ethnic Relations at the University of Warwick. His interests include the role of the voluntary sector in the delivery of welfare services, and the role of the churches in a multi-racial and multi-cultural society. Recent publications include chapters on social mobility of Afro-Caribbean migrants in Britain, and on housing, the churches, and social services, and he has co-authored *A Tree God Planted*, a study of black people and the methodist church.

Iris Kalka completed her doctorate on Gujaratis in Harrow at the London School of Economics in 1987. In Israel, where she lectured (1987–9) in the Public Health and Community Medicine School of the Hebrew University, she has conducted research on Ethiopian Jewish immigrants, and has published several journal articles and book chapters on British Gujaratis and Ethiopian Jews. She is currently completing a book on Gujaratis in Britain. Her special interest is in the cultural transformation of food habits and the symbolic aspects of food and cuisine among immigrants.

Pnina Werbner is a Research Associate in the Department of Sociology, University of Manchester and presently is a Research Fellow with the Leverhulme Foundation. She has conducted fieldwork in Britain and Pakistan, and is currently working on the extension of Sufi cults into Britain and the local political aspects of Islamic revival. She is the author of *The Migration Process: Capital, Gifts and Offerings among British Pakistanis* (Berg, 1990), co-editor of *Economy and Culture in Pakistan: Migrants and Cities in a Muslim Society* (Macmillan, 1990) and editor of *Person, Myth and Society in South Asian Islam* (special issue of *Social analysis*, 1990), and has published extensively in academic journals and collections.

Sallie Westwood teaches at the University of Leicester. Her publications include *All Day, Every Day: Factory and Family in the Making of Women's Lives* and, with Parminder Bhachu, *Enterprising Women: Ethnicity, Economy and Gender Relations* (Routledge, 1988). Currently she is involved in a research project on racism and mental health with the Leicester Black Mental Health Group.

Introduction I

The context of leadership
Migration, settlement and racial discrimination

Muhammad Anwar

Over the centuries, Britain has received and absorbed large numbers of people from other countries and many Britons went abroad to the colonies as rulers, administrators, soldiers, business people, etc., to represent the Empire. But it is only in the last forty years that Britain has received in significant numbers from the former colonies workers and their dependants whose colour differs from that of the indigenous population. The main sources of this immigration are the New Commonwealth countries (including Pakistan) of the Indian subcontinent and the West Indies. The estimated present-day number of ethnic minorities is about 5 per cent of the total population of 54 million. Of these, almost 50 per cent are now British born. Thus, half of the ethnic minority population is not 'immigrant' but native born British and most of the others now have British nationality.

Migration

Commonwealth citizens had free entry into Britain under the Commonwealth rules. With the colonial links and the knowledge about Britain of several thousands of soldiers and seamen from the West Indies and India during the Second World War, some of them decided to stay in Britain and others came back to work in the expanding industry after the war. They were initially welcomed by the British public as allies, who had defended their nation (Cabinet Papers 1950). Before this seamen had come to this country for many years, thus founding ethnic minority communities in the ports – notably Bristol, Cardiff, and Liverpool. However, the start of post-war mass migration was the arrival of the *Empire Windrush* ship in June 1948. It docked at Tilbury with 492 immigrants from Jamaica; most of these had been in Britain during the war, had returned to the Caribbean and were unable to secure work either there or in the USA. After this the immigration progressed slowly and during the

1950s the number of immigrants from the West Indies increased, reaching an annual rate of 30,000 in 1955 and 1956. Although the Conservative Party, elected to power in 1951, encouraged both immigration and emigration, some concern was expressed about the number of coloured immigrants. Nevertheless, the government's policy was clear even in 1954, as Henry Hopkinson, Minister of State for the Colonies, said:

> in a world in which restriction on personal movement and migration have increased we can still take pride in the fact that a man can say *Civis Britannicus Sum* whatever his colour may be, and we take pride in the fact that he wants to and can come to the mother country.
>
> (Hansard, 5 November 1954, col. 827)

However, as pressure for immigration control grew, the Conservative Party changed from its policy of free entry for all Commonwealth citizens to a policy of immigration control, publishing a Bill on 1 November 1961 to restrict immigration. The pressures and debates which led to the Commonwealth Immigrants Act of 1962 have been discussed elsewhere (Rose *et al.* 1969).

As the debate on immigration control started, more and more West Indians emigrated to Britain to beat the impending ban. For example, between the beginning of 1961 and the middle of 1962, when the Commonwealth Immigrants Act came into force, 98,000 persons emigrated to Britain from the West Indies. Immigration from India and Pakistan started later than that from the West Indies, but also reached a high level from 1960 onwards as people tried to enter Britain before the ban. The figures for the intercensal period of 1951–61 show that the number of New Commonwealth immigrants doubled from 276,000 to 541,000. Those who came to Britain during this period were economically active persons. They included a high proportion of women among the West Indians, while the overwhelming majority of the Indians and Pakistanis were men.

The voucher system which was introduced under the 1962 Act gave the opportunity for those who were already here to arrange jobs and vouchers for their relatives and friends. This increased the element of sponsorship and patronage. Dependants of those already in Britain were allowed to come without vouchers. As a result, between July 1962 and December 1968 only 77,966 voucher holders were admitted compared with 257,220 dependants. This led to the establishment of small ethnic communities in the settlement areas, reinforced by kinship and friendship bonds (Anwar 1979)

Between 1969 and 1971, out of 318,521 people arriving for settlement from the New Commonwealth countries, 259,646 were dependants and only 58,875 were male workers. This pattern of decline for male workers, and now for dependants as well, has continued. For example, the 'primary' immigration, i.e. men accepted here on arrival – 17,900 in 1972 – was reduced to a trickle – 1,700 in 1982 – and has now virtually stopped. Even the number of dependants, women, and children arriving was more than halved from about 50,000 in 1972 to about 23,000 in 1982. In 1988 it was further reduced to 6,320 dependants accepted for settlement on arrival. Total immigration from the New Commonwealth countries and Pakistan (NCWP) had declined sharply from 68,000 in 1972 to 24,800 in 1984 and 22,700 in 1988. On the basis of these figures it is fair to conclude that large-scale immigration from the NCWP countries is now over. On the other hand, between 1971 and 1983 more people had left Britain than had entered it. Overall, the net loss of population by migration during this period was 465,000, mainly as a result of emigration to Australia, Canada, South Africa, and the EC countries.

It is worth mentioning here that the British public's reaction to immigration from the NCWP was the same as it had been to the previous waves of migrations (for details see Anwar 1979). Signs such as 'All blacks go home' and 'Send them back' were quite common. 'Paki-bashing' and other anti-immigrant demonstrations and activities are still common. The British Campaign to Stop Immigration and the actions of the National Front and British National Party have been prime examples in this context. Racial attacks and racial harassment are unpleasant facts of life for many ethnic minorities as are racial discrimination and racial disadvantage because of their colour and religious and cultural backgrounds (CRE 1987: Home Office 1981, 1989). Therefore, as migrants became settlers, discrimination in employment, housing, and other areas became a daily reality for ethnic minorities.

Demographic characteristics

Ethnic minorities are not evenly distributed throughout the country. They are mainly settled in inner-city and industrial areas, as most of them came to Britain as economic migrants. This applied both to those who initially had freedom of movement and to those who came through government and employers' recruitment efforts.

In 1981, 56 per cent of ethnic minorities were found in London and the South East, 23 per cent in the Midlands, 16 per cent in the North and North West, 4 per cent in the South West and Wales, with relatively few (2 per cent) in Scotland (OPCS 1983). The contrast between the general population in Greater London and the South

Table 1 Persons resident in private households: total population and persons with head of household born in the New Commonwealth and Pakistan (NCWP)

GB regions	Total population No.	(%)	NCWP population No.	(%)	NCWP % of total population
Scotland	4,954,32	(9.4)	46,188	(2.1)	0.9
North, Yorkshire & Humberside, and North West	14,075,451	(26.7)	349,286	(15.8)	2.5
Midlands and East Anglia	10,598,267	(20.1)	495,943	(22.5)	4.7
South East:					
Greater London	6,492,642	(12.3)	945,148	(42.8)	14.6
Remainder	9,759,911	(18.5)	282,606	(12.8)	2.9
South West and Wales	6,879,732	(13.0)	88,074	(4.0)	1.3
	52,760,331	(100)	2,207,245	(100)	4.2

Source: Registrar General, Scotland, and OPCS, Census 1981: National Report, Great Britain, part I, Table 11, HMSO, 1983

East (31 per cent) and the ethnic minority population (56 per cent) is particularly marked as shown in Table 1. Moreover, they are heavily concentrated within these regions.

The 1981 census figures show that of the 2.2 million ethnic minority population, an estimated 1.2 million (55 per cent) are of Asian origin, about 0.55 million (25 per cent) are of Afro-Caribbean origin, and the remaining 20 per cent of ethnic minorities have their origin in South-East Asia, the Mediterranean, and other parts of the New Commonwealth (see Table 2).

The recent Labour Force Surveys show a similar pattern, that just under one-third of the ethnic minority population are of Indian origin, just over a quarter are of West Indian, Guyanese, and African origin and one-fifth are of Pakistani and Bangladeshi origin (OPCS 1987).

Further analysis of the 1981 census data shows that Afro-Caribbeans were highly concentrated in the South East (65 per cent) with over half of these (56 per cent) in the Greater London area. Nearly half (48 per cent) of Indians were also living in the South East; as were 57 per cent of Bangladeshis and 65 per cent of East African Asians, but only 31 per cent of Pakistanis. Almost two-thirds of the total population of Pakistani origin live in the conurbations of the West Midlands (22 per cent), Yorkshire and Humberside (21 per cent), and the North West (16 per cent). As mentioned above, the

Table 2   Persons resident in private households with head of household born
in the NCWP, by country of origin

	All persons		
	Born inside UK	*Born outside UK*	*Total persons*
Caribbean	273,558	272,186	545,744	(24.7)*
India	261,206	412,498	673,704	(30.5)
Pakistan	118,252	177,209	295,461	(13.4)
Bangladesh	16,939	47,662	64,561	(2.9)
East Africa	48,673	132,648	181,321	(8.2)
Far East	39,742	80,381	120,123	(5.4)
Mediterranean	79,315	90,763	170,078	(7.7)
Remainder	57,907	98,346	156,253	(7.2)
Total NCWP	895,592	1,311,653	2,207,245	(100)

Source: Registrar General, Scotland, and OPCS, census 1981: National Report,
       Great Britain, part I, Table 11, HMSO, 1983.
Note: * Figures in parentheses = Great Britain %

settlement patterns of the ethnic minorities were determined by the availability of work in different areas. Also the settlement patterns in various regions and in some cities and towns within these regions are not a chance phenomenon. They came about as a result of the active kin–friend 'chain migration' (Anwar 1979).

The migration from NCWP countries was initially predominantly male. Now the balance of sexes among Afro-Caribbeans is almost the same as for the general population, but there is still a relatively high ratio of men to women in the Asian communities, particularly among Pakistanis and Bangladeshis. However, with the arrival of dependants from the Indian sub-continent, the Asian sex ratio is moving towards that of the rest of the population.

Ethnic minority households are larger, mostly four persons, than those in the rest of the population, mostly one or two persons. Among ethnic minorities, Indian, Pakistani, and Bangladeshi households tend to be the largest. For example, 60 per cent of Pakistani or Bangladeshi households have five or more persons compared with 9 per cent of white households. West Indian households, on the other hand, comprising three persons, tend to be only slightly larger (18 per cent) than white households (17 per cent). The average household size among Asians is 4.9 persons and for West Indians 3.0 persons compared with 2.6 persons for all ethnic groups. (OPCS 1986; see Figure 1 for details).

The 1981 census and the recent Labour Force Surveys' data show that the ethnic minority population has a different age structure from the white population, the ethnic minority population is younger, and

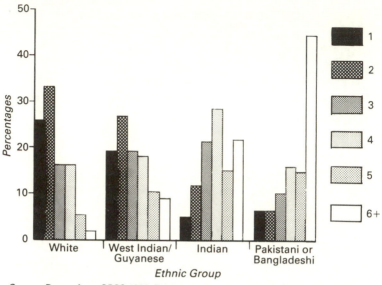

Source: Drawn from OPCS 1985, Table 5.9

Figure 1 Household size, by ethnic group of head of household, UK, Spring
1984

that there is also variation in age structure between different ethnic
groups. For example, only 3 per cent of the ethnic population is over
state pension age, compared with 19 per cent of the white population. One-third are under 16, compared with one-fifth of the white
population. The proportion of under-16s is around half of the
Pakistani and Bangladeshi populations. Table 3 shows the age structure
of the population.

Table 3 also shows an increasing number (43 per cent) of the
ethnic minority population born and growing up in this country.
According to the 1981 census, almost 93 per cent of ethnic minority
children aged 0–4 and 81 per cent of those aged 5–15 were born in
Britain. The majority, 60 per cent, aged 16–19, were also born in this
country. Although 43 per cent of ethnic minority populations in Britain were born in this country, there are differences between the two
main groups, the West Indians and Asians. Over half of the West Indians were born in this country compared with under 40 per cent of
Asians. One reason for this is the difference in timing of the principal
migration period for the two groups. Table 4 gives the age structure
by sex from the 1985–7 Labour Force Surveys.

Table 3a Persons resident in private households: total male population and males with head of household born in the NCWP, age distribution, by country of origin

Males age	Total male population		Total NCWP males		Caribbean		India		Pakistan		Bangladesh		East Africa		Remainder	
0–4	1,646,866	(6.4)*	121,107	(10.7)	18,462	(7.0)	34,686	(10.2)	28,106	(17.4)	5,945	(14.9)	11,546	(12.6)	22,362	(9.7)
5–15	4,450,302	(17.3)	258,110	(22.9)	67,757	(25.6)	79,663	(23.4)	43,176	(26.8)	8,833	(22.1)	15,787	(17.2)	42,894	(18.7)
16–19	1,768,867	(6.9)	95,852	(8.5)	35,568	(13.4)	26,726	(7.9)	8,645	(5.4)	2,489	(6.2)	5,645	(6.1)	16,799	(7.3)
20–29	3,735,081	(14.5)	212,517	(18.8)	37,119	(14.0)	59,803	(17.6)	29,924	(18.6)	6,604	(16.5)	24,149	(26.3)	54,918	(23.9)
30–44	5,209,181	(20.3)	220,936	(19.5)	42,986	(16.2)	66,179	(19.4)	26,138	(16.2)	7,706	(19.3)	23,758	(25.8)	54,169	(23.6)
45–64	5,797,328	(22.6)	189,475	(16.8)	57,814	(21.8)	59,524	(17.5)	23,127	(14.3)	7,996	(20.0)	9,207	(10.0)	31,807	(13.9)
65 +	3,073,799	(12.0)	30,718	(2.8)	5,530	(2.0)	14,074	(4.0)	2,166	(1.3)	420	(1.0)	1,845	(2.0)	6,683	(2.9)
All ages	25,681,424	(100)	1,128,715	(100)	265,236	(100)	340,655	(100)	161,282	(100)	39,993	(100)	91,937	(100)	229,612	(100)

Note: * Figures in parentheses = Great Britain %

Table 3b Persons resident in private households: total female population and females with head of household born in the NCWP, age distribution, by country of origin

Females age	Total female population		Total NCWP females		Caribbean		India		Pakistan		Bangladesh		East Africa		Remainder	
0–4	1,564,277	(5.8)*	115,813	(10.7)	18,052	(6.3)	33,499	(10.1)	26,604	(19.8)	5,579	(22.7)	10,857	(12.2)	21,222	(9.8)
5–15	4,231,300	(15.6)	242,977	(22.5)	67,767	(24.2)	76,349	(22.9)	35,989	(26.8)	6,318	(25.7)	15,611	(17.5)	40,943	(18.9)
16–19	1,718,776	(6.4)	92,183	(8.6)	35,786	(12.8)	26,022	(7.8)	7,184	(5.4)	1,324	(5.4)	5,608	(6.3)	16,259	(7.5)
20–29	3,689,750	(13.6)	215,828	(20.0)	46,710	(16.7)	59,434	(17.9)	27,594	(20.6)	4,687	(19.1)	25,374	(28.4)	52,029	(24.0)
30–44	5,187,626	(19.2)	225,844	(20.9)	57,444	(20.5)	65,790	(21.0)	22,590	(16.8)	4,890	(19.9)	20,519	(23.0)	50,611	(23.3)
45–59	4,627,979	(17.0)	129,846	(12.1)	44,047	(15.7)	42,558	(12.8)	11,215	(8.4)	1,507	(6.1)	7,703	(8.5)	22,816	(10.5)
60 +	6,059,199	(22.4)	56,039	(5.2)	10,702	(3.8)	25,397	(7.5)	3,003	(2.2)	263	(1.1)	3,712	(4.1)	12,962	(6.0)
All ages	27,078,907	(100)	1,078,530	(100)	280,508	(100)	333,049	(100)	134,179	(100)	24,568	(100)	89,384	(100)	216,842	(100)

Note: * Figures in parentheses = Great Britain %
Source: OPCS, Census 1981: Country of Birth, Great Britain, Table 3, HMSO, 1983

Table 4 Age structure, by sex, of ethnic groups

	Males %				Females %			
	Under 16	16–29	30–44	45+	Under 16	16–29	3 0–44	45+
White	21	23	21	35	19	21	20	40
Indian	32	24	24	20	31	30	23	16
West Indian	26	31	13	30	25	35	18	23
Pakistani	42	22	19	16	44	28	17	12
Bangladeshi	50	19	11	21	50	23	19	8
African	28	30	27	15	24	32	30	14
Chinese	30	28	26	16	28	23	34	15
Arab	18	36	28	17	25	35	24	16
Mixed	54	26	10	9	55	27	10	8
Other	28	27	29	15	26	28	31	16

Source: Adapted from Haskey 1988: 31, Table 3

The position of ethnic minorities in the labour market is a fundamental aspect of their position in British society. The type of work available to them not merely governs their incomes, it also helps to determine in which area they live, where their children go to school, how they interact with the indigenous population, their chances of participation in civic life, and their overall status in society. The Labour Force Survey shows that some 4.6 per cent of the population of working age in Britain, or about 1.5 million people, were from ethnic minority groups (Department of Employment 1988).

It needs to be stressed here that the occupations which most of the immigrants have taken up in Britain helped the post-war expansion of industries and services and even today the contribution of ethnic minority workers to its economy is enormous. To mention one example, almost one-third of the hospital doctors in the National Health Service are from overseas (Anwar and Ali 1987).

Research undertaken by the Commission for Racial Equality and others (Anwar 1982, 1986b; Brown 1984) shows that ethnic minorities are more likely than white people to be unemployed; the level of unemployment is highest among young people. One in three of the ethnic minority people aged 16–24 was unemployed compared with one in six of white people, with the rate for Pakistanis and Bangladeshis being 43 per cent (Department of Employment 1987). But in some London boroughs the overall unemployment rate for ethnic minority young people was 60–70 per cent. And those who were working generally had jobs with lower pay and lower status than those of white workers. There is also widespread racial discrimination in employment, both direct and indirect. All the available

Table 5 Job levels of men: all employees by ethnic group

Job level	White %	West Indian/ Guyanese %	Asian %	Indian %	Paki- stani %	Bangla- deshi %	African– Asian %	Muslim %	Hindu %	Sikh %
Professional, Employer, Management	19	5	13	11	10	10	22	11	20	4
Other non-manual	23	10	13	13	8	7	21	8	26	8
All manual of which:	46	83	73	75	82	82	56	80	51	87
Skilled manual and Foreman	42	48	33	34	39	13	31	33	20	48
Semi-skilled	13	26	34	36	35	57	22	39	28	33
Unskilled	3	9	6	5	8	12	3	8	3	6
Base: male employees Weighted	1,490	972	2,167	847	611	177	495	998	571	452
Unweighted	591	467	1,041	401	298	96	227	507	258	213

Source: Adapted from Brown 1984

research evidence suggests that racial discrimination is a major contributory factor to the higher unemployment rate of ethnic minorities and their lower-pay jobs (CRE *Annual Reports* 1981–9). An overwhelming majority of people from ethnic minorities are employed in manufacturing industries. Ethnic minorities are under-represented in the distribution trade, which forms the largest single area of employment for the total population of Britain. However, recent trends show that the number of self-employed Asians is increasing at a faster rate than among the white population.

Looking at the types of jobs, the Policy Studies Institute (PSI) survey found that male West Indians and Asians were more likely to be in manual work than whites; respective figures for all manual work were 83 per cent, 73 per cent and 46 per cent. Ethnic minority people were more likely to be doing skilled and semi-skilled work. Fewer were employers, managers, and professionals (i.e. West Indians 5 per cent, Asians 13 per cent, and whites 19 per cent). Variations were found within Asian communities, e.g. 69 per cent of Bangladeshis were in semi-skilled and unskilled manual jobs compared with 41 per cent of Indians, 43 per cent of Pakistanis, and 25 per cent of African–Asians (Brown 1984). For details, see Table 5.

It appears that even well-respected professionals from ethnic minorities are not free of problems. A study of doctors showed that while overseas doctors make up almost one-third of all hospital doctors in England and Wales, they are concentrated in the lower grades and in unpopular specialities. The study also shows that overseas doctors wait longer for promotion and that they have to make more applications for posts than their white colleagues (Anwar and Ali 1987).

On the other hand, a study of teachers in eight local education authorities showed that only 2 per cent were from ethnic minorities and that they were found disproportionately on the lowest scales: 78 per cent on Scales 1 or 2 compared with 57 per cent of white teachers. At the senior levels, only 5 per cent of ethnic minority teachers were head or deputy head teachers compared with 13 per cent of white teachers (Ranger 1988).

A study of graduates also showed that it was harder for ethnic minority graduates to obtain jobs than for their white counterparts with similar qualifications (Brennan and McGeevor 1987). The second study by Brennan and McGeevor (1990) shows similar patterns. It shows that ethnic minority graduates believe that their ethnicity hinders the search for jobs, that their opportunities for promotion are more limited, and that the work they take is more often not the most preferred.

In short, racial disadvantage and racial discrimination in employment is still widespread.

As far as the overall housing tenure pattern is concerned, there are differences between ethnic groups. Over 70 per cent of Asians are owner-occupiers, compared with just over 40 per cent of West Indians and about 60 per cent of whites. Owner-occupation among Asians in some areas outside London is as high as 90 per cent. But as most of them live in inner-city areas, the quality of their housing is very poor. They face the problems of the inner cities and these lead them to suffer an overall pattern of racial disadvantage and racial discrimination in housing, in both the private and public sectors (CRE 1984, 1988a, 1989). There is also an increasing number of racial attacks which take place on some local authority housing estates. Many individuals are now coming forward to complain to the CRE about racial discrimination in housing (CRE *Annual Report* 1989).

Overall, the housing conditions of ethnic minorities are inferior to those of the general population. There is, for example, more overcrowding among ethnic minorities with a much higher proportion in housing with one or more persons per room (19.87 per cent) than in the general population (3.36 per cent). Also a higher proportion of people from ethnic minorities live in flats (16.44 per cent) than in the general population (10.65 per cent). Bangladeshis have the worst housing conditions of any ethnic minority group: only 83.6 per cent of Bangladeshis have exclusive use of a bath and inside WC, nearly half of the households are overcrowded (47.95 per cent), and more than twice the proportion in the total population (22.1 per cent) live in purpose-built flats (CRE 1988b).

In education several studies have revealed the racial discrimination which ethnic minorities face. Some of these studies are referred to in the government-appointed Swann Committee report, *Education for All* (1985). Institutional racism and the underachievement of some ethnic minority groups in education were highlighted among many other aspects of education covered by the report. However, some more recent research about secondary education has shown that quality of schools determines the achievement levels of students (Smith and Tomlinson 1989). This research also suggests that there is much to be done to make secondary education reflect the broader outlook that is needed in a multi-cultural society. Furthermore, recent research shows that racial discrimination and differential treatment of ethnic minority children begin as soon as they enter primary schools (Wright forthcoming).

Racial discrimination in the provision of public- and private-sector services is still widespread, although this happens discreetly and often the victim is not aware of it (Anwar 1986b). The discrimination, for example, in health and the caring services is usually indirect or sometimes unintended.

The phenomenon of racial attacks and harassment has shocked people in recent years. In a Home Office study in 1981, it was revealed that Asian and Afro-Caribbean people were far more likely than white people (50 times and 36 times respectively) to be victims of such attacks. In 1986 the Race Relations and Immigration Sub-committee of the Home Affairs Committee in its inquiry into racial attacks concluded that the incidence of racial attacks and harassment remained 'the most shameful and dispiriting aspect of race relations in Britain', and added that the common and widely held view in many areas was that the problem was increasing.

In London, according to the Metropolitan Police, racial attacks had increased from 2,179 in 1987 to 2,214 in 1988. Campaigning organisations believe, however, that many attacks go unreported and the problem has been highlighted once again recently by a report produced by the Inter-departmental Racial Attacks Group (Home Office 1989).

Another problem is the disproportionate number of young black males who are stopped and searched under the Police and Criminal Evidence Act (Willis 1983); young Afro-Caribbean males were stopped ten times as often as whites. Also black defendants are more likely to be held in custody to await trial than whites: 9 per cent of Afro-Caribbeans, 9 per cent of Asians, and 5 per cent of whites were remanded (Home Office 1989). However, a higher proportion of Afro-Caribbeans remanded are subsequently acquitted than white defendants: 7.5 per cent compared with 3.9 per cent. These figures create strong feelings and concern in the ethnic minority communities.

Redressive action policies which are needed to tackle racial disadvantage and racial discrimination by central and local government, employers, trade unions and the voluntary sector are presented elsewhere (Anwar 1986b). Here I would like to point out that ethnic minority organisations and leaders have regularly spoken about the issues of racial disadvantage and discrimination, and racial attacks and harassment. However, their powers to take any direct redressive action to tackle these issues are very limited as they still do not hold many influential positions in the institutions of the society. But because of their activities and protests, more ethnic minority people are coming forward to complain about the injustices and racial discrimination (see CRE *Annual Reports* 1986–8). They are also becoming more politicised, as is shown in several of the contributions in this volume.

It is estimated that there are over two thousand ethnic minority organisations in the UK. Almost 300 of these are in the Greater London area. (For the types of organisations see Anwar, this volume.) In addition to ethnic minority organisations, race relations workers and ethnic minority MPs, councillors, and trade union officials, and many others provide the ethnic leadership in various fields and at different levels. These leaders regularly raise the issues outlined above and demand appropriate action.

References

Anwar, Muhammad (1979) *The Myth of Return*, London: Heinemann.

Anwar, Muhammad (1982) *Young People and the Job Market*, London: Commission for Racial Equality.

Anwar, Muhammad (1986a) *Race and Politics*, London: Tavistock.

Anwar, Muhammad (1986b) 'Redressive action policies in the United Kingdom', paper presented at the XIth World Congress of Sociology, New Delhi.

Anwar, Muhammad and Ali, Ameer (1987) *Overseas Doctors: Experience and Expectations*, London: Commission for Racial Equality.

Brennan, John and McGeevor, Philip (1987) *Employment of Graduates from Ethnic Minorities*, London: Commission for Racial Equality.

Brennan, John and McGeevor, Philip (1990) *Ethnic Minorities and the Graduate Labour Market*, London: Commission for Racial Equality.

Brown, Colin (1984) *Black and White Britain*, London: Policy Studies Institute.

Cabinet Papers (1950) *Coloured People from British Colonial Territories*, London: Public Records Office.

Commission for Racial Equality (1981–9) *Annual Reports*, London: Commission for Racial Equality.

Commission for Racial Equality (1984) *Housing in Hackney*, London: Commission for Racial Equality.

Commission for Racial Equality (1988a) *Homelessness and Discrimination* (Report of a Formal Investigation into the London Borough of Tower Hamlets), London: Commission for Racial Equality.

Commission for Racial Equality (1988b) *Housing and Ethnic Minorities: Statistical Information*, London: Commission for Racial Equality.

Commission for Racial Equality (1988c) *Learning in Terror. A Survey of Racial Harassment in the Schools and Colleges*, London: Commission for Racial Equality.

Commission for Racial Equality (1989) *Racial Discrimination in Liverpool City Council*, London: Commission for Racial Equality.

Department of Employment (1987) *Employment Gazette*, January, London: HMSO.

Department of Employment (1988) *Employment Gazette*, March, London: HMSO.

Haskey, John (1988) 'The ethnic minority populations of Great Britain: their size and characteristics', *Population Trends*, 54, London: HMSO.

Home Office (1981) *Racial Attacks: A Report of a Home Office Study*, London: HMSO.

Home Office (1989) *The Response to Racial Attacks and Harassment: Guidance to the Statutory Agencies* (Report of the Inter-departmental Racial Attacks Group), London: Home Office.

Office of Population Censuses and Surveys (1983) *Census 1981: Country of Birth, Great Britain*, London: HMSO.

Office of Population Censuses and Surveys (1986) *Labour Force Survey*, London: HMSO.

Office of Population Censuses and Surveys (1987) *Population Trends*, London: HMSO.

Ranger, Chris (1988) *Ethnic Minority School Teachers*, London: Commission for Racial Equality.

Rose, E.J.B. in association with Deakin, N., Abrams, M., Jackson, V., Preston, M., Vanags, A.H., Cohen, B., Gaitskell, J. and Ward, P. (1969) *Colour and Citizenship*, London: Oxford University Press.

Smith, David, and Tomlinson, Sally (1989) *The School Effect: A Study of Multi-racial Comprehensives*, London: Policy Studies Institute.

Swann Committee (1985) *Education for All*, London: HMSO.

Willis, Carole (1983) *The Use, Effectiveness and Impact of Police Stop and Search Powers*, London: HMSO.

Wright, Cecil (forthcoming) *The Early Years: How Children of Ethnic Minority Groups Experience Schools*, London: Commission for Racial Equality.

Black and ethnic leaderships in Britain

A theoretical overview[1]

Pnina Werbner

If it is true that men and women make their own history, they do so through organised action and the formulation of common, culturally constituted, objectives. In attempting to rescue the multitude of nameless British black and ethnic leaders from collective obscurity, this book looks beyond social movements to their incipient formative bases. Castells (1983: 319–20) has argued, it will be recalled, that urban movements have three major goals – mobilisation for improved collective consumption; a search for cultural identity and autonomy, either ethnically based or historically originated; and a struggle for increasing local and neighbourhood power. Seen processually, such movements often lose their impetus, he argues, once they achieve some of their aims: they are destroyed by internal dissent or contradiction, or their leaders are continually incorporated by the political apparatus, and the initial drive is lost (Castells 1983: 325).

But what sets an urban protest movement into motion? To become a *movement*, we argue here, a collectivity must go through three critical stages – from *localised associative empowerment* to *ideological convergence*, and, finally, *mobilisation*.

The first stage, *localised associative empowerment*, is marked by the formation of a 'web of filiations and affiliations', to borrow Said's term (1983: 145), of an associative network focused on distinctive cultural or political issues. In urban ethnic groups associative empowerment often takes the form of associational efflorescence. Local ethnic communities form a multitude of associations, both formal and informal, concerned with group welfare and collective consumption, cultural and religious activities, or political objectives.

In the present volume, contributors touch on various dimensions of this associational efflorescence. Werbner's essay discusses some of the ideological bases for associational proliferation among British Pakistanis and the new drive in ethnic communities to compete for state-allocated resources. Carnival, Cohen demonstrates, builds on a multitude of local groups, both formal and informal, which work throughout the year in order to stage this major event. Westwood analyses the process which led to a sports organisation for young black people becoming the basis for a battle for autonomy and territoriality with the local state.[2] Banks argues in his essay that the changing definitions of a project to build a Jain temple are the outcome of struggles between various groups and associations, on the one hand, and variously defined constituencies on the other. In Tower Hamlets, Eade reports, activists in different Bangladeshi associations compete through local council elections for power and leadership positions. In Harrow, far removed economically from the East End, Gujarati activists fight for equal opportunity policies while forming a plethora of more specific Gujarati associations, as Kalka shows. The national Indian Workers Association, Josephides reports, evolved partly through a federation of many local groups in many cities, and has periodically been riven by ideological and personal conflict. Johnson, in his essay, discusses the efflorescence of black-led churches in Britain and the increasing pastoral role they are assuming.

During the initial stage, then, of social movement formation, associations remain relatively discrete and often compete with one another, both for state allocations and on ideological grounds. Nevertheless, the web of affiliations, seen as a whole, is united in its drive to establish distinctive cultural and political institutions and thus to increase its relative autonomy in relation to the urban locality and the wider society. Even when, as Goulbourne argues, black activists reject the 'communal option' and form organisations with a broad, universalistic agenda, they nevertheless aim, through these organisations, to recapture control and self-determination from a remote bureaucratic state apparatus.

The second stage of a social movement, *ideological convergence*, involves the formulation of a common discourse and set of objectives in relation to the state or local state, and with regard to the contemporary condition of the group within the larger society.

The trend towards ideological convergence is highlighted in many of the essays here. Eade's essay analyses the dialectical formulation of a common political discourse among Bangladeshi activists fighting local-level elections in the East End. Jeffers shows how the Black Section movement had to justify its distinctive political discourse within the broader socialist labour camp. In Kalka's essay, representatives on a multi-ethnic committee had to thrash out a joint discourse and set of objectives. Josephides highlights the debates within the Indian Workers Association regarding the limits of the black versus socialist discourse and its political objectives. According to Cohen, West Indian Carnival leaders have progressively widened the cultural discourse of Carnival to embrace new forms of music and artistic expression, and new social collectivities, while debating whether or not Carnival should highlight political issues explicitly. In Werbner's essay, the discourse on internal 'class' relations within the British Pakistani community finds expression during a battle to secure funding from the state for a community centre. Banks, like Eade, analyses how a discourse can be manipulated in relation to different constituencies and audiences.

The final stage in the formation of an urban social movement, *mobilisation*, is the stage in which the movement emerges as a recognisable, public *protest* movement. Mobilisation usually occurs in response to a particular issue or event threatening group autonomy or solidarity, and the cultural or religious ideals constituting it.

Several of the case studies in the volume analyse the emergence of such a protest movement. Westwood's essay shows how a group of young black people mobilise when the local state attempts to take their corporate property away from them. Jeffers's essay discusses the mobilisation process in the Black Section movement as a response to local issues and wider objectives. His argument is complemented by Cohen's analysis of the historical processes which led to the emergence of the Notting Hill Carnival as a major movement.

In a sense, then, this book is about *potential* urban social movements in their early formative stages. This early stage is characterised by the emergence of valorised associative networks and a series of local, or, exceptionally, national, discrete movements all aiming to increase the cultural autonomy, political influence and economic independence of post-war immigrants to Britain from the Caribbean and South Asia. Few of these localised associations or movements are headed by widely acknowledged and legitimised exemplary leaders. Many will never become fully fledged movements.

There are several reasons for the absence of an exemplary, charismatic 'black', Asian, or Caribbean leadership in Britain. The first and most important of these is that members of the various ethnic communities share a deep suspicion of their own ethnic representatives. This is because the majority of ethnic leaders at the local level deal with the state *within the parameters defined by state*. Their intercalary position is necessarily the focus of both conflict and co-operation. On the one hand, they negotiate with the state for communal grants and individual welfare provisions, or debate policy issues on multi-ethnic committees established under the auspices of the local state. On the other, they protest against state policies through their individual associations. But their access to patronage makes them suspect, even as they are often esteemed for their communal work. This access to patronage is after all a primary source of their 'internal' influence and prominence. Since there is a vast multitude of these functionaries, none achieves any real prominence. At the same time, as several of the essays in this volume show, a new generation of such leaders is increasingly *confronting* the local state: ethnic leaders on multi-ethnic bodies, as well as local state employees such as youth leaders, are making increasingly more radical and far-reaching demands from the state to fulfil immigrant or minority rights, and rectify the hidden consequences of institutional racism.

The situation in Britain today is, from this perspective, not comparable to that in the USA at the outset of the post-reconstruction era. Early American black exemplary leaders were accorded their emblematic status *precisely within* the state patronage system in which they acted as *sole* representatives (see Huggins 1978). However, in modern-day Britain, with its multitude of ethnic brokers, multiplicity of communication channels and variety of black activists, the rise of a single exemplary black leader is likely to be very different. In common with leaders of contemporary American movements such a leader is likely to be accorded widespread legitimacy only if he or she is seen to be *independent* of the state patronage system and its buffer institutions (on such institutions see Katznelson 1973; Lawrence 1974). Such a leader must be able, moreover, to transcend internal divisions within the ethnic community and mobilise widespread support. To do so, a leader must define broad policy aims and have the autonomous organisational infrastructure allowing for broad-based political mobilisation. He or she must, in other words, head a social movement.

This leads to the second reason for the present absence of a widely recognised black or ethnic leadership: namely, the very recent historical emergence of the various ethnic communities discussed in this volume – most were formed as self-reproducing communities during the 1960s and have had little time to create powerful national federal organisations or territorially based communal alliances. True exemplary leaders emerge in response to major issues, either national or communal, and their emergence is conditional on the prior creation of either national federative organisations or a network of local affiliations.

Both anti-colonial struggles and the American civil rights movement seem to show that great, mythical leaders emerge during periods of great challenge or crisis. They tend to rely on broad alliances, in which key associations within the wider society – the church, trade unions, liberal organisations – support the causes of the movement (see Marable 1985; on a less broadly based British alliance formed in the 1960s to influence anti-discrimination legislation see Heineman 1972: 126). In Britain today, Johnson argues in his essay, the various denominational churches are at present rallying to the cause of anti-racism, and have condemned government policy in the inner cities publicly and vocally. Liberation theology has come home to Britain and the various churches, all powerful international organisations, are key partners in the anti-racist battle.

As the confidence and experience of leaders grow, so too does their ability to lead organised campaigns. Jeffers, Anwar, and Goulbourne show that recognisable black or ethnic leaders are beginning to emerge before the public eye as members of the various minority communities enter, like Jewish activists before them, into mainstream politics, or achieve important positions in central mainstream organisations. Goulbourne, in a major theoretical discussion of leadership and authority, argues that West Indian public personalities, although engaged primarily in *non*-communal, broader issues, are nevertheless increasingly identifying themselves publicly, as members of the *black* community, with the fight against racial subordination.

Racism in Britain has until recently either been associated with the far right or, more commonly, it has remained mostly unofficial, disguised, fragmented, and individually perceived. Immigration laws have been changed through a gradualist process, affecting at any time only part of the immigrant population and its descendants. Recently, however, there has been a resurgence of crude racism in the form of racial physical attacks and public verbal abuse, and these, coupled with police violence and judicial indifference, periodically force racism onto the government's agenda. The inner-city riots and, more recently, the Muslim community's mass protest movement against Salman Rushdie and the *Satanic Verses* have made clear that ethnicity and racism must be taken seriously. However, as Benyon points out, while the powerless can force issues onto the agenda through riots or massive protests, the political construction of these events is easily distorted (Benyon 1984, 1987). Anti-racist campaigns, to be effective, thus require unifying causes and articulate, clear aims (see Ben Tovim *et al.* 1986; also Heineman 1972). At the time of writing, no single, clear-cut, 'new' national cause exists around which a unified black social movement can emerge. Instead, anti-racist battles are being fought throughout the country on many lesser fronts, and through minor, local, little recognised campaigns.

To understand the roles of both local and national leaders, the need is thus to begin by analysing the organisational and structural contexts in which they emerge, mobilise support, and engage in struggles for communal rights. Rather than simply focusing on 'cultural' or 'political' communities, however, the discussion of ethnic leadership here locates such leaders within four types of mutually

19

constitutive 'communities', defined analytically: 'imagined' communities, 'interpretive' communities, communities of 'suffering', and 'moral' communities.

Imagined communities: processes of associational efflorescence

If the post-war immigrant population of Britain is divided into ethnic groups, variously and situationally defined, then ethnic groups themselves are *internally* divided. Associational activities and leaders emerge along the lines of these divisions, generated by several oppositional principles: segmentary, class, centre–periphery, and ideological. The four major oppositional principles are interrelated. Hence, for example, burial and friendly societies are often organised on the basis of segmentary *regional* divisions, and along *class* lines – they are mostly run by working-class migrants. Such associations form the base of a broad pyramid. Above them, elite migrants – professionals, businessmen, and an emergent 'salariat' (see Alavi 1988) – establish formal organisations with more global aims – cultural, political, religious – usually claiming, by virtue of these aims, to represent the interests of the whole ethnic or religious group. It is at this level that both *class* and *ideological* oppositions, as well as political strategies, emerge.

Despite this apparent divisiveness, and the internal debate it generates, such oppositions reflect, Josephides and Werbner argue, the enormous cultural vitality of ethnic or religious groups, and the commitment they have to the long-term continuity of the group and to its perpetuation. Divisiveness at one level thus implies a transcendent unity at another level. If the group's sacred values are perceived to be seriously violated, these different and opposing factions can and will unite and mobilise for joint action. When black women were physically attacked and injured by police in Brixton and Tottenham, the community responded fiercely and unequivocally: such attacks violated the sacred value attached to motherhood in the Afro-Caribbean community (and, indeed, in many other ethnic groups). The perceived violation of central Islamic sacred values has mobilised the normally fragmented Muslim religious community in a broad unified alliance.

It is important to take theoretical account of the internal class structure of the various British post-war immigrant groups. These groups do not simply constitute a monolithic 'underclass', for their middle-class members have access to broader resources well beyond the reach of such an underclass. Indeed, Wilson has argued that the plight of American inner-city black ghettos is linked to the flight of the black urban middle and working classes to the suburbs. It is these classes which sustain communal buffering institutions and create a sense of confidence and self-reliance; elite members of a ghetto community are the ones who, with their greater resources, help tide the community over periods of severe recession and provide models of mainstream lifestyles. By 'their very presence [they enhance] the social organisation of ghetto communities' and endow it with 'a sense of community, and positive neighbourhood identification' (Wilson 1987: 143). And, as Rex and Tomlinson also point out (1979: 293), it is the radicalisation of this class which is likely to change the course of British minority politics.

The central role of ethnic intellectual and class elites in the foundation and day-to-day running of associations is evident in virtually all the essays in this book: black activists in a London Labour Party constituency, local-level Bangladeshi activists in East London, middle-class Gujarati activists in Harrow, Pakistani activists, both businessmen and workers, in Manchester, a university graduate black youth leader in Leicester, Indian socialists throughout Britain, West Indian cultural activists in Notting Hill, a Jain professional in Leicester – all are politically self-conscious, elite members of their communities. As such, they all share greater involvement and knowledge of the wider society.

Ethnic communities are 'imagined' in two different senses. They are imagined, as Goulbourne and Werbner argue, by the state and local state which must reify ethnic segments as perpetual communities in order to control conflict or allocate resources in an 'equitable' manner. They are also imagined, as Eade, Kalka, and Banks show, by the various leaders who claim to represent them. In creating associations with global cultural, political, or religious aims, such leaders define and invent communities out of segments. The field of ethnic relations is thus imaged and transformed, by both ethnic leaders *and* the state, into a struggle between culturally bounded 'communities'.

Yet, as Kurt Lewin argued, urban ethnic leaders are located in fact within an unbounded 'social field' rather than within a bounded community. Leaders may be located at the 'centre' or 'periphery' of this field (see Higham 1978 for a recent discussion). The 'ethnic centre' is constituted by its close-knit networks and intense, ethnic-specific, sociability. Within it 'organic' ethnic leaders and elites foster and develop distinctive ideologies, values, and institutions. Most 'internal' cultural and religious organisations are manned by leaders from the 'centre', concerned to a great extent with parochial, exclusive issues. 'Peripheral' leaders are those who, in one sense or another, move with greater ease and have greater contact with the wider society. As Westwood, Cohen, Kalka, and Eade all show, such leaders may be organically embedded within the ethnic community, sharing its fundamental values and aspirations and closely involved in its social life, or they may be truly peripheral, 'external' to the group. Their leadership then often becomes, as Banks and Werbner highlight, a key facet of their continued membership in the community.

It is the latter class of leaders, however, who are most often suspected of collaboration, accused of self-interested social climbing, and regarded as convenient brokers manning 'buffering' institutions (Katznelson 1973; Pryce 1979: 223–40; Pearson 1981). They may also play, however, a very significant mediatory role once anti-racist social movements gather momentum. It is often, indeed, leaders who are – at least in some significant cultural sense – of the 'periphery' who become the most radical activists and organisers of such social movements. It is they who most clearly 'politicise' culture, transforming it into an ideological agenda. (Indeed, leaders may come from beyond the group altogether. See Higham 1978, and Heineman 1972 on the key role of white liberals and socialists in the Campaign Against Racial Discrimination.)

In addition to the multitude of *local* associations representing *specific* cultural, religious, political, or welfare interests and platforms, ethnic communities also develop *territorial* organisations. Such organisations usually build corporately owned buildings which serve the needs of a whole neighbourhood or urban ethnic group, and establish cultural claims to urban territorial *ownership* through the creation of public, tangible landmarks (see Mellor 1989). Mosques, churches, or Gurdwaras, ethnic community centres, youth clubs, neighbourhood advice centres, or religious schools are examples of such territorial organisations. Street festivals, such as Carnival, the Chinese new year celebrations, or Muslim processions on the Prophet's birthday, which temporarily take over and occupy urban territory, may also be regarded as territorial organisations. So too, local umbrella organisations, such as West Indian Co-ordinating Committees (see Pearson 1981), come to be territorially defined. Ownership is fiercely defended as Westwood documents evocatively, precipitating a group of young black people into protest; the very success of Carnival, Cohen argues, its territorial control and cultural challenge, creates an imperative for the state to attempt to co-opt and control it. Werbner and Banks both demonstrate that the control of territorial organisations is a hotly contested prize *within* ethnic communities. So too the success of the Southall Indian Workers Association, according to Josephides, stems partly from its ownership of a major building.

Territorial organisations are often *hierarchical* forums in which *internal* ideological and class divisions are given clear public political expression in debates or politically fought elections over the control of the organisation (see Werbner 1985, 1990). Whereas *local* associations are founded upon agreement and social cohesion, and usually split when disagreements emerge, some central ethnic *territorial* organisations – corporately owned – often become major ethnic arenas in which internal disagreements and rivalries emerge publicly. It is in this context that the battle for important, internally recognised, local leadership positions is often fought. Yet as an immigrant community sinks roots, territorial organisations begin to multiply. Instead of one organisation, symbolically objectifying the whole imagined community, there come to be many organisations, objectifying its fragmentation. At this point major leadership struggles often shift to wider forums.

Ethnic associations follow predictable developmental processes: from informal to formal, voluntary to professional, local to national (see Thomas and Znaniecki 1958, Higham 1978). As they federate, the locus of ethnic elite competition for positions of power often shifts from the local to the national context.

Trans-local, *federated* associations are composed of local associations *sharing specific goals* rather than of the whole urban ethnic territorial community. Such national organisations thus serve to evoke imagined communities on a broader national scale – it is as if the whole ethnic community is composed of poetry lovers, religious devotees, political activists, doctors, etc., depending on the global aims the various federated organisations foster. Thus, for example, each religious denomination or strand of British Islam has its local, territorial, and national organisational expressions. The different Islamic federated associations may unite temporarily, as in the current protests against the *Satanic Verses*, but both local and federated national associations remain discrete organisationally while claiming to represent the 'true' Islam and the '*whole*' British Muslim community. In this volume Josephides traces the history of the Indian Workers Association as a federal organisation. Although internal rivalries and splits have plagued the organisation it has nevertheless succeeded in creating and maintaining a socialist constituency of Indian workers throughout Britain, concerned with defending the interests of black workers, and evoking this imagined community ideologically and politically.

The fact that ethnic segments are situational, and ultimately imagined, points to some of the dilemmas and contradictions inherent in ethnic and black political activity.

Interpretive communities: radicals, reformers, and the politicisation of culture

The increasing radicalism of black, religious, and ethnic politics in Britain has been widely noted (see, for example, Rex and Tomlinson 1979: 292). As their subordinate position in British society has become more evident, black activists have returned to their experiential and social roots, and thus to the wider diaspora to which they belong (Gilroy 1987). Pan-Africanism, World Islam, Third World anti-colonialism or neocolonialism, the Black Power movement in the USA and the Caribbean – all provide themes and symbols in the fight against racism and material subordination in Britain itself. In these ethnic and religious politics, both local and national, culture is 'politicised' – it is no longer constituted by the unquestioned, taken-for-granted premises of a living, day-to-day social environment, but by a fetishised ideology, a political agenda. This is particularly so in broad, inter-ethnic arenas or in relation to the state. Here, in the battle for specific religious schools, for example, for separate radio and television programmes, for special ethnic communal collective consumption allocations, for jobs and quotas, culture is reified (Kapferer 1988: 114–15; Geertz 1973; also Anderson 1983). Highly selective features of a much broader tapestry of cultural practices and implicit understandings are highlighted, and claimed to objectify the group and its values. At the same time broader themes drawn from erstwhile battles against a prior British colonial regime are relocated in the present context.

In a recent essay Edward Said points to the dangers inherent in the development of radical discourses which come to be acceptable *within* a group, without gaining any wider currency or recognition (Said 1983). What he describes is a kind of radical communal solipsism. One of the primary dilemmas of anti-racist and religious or ethnic-based movements is how to assert autonomy, separation, and communal rights while reaching out simultaneously to other groups who might be potentially sympathetic to the movement. It was not by chance that church-based and labour-based black leaders were at the forefront of the American civil rights movement or that the success of the Campaign Against Racial Discrimination (CARD) in Britain stemmed from its close connections with the Labour Party. The Black Power separatist movements of the 1970s asserted autonomy and the potential for urban disruption, but ultimately they had to evolve modes of alliance and co-operation with other organisations. In Kalka's essay in this volume we see how a radical discourse by ethnic representatives is basically ignored or disattended to by state officials serving on a multi-ethnic committee. Young blacks in

Leicester find their case consistently misinterpreted by the media and the local Labour council. On the other hand, as Werbner shows, an alliance between Pakistani workers and white socialist activists, while utilising a radical discourse, creates the basis for a successful funding application.

Radicals do, of course, want to be effective, to reach beyond the group. The movement of ethnic associations and their leaders tends thus towards a dialectical progression: on the one hand, towards greater integration and penetration of mainstream organisations, and the formation of broad-based alliances; on the other hand, alongside this integration a more strident assertiveness of the distinctiveness, separateness and autonomy of ethnic, black, or religious collectivities and their distinctive predicaments. Sometimes these counter-movements undermine each other. Muslim demonstrations against the *Satanic Verses* assert the total separation of the Muslim community (itself a collectivity transcending ethnicity and race) and strike at broader potential alliances and a unified 'black' movement. In the long run, however, what started as a specific religious movement may be transformed into a wider movement against racism, a defence of the *emotional* right to have one's beliefs respected, 'not to be offended', thus incorporating the previously conservative Muslim community into a more radical black struggle. Given the complex dialectics involved, outcomes are often unpredictable. Black professionals co-opted by the state become its most vocal critics. Carnival, initiated by black cultural radicals, is taken over by a more moderate leadership, co-opted by the state, yet continues to retain its radical potential.

But how do black radicals reach out across the communicative abyss? Eade demonstrates that they do so by using the rhetoric of 'community' and 'localism', both ambiguous concepts open to broader or narrower interpretations. Once again, then, community is reified, this time ambiguously as local and multi-ethnic, local and 'black', or local and 'Bangladeshi'.

Radical discourses are not 'invented' by individual leaders; they reflect and embody particular historical moments. Moderates adopt a radical discourse once it becomes accepted currency in the group. Nevertheless, radicalism often spells isolation. To be effective, leaders must learn the discourses acceptable in specific domains: in British politics the stress is on class, community, and economic issues; a stress on other values – spiritual, emotional, cultural, or racial – is regarded, at best, as eccentric; at worst it is seen, as both Jeffers and Westwood show, as an unwarranted attack on implicit institutional norms. Moreover, radicalism is to a large extent a matter of rhetoric. Ethnic monitoring is regarded as mildly reformist when promoted by the Commission for Racial Equality (CRE), as a radical policy when promoted by left-wing councils. Then again, radicals often disagree with one another, as Eade and Josephides highlight: within the post-war British immigrant community there are radical socialists who reject black separatism, radical religious leaders who reject both socialism and any secular-based movement, radical anti-racists who reject liberalism.

Radical rhetoric and tactics are not, then, in themselves, a guarantee of effective reform. It is for this reason that many ethnic activists, strongly committed to their groups' causes, adopt a more moderate stance. They prefer to win small battles through negotiation and lobbying, rather than dream and proclaim about major, unwinnable battles.

The question remains, however: does the more militant, radical rhetoric increasingly used by 'black' activists signify a real change? We suggest that in some respects it does. In creating a new, shared, symbolic discourse, radicals are creating a *cultural* basis for unified *political* action which can encompass the different ethnic and immigrant segments. A multi-cultural committee is precisely that: a fragmented aggregation of representatives, separated by a variety of group-specific aims. A 'black' committee with exactly the same composition is a symbolic unity. It is capable of formulating joint policies and engaging in joint action. Its imagined community is a unified one. Its ontology is linked to shared experiences. It represents a community of suffering.

The emergence of a community of suffering

A significant theme emerging from many of the essays in the volume is the drive throughout Britain, in local communities and in many different forums or contexts, towards the creation of a transcendent 'black' unity – a unity composed out of the diverse ethnic and religious immigrant groups from Asia and the Caribbean.

Hence, alongside the movement towards the establishment of specific ethnic cultural, religious, or political institutions is an increasingly more dominant move to articulate the experience of racism, and thus to reconstruct the post-war immigrant community, symbolically and culturally, around this single dominant experience. British Asians and Caribbeans in this country are increasingly conscious of themselves as members of a 'community of suffering'. As Turner (1957: 302) says: 'The affliction of each is the concern of all; likeness of unhappy lot is the ultimate bond of ritual solidarity.' To appreciate the emergence of this common consciousness, we need to reflect briefly on the nature of racism.

Racism is manifested by a series of violations and acts of violence. These violations are directed against a person's inviolable humanity: his or her body, sacred cultural values, personal and communal property, right to civilised public treatment, and equal citizenship rights or allocations (to housing, jobs, etc.). Violence generates moral and social alienation and sometimes counter-violence, often within an escalating cycle. The current victims of racism in Britain, primarily post-war immigrants from South Asia and the Caribbean and their descendants, are increasingly cognisant of these acts of violence perpetrated against them as individuals and as communities. To confront this experience culturally and symbolically they must redefine themselves historically.

This process of historical redefinition can only be understood if we recognise the fundamental nature of ethnicity as a segmentary structure. Axiomatic or primordial loyalties define different principles of ethnic segmentation: familial, religious, cultural, linguistic, regional, or national – and different *levels* of segmentation: village kin group, caste, nation; religious sect, denomination, global community of believers (see also Keyes 1981). Not all the segments are objectified symbolically in lasting organisational structures. In post-war Britain religious communities – Muslims, Hindus, Jains, Sikhs; national communities – Pakistanis, Indians, Bangladeshis, West Indians, or Afro-Caribbeans (including Jamaicans, Trinidadians, Barbadens, Guyanese, etc.); and linguistic communities – Punjabis, Gujaratis, Bengalis – all receive some organisational expression and state recognition in the form of special provisioning for collective consumption. On the whole, however, racial categories – social collectivities defined on the basis of colour (black or white) – are not the object of state largesse. Black people are regarded as members of broader collectivities – of the underprivileged, inner-city residents, the unemployed, and so forth. Racial categories as the basis for a legitimate discrete identity are usually formally denied both by the right and the left (see Rex and Tomlinson 1979: 36–69; Ben Tovim *et al.* 1986). Officials sustain a 'colour-blind' or culture-specific policy. At the same time, unofficial and euphemistic acknowledgement of this dominant cleavage in British society is variously expressed in anti-immigrant pronouncements and legislation (Ben Tovim and Gabriel 1982), discussions about the 'problems' of the 'inner city', police harassment and the criminalisation of some sections of the black community (Hall *et al.* 1978).

One aim of the incipient social movements discussed here is to redefine the black–white dominant cleavage, to use Gluckman's term (Gluckman 1958; see also Rex 1986), as a *morally* paramount division within the series of segmentary ethnic and religious divisions which make up Britain's post-war immigrant society. Because this dominant cleavage is born in violence and generates a community of suffering, black activists believe that its moral claims subsume and encompass other ethnic-type divisions within a transcendent unity. Thus they often deny the validity of specific ethnic or religious claims, and argue that the state as provider of 'ethnic' collective grants, or co-opter of 'ethnic leaders' to representative posts, is acting divisively. The same criticism applies to other mainstream organisations such as the Labour Party. This point of view is put forward forcefully by Goulbourne who argues that the state is increasingly moving towards the 'communal option'.

Goulbourne's argument requires further examination. The 'communal option', he appears to argue, is determined, indeed overdetermined, by the state and wider society, and is a singular, unidirectional trend. Against this we would argue that the process of emergent ethnicity is a dialectical one: on the one hand are attempts by the state and local state to resolve major structural–economic problems affecting minorities through minor hand-outs and hopeful co-option onto multi-cultural committees (see Lawrence 1974). In doing so apparently harmless communal fictions are created which confine and contain ethnic leaders. On the other hand, ethnic groups themselves claim their *rights* to state provisioning or religious autonomy as equal *but different* citizens. The process is dynamic and interactive. At the same time it is it is unlikely that the 'communal option' will ever be much more than a *laissez-faire* local policy. A more extreme communalism would entail either legal pluralism or apartheid, both equally unacceptable: the former would undermine the universal powers of the state, the latter would generate internal civil strife. Instead, the 'communal option' is best viewed as a kind of pragmatic liberal compromise, and the current status quo with all its inconsistencies is, in our view, unlikely to change radically unless the democratic fabric of the whole society is undermined.

'Ethnic' claims to collective consumption or representative status are, it must be remembered, made by associations and their leaders in the name of deeply felt symbolic requirements and experiences; these appear to the people themselves to be just as valid in the specific contexts in which they are made as the experience of racism is. The primary aim of these associations is, after all, to ensure the autonomy of the immigrant community and establish the basis for its future cultural continuity and reproduction. Hence the study of ethnicity as a series of segmentary systems must, as anthropologists have long recognised, account for the situational relevance or salience of ethnic segments. At certain levels, and in certain contexts, ethnic, religious, or national–communal issues are paramount. But at the level of confrontation with the state on matters of poverty, under-privilege, police violence, racial harassment, or political representation immigrant activists are fighting to establish both the overriding principle and the cultural articulation of the black experience as a primary basis for political mobilisation. 'Blackness', in other words, is first and foremost a *political* category encompassing the material, political, and symbolic subordination of post-war British immigrant communities. It is in this sense that race and class coincide, and that immigrants from the Caribbean and Asia constitute a 'class fraction'. Yet as Jeffers and Eade both show, such a class fraction must be actively constructed and defended.

In Britain the battle against racism is still in its early phase. The most significant national movements this struggle has generated so far were CARD, in the 1960s, which Heineman describes as 'an organisation representing a movement that did not exist' (1972: 2), and the Anti-Nazi League alliance, articulated in the Rock Against Racism movement in the 1970s. While CARD had little success in tapping local, grass-roots organisations and was elitist throughout, it did create during its shortlived existence a relatively broad alliance with major influence on the course of anti-racist legislation in Britain. In a sense, as Heineman recognises, it rode on the crest of the American civil rights movement's wave. Once its legislative programme was accepted, it collapsed in disarray, amidst mutual recriminations and internal divisions between Black Power radicals and liberal/socialist reformers.

Rock Against Racism arose in response to Powellism and the mounting electoral successes of the National Front (for an extensive discussion see Gilroy 1987). The movement, Gilroy suggests, was remarkable for the way it mobilised working-class white British youth to the cause of anti-racism through music and grass-roots activism. However, Gilroy argues, the very success of the movement also spelled its demise: the failure of the National Front to win broad electoral support was followed by a gradual dissipation of the anti-racist forces.

The anti-racist movements of the 1980s have been more purely 'political'. They have involved an increasingly concerted effort on the part of various black and ethnic activists to enter into mainstream politics, as Anwar shows in his essay (see also Anwar 1986). It is important, however, to recognise, as Eade, for example, stresses, that while ethnic groups may share fundamental political goals, entry into both local and national mainstream politics also reveals, simultaneously, internal divisions and disparate goals within these communities and among the various activists seeking to represent them.

It is also very importantly the case that the drive to enter politics has, as Jeffers shows, both cultural and ideological dimensions. The problems British Asian and Caribbean entrants into mainstream politics confront are more than simply political. They involve a major reconstruction of ideology, group identity, and the organisational definition of 'blackness', race, and community. The ideological battle is one of establishing the primacy of 'blackness' against 'class' as a legitimate basis for political organisation and representation, its moral *encompassment*, in Dumont's terms, of other cultural and religious group definitions (Dumont 1983). Just as 'community' has to be actively constituted ideologically and defined organisationally, so too the 'black' constituency must be given moral legitimacy against, on the one hand, universalistic ideologies such as socialism and liberalism (see Ben Tovim *et al.* 1986) and, on the other, over more specific loyalties. Ethnic, as against black, activists may seek to enter mainstream politics in order to further particularistic causes (such as those of world religions like Islam). For black activists 'blackness' is a universalistic category because it encompasses a variety of ethnic groups, united by a common shared experience of victimisation. It is particularistic in making claims to unique predicaments, generated by racism. These predicaments, activists argue, require special privileged access to state resources in order to rectify unwarranted, but often hidden, discrimination. The experience of racism itself qualifies the people who suffer racism to be leaders.

Yet the issues raised by black activists are countered by powerful arguments: to recognise the legitimacy of racial categories as a basis for political mobilisation and representation is not only to deny universal socialism or liberalism, but to risk a white backlash, to create a prescription for tokenism, and to undermine cross-racial alliances. Such demands are intolerant of other ethnic segmental needs and rights to state support. Most importantly, perhaps, black demands for political representation are unlikely, even if successful, to resolve the major problems of the post-industrial society: the restructuring of the economy which has generated structural unemployment and inner-city decline (Miles and Phizacklea 1980; Miles 1982; Wilson 1987).

Moral communities: autonomy and internal colonialism

A community of suffering is also a moral community. Moral communities are constituted not only through shared suffering but also through mutual welfare and internal giving to religious or communal causes (Werbner 1990). Collective provision for communal needs is thus at the heart of communal identity/organisation.

State provision – allocations made by the state for 'collective consumption' – constitutes both a right and a means of indirect state control. In both senses such provision has profound symbolic connotations. Because of this, political (as well as academic) debates in Britain regarding state provision or institutional racism are implicitly also debates about more complex symbolic issues such as national and cultural identity, or immigrants' position as integral and genuine members of the nation.

The economic, political, and social subordination of certain ethnic minorities within industrial societies has been analysed as a form of 'internal colonialism' (Blauner 1972). At first glance, the brokerage or buffering role of ethnic leaders seems simply to strengthen this analogy. Werbner argues, however, that while the role of ethnic leaders is, indeed, initially analogous to the role such leaders had in the colonial administration, it also comes to exemplify – over time – the processes of change which characterised the battle *against* colonialism. Hence, if the analogy between colonial societies and underprivileged, encapsulated minorities in western industrial societies is to be fully drawn out, it must incorporate within its theoretical framework the processes and contradictions which have led, ultimately, to the *overthrowing* of colonialism.

Radical institutions are often born out of accommodationist, state-sponsored buffer institutions. The doubts expressed by Rex (1979: 88), for example, about the political effectiveness of 'paternalistic' institutions such as the Commission for Racial Equality or local Community Relations Councils (CRCs) need, perhaps, to be re-examined. Ben Tovim *et al.* (1986) have argued, against this view, that CRCs represent *potentially* the most promising organisation for campaigning on broad policy issues, and especially for pressing for the implementation at the local level of national, legally approved anti-racist policies. This is because CRCs have administrative continuity and constitute a forum for the formation of broad, multi-ethnic alliances. What CRCs critically lack, however, is a *cultural* dimension which, as the essays in this volume illustrate, underlines effective social movements and upholds transcendent unities. Nevertheless, CRCs constitute a learning ground; they make activists aware of central legal and economic issues and create opportunities for forging alliances.

Co-ordinated campaigns require a strong leadership. Strong leadership is ultimately born within cadres of committed activists who form alliances, often temporary, with other committed activists within related fields. Such activists are often elitist. Their strength lies in their mutual linkages. Marable's description of the civil rights movement in the USA illustrates this process. In Britain in the 1960s 'a "race relations constellation" developed, comprising a number of organisations linked informally by common concerns and common attitudes, and a group of "race relations professionals" who worked both within and outside the government' (Heineman 1972: 126).

A powerful movement not only entails a strong central leadership representing nationally federated local groups; it also requires major funding and large-scale mobilisation. At present what we have in Britain is the incipient basis for such an alliance as national ethnic, religious, and black umbrella organisations gather strength, and as other powerful organisations – such as the church – commit themselves explicitly and specifically, as Johnson demonstrates, to the causes of ethnic minorities and the fight against racism.

The issue of funding is central here. Strong organisations and concerted campaigns require adequate funding. Almost all the essays in this volume touch on this issue and thus it needs to be examined more closely. Ethnic communities can mobilise funding internally and this gives them a great measure of autonomy. Jewish and European immigrant friendly societies in the USA, faced with a virtual absence of state-provided welfare, created powerful mutual assurance national umbrella organisations (Barton 1978), as well as hospitals, schools, and universities (Glazer 1978). In Britain most religious territorial organisations are built with internal funding. Giving to communal causes, as Banks shows in this volume, is for Jains a symbolic act, modelled upon ritual giving. It defines a series of moral communities (Werbner 1985). Fund-raising also articulates internal organisational hierarchies and leadership positions not dependent on external state recognition. For this reason ethnic groups and radical organisations are often reluctant, as Josephides indicates, to apply for state funding. Yet community groups are *entitled* to state funding as citizens and taxpayers; they often need this funding in order to build up ethnic institutions which are not dependent on the largesse of wealthy community members. State giving thus also, in a sense, implies the symbolic incorporation of ethnic groups into the wider moral community. It objectifies equality and citizenship rights. Such giving therefore has a symbolic dimension, whatever its instrumental utility. But if state largesse or provisioning is perceived by minority group members to be inadequate – given, from their point of view, the enormous resources of the state – then such allocations will increasingly be regarded by them as merely tokenistic.

Internal fund-raising and external funding applications depend on different leadership talents. In the latter case, as Banks and Werbner show, familiarity with bureaucratic and administrative procedures is all-important. The causes for which funding is required must be presented in terms comprehensible and acceptable to the state, and must be negotiated through a labyrinth of committees. In this connection Rex and Tomlinson comment dismissively that 'Fast-talking operators become skilled at knowing how to apply for money and a further stratum of the immigrant community finds itself effectively bribed into silence' (1979: 58).

State funding also depends on 'fictions' of communal unity; it both divides immigrant communities, somewhat arbitrarily, into discrete ethnic groups, and implies that each such group is an undivided unity. Hence it might be argued that state largesse has almost entirely negative implications: it undermines 'natural' leadership formations, substituting for them systems of patronage. It creates dependency. It is open to manipulation by unscrupulous brokers. It divides and rules. It is, as such, an instrument of internal colonialism.

In the long run, however, state funding also has positive implications, and, indeed it may generate a more radical movement. In creating 'fictions' of communal unity, it demands a regularisation of election procedures and public accountability in ethnic associations. In the course of negotiations over funding, the divisions within an ethnic group and the inadequacy of the services provided by voluntary associations are revealed. The state is gradually compelled to appoint professional (and, increasingly, black) state employees – youth leaders, social workers, community workers, etc. Voluntary groups come to be semi-permanently funded by the state. Such state and para-state employees often emerge, as they did indeed in the anti-colonial movements, as a radical salariat, spanning the ethnic and wider society culturally, yet politically highly committed (Alavi 1988; Anderson 1983: 104–28). They may be paid by the state, but they cannot be 'bribed into silence'.

Finally, in conclusion, we need to ask how the different dimensions of community, reviewed here, relate to social movement formation. The argument we have put forward suggests that paralleling the three phases which characterise the emergence of a social movement – 'associative empowerment', 'ideological convergence' and 'mobilisation' – are processes or organisational, ideological and experiential expansion. Ethnic segments forge greater unities, as interpretive and moral communities, by formulating joint discourses and creating broader associational networks or alliances. In doing so they draw on a growing realisation of common predicaments and experiences which unite them as communities of suffering. The move is from narrow associational loyalties and interests to encompassing unities. The imagined communities evoked in the course of this process come, over time, to refer to larger collectivities. When and if members of such collectivities mobilise for common protest or joint action, a social movement is born.

As transcendent unities such movements include, however, a variety of groups with different, and sometimes even opposing, aims. They are subject to internal power struggles over competing cultural objectives.

Ethnic and black politics are thus located within a normative or cultural field of action, of contested interpretations, and claims to power and dominance. It is a field in which the primacy of the social, cultural, symbolic, or political is asserted over the purely economic; in which the economic is culturally and politically constituted (Cohen 1969, 1974; CCCS 1982). Ethnicity, as anthropologists have long noted, reifies and fetishes culture; in ethnicity, as in nationalism, cultural mythologies and selective discourses and languages are constructed and commoditised.

We find here, then, a convergence between well-established anthropological positions and those of contemporary historians and sociologists of ethnicity, race, nationalism, and urbanism. The need is, however, to retain the specific recognition of division within unity, and of recurrent internal organisational patterns, which is the strength of ethnographic social structural approaches. The contributors to this volume analyse the *processes* underlying the emergence of local ethnic or black leaders, as historically and situationally located social agents.

The pull towards autonomous self-reliance, on the one hand, and the right to benefit from state largesse which implies dependence, on the other, is only one of a series of dilemmas and dialectical processes the study of ethnic organisations and their leaders reveals. Ultimately, the fight against racism, like the fight for cultural, religious, and political autonomy, is often a matter of combining apparently contradictory leadership styles and strategies (see Glazer's revision of Myrdal's contrast: Glazer 1978; Myrdal 1944: 709–56): of protest *and* accommodation, black power *and* social liberalism, universalism *and* particularism. Negotiation, reform, and protest tend therefore, in reality, to coexist in contemporary ethnic and anti-racist movements; if the combination is effective, the movement makes real political and economic gains. If it is counter-productive, racist and anti-immigrant forces gather support. It is essential, then, to take a broader perspective: to see the combined effect of a multitude of localised battles and different styles of leadership. This volume is intended to provide such a broad, and yet complex, view of immigrant associations and their leaders.

Notes

1 I am grateful to Iris Kalka, Rosemary Mellor, Mary Chatterjee, Muhammad Anwar, and Richard Werbner for their incisive comments on an earlier draft of this essay.
2 'Local state' follows Castells' usage and is a general term referring to local government, municipal or local authorities.

References

Alavi, Hamza (1988) 'Pakistan and Islam: ethnicity and ideology', in Fred Halliday and Hamza Alavi (eds) *State and Ideology in the Middle East and Pakistan*, London: Macmillan.

Anderson, Benedict (1983) *Imagined Communities: Reflections on the Origin and Spread of Nationalism*, London: Verso.

Anwar, Muhammad (1986) *Race and Politics: Ethnic Minorities and the British Political System*, London: Tavistock.

Barton, Josef J. (1978) 'Eastern and southern Europeans', in John Higham (ed.) *Ethnic Leadership in America*, Baltimore, Md: Johns Hopkins University Press.

Ben Tovim, Gideon and Gabriel, John (1982) 'The politics of race in Britain 1962–79: a review of the major trends', in Charles Husband (ed.) *Race in Britain: Continuity and Change*, London: Hutchinson.

Ben Tovim, Gideon, Gabriel, John, Law, Ian, and Stredder, Kathleen (1986) *The Local Politics of Race*, London: Macmillan.

Benyon, John (ed.) (1984) *Scarman and After*, London: Pergamon.

Benyon, John (1987) 'Interpretations of civil disorder' and 'Unrest and the political agenda', in John Benyon and John Solomos (eds) *The Roots of Urban Unrest*, London: Pergamon.

Blauner, Robert (1972) *Racial Oppression in America*, New York: Harper & Row.

Castells, Manuel (1983) *The City and the Grassroots: A Cross-cultural Theory of Urban Social Movements*, London: Edward Arnold.

Centre for Contemporary Cultural Studies (1982) *The Empire Strikes Back: Race and Racism in 70s Britain*, London: Hutchinson.

Cohen, Abner (1969) *Custom and Politics in Urban Africa*, London: Routledge & Kegan Paul.

Cohen, Abner (1974) *Two Dimensional Man*, Berkeley, Calif.: University of California Press.

Dumont, L. (1983) 'A modified view of our origins: the Christian beginnings of modern individualism', *Contributions to Indian Sociology* (NS) 17 (1): 1–26.

Geertz, Clifford (1973) 'After the revolution: the fate of nationalism in the new states' and 'The integrative revolution: primordial sentiments and civil politics in the new states', reprinted in *The Interpretation of Cultures*, New York: Basic Books.

Gilroy, Paul (1987) *There Ain't No Black in the Union Jack: The Cultural Politics of Race and Nation*, London: Hutchinson.

Glazer, Nathan (1978) 'The Jews', in John Higham (ed.) *Ethnic Leadership in America*, Baltimore, MD: Johns Hopkins University Press.

Gluckman, Max (1958) (1940, 1942) *Analysis of a Social Situation in Modern Zululand*, Rhodes-Livingstone Paper 28, Manchester: Manchester University Press for the Rhodes-Livingstone Institute.

Hall, Stuart, Critcher, C., Jefferson, T., Clarke, J. and Roberts, B. (1978) *Policing the Crisis: Mugging, the State and Law and Order*, London: Macmillan.

Heineman, Benjamin W. (1972) *The Politics of the Powerless: A study of the Campaign Against Racial Discrimination*, London: Oxford University Press for the Institute of Race Relations.

Higham, John (1978) 'Introduction: the forms of ethnic leadership', in John Higham (ed.) *Ethnic Leadership in America*, Baltimore, Md: Johns Hopkins University Press.

Huggins, Nathan I. (1978) 'Afro-Americans', in John Higham (ed.) *Ethnic Leadership in America*, Baltimore, Md: Johns Hopkins University Press.

Kapferer, Bruce (1988) *Legends of People, Myths of State: Violence, Intolerance and Political Culture in Sri Lanka and Australia*, Washington, DC: Smithsonian Institution Press.

Katznelson, Ira (1973) *Black Men, White Cities*, Oxford: Oxford University Press for the Institute of Race Relations.

Keyes, Charles F. (1981) 'The dialectic of ethnic change', in Charles F. Keyes (ed.) *Ethnic Change*, Seattle, Wash.: University of Washington Press.

Lawrence, Daniel (1974) *Black Migrants, White Natives: A Study of Race Relations in Nottingham*, Cambridge: Cambridge University Press.

Marable, Manning (1985) *Black American Politics: From the Washington Marches to Jesse Jackson*, London: Verso.

Mellor, Rosemary (1989) 'Urban sociology: a trend report', *Sociology* 23 (2): 241–60.

Miles, Robert (1982) *Capitalism, Racism and Migrant Labour*, London: Routledge & Kegan Paul.

Miles, Robert and Phizacklea, Annie (1980) *Labour and Racism*, London: Routledge & Kegan Paul.

Myrdal, Gunnar (1944) *An American Dilemma: The Negro Problem and Modern Democracy*, vol. II, New York: Harper Brothers.

Pearson, David G. (1981) *Race, Class and Political Activism: A Study of West Indians in Britain*, Westmead: Gower.

Pryce, Ken (1979) *Endless Pressure: A Study of West Indian Lifestyles in Bristol*, Bristol: Bristol Classical Press.

Rex, John (1982) 'Black militancy and class conflict', in Robert Miles and Annie Phizacklea (eds) *Racism and Political Action in Britain*, London: Routledge & Kegan Paul.

Rex, John (1986) 'The role of class analysis in the study of race relations – a Weberian perspective', in John Rex and D. Mason (eds) *Theories of Race and Ethnic Relations*, Cambridge: Cambridge University Press.

Rex, John and Tomlinson, Sally (1979) *Colonial Immigrants in a British City: A Class Analysis*, London: Routledge & Kegan Paul.

Said, Edward W. (1983) 'Opponents, audiences, constituencies and community', in Hal Foster (ed.) *Post Modern Culture*, London: Pluto Press.

Thomas, William I. and Znaniecki, F. (1958) *The Polish Community in America*, vol. II, Chicago: Dover. Originally published in 1918.

Turner, V.W. (1957) *Schism and Continuity in an African Society: A Study of Ndembu Village Life*, Manchester: Manchester University Press for the Rhodes-Livingstone Institute.

Werbner, Pnina (1985) 'The organisation of giving and ethnic elites', *Ethnic and Racial Studies*, 8 (3): 368–88.

Werbner, Pnina (1990) *The Migration Process: Capital, Gifts and Offerings among British Pakistanis*, Explorations in Anthropology Series, Oxford: Berg.

Wilson, William J. (1987) *The Truly Disadvantaged: The Inner City, the Underclass, and Public Policy*, Chicago: University of Chicago Press.

Part one

Community, Party Politics, and the Black Experience

Chapter one

Ethnic minorities' representation

Voting and electoral politics in Britain, and the role of leaders

Muhammad Anwar

Introduction

Leadership in the ethnic minority communities is as important to study as the areas of kinship, employment, and housing (Anwar 1979). Ethnicity has social significance in structuring wider authority relationships between various groups in Britain. Through their ethnic organisations, the leaders might find ways of promoting the participation of their communities in the institutions of British society, including political participation. But what type of ethnic minority leaders exist in Britain?

I have suggested elsewhere that there are 'formal' and 'traditional' leaders who represent the ethnic communities (Anwar 1979). Formal leaders are those who represent ethnic communities through their organisations, whether elected, nominated or self-appointed. They are mainly educated, and are professionals who have contacts with the wider society. Their role is important in inter-ethnic situations.

The traditional leaders draw their support from kinship groups. Their leadership depends on age, length of stay in this country, and sometimes the number of relatives sponsored and patronised. The traditional leaders usually play their part in intra-ethnic situations and formal leaders depend on their support in an inter-ethnic situation, because sometimes the traditional leaders are more effective in mobilising support, particularly on religious issues, as we have recently seen with the Rushdie affair and at the recent local elections.

It must be pointed out that we will find some differences between Afro-Caribbeans and Asians when looking at formal and traditional leaders. This is partly due to their different cultural backgrounds and partly the nature of different migrations. 'The notion of the "brothers-on-the-block" is a central notion amongst West Indians in Britain as it is in the USA, and amongst Asians, kin-organisations are a prime focus of trust' (Rex and Tomlinson 1979). Therefore, for any study of ethnic group mobilisation and political participation in Britain, these differences are important to bear in mind.

The distinction of 'leaders from the periphery' and dynamic leadership oriented towards the centre of the group (Lewin 1948), and the leadership of accommodation and the leadership of protest suggested by others (Higham 1978), are also useful contributions to a sociology of ethnic leadership. Higham points out that the distinction between accommodation and protest, as alternative strategies for dealing with the host society, was given classic formulation in Gunner Myrdal's great work *An American Dilemma* (1969). It is clear from several other studies of ethnic groups in the USA that ethnic leadership and ethnic organisations have played an important role in the development of that society. However, in Britain this is a relatively new subject for study.

I have suggested in the Introduction I that there are more than two thousand ethnic minority organisations throughout the country. These include social, welfare, religious, educational, political, and professional organisations at local, regional, and national levels. These are mainly based on ethnic, regional, or national origin, or on religion, except some professional ones, e.g. the Overseas Doctors Association (ODA). The role of ethnic minority leaders and these organisations is crucial as they provide the channels of communication with the wider society.

Currently, some well-established national ethnic organisations exist, including the West Indian Standing Conference, the Confederation of Indian Organisations, the Standing Conference of Pakistani Organisations, and the Federation of Bangladeshi Organisations. There are also several national minority religious organisations, which include the Union of Muslim Organisations (UMO), the UK Islamic Mission, the Supreme Council of Sikhs, and several Hindu organisations and black churches.

However, there is no one representative national organisation covering all ethnic minority groups, say, on the lines of the Jewish Board of Deputies, which was established in 1760, and constitutes the lay leadership of Anglo-Jewry and provides a united front in relation to the wider British society. Although some attempts by ethnic minority leaders have been made in the past to form a national civil rights organisation, as found in the USA, there seems no prospect in the near future for such a development.

Following a visit to Britain by the Revd Martin Luther King, the Campaign Against Racial Discrimination (CARD) was set up in December 1964. This organisation hoped to influence central government, Parliament, and the media and to 'build a mass united front for coloured immigrants and their children'. However, the tensions between these two roles and between the West Indians, Indians, Pakistanis, and white British who comprised CARD caused the failure of a unique pressure group within the British political system. It collapsed after three years, in the autumn of 1967, and left a large ethnic minority population without a national spokesman (for details see Heineman 1972).

In February 1965 the Racial Adjustment Action Society was formed. In June 1967 the Universal Coloured People's Organisation was set up, and it invited Stokely Carmichael, the then American black student leader, to speak. These organisations were joined mainly by the West Indians. These and other organisations which were formed 'began to explore new possibilities of independent political and industrial action by immigrants' (Rex and Tomlinson 1979).

Another attempt to form a national umbrella organisation of ethnic minorities was made in the mid-1970s with the general encouragement of the then Community Relations Commission and with financial support from the Calouste Gulbenkian Foundation. A conference, Black People in Britain, took place in 1975, followed by another one in 1976 (for details see Dhavan 1976). An organisation was formed, but it slowly disappeared.

However, as already mentioned, several national, regional, and local ethnic organisations are playing an important role in interethnic relations.

The colonial links of British ethnic minorities and the struggle of blacks for political rights in the USA are important factors to bear in mind when comparing the two countries. Because of the historical links of ethnic minorities from the New Commonwealth and Pakistan, in Britain they have always had a legal right to participate fully in politics. This includes the right to vote and to be a candidate in elections. On the other hand, the civil rights movement in the 1960s in the USA (Morris 1984), among others, achieved the Voting Rights Act of 1965. The civil rights movement in the process produced several well-known leaders who were later elected as officials. Overall, the political participation of blacks, in particular, expanded. The number of black voters and the number of black elected representatives increased every year. However, in the absence of such a mass movement in Britain, what role are ethnic minority leaders playing?

The role of ethnic minority leaders and ethnic minority organisations is very important in the political process. Therefore, in this chapter, first, I analyse the participation of ethnic minorities in the electoral process, and then present the role of their leaders in this context. The participation of ethnic minorities in the British political process is an important indication of their involvement in the society.

The importance of the ethnic minority vote

Since, as outlined in Introduction I, ethnic minorities are not randomly distributed throughout the country, their concentration in particular conurbations means that statistically they are in a position to influence voting strength in those areas. Within these conurbations, they are even further concentrated in some parliamentary constituencies and local wards and are therefore in a position to make an impact on the overall voting turnout in those inner-city constituencies and wards. For example, according to the 1981 census, there were fifty-eight constituencies with more than 15 per cent of their total population living in households with the head born in the New Commonwealth or Pakistan. Nineteen of them had more than 25 per cent and seven had over 33 per cent (with three approaching almost half: Birmingham Ladywood, Brent South, and Ealing Southall). There are many others with an ethnic minority population of between 10 and 15 per cent. These figures do not take into account ethnic minorities where the head of household was born in this country. However, it is estimated that in 1987 there were about a hundred parliamentary constituencies in England with an ethnic minority population of over 10 per cent.

As far as the local election wards are concerned, there are now several hundred with more than a 15 per cent ethnic minority population, and several with almost 50 per cent. In 1981, the highest proportion of ethnic minority population, 85.4 per cent, was in Northolt Ward in the Borough of Ealing, where it was estimated that almost 76 per cent of electors were Asians out of a total of 8,148 electors on the register. Glebe Ward in the same borough had almost 60 per cent Asian electors. It must be pointed out, however, that counting Asian names on the register is an underestimation of their actual numbers in the population as some Asians do have anglicised names. There is also under-registration among Asians compared with whites. This means that the real number of Asians eligible to register will be greater than estimated. The same applies to other ethnic minorities.

The level of political awareness among ethnic minorities has increased over the past two decades. This is partly because they have come to recognise that their sense of security in this country can be buttressed by such an awareness, and partly because an increasing number of ethnic minority organisations are articulating issues which impinge on their sense of security. The ethnic press has also played an important role in the creation of this awareness. In this regard, ethnic minorities are responding to speeches and comments that are widely disseminated by the mass media, including the ethnic press, and particularly during election campaigns, and are thus in a position to take action, both individually and through their leaders, in order to guarantee their own future in this country.

The response of the major political parties in this context is important too. These parties have not only felt the need to take steps to involve ethnic minorities in their activities and campaigns, but have also openly sought their votes in various elections between 1974 and the general election in 1987, a pattern which applies to local elections too.

The participation of ethnic minorities in the political process thus depends on several factors. These include whether they register on the electoral register; if they are on the register, whether they come out to vote; and how they compare with white people in this respect.

Registration

To what extent do ethnic minorities register? We have examined this phenomenon since 1974. (Anwar 1975, 1980, 1984, 1986). In 1974, a sample survey showed that 27 per cent of Asians, compared with 37 per cent of Afro-Caribbeans and 6 per cent of whites from the same areas, were not registered. In 1976, checks in two areas where field-work had taken place in 1974 showed a great improvement in the registration level of ethnic minorities. In Birmingham it was found that 5 per cent of Asians and 13 per cent of Afro-Caribbeans were not on the register, compared with 4 per cent of whites. In Bradford, 9 per cent of Asians were not registered as against 5 per cent of whites from the same areas.

At the 1979 general election a survey in 24 constituencies spread throughout the country, however, showed that 23 per cent of Asians, 19 per cent of Afro-Caribbeans, and 7 per cent of whites were not registered. Compared with the 1974 survey, the level of registration among Afro-Caribbeans rose by 18 per cent (from 63 per cent in 1974 to 81 per cent in 1979), while among Asians it increased marginally from 73 per cent in 1974 to 77 per cent in 1979. Among the white population, it remained virtually constant (94 per cent in 1974 and 93 per cent in 1979). However, it is relevant to point out that the results showed wide variations from area to area. Part of this variation was linked with the policies of local electoral registration offices and with the interest taken by the political parties and ethnic minority organisations and leaders in persuading and helping members of their groups to register.

45

The results of the 1979 survey were confirmed by an OPCS study undertaken in 1981 at the time of the census. The study showed that in Inner London both the Asian and Afro-Caribbean people had about double the non-registration rate of white people (27 and 24 per cent as opposed to 12 per cent) (Todd and Butcher 1982). We again monitored registration in 1983 in the same areas as in 1979. This survey showed that among those qualified to be registered, Asians' level of registration had increased from 77 per cent to 79 per cent. But the level of registration among Afro-Caribbeans had fallen to 76 per cent in 1983, from 81 per cent in 1979 (see Table 1.1). The fieldwork for the survey was undertaken in inner-city wards where registration levels are generally low.

When we looked at the 1983 survey results at constituency level, these showed that there was a good deal of variation in registration levels as far as ethnic minorities were concerned. For example, particularly low levels of registration (60 per cent or less) were recorded in Ealing Southall, Croydon North-East, Hackney North and Stoke Newington, Norwood and Walsall South constituencies. On the other hand, Wolverhampton South-West, Preston, Rochdale, Sheffield Heeley, Leicester South, Manchester Gorton, Birmingham Sparkbrook, and Battersea constituencies had over 80 per cent registration among ethnic minorities.

During 1986, in a research project funded by the Commission for Racial Equality (CRE) in five areas in the North of England, Mich Le Lohe found that 18.2 per cent of Asians and 14.6 per cent of Afro-Caribbeans were not registered compared with 18.1 per cent of whites from the same areas. However, after taking out those who had 'good reason' for non-registration (moving house, not eligible because of nationality, etc.), 4.7 per cent of Asians, 8.4 per cent of Afro- Caribbeans, and 3.9 per cent of whites were not registered (see Le Lohe 1987).

Although steady improvement has taken place in the registration levels of ethnic minorities in the last thirteen years, the high level of non-registration among ethnic minorities and, also now, among whites in the inner cities needs action. Reasons for non-registration include recent arrival, the language difficulty that Asians and various other ethnic groups face, the general alienation of some groups, and feared harassment and racial attacks from the National Front and other such organisations, who could identify Asians from their names on the register. There is also the fear of 'fishing expeditions' by immigration authorities. A final reason for non-registration could be the administrative inefficiency of the registration offices.

At present, steps are being taken to reduce the higher level of non-registration among ethnic minorities. Several areas now use either

Table 1.1 Registration by racial groups: comparison of general elections

	White			Total ethnic minority			Afro-Caribbean			Asian			Other ethnic minority		
	1983 (994) %	1979 (1,041) %	1974 (150) %	1983 (1,020) %	1979 (774) %	1974 (183) %	1983 (152) %	1979 (145) %	1974 (41) %	1983 (822) %	1979 (570) %	1974 (142) %	1983 (46) %	1979 (59) %	1974 – %
Registered	81	93	94	78	77	70	76	81	63	79	77	73	78	71	–
Not registered	19	7	6	22	23	30	24	19	27	21	23	27	22	27	–

Note: Percentages are based on those eligible to vote
Source: Anwar 1984

Table 1.2 Asian and non-Asian turnout in Bradford West, Burnley, and Rochdale: 1979 General Election

Polling station	Asian electors	Non-Asian electors	Asian proportion %	Asian voters	Asian turnout %	Non-Asian voters	Non-Asian turnout %
Bradford Drummond	773	398	66.0	531	68.9	206	51.8
Bradford Grange	1,692	1,894	47.2	1,333	78.8	998	52.7
Bradford St. Andrews	332	253	56.7	185	55.7	162	64.0
Bradford Southbrook	1,093	2,006	35.3	821	75.1	905	45.1
Bradford (4) total/av	3,890	4,551	46.1	2,870	73.8	2,271	49.9
Burnley Stoneyholme	472	1,038	31.2	355	75.2	729	70.2
Rochdale West St	326	285	53.4	199	61.0	187	65.6
Rochdale Silver St	137	1,135	10.8	112	81.8	735	64.8
Rochdale Shepherd	581	477	54.9	415	71.4	308	64.6
Total/av (8) above	5,406	7,486	42.0	3,951	73.1	4,230	56.5

Source: Anwar 1980

special leaflets designed for ethnic minorities in several languages which go with Form A, or a translation of Form A into different languages. Some registration offices – Ealing, for example – now employ full-time, year-round fieldworkers who visit homes from which no Form A has been received during the previous year. Among others, registration offices in Lambeth and Haringey, London, in Birmingham, and in Bradford have made special efforts to register ethnic minority electors. Hackney in London started a special registration campaign. The Home Office has issued a Code of Practice for Electoral Registration Officers (EROs), which is also relevant in this context. The ethnic minority press has been used and ethnic programmes on radio and television have also helped to make people aware of the importance and the timing of registration. Political parties in some local areas, ethnic minority leaders and organisations, and some local Community Relations Councils have all made special efforts to increase registration levels in their areas.

It is due to such efforts, and an increasing awareness among the ethnic minorities of the political process, that their registration levels are edging nearer to those of white people. But do those who register come out to vote at elections?

Turnout

Over the last two decades, surveys at the time of various local and general elections have shown that, on average, Asian turnout is always higher than that of non-Asians (including whites) from the same areas; e.g. at the October 1974 general election a survey in Bradford and Rochdale showed that the turnout rate among Asians was 57.7 per cent compared with 54.6 per cent for non-Asians (Anwar 1986).

At the 1979 general election, turnout rates at certain polling stations in 19 constituencies were calculated for Asian and non-Asian voters. In 18 of the 19 areas the Asian turnout was higher than that of non-Asians. On average it was 65 per cent for Asians and 61 per cent for non-Asians. Eight selected polling stations in the three constituencies of Bradford West, Burnley, and Rochdale were also covered at the same election. Once again, it was confirmed by the findings that the level of turnout among Asians was higher than that of non-Asian voters (73.1 per cent compared with 56.5 per cent), as shown in Table 1.2.

To look at this trend, we monitored another type of election, the European Parliamentary election in June 1979. Again it was found that the Asian turnout in Bradford and Burnley (for four polling stations monitored) was higher than that of non-Asians – 38.5 per cent compared with 21.3 per cent. It is indeed significant that, while the turnout rate among all electors nationally for the European Parliamentary election was lower than their turnout rate for the general election a month earlier, the turnout rate among Asians was not only higher than that of their non-Asian neighbours who voted at the same polling stations, but also higher than the national turnout rate of 32.1 per cent. The Asian turnout rate of 38.5 per cent was almost twice that of their non-Asian neighbours, and this rate was achieved at an election which the general electorate clearly did not consider to be as important as the general election a month previously (Le Lohe 1984).

Although there are methodological difficulties in calculating the rates of turnout for Afro-Caribbeans, and for other ethnic groups who have anglicised names which are not easily identifiable from the electoral register, some studies have shown that the Afro-Caribbean turnout was also higher than that of whites from the same area.

Some further work during the 1980–2 local elections also confirmed this trend. For example, in Ealing in one ward at the 1981 local election, the turnout rate among Asians was 59.1 per cent compared with 32.8 per cent for non-Asians. In 1982 in Bradford, results for one ward showed that the Asian turnout was 58.4 per cent compared with 23.1 per cent for non-Asians.

Twenty constituencies were monitored at the 1983 general election as part of a survey designed to look at the turnout of different ethnic groups. Some of these constituencies were those that were covered in the 1979 survey referred to above. Interviewers recorded the total number of voters leaving the polling stations, as well as each voter's ethnic group. At this election, 81 per cent of Asian voters turned out to vote compared to 60 per cent of non-Asian voters. In 18 of the 20 constituencies covered, turnout among Asian voters was higher than that among non-Asians. Almost a quarter of the electors on the register in the areas surveyed were Asian, and the greater likelihood of their turning out to vote suggests that they had a significant impact on the final outcome in each constituency (Anwar 1986).

All these results show that Asian and other ethnic minorities may be more reliable voters than their white neighbours and are consequently in a better position to influence the outcome of elections where they vote.

Voting patterns

We will now look at who the various ethnic groups, including whites, voted for in the last three general elections, 1979, 1983, and 1987. It must be pointed out that the CRE surveys in 1979 and 1983 were mainly undertaken in inner-city areas where support for the Labour Party is usually higher.

At the 1979 general election a sample of voters from twenty-four constituencies were asked to record (on duplicate 'ballot' papers) the way they voted in the polling stations. The 'ballot' papers were similar to those used in the real election, except that they were marked by the interviewers to record the voter's ethnic group. The 'ballot' papers were placed in a box by the voters as they left the polling booth. Out of a total sample of 3,225 voters involved in this exercise, 1,205 were from ethnic minority groups. The results showed that the majority of ethnic minority voters actually voted for the Labour Party as against other parties. While 50 per cent of whites voted Labour, 90 per cent of Afro-Caribbeans and 86 per cent of Asians in the sample voted Labour.

Among whites in the sample, Labour had an 11 per cent lead over the Conservatives compared with a 78 per cent lead among Asians and 85 per cent among Afro-Caribbeans. When we compare the 1979 survey results with another undertaken in 1974, we find that in the wards in seven constituencies where comparisons of voting were possible, it appeared that the Conservative vote among ethnic minorities, particularly Asians, had increased in 1979. It was found that ethnic minority 'swings' to the Conservative Party were largely accounted for by the voting pattern of Asian voters as against Afro-Caribbean voters. Whereas Afro-Caribbean voters solidly backed the Labour Party, Asian voters spread their votes between the Labour and Conservative parties in such a way that higher proportions voted for the Conservative Party in some constituencies than in others. In seven constituencies out of the twenty-four we surveyed, over 15 per cent of Asian voters cast their votes for the Conservative Party.

The CRE's exit poll of the 1983 general election based on 4,240 voters in twenty-five constituencies showed that 71 per cent of Asians voted Labour, 5 per cent Conservative, and 11 per cent for the Liberal/SDP Alliance candidates, as shown in Table 1.3. As a group, 70 per cent of ethnic minority voters voted Labour. It must be pointed out that most of the twenty-five constituencies covered in this survey were Labour-held at the time of the 1983 general election and this had some bearing on these results. However, a national exit poll which was conducted by the Harris Research Centre (1983) for ITN also confirmed this trend. It showed that the majority of ethnic minorities had voted Labour (57 per cent) but 24 per cent and 16 per cent of them had voted Conservative and Alliance respectively.

The comparison of the two CRE surveys showed that the Asian support for Labour had decreased from 86 per cent in 1979 to 71 per

Table 1.3 Voting patterns by ethnic group: 1983 General Election

	Ethnic group					
	Total (4,240) %	White (2,190) %	All ethnic minority (2,050) %	Afro-Car. (603) %	Asian (1,375) %	Other ethnic minority (72) %
Labour	48	35	70	72	71	49
Conservative	20	29	6	6	5	22
Alliance	14	17	9	4	11	9
Others	1	1	1	1	1	–
Refused	16	18	13	17	12	19

Source: Anwar 1986

cent in 1983. Another survey showed that 21 per cent of ethnic minority voters who had voted for the Labour Party in 1979 switched from Labour to other parties at the 1983 election (*Guardian*, 13 June 1983). But, in comparison, the Labour vote had remained strongest among Afro-Caribbeans. Only the Liberal/SDP Alliance had substantially increased its share of the vote in these constituencies among both white and ethnic minority voters. The highest recorded ethnic minority vote for the Labour Party was in Bristol East (93 per cent), for the Conservatives in Croydon North-East (27 per cent), and for the Alliance in Rochdale (54 per cent), the last two with a predominantly Asian electorate. This pattern was consistent with the CRE survey of the 1979 general election referred to above. Monitoring of these three constituencies had shown that the personal popularity of the respective candidates for these parties was one of the key factors in attracting the ethnic minority vote.

A survey for the Hansib group of papers conducted by the Harris Research Centre during the 1987 general election campaign (25–9 May) about the voting intentions of Afro-Caribbeans and Asians showed that 86.8 per cent of Afro-Caribbeans and 66.8 per cent of Asians intended to vote for the Labour Party compared with 5.7 per cent and 22.7 per cent respectively for the Conservative Party. Ten per cent of Asians and 7 per cent of Afro-Caribbeans intended to vote for the Alliance. No white electors were included in the survey. As these were only intentions, we do not know how these ethnic minorities actually voted on the polling day (*Asian Times*, June 1987).

Another poll conducted by the Harris Research Centre, in London on 8–9 June 1987, however, showed that 64 per cent of ethnic minority voters intended to vote Labour, 23 per cent Conservative, and 11 per cent Alliance. On the other hand, 32 per cent of whites intended to vote Labour, 45 per cent Conservative, and 23 per cent Alliance.

The indication of ethnic minority voting patterns at the 1987 general election came from an ITN poll also conducted by the Harris Research Centre. It showed that 61 per cent of Asians and 92 per cent of Afro-Caribbeans had voted for Labour compared with 31 per cent of whites. On the other hand, 20 per cent of Asians, 6 per cent of Afro-Caribbeans, and 43 per cent of whites had voted for the Conservative Party. The Alliance received 17 per cent of votes from Asians, 24 per cent from whites, and none from Afro-Caribbeans in the sample. It must be pointed out that these results are based on a small sample of ethnic minorities.

A recent Harris poll revealed that nearly 60 per cent of the 542 ethnic minority respondents said they voted Labour in the 1987 election and 62 per cent hope to vote Labour in the next general election. Seven per cent said they voted Conservative and will continue to do so. However, 27 per cent did not vote at the last election and 16 per cent did not intend to vote in the next (*Guardian*, 4 July 1989).

The voting patterns of ethnic minorities depend on many factors. However, it appears that regular contacts between political parties and ethnic minorities, their organisation and mobilisation at elections, whether the candidate is personally known to the ethnic minority electors, and their party policies generally and about race and immigration issues in particular are important factors in attracting ethnic minority votes. Also, recent research shows that the ethnic minorities now vote on party lines and not on ethnic lines (Anwar 1984). This was demonstrated recently in a parliamentary by-election in Vauxhall where two ethnic minority candidates stood in protest against the Labour Party candidate (who was later elected) as that party had not selected an ethnic minority candidate. The two ethnic minority candidates received very few votes (see *The Times*, 17 June 1989).

The political parties' response

The participation of ethnic minorities in the political process is importantly affected by the policies and initiatives taken by the political parties. The major political party leaders have openly sought ethnic minority voters' support in the last few years without the fear of losing white voters. Some political parties have set up special bodies whose role is to attract ethnic minorities' support. For example, the Conservative Party has had an ethnic minority unit in the Conservative Central Office's Department of Community Affairs since 1976. Its objective is to make party members aware of the growing electoral importance of Asian and Afro-Caribbean electors, and to influence party policy so as to improve the image of the party among ethnic minorities and, thus, attract their support. The unit helped form an Anglo-Asian Conservative Society through which it recruited Asians directly into the party. This was followed by the formation of the Anglo-West Indian Conservative Society with the same objective. However, at national level the Anglo-Asian and Anglo-West Indian societies have now been replaced by another organisation called the One Nation Forum with roughly the same objectives. It appears that the societies at the local level will continue as before.

These societies have representation on the area and national committees of the National Union of Conservative and Unionist Associations. At the last count, there were twenty-seven local Anglo-Asian Conservative societies throughout the country. Among their activities, they arrange meetings between Conservative candidates and Asian and Afro-Caribbean groups at election times.

The Labour Party Race and Action Group (LPRAG) was set up in 1975 as a pressure group to educate and advise the party on relevant issues. More recently Labour's National Executive Committee (NEC) set up a Black and Asian Advisory Committee similar to the party's women's and local government committees, to attract ethnic minorities' support for the party (for the controversy surrounding this committee, see Jeffers, this volume).

The Liberal Party did not have special arrangements for ethnic minorities within its constitutional framework, but it had a Community Relations Panel which included ethnic minority members. It met regularly to discuss issues relevant to these minorities and also formulated policies which the party implemented to attract ethnic minority members, as well as campaign strategies at elections specially directed at them.

Like the Liberal Party, the SDP had not got any special arrangements for ethnic minorities within the party's constitution. However, it encouraged ethnic minority candidates to become members of its National Council. There were in 1984 two such directly elected members on the council. The SDP had started a Campaign for Racial Justice which was asked to nominate two ethnic minority candidates to the council in order to make it more broad-based and reflective of the composition of its membership. However, with the newly merged Social Liberal Democrat and SDP parties, there may be a new framework to attract ethnic minority support in the future.

Ethnic minority candidates

Another way to examine the response of the political parties to the question of ethnic minority participation is to look at the number of candidates adopted by the main political parties in the last few years. What sort of constituencies did they contest? What support did these candidates receive from the party machinery? What success rate did the ethnic minority candidates achieve? Why did a lot of 'independent' and 'fringe' party ethnic minority candidates stand at elections? Do they succeed, and how does their success rate compare with that of ethnic minority candidates who stand for the main political parties?

Three MPs from the Indian sub-continent were elected to the House of Commons before the Second World War. The first, Dadabhai Naoroji, was elected as long ago as 1892, as a Liberal with a majority of five at Finsbury Central. The second, Sir Mancherjee Bhownagree, was twice elected as a Conservative for Bethnal Green North-East, in 1895 and 1900. The third, Shapurji Saklatvala, was twice elected for Battersea North – as a Labour Candidate in 1922 and as a Communist in 1924. In the House of Lords, there was one member from the Indian sub-continent, Lord Sinha of Raipur (1863–1928). However, since the Second World War there had been no MPs from the ethnic minorities until 1987, although there have been three members of the House of Lords, Lords Constantine, Pitt, and Chitnis (Anwar 1986).

The first ethnic minority candidate since the Second World War put forward by a major political party for a general election was Sardar K.S.N. Ahluwala, who contested Willesden West for the Liberal Party in 1950. Dr David Pitt (now Lord Pitt) contested Hampstead in 1959 and Clapham in 1970 for the Labour Party. In 1970, there were also three ethnic minority candidates who stood for the Liberal Party. In February 1974 the Labour Party put forward a Pakistani, Councillor Bashir Mann from Glasgow, to contest East Fife. Dhani Prem (Coventry South-East) stood for the Liberals. None of them had any chance of winning. In the October 1974 general election there was only one ethnic minority candidate, Cecil Williams who stood for the Liberal Party. In the 1979 general election there were five ethnic minority candidates put forward by the three main political parties: one Labour candidate, two Liberals and two Conservatives. This was the first time since 1945 that the Conservative Party had nominated ethnic minority candidates. In the event, none of the candidates was elected because they contested seats where they had no chance of winning.

At the 1983 general election there were eighteen ethnic minority candidates who stood for the major (four) parties. How did they perform as candidates? Most of them performed like any other candidate for their respective parties. For example, in 17 of the 18 constituencies contested, where comparison with the notional party position in 1979 was possible, the parties' position was unchanged (Anwar 1984). However, as in 1979, no ethnic minority candidate contested a winnable or 'safe' seat (except Paul Boateng who fought Hemel Hempstead, a notionally winnable seat on the basis of the redrawn boundaries).

The analysis of the Independent or fringe party ethnic minority candidates who stood in general elections between 1950 and 1983 shows that their performance, on the whole, had been 'poor' compared with those who stood for the main political parties. But why did these candidates stand in those elections? A close examination of their campaigns shows that some, like other fringe or Independent candidates in elections, stood because they wanted to air some issues, others stood for small parties, and still others stood because they wanted to protest against the lack of ethnic minority representation in the House of Commons.

At the 1987 general election, out of the twenty-seven ethnic minority candidates for the four main political parties, four were elected. The four, all Labour, were Keith Vaz (Leicester East), Diane Abbot (Hackney North and Stoke Newington), Paul Boateng (Brent South), and Bernie Grant (Tottenham). The three London MPs were all elected in 'safe' Labour seats. However, Keith Vaz won with a swing of over 9 per cent from the Conservative candidate, Peter Bruinvels, compared with a swing of just over 2.2 per cent for Labour candidates in other seats in the East Midlands. The performance of other ethnic minority candidates was, in general terms, like that of other party candidates in the same regions.

However, it must be pointed out that the phenomenon of the performance of an ethnic minority candidate is a complex matter. There are many factors affecting such performances and these could vary according to his or her party label, the characteristics of the area of contest, the personal popularity of the candidate, rejection by some white voters on grounds of colour, and whether the seat is 'safe' or 'winnable'. Some of these reasons could equally apply to a white candidate. However, there is enough evidence to indicate that now ethnic minority candidates are increasingly being accepted as 'party' candidates. Many have been successful in local elections in the last few years, and in the 1987 general election. For example, in the Greater London boroughs elections in May 1986, over 150 ethnic minority councillors were elected. Others were elected in Leicester,

Bradford, and Birmingham, to mention but a few areas. Altogether, it is estimated that there are over 200 ethnic minority councillors throughout the country.

The main political parties have continued their efforts to attract ethnic minority electoral support. Some of these efforts were reflected in the selection of several ethnic minority candidates for the 1987 general election and the recent local elections. In the 1988 local elections, monitored by the CRE, out of the 58 ethnic candidates, 30 were elected, 29 for the Labour Party and one for the Conservative Party.

Ethnic minority organisations and the role of leaders

The history of ethnic minority organisations in Britain is as long as the presence of ethnic minorities themselves. For example, there was an Indian Workers Association in the 1930s (John 1969). At present, the number of these organisations runs into thousands. One recent analysis I undertook based on several sources showed that there were over two thousand ethnic minority organisations. These organisations include social, welfare, self-help, women's, religious, professional, and political groups. Some cover a combination of these interests. Their leaders play a crucial role in the political context in organising their members and mobilising support for the political parties. Both 'formal' and 'traditional' leaders play their due role in the political participation of ethnic minorities. Young people are, however, sometimes critical of the ineffectiveness of ethnic minority organisations and their leaders (Anwar 1976). Some of them prefer to participate directly in the political parties' machinery rather than through ethnic minority leaders. But as a consequence of this participation, they often themselves become ethnic minority leaders.

The activities of ethnic minority leaders and ethnic minority organisations in terms of political participation or as pressure groups take place regularly, but their 'overt' role is more noticeable at election times. I have presented in some detail the role of Pakistani organisations and their leaders in various elections in Rochdale (Anwar 1979). For example, in 1972 the Pakistani associations held meetings to make Pakistanis aware of the dangers of the British Campaign to Stop Immigration. The Pakistan Welfare Association asked the Pakistanis to support the Liberal candidate, Cyril Smith, as he was more sympathetic towards their problems. Pakistani leaders acted as polling agents and campaigned actively. Later elections in Rochdale have followed similar patterns. The participation of ethnic minority leaders and organisations in election campaigns in Bradford has been documented by Mich Le Lohe (1975, 1982).

At national level in the 1979 general election, for example, various ethnic minority organisations mobilised support among their members. Some of them issued political statements in this connection. The Standing Conference of Pakistani Organisations (SCOPO), for example, advised its members and other Pakistanis to vote Liberal in constituencies where the Liberal candidate had an advantage, but otherwise to vote Labour. On the other hand, the President of the Confederation of Indian Organisations made a public plea for Asians to vote Conservative (Anwar 1986). The Black People's Manifesto Conference issued a manifesto which demanded action on sixteen specific issues and was sent to candidates standing in areas with ethnic minority electors.

At the 1983 and 1987 general elections, many local and national representatives of ethnic minority organisations made statements about their participation. At the 1983 general election, the Confederation of Indian Organisations, in conjunction with the West Indian Standing Conference and the Federation of Bangladeshi Organisations, even decided to put forward three ethnic minority candidates as a protest. One of their spokesmen said, 'we are not creating a different party or racial group. We are doing it in order to teach a lesson to the political parties not to take us for granted' (*Sunday Times*, 29 May 1983). Because of some disillusionment with the Labour Party among ethnic minority activists for not selecting ethnic minority candidates for safe seats, the action of putting forward Independent candidates at the 1983 general election was taken. It is assumed that one such candidate, R. Ganatra (Independent) in Leicester East, who received 970 votes, cost the Labour Party this seat, because the Conservative candidate, Peter Bruinvels, won the seat by only 933 votes (for details, see Anwar 1986). At the 1987 general election, Leicester East was won by Keith Vaz, the first Asian to enter the House of Commons after the Second World War.

Recently, the ethnic minority organisations and ethnic leaders have become more active in the political process. Some have joined the Conservative Party's One Nation Forum. Several others are active in the Labour Party's unofficial Black Sections. The Black Sections recently launched a campaign, for example, to target more than thirty parliamentary constituencies in an attempt to increase the number of ethnic minority Labour MPs (*Guardian*, 26 February 1989). At the 1987 general election, Labour had twelve ethnic minority candidates and four of these were elected. With the process of re-selection of Labour MPs which has recently started, the Black Sections are increasing the pressure for the adoption of more ethnic minority candidates for the next general election.

At the 1989 local elections ethnic leaders and organisations played an active part in the election campaign. Muslims, in particular, due to the Rushdie affair, were very active. They also put forward Independent candidates and achieved up to 30 per cent of the vote in Leicestershire, and one Muslim won a seat in Blackburn with the help of some Conservative support. This showed that organised co-operation could put pressure on the political parties for action for their demands.

It appears from the recent trends that the role of the ethnic minority organisations and their leaders, some of whom are now elected as local councillors and MPs in the political process, and also those who are appointed on public bodies, is going to increase in the future.

Conclusions

The concentration of ethnic minorities in several inner-city areas of Britain has maximised their importance as electors. They are becoming increasingly involved in the British political process, quite often with the help of their leaders and ethnic minority organisations. Their numbers, turnout patterns, and voting behaviour are having an impact on the outcome of elections in the areas of their settlement. However, the participation of ethnic minorities in general, and their leaders in particular, must be seen in a wider context of British society in which racial disadvantage and racial discrimination are a daily reality for far too many members of these groups. Undoubtedly, members of political parties, being part of the society, are not free of prejudice and discrimination, whether conscious or unconscious. Some ethnic minority members of political parties and leaders have, publicly and privately, complained to me about such treatment. Marian Fitzgerald also showed in her study that at constituency and ward level there was considerable reluctance by white workers of political parties to canvass ethnic minority electors and to support ethnic minority candidates (Fitzgerald 1984).

The importance of ethnic minorities in the political process is unquestionable. So is the importance of ethnic minority leaders and their organisations. However, the integration of ethnic minorities into the political process requires their 'effective' representation and involvement in the political parties and not 'tokenism'. The American experience in this connection suggests that ethnic leaders could play an important role in making the political participation of their members really effective. In the USA in the 1970s, both the political parties and black leaders made concerted efforts to achieve a breakthrough in the political process for blacks. As a result, the representation of blacks increased dramatically (Cavanagh 1984).

The voting patterns of blacks in the USA exhibit bloc voting characteristics and they vote mainly for the Democratic Party (Keech 1968; Wilson 1970; Halloway 1971; Henderson 1982). This tendency was exhibited among ethnic minorities in the UK in the 1960s and 1970s when most of them voted for the Labour Party. However, recent trends show that ethnic minority electors do not vote as a bloc and also that they do not necessarily vote on ethnic lines (Anwar 1984).

Even for other ethnic minority groups in the USA, their organisations and leaders have played an important role in the political process (Goren 1970; Daniels 1978; Barton 1978; Shannon 1963). However, blacks are still less well represented than other ethnic minority groups in the USA in economic and political power. But there are also differences between these other ethnic groups. The Irish have shown, for example, remarkable political success, the Jews organisational and economic success, and the Japanese educational success (Glazer 1983). In Britain, Jews, not more than half a million in number, are a good example of success in education, economics, and politics (for political participation, see Alderman 1983). William Fishman has described some of the struggles which took place between 1875 and 1914 to unite and politicise Jewish workers (Fishman 1975). Jews joined the political parties, sought office, and worked hard through the political parties to become candidates and to get elected. Their leaders and organisations also helped in this process. There are clear lessons from the Jewish experience for other ethnic minority leaders and organisations.

So far, what results have ethnic minority leaders achieved in the political process? Some but not enough. In addition to the four ethnic minority MPs, at local level ethnic minority concentrations have helped to elect ethnic minority councillors in several areas, though they are still under-represented in proportion to their numbers. Generally, ethnic minority candidates are increasingly being accepted as 'party candidates' and also get white people's support. However, in some areas white electors still discriminate against ethnic minority candidates. Even the recent record of ethnic minority candidates shows that if they are given 'safe' or 'winnable' seats, they can win. Their performance has certainly improved in the last few years, as white electors are getting used to them.

Several ethnic minority councillors have also become mayors (two lord mayors) and leaders of councils. These mayors belonged to either the Labour or the Conservative parties.

A few years ago, ethnic minority councillors (mainly in London) set up their own forum to discuss issues which they and ethnic minority communities faced. A Parliamentary Black Caucus was launched in April 1989, by three of the four ethnic minority MPs and a black peer, Lord Pitt of Hampstead, to highlight issues and problems that black people face in this country (*Guardian*, 1 April 1989). The group hopes to follow the 18-year-old US Congressional Black Caucus which has put on the political agenda issues affecting US blacks. Also, the argument about the establishment of Black Sections in the Labour Party goes on (see Jeffers in this volume).

Ethnic minorities in Britain are not homogenous groups. They are ethnically, socially, religiously, economically, and politically diverse. Furthermore, the styles of leadership in various communities are different. Some believe in 'accommodation', others in 'protest', and still others prefer a combination of both accommodation and protest. There are sometimes tensions between ethnic groups and ethnic leaders, particularly in local situations, as has emerged from several Community Relations Councils, where these leaders represent their communities.

In addition to those who are elected as councillors and MPs, it seems important that other ethnic minority leaders have some official recognition in order to be accepted by the wider society and the media. This would include recognition by local Community Relations Councils, local authorities, political parties, the Commission for Racial Equality, etc., and the ethnic press. It is by getting recognition by these bodies that ethnic leaders achieve some credibility, whether they are effective or not.

The activists in the ethnic minority communities are conscious that they need to produce effective leaders to participate in activities with other ethnic groups and to compete with white leaders to secure the positions of authority in the political process. Some ethnic groups give ethnic leadership so much importance that, to achieve this aim, an Ethnic Minority Leadership project was set up ten years ago, based in Lewisham, 'to train black people to take part in public life'. It recently held a seminar on Black Leadership, where the importance of leadership training was reiterated by several speakers (*Caribbean Times*, 11 August 1989).

During my interviews with ethnic minority young people as part of another project, most of them expressed the desire to undergo leadership training at some stage, and almost all of them agreed that such training is needed for the existing leaders to make them more effective.

The overall trends show that some progress has been made in politics by the ethnic minority leaders, but they have a long way to go to really influence the decision-making process and help tackle the disadvantage and discrimination many of their members still face in this country.

References

Alderman, Geoffery (1983) *The Jewish Community in British Politics*, Oxford: Clarendon Press.

Anwar, Muhammad (1975) 'Asian participation in the 1974 autumn election', *New Community* III (4).

Anwar, Muhammad (1976) *Between Two Cultures*, London: Community Relations Commission.

Anwar, Muhammad (1979) *The Myth of Return*, London: Heinemann.

Anwar, Muhammad (1980) *Votes and Policies*, London: Commission for Racial Equality.

Anwar, Muhammad (1984) *Ethnic Minorities and the 1983 General Election*, London: Commission for Racial Equality.

Anwar, Muhammad (1986) *Race and Politics*, London: Tavistock.

Anwar, Muhammad and Kohler, David (1975) *Participation of Ethnic Minorities in the General Election, October 1974*, London: Community Relations Commission.

Barton, Josef (1978) 'Eastern and Southern Europeans', in John Higham (ed.) *Ethnic Leadership in America*, Baltimore, Md, and London: Johns Hopkins University Press.

Cavanagh, T.E. (1984) *The Impact of the Black Electorate*, Washington, DC: Joint Centre for Political Studies.

Daniels, Roger (1978) 'The Japanese', in John Higham (ed.) *Ethnic Leadership in America*, Baltimore, Md, and London: Johns Hopkins University Press.

Dhavan, Rajeev (1976) *Black People in Britain: The Way Forward*, London: Post Conference Constituent Committee.

Fishman, William (1975) *East End Jewish Radicals 1875–1914*, London: Duckworth.

Fitzgerald, Marian (1984) *Political Parties and Black People*, London: Runnymede Trust.

Glazer, Nathan (1983) *Ethnic Dilemmas 1964–1982*, Cambridge, Mass.: Harvard University Press.

Goren, Arthur (1970) *New York Jews and the Quest for Community*, New York: Columbia University Press.

Halloway, H. (1971) *There is a River: The Black Struggle for Freedom in America*, New York: Vintage.

Harding, Vincent (1981) 'The negro and the vote: the case of Texas', in A. Meier and E. Rudwick (eds) *The Making of Black America*, New York: Atheneum.

Harris Research Centre (1983) Survey for ITN in June.

Heineman, Benjamin (1972) *The Politics of Powerlessness*, London: Oxford University Press for the Institute of Race Relations.

Henderson, L. (1982) 'Black politics and American presidential elections' in M. Preston, L. Henderson and P. Punyean (eds) *The New Black Politics*, New York: Longman.

Higham, John (ed.) (1978) *Ethnic Leadership in America*, Baltimore, Md and London: Johns Hopkins University Press.

John, D.W. (1969) *Indian Workers' Associations*, London: Oxford University Press.

Keech, W. (1968) *The Impact of Negro Voting*, Chicago: Rand McNally.

Killian, Lewis (1975) *The Impossible Revolution Phase II: Black Power and the American Dream*, New York: Random House.

Le Lohe, M.J. (1975) 'Participation in elections by Asians in Bradford', in I. Crewe (ed.) *The Politics of Race*, London: Croom Helm.

Le Lohe, M.J. (1982) 'The participation of the ethnic minorities in the British political process', a report submitted to the Commission for Racial Equality.

Le Lohe, Mich (1984) *Ethnic Minority Participation in Local Elections*, Bradford: University of Bradford.

Le Lohe, Mich (1987) 'A study of non-registration among ethnic minorities', a report submitted to the Commission for Racial Equality.

Lewin, Kurt (1948) *Resolving Social Conflicts: Selected Papers on Group Dynamics*, New York: Harper & Row.

Morris, Aldon (1984) *The Origins of the Civil Rights Movement: Black Communities Organizing for Change*, New York: Free Press.

Myrdal, Gunnar (1969) *An American Dilemma*, New York: Harper.

Rex, John and Tomlinson, Sally (1979) *Colonial Immigrants in a British City*, London: Routledge & Kegan Paul.

Shannon, William (1963) *The American Irish*, New York: Macmillan.

Todd, J. and Butcher, B. (1982) *Electoral Registration in 1981*, London: Office of Population Censuses and Surveys.

Wilson, J. (1970) 'The negro in politics', in S. Fisher (ed.) *Power and the Black Community*, New York: Random House.

Chapter two

Black Sections in the Labour Party
The end of ethnicity and 'godfather' politics?

Sydney Jeffers

> The main reason we want to see Black Sections recognised is be-
> cause we believe the only way that appropriate strategies for
> overcoming racism will be devised, is when we as Black people
> come together and decide on effective anti-racist policies which
> we can take to a wider political audience. As victims of racism, we
> have a right to be in the forefront of the anti-racist struggle.
>
> (Labour Party Black Sections 1988)

Introduction

The Black Section movement of the Labour Party has consistently
rejected a politics of race based on 'ethnicity'; a politics which reduces
racism to cultural difference, a politically divisive ethnic particularism.[1]
The movement has sought instead to work with a more political, historically contingent, conception of race that views blackness as being
a product of racism, but not just that.

The Black Sections' definition of black is essentially political, and
based on people's direct, first-hand, experience of racism; it has to do
with how they are treated by 'white' society, rather than what culturally distinct groups they belong to.

The present chapter argues that Black Sections face at least two
major obstacles. First, although their use of a more political definition of black does not rely on any assumed ethnic differences, it still
risks the danger of substituting one essentialist definition for
another. A one-dimensional definition of black people as, simply, the
victims of racism may guarantee their place at the vanguard of the
anti-racist struggle. However, the problems black people face are not
simply ones of racism. There is the danger of inflating the concept of
racism so as to cover all social ills black people encounter.

The second set of problems has more to do with the Sections'
location within the Labour Party and within a Labour movement still

primarily committed to capturing the state on behalf of the oppressed working class. This traditional 'statist' strategy highlights problems of representation for the Black Sections. On the one hand, they want to represent black people who still overwhelmingly vote for Labour. But if they are to make interventions from *within* the state, they must get selected by the party and elected by a white majority. The strategy of working 'in and against the state' involves obvious tensions, and it is unclear whether it can be made to work effectively.

The chapter begins with a fairly detailed sketch of key episodes in the history of one particular Constituency Labour Party (CLP) Black Section in London during the first three years of its life. By presenting an ethnographic case study I hope to highlight some of the key issues and conflicts which the Black Section movement has generated. My aim is to provide some insight into what is probably the most significant development in black British politics in the 1980s.[2]

At this point I should come clean and situate myself in this picture. The chapter is based on unfunded research on Black Sections during a time when I was myself actively engaged in the movement as the Secretary of a local Constituency Labour Party Black Section. I was able, because of my active involvement, to trace the development of the section over several years from its inception. My comrades were aware that I was wearing two hats – one as activist, one as observer – but were generous enough to think that this was no bad thing, and that, indeed, it was good that something be written on the subject. I hope I can do them justice.

The development of a Black Section: a case study

Setting up

The establishment of a Black Section in our CLP came about when a black councillor called a meeting for black members to discuss the idea in January 1985.

Only five people turned up to the initial meeting. This group, all men and experienced members of the Labour Party, was to form the core of the section over the next few years. As there were so few of us, we decided that we should reconvene the meeting for the following month and not take any decisions. We stayed, however, to discuss the issues; so long in fact that we got locked in the building by the caretaker and had to break out by climbing over a wall.

The main topics of that initial meeting were focused on the definition of 'black' and the merits of adopting a caucusing strategy within the party.

The question of identity, who should the Black Section be for, prompted a heated debate as one member made it clear that he thought the Black Section should refer to Afro-Caribbean people, not to Asians. The reason was that if the purpose of such a group was to fight racism and help those racially discriminated against, then it should be primarily for Afro-Caribbeans because they were worse off, they had no small businesses to fall back on, they were the ones the police picked on, and it was they who were getting messed up by the welfare state, e.g. underachieving in schools. Furthermore, he said, it was always the Asians who with their qualifications profited from race initiatives; they were the ones who got the cushy race relations jobs with the council whilst the 'blacks' had only just managed to break into the council's direct labour force, doing dirty and poorly paid manual jobs.

This proved to be a minority view within even this small group whose ethnic breakdown included one Bengali (an advice worker and councillor), one Jamaican (ex-director of a local authority funded police monitoring project), one Guyanese (a twenty-year veteran of the Labour Party, CARD and sponsor of the black performing arts), a young Asian from Leicester (a radical social worker), and myself – a black Londoner (with academic pretensions).

We argued that Asians should not be lumped together, and against the assertion made by our colleague that they did not experience racism of a direct and indirect nature. Who was it, we asked, that was getting the bulk of individual racial attacks and state harassment over immigration?

. The second topic concerned the wisdom of setting up a Black Section at all and making race an issue within the party, particularly at the local level. The majority of us remained to be convinced that there was something positive to be gained. We had no problem with the principle of caucusing. The question was more tactical: would this achieve anything other than the alienation of our white comrades and our own marginalisation?

The obvious examples of caucusing within the party were the Women's Sections. Comparisons were drawn between their position and our own; gay and lesbian politics were brought into our discussion, which concluded tentatively that if the party were prepared to accept positive action for women, why not for blacks?

At our next meeting the councillor argued in favour of forming a Section on the grounds that black members of the party, especially councillors, needed the support of a collective platform if they were not to be tokenised and rendered marginal. Elected to the council in 1982 when the 'new left' had finally managed to displace the 'old guard' who, in turn, had promptly defected to the newly formed SDP,

he was very wary of becoming a political 'mascot', the token representative of the black community on the council's Labour group.

There was a major discussion about the role of a Black Section in
the party. Would it be a black pressure group or just a recruiting unit
for the party? The establishment of a Turkish Section in the local
CLP was seen as evidence of a patronising divide and rule strategy
being exercised by the white leadership locally.

It was felt that somehow the real power lay on the streets and that
our section would, or should, be a popular organisation trying to
bridge the gap between the local black community, which was under-
represented in the party, and the local party whose leadership ran the
borough. Racism within the council was seen as a major problem that
we should address. It was no longer a question of whether we should
set up a Black Section, but how.

The second meeting was one of the biggest we ever had, with sixteen people. This meeting was different from the first in that we had
invited a speaker from the Westminster CLP Black Section. The
speaker pre-empted a repeat of some of the arguments we had had
before, by bringing with him the National Black Section 'package'
outlined in a pamphlet: *Seven Steps to Forming a Black Section*. This
contained the following definition:

> 'Black' is a political concept. It is used to include all racially op-
> pressed minorities. Each geographical area, therefore, is likely to
> reflect its own 'black' communities. In most areas this will inevit-
> ably mean people of Afro-Caribbean or Asian descent. However,
> in Haringey, for example, Cypriots have chosen to be, and are,
> involved in local Black Sections.
>
> (Labour Party Black Sections 1985)

This definition made it much easier not to fall out over the question
of identity and membership. It provided a ready-made formula which
could be defended politically as being inclusive and, at the same time,
a rejection of the entrenched neo-colonial model, a model based on
splitting up subject populations along ethnic or racial lines. Our attention was drawn to the Labour Party's own consultation document
which employed divisive and confused ethnic and national categories
but still argued that greater black representation was needed in the
party.

At this point we were also being invited to join the National Black
Section movement; this offered, as it were, a political franchise which
was attractive in itself.

The net result of the meeting was that we agreed to constitute ourselves formally as a Black Section at the next monthly meeting. We
would then make a bid to the organs of the local party to gain repres-

entation on the various committees that make up a local CLP. It was felt that the party would not oppose the creation of a black caucus, but we were concerned about its reaction to the demand for the same kind of representational rights that Women's Sections had.

The local party appeared to have no great objections to our establishment. We were granted representative rights and were very quickly drawn into the preparations for the forthcoming local elections, which included the drafting of the local party manifesto.

Racism and the council

Having formally established ourselves in April 1985, we walked straight into a dispute over the council's handling of racist staff in its Housing Department. This was to bring us into conflict with the party leadership and to set a pattern for the future of the section; we found ourselves more often responding to issues than initiating policies.

The case surrounded four black workers in the Housing Department who had moved out of their jobs in response to alleged racial harassment by three of their colleagues. The council had investigated the complaints and found that the three had been guilty of harassment and had, moreover, been involved with the National Front.

The disciplinary measures taken by the council were, first, to reprimand the staff, and second, to send them on a race awareness course. However, a further proposal was to move the main perpetrator to a neighbourhood office, a position which would put her in close contact with the public.

The local NALGO branch and the council's black workers' group regarded the council's action as being too light-handed and the final proposal as an affront. Consequently, they demanded the dismissal of the three workers. To underline their demands, they refused to cooperate with the three staff involved. Personnel wrote to NALGO to ask them to drop the action. NALGO lobbied the council publicly. A dispute had developed.

Our Black Section, newly formed to combat racism and encourage greater participation and representation within the party, particularly within the local council, felt that it should become involved directly. The section had by now a considerable local government bias, with two councillors and a number of council workers, including a member of the Race Relations Unit, in it. When the dispute was discussed, other cases of racism in the council were cited. Some members alleged that the council was guilty of complicity in its dealing with these racists in its ranks, and that this went right up to senior officer and committee level.

At our next meeting we were addressed by a NALGO representative about the dispute and we were asked to support their anti-racist campaign. Naturally, we agreed (how could we not?). We were aware, however, that the Socialist Workers Party were using this dispute and the campaign for their own purpose, and we did not want to be seen merely as passive supporters. Our immediate response was to call for an independent public investigation. This demand was not met, but an academic report on the delivery of council services in housing did find racism in the allocation of housing. The report was felt by the group to be too equivocal and we decided to pursue another strategy.

Our next move was to table a number of motions for the joint meeting of the local government committee (LGC) and the council's ruling Labour group. The substance of these motions was directed at the council's manifesto commitments to anti-racism, arguing that really they were too insubstantial for us to support them. The motions threatened that unless the situation was rectified we would need to adopt more drastic measures. These might include the public resignation of the only two black councillors, one of whom was the chair of the Race Relations Committee, and the other being Chair of our Black Section.

We demanded that the council 'beef up' its commitments and take the following action:

1 It should rename the Race Relations Committee the Race and Community Affairs Committee, to signal the legitimacy of the increased community involvement in that committee.
2 It should grant the Race Committee full independent programme status – i.e. a budget.
3 It should change the reporting lines of its race advisers from Personnel Department to the Chief Executive's Department.
4 It should introduce ethnic monitoring for its staff.
5 It should institute a new disciplinary code that would make racism a matter of 'gross misconduct' and therefore a sackable offence.
6 It should place advertising for jobs in the ethnic press.

The joint LGC/Labour group meeting that had discussed the manifesto was hastily reconvened at our insistence. It had been called on a Sunday without sufficient notice being given, and had been far too hurried to discuss the issues. We had made an effort to turn out in force to lobby the meeting and visibly support the black councillor and committee chair, at their request.

The meeting was largely successful. First, in that it had taken place at all. And second, in that all of our demands were met except the key movement of race advisers to the Chief Executive's Department.

In the course of the meeting, however, tempers flared and bad feeling was generated within the Section. This situation has continued up to the present with some members accusing others of being 'Uncle Toms' and careerists only interested in using the Section and black people to get on in the world.

Public meetings and the local elections

As part of the campaign for the 1986 London local government elections we decided to hold a public meeting. The title of the meeting was 'Why Black Sections in the Labour Party?', and it was to be held on a Wednesday evening at the local Labour Club.

The speakers were to include the Leader of Haringey Council and prospective parliamentary candidate (PPC), Bernie Grant; Hackney Councillor and PPC, Diane Abbott; Lewisham Councillor and PPC Russell Profitt; Haringey Councillor and Secretary of the Black Section National Steering Committee, Narendra Makenji. It was chaired by one of our black councillors who was also chair of our Black Section.

At an early stage MPs Clare Short and Jo Richardson were invited. Jo Richardson had chaired the Labour Party National Executive Committee (NEC) Working Party charged with the investigation and consultation into the position of black people and the party. The premiss of this investigation was that black people were 'underachieving' within the party and in British politics generally, and the brief was to look at ways to encourage greater participation.

The committee had basically come out in favour of, or at least could see no principled objection to, the recognition of Black Sections. Its findings were, however, squashed by the leadership which objected to the establishment of the principle of 'apartheid within the Labour Party'. A Black and Asian Advisory Committee was established instead.

Richardson and Short proved to be unavailable as did Grant and Abbott. But the meeting was a success in terms of attracting media coverage, if not the attention of local people directly. The local press were there, having already run a headline 'Two fingers to Kinnock: Labour rebels launch party Black Section'; so too were a camera crew from BBC TV's current affairs programme *Newsnight*. The audience was mainly composed of active Labour members, although not many members of the public attended.

The original thinking behind the meeting had been to try and get a local public audience for a discussion of the merits of Black Sections in the Labour Party. We decided that such a meeting might prove too risky. We might draw a barrage of criticism, especially from the 'class warriors' of Militant and the far left who often attended Black

69

Section public meetings to barrack and undermine them. The meeting would thus run the risk of being counter-productive.

Instead we went for the safer and more conservative approach: simply to answer the question implied by the title, namely, Why Black Sections?

The arguments in favour put by the speakers were the, by now, familiar ones:

- that the loyalty of the black voter has been taken for granted by the party;
- that the party as a major institution of a racist society is itself likely to be institutionally racist;
- that institutional racism manifests itself in the low representation of black people in positions of power within the party;
- that the explanations given for this – e.g. that black political activity was underdeveloped, immature, or apathetic – were unsatisfactory.
- that the way forward lay in the self-organisation and representation of black people in the party through Black Sections;
- and that this would help radicalise and develop the party itself.

The speakers remained somewhat ambiguous over the actual role Black Sections could play in mediating between the interests of the party and those of the community. When the crunch came, which side would Black Sections be on? The line between representing the black members of the party and representing the black community as a whole was left unclear. The high degree of electoral support given to Labour by the black communities made it easy to make the assumption that the two constituencies would share the same outlook.

Positive action an electoral liability?

The results of the local elections were very uneven. In the north of the borough there was a swing to Labour, but in the south the Tory vote collapsed and the SDP–Alliance gained thirteen wards, to add to their rump of three that had defected to the SDP.

In the north five black councillors were elected, three of whom were active in Black Sections, and one of whom was a member of the Turkish Section. Of the two black councillors who were not members of Black Sections, one was thought to be 'in the pocket' of the leadership, working for an ethnic organisation funded by the council; the other was thought to be reluctant to join for personal reasons. Significantly, of the five councillors the two non-members were women, while the Black Section supporters were men, a split reflecting the overwhelming male bias in our local membership.

Given the electoral disaster in the south of the borough, there was bound to be some recrimination. It came in the form of accusations that the party in the south had suffered from a backlash to the 'loony-left' image of the council, and that part of this backlash was racial. The south contained a more traditional white working-class population than the north, which was held to be inhabited by a mixture of blacks and yuppies.

The implications were clear – if, as a party, we were to recapture the white working-class vote, we would have to ditch the 'loony-left' image and drop the political baggage that went along with that; in particular, commitments to equal opportunities for blacks, lesbians, and gays.

The scramble for committee chairs that followed the elections caused further disputes. It emerged that through the fine interpretation of the rules, the leadership's allies on the council had done rather well, and the black councillors had no representation on any of the key committees, including Direct Labour, Housing, Environmental Services, and two Policy sub-committees – Decentralisation and Police.

The argument was advanced that the black community, through these newly elected black councillors, should be on some of these committees as they were so central to the delivery of services to the black communities. And the counter-argument was made that it was just too bad the councillors didn't read the small print, and anyway, the view that no direct black representation on these committees meant that black people's interests would not be served was tantamount to an allegation of racism that could not be supported. The result was a widening of the gap between the leadership and the Black Section, other 'outsiders' in the Labour group.

The 'way forward' debate

The year 1988 saw our Black Section consider the question of the National Black Section's overall strategy. This had consisted of a constitutional struggle for full recognition by the party, waged at the Annual Party Conference. Motions which local CLP Black Sections had managed to get adopted by their CLPs, when put to the conference, were voted down by conservative trade unions by a huge majority; the reason being that these unions still held a 'race-blind' ideology in which the acknowledgement of race as such was almost tantamount to discrimination in itself (see Ben Tovim *et al.* 1986).

The debate which was already taking place was put at the top of our agenda by Bill Morris's proposal. The proposal was that the Black Section dispute within the party be resolved by the establishment of a black socialist society that could seek affiliation to the party in the same way as the Fabian Society.

Bill Morris, the black Deputy General Secretary of the Transport and General Workers Union, put forward his proposal in the *Tribune* on 8 January 1988. The same article, 'Time for new thinking in the Black Section debate', was reprinted in the *Caribbean Times* on 22 January 1988.

In this article Morris opened by saying,

> It would be unkind to say that Black Sections are an idea whose time has gone. After all, the debate on black representation in the Labour Party has helped to give us four black MPs and to raise the party's – and the nation's – consciousness of racism and discrimination.
>
> The debate on Black Sections has been described as 'establishment tree shaking' – which of course has a value. But the time has come to move on.
>
> The motion to establish Black Sections has been defeated at successive party conferences, and the majority against it shows no signs of shrinking.

On the struggle to get the Black Section motion passed at the Annual Party Conference, he said that it

> had become little more than a ritual gesture of protest – however justified – about the exclusion of black people from the centres of power in the party.

(Morris 1988)

A more important issue required attention, in Morris's view: namely, the sharp decline in Labour support among black people. The failure of the Black Section campaign to reverse this trend or to mobilise real mass support, together with the collapse or marginalisation of the issues, meant that a new solution was required.

The solution proposed was to form a black socialist society much along the lines of a proposal made by Eric Heffer back in 1985 for black members to join societies and affiliate at all levels like Poale Zion. A black socialist society would avoid the eligibility question, preserve the principle of self-representation, and allow black people to be incorporated in the extensive policy review process that was being conducted. There were a number of questions to be resolved, but with good will on both sides, political self-discipline, and an eye on the prize, these details could and should be ironed out.

The response of the National Black Section to these proposals was to try and keep the doors to negotiation open without going back on the basic principle that the section, or whatever it proved politic to call such an organisation, should be located within the party. As the Black Section National Secretary Kingsley Abrams stated in a letter to the *Guardian*: 'the Black Section is still fully committed to Black self-organisation within the Labour movement. We continue to seek a change in Labour's constitution which will guarantee Black representation at all levels of the party' (Abrams 1988).

The National Executive of the Black Section had already begun an extensive consultation exercise after the last defeat at the Annual Party Conference. A number of alternatives, including affiliation, were tabled for discussion with a view to making a decision at the national conference in Manchester.

Our discussion of the way forward was lengthy and passionate. Criticisms of the National Black Section leadership were that the movement had become locked into a destructive and often personal confrontation with the leadership of the party, and even with some of the newly elected black MPs.

Another complaint was that the Black Sections had become bogged down in a constitutional war of attrition, and were failing to do anything more. The pronouncements on policy were very sporadic and weak. The attempt to engage with some of the larger issues such as foreign policy and Northern Ireland had meant that the organisation was becoming overstretched and apparently failing to deal with the local bread and butter issues for which it was founded.

There had been too much talk, not enough action, and no follow-up. The Black Sections had been blown from one issue to another as the political winds blew. More general issues like the poll tax, housing, and social service provisions needed addressing as they would have an acute impact on the black population. The complaint was that the movement was getting trapped in a political dead end.

Counter-arguments were put that, on the contrary, Black Sections had been successful in their primary aim of increasing black representation. We only had to look at our own borough to see the increase in the number of councillors, school governors, and party officials. Of course, nationally there were now four black MPs, all of whom were, or had been, supporters of Black Sections.

Another consideration was that a realistic time-scale for achieving fundamental changes in the party should be used. It had taken women fifteen years to win their argument so it was probably premature to write off the campaign so quickly.

We were agreed that the section had been too inward looking and had failed to recruit a significant number of new members to join the party. Although it had certainly increased the activity and effectiveness of those already in it, our section had never come to terms with the obvious male bias. It had only managed to attract a couple of women on a regular basis, as against a core of about eight men.

Although we had managed to hold a joint meeting with the Turkish Section at the time of the general election, there had been little other contact between our sections. We had, however, helped members in the south party, the neighbouring CLP in the south of the borough, to form their own Black Section and had regular contact with them and other neighbouring Sections.

Overall we decided that we should persevere with the Black Sections' original strategy of seeking full recognition by the Labour Party but send a message of warning to the leadership that things had to be sorted out. The present impasse could not continue indefinitely.

As it turned out, this position appeared to be quite typical of local sections nationally. At the 1988 national conference only Tottenham came out in favour of trying affiliation. And Bernie Grant, who came to the conference to bash heads together, avoided a split by reaffirming his support for the principles of self-organisation and representation. This was neatly done by introducing himself as 'Bernie Grant, MP for Tottenham and Secretary of the Parliamentary Labour Party Black Section' (Bernie Grant, 27 March 1988, Black Section National Conference, Manchester). After the cheers had died down, he proceeded to convince the national conference that he could serve as a trusted go-between and negotiate on behalf of the section with the party leadership. This was later agreed, with the proviso that any decision would require the agreement of a reconvened national delegate conference.

This was the news we brought back to our section. The reaction to it was cautious approval. Some of the other messages we brought back, such as the need to get out into the community and work in our unions, were already familiar themes in our own discussions.

Conclusions: the dilemmas of a progressive politics of anti-racism

While the immediate effect of black militancy may be a white backlash in the labour movement as elsewhere, there is certainly more likely to be a place found for black workers in the labour movement if they are militant than if they rely upon the paternalism of labour leaders; it may take time before this is learned either by black leaders or trades unionists and Labour politicians.

(Rex 1979: 91)

The Black Sections face two dilemmas. The first one concerns the attempt to reconstruct a politics of anti-racism that is not based on ethnic particularism but on a shared opposition to racism. The success of this approach requires that the sections recognise the variety of forms that racism may take and that they do not reify the concept itself and render it a fixed unchanging essential thing, insulated from the experience of people living in a complex world. The danger is that the tendency to oversimplify will prove too strong.

This danger was apparent in Bernie Grant's argument, made at the black MPs' fringe meeting during the 1989 Black Section conference, that we (members of Black Sections), as supporters of black people in the struggle, must therefore support the anti-Rushdie demonstrators in Bradford, because they are black. Yet these demonstrators were out on the streets not as blacks, but as outraged Muslim fundamentalists. Not all Muslims are black, and not all Muslims take the fundamentalist position. Why then should black socialists give support to hardline religious leaders?

The Rushdie affair illustrates the difficulties that the section must face in trying to move beyond the dominant constructions of race as ethnicity. The Black Sections' Executive came to the position that, rather than accept Bernie Grant's argument, they would reject the calls to extend the blasphemy laws to cover minority religions and call for the repeal of all blasphemy laws.

Perhaps as revealing as the rejection of the arguments about Rushdie, put by MPs Bernie Grant and Keith Vaz, was the way in which the Black Section National Executive managed to retain control of the conference by keeping this debate off the agenda altogether. This brings us to the Black Sections' other set of problems which has to do with representation and the Labour movement.

The Black Sections are part of the Labour Party whether the leadership chooses to acknowledge them or not. As such they suffer from many of the problems of the party itself: the over-reliance on activists who have to really commit themselves full-time to the party machinery, the unrepresentative relationship between the party and the Labour voters, the male orientation and domination of the party machine, and the problems of taking the electoral road to socialism.

The struggle the Black Section Executive had to keep the Rushdie affair from taking over the 1989 annual conference highlighted some of the problems it faces in keeping control of the movement and preventing it from becoming merely the back-up for black MPs. Had the conference been bounced into discussing the Rushdie issue, the essential business of conference, which included agreeing negotiating positions for the meeting with the party, would not have been concluded. This would have left the door open for the MPs to assume the role of negotiators and effective leaders of the movement.

A major plank in the section campaign was to have black representation in the House of Commons. Having achieved this, or at least been instrumental in it, how were they to have any control over the black MPs? The Black Sections' response was to try and construct a clear political platform, a black agenda, that MPs might support or be judged by.

The relationship of the Black Section movement to the Labour movement more generally is inevitably strained by the fact that the sections are accusing Labour of being racist in so far as it fails to recognise the special predicament of blacks, and prevents them from taking an active part in the movement. The sections' call to put racism back on the political agenda is not going to be met with great enthusiasm by a Labour leadership that is trying to regain the political middle ground in which race is an uncomfortable issue.

The emergence of the Black Section movement is, in my view, indicative of the development of a local government based anti-racist politics, that has seen the number of black workers and race-specific workers increase over the period of the 1970s and 1980s. A decade of formal commitment to equal opportunities and anti-racism raised expectations and a sense of frustration when nothing much happened.

This may help explain the motivation of some black activists who wanted to ensure that something more did happen through getting more involved and claiming the right to appeal to the party leadership, locally and nationally, on behalf of black people generally.

However, in recent years the ability and legitimacy of metropolitan Labour local authorities, in particular, to intervene, in an attempt to achieve some redistribution of social goods, has been severely restricted by the Conservative government. The mood of the Labour leadership nationally has been to try and retake the sensible middle ground and distance itself from the 'London effect' of left-wing, sometimes black-led, Labour local authorities.

In this context the emergence of the Black Sections' movement seems certain to focus attention upon the degree of commitment the Labour Party has to the cause of anti-racism. This it apparently views as a potential vote and credibility loser. The key problem for the Black Sections' movement is to make itself essential to the success of the party.

For example, the Section's inability to defend its National Vice-Chair, Martha Osamor, from de-selection as a PPC in the 1989 Lambeth by-election demonstrated that the party leadership were ready to call the Section's bluff and count upon the loyalty of black electors who remain willing to ignore the complaints of the Section and still vote for the party regardless.

Central to the arguments of the Black Sections has been their rejection of a politics of race based simply on ethnic identification and their attempt to act as brokers within the party for the interests of a politically united (in their common experience and opposition to racism) black community. The attempts of the Labour leadership to set up a rival Black and Asian Advisory Committee, which was intended to take the steam out of the Black Section campaign, could not have been better designed to have the opposite effect.

What this initiative did was to confirm the opinions of many Black Section members and sympathisers that the leadership was engaged in a divisive attempt to revive a neo-colonial, ethnic politics of race, a politics that would only serve to splinter various ethnic constituencies and keep them firmly on the margins of power. By restricting them to a merely consultative role within the Labour Party the suspicion that the party only wanted black votes, not black involvement, was also confirmed.

The Black Sections maintained that what they represented was a more progressive politics of anti-racism, based on a voluntary and inclusive definition of race that was fundamentally political and progressive. According to their view, the shared and direct personal experience of racism itself conferred the right to self-representation, as well as to self-definition and self-organisation.

Hence, my argument is that what is progressive about the Black Section project is precisely its attempted rejection of ethnicity as a basis of political mobilisation. At the same time, however, as a section within the Labour Party, the movement starts from a position that tends to frustrate its radical pretensions. It has thus encountered real problems in its attempt to shift the Labour movement's conception of race beyond that of one based on a reduction of race to ethnicity.

Black Sections have to combat two opposing positions: one which takes a romantic view of blacks as a super-exploited vanguard of the working class, the other which regards blacks as a passive and captive constituency of Labour support. Both are restrictive and unhelpful. Both are reductive and fail to recognise that black people are more than just victims of racism or capitalism.

Black Sections claim to represent and speak for black people. Yet this claim is clearly inflated and ambiguous. The sections can only really claim to represent a certain group of black activists in the Labour Party. Beyond that they occupy, I would argue, a symbolic position in the field of race politics, along with other key agencies, such as the black churches or other black voluntary organisations.

This is not to say that their effect is merely symbolic but, rather, that they are engaged in a politics which is conducted at a largely symbolic level. The efforts of the section have been directed at getting the Labour Party to change their ideas of what black means, and to recognise the authenticity of this black experience.

In so doing they have challenged an ideology and conception of what blackness is, primarily a notion that it consists of being a member of some static foreign, ethnic minority, rather than being a member of a group, defined as being different, other, subordinate, and threatening on racial grounds.

The collapsing of race into ethnicity is part of the problem that the sections seek to address. However, their problem is that the ethnic component does not evaporate, having been separated from the racial part; it too has an authenticity that cannot be reduced.

As to the prospects for Black Sections, Z. Layton-Henry (1984), following Lawrence (1974: 156) and others (e.g. Miles and Phizacklea 1980), outlined four ways in which 'the growing population of black Britons may be linked to the wider political system' (Layton-Henry 1984: 166).

1 Increasing black integration within traditional class-based politics. This strategy implies that issues of distributional justice will ultimately overtake those of access rights, such as immigration.
2 Black unity arising from the development of a black racial consciousness, as white society continues to discriminate against and disadvantage black people.
3 The disarming of black politics by buffer mechanisms which sidetrack and patronise black activists under the guise of providing special help for the politically underdeveloped ethnic minorities.
4 Growing disenchantment, alienation, and withdrawal from the political process, which might result either in alternative forms of communal organisation such as religion, or in more disruptive, violent expressions of individual alienation, such as the periodic eruption of black riots in the inner cities (on riots as a political strategy, see Benyon 1984, 1987).

Layton-Henry rejects the view that any one of these scenarios will be followed exclusively, opting for what I think is the more realistic conclusion, that future developments will depend on a number of complex factors, and that these will result in tensions and a diversity of strategies, themselves arising from the diversity represented within the black communities.

Seen in terms of this typology Black Sections clearly exhibit elements of both the first and second options: on the one hand, their aim is to be included in the mainstream of Labour politics. At the same time, however, there is a tension between this demand and the basis of their mobilisation – a call for black political unity.

The tension is primarily, however, between black socialists who claim that to ignore the political construction of race and racism denies their primary experience, and the Labour movement in which a race-blind but ethnically sensitive multi-cultural attitude persists, with the recognition of race and racism being regarded as almost the height of uncomradely behaviour, and likely to alarm the voters to boot.

The danger of becoming a 'buffer' for the Labour Party, and not mobilising the black community, is a fate that the Black Section movement has had to fight against. There is, however, another danger: that the Black Sections may themselves make their appeal too narrow, defining black people purely in the negative, as merely the victims of racism.

The political feat that the Black Sections have to pull off is the construction of a black British political identity that does not ignore the lived reality of cultural difference but does not succumb to it either. A position that does not simply state that we are non-white victims of a singular 'racism' and therefore a unitary political force. The question then becomes, how can Black Sections achieve this aim, given the meagre resources at their disposal?

It has never been possible to deliver the black vote in Britain in the sense that it has in the USA. Yet Black Sections have implied that it is possible, or at least that the black vote might be lost if the Labour Party did not take their demands more seriously.

The movement's major weapon has been the potential it has to embarrass the Labour Party. The unsuccessful expulsion of Amir Khan in Birmingham, and the de-selection and attempt to discipline Sharon Atkin, demonstrate the sensitivity of the Labour leadership to accusations of racism. They also demonstrate the unwillingness of the leadership to accept in public an alternative view of race constructed along non-multi-cultural lines.

The leadership of the Labour Party seemed content to tolerate the existence of Black Sections locally so long as they remained local phenomena and did not interfere with major public electoral issues.

Some of the Black Sections' best coverage in the national press comes from the *Daily Express* which must relish stories such as the following:

> *Black Power Struggle that is Tearing Labour in Two*: Black Sections are the new albatross around the neck of Labour leader Neil Kinnock. Months after the head of the Militant body was cut off, it seems to have sprung up again in the form of defiant black extremists.

> (Miller 1987)

The selection of black prospective parliamentary candidates in the run-up to the 1987 general election highlighted another problem for the Black Sections: how were they to mandate or retain the allegiance of these individuals, and who would the successful elected MPs represent?

During the 1987 general election campaign, after Sharon Atkin was de-selected in Nottingham East, it was apparent that there was a great deal of tension between the remaining black PPCs and the Black Section National Executive over the need to get on with getting elected locally as representatives of the Labour Party, and that of defending Sharon Atkin who was de-selected for allegedly saying at a campaign meeting in Birmingham on 7 April, 'I don't give a damn about Neil Kinnock and a racist Labour Party' and 'I don't want a parliamentary seat if I can't represent black people' (reported on the front page of *The Times* on 30 April 1987).

I would argue that the failings of Black Sections are essentially those of the Labour Party itself. The criticism from Darcus Howe, that

> The black middle-class has every right to protest, every right to organise itself independently so as to demand that they join the decaying, mediocre, ruthlessly competitive, self-perpetuating centres of power. They ought not to be kept out because they are black. For that is what the Black Sections are really about, the quest of the black, professional middle-class for power-sharing with its white counterpart.
>
> (Howe 1985: 15)

is partially supported by the experience of our local Black Section.

In so far as our strategy was simply to reproduce the 'new urban left' strategy, to capture what we could of the local state on behalf of the oppressed, then the section was guilty of an attempt to get hold of or share power. The patronising aspect of the statist project of the Labour Party, to wield the power of the state on behalf of the working class, is difficult to move beyond, but if the Black Sections are to represent a way forward, then they will have to do just that.

© 1991 Sydney Jeffers

Appendix

Brief Black Section chronology

1983   Early sections formed in London: Vauxhall and North
       Westminster. Four resolutions go to party conference;
       these are rejected but working party under Jo Richardson
       set up to report to the NEC the following year.

1984   Kinnock, Kaufman, and Hattersley announce opposition to
       Black Sections as a ghetto option. They see the real prob-
       lem as black political inactivity. First Black Section
       conference in Birmingham. About 20 sections formed,
       mostly in London. Some 25 CLPs and the Electrician's
       Union (EEPTU) submit 18 resolutions and 7 amendments
       to party conference. Richardson's working party fails to re-
       port and submits a consultative document 'Black people
       and the Labour Party'. Conference rejects Black Section
       proposal again.

1985   NEC consultation finds in favour of Black Sections. Leader-
       ship rejects NEC report and sets up the Black and Asian
       Advisory Committee instead. This is immediately boycotted
       by the Black Section.

1986   Local government elections see increase in number of black
       councillors. Black Section claims the credit. Amir Khan ex-
       pelled from Birmingham CLP for bringing the party into
       disrepute over allegations of corrupt 'Godfather' politics.

1987   Sharon Atkin de-selected from Nottingham East after
       addressing meeting in Birmingham and accusing the
       Labour Party of being racist. Four black MPs elected:
       Boateng, Abbott, Vaz, and Grant. Black Section National
       Executive suspends Sharma and Patel for talking out of
       turn to the press.

1988   Bill Morris re-floats Eric Heffer's 1985 'Poale Zion' affili-
       ation option. Black Section conducts 'way forward' debate
       at Manchester annual conference and rejects the Morris
       proposal. However, the door is left open for Bernie Grant
       to negotiate a settlement with the party leadership. First
       Black Section Women's Conference held. The *Black
       Agenda* document produced. Sharon Atkin charges re-
       duced to disrepute after NEC threatened with legal action.

1989   Negotiation between Black Section representatives and
         Larry Whitty over Morris's proposals and the resolution of
         the dispute. Visit by US Congressional Black Caucus to
         black MPs. Black Section Vice-Chair, Martha Osamor,
         removed as a candidate for the Lambeth by-election.
         Labour retain the seat easily: two Independent black candi-
         dates lose deposits.

1990   Attempts by Parliamentary Black Caucus, led by Bernie
         Grant MP, to form a coalition of black politicians and
         academics, and to establish a black think-tank or race and
         social policy institute.

Distribution of Black Sections

At present there are about 35 Black Sections of which 20 are in London. The rest follow the pattern of black residence in the major
metropolitan areas with the notable exceptions of Liverpool and
Bradford. In Liverpool the Militant-dominated Labour Party would
not tolerate Black Sections. In Bradford and Leicester the politics of
ethnicity, focused on religion, has to date prevented the establishment of a non-ethnic black political organisation.

Notes

1 On different constructions of race and ethnicity, see Banton 1987; Gilroy
   1982 and 1987; and for the United States, Omi and Winant 1986.
2 On black British politics more generally, see Anwar 1986; Barnett 1982;
   Fitzgerald 1984 and 1987; Jacobs 1986; Layton-Henry and Rich 1986.
   On local Labour politics, see Ben Tovim *et al.*, 1986 and Wainwright
   1987.

References

Abrams, Kingsley (1988) In the *Guardian*, 16 January.
Anwar, M. (1986) *Race and Politics: Ethnic Minorities and the British
    Political System*, London: Tavistock.
Banton, M. (1987) *Racial Theories*, Cambridge: Cambridge University Press.
Barnett, M. (1982) 'The Congressional Black Caucus: illusions and realities
    of power', in M. Preston *et al.* (eds) *The New Black Politics: The Search
    for Political Power*, New York: Longman.
Ben-Tovim, G. Gabriel, J., Law, I., and Stredder, K. (1986) *The Local
    Politics of Race*, London: Macmillan.
Benyon, John (ed.) 1984 *Scarman and After*, Oxford: Pergamon Press.

Benyon, John (ed.) (1987) 'Interpretations of civil disorder', in John Benyon and John Solomos (eds) *The Roots of Urban Unrest*, Oxford: Pergamon Press.

FitzGerald, M. (1984) *Political Parties and Black People: Participation, Representation and Exploitation*, London: Runnymede Trust.

FitzGerald, M. (1987) *Black People and Party Politics in Britain*, London: Runnymede Trust.

Gilroy, P. (1982) 'Steppin' out of Babylon – race, class and autonomy', in CCCS, *The Empire Strikes Back*, London: Hutchinson.

Gilroy, P. (1987) *There Ain't No Black in the Union Jack: The Cultural Politics of Race and Nation*, London: Hutchinson.

Howe, D. (1985) 'As I see it: black sections for the black middle classes. I say yes', *Race Today*, London: Race Today Collective.

Howe, S. and Upshal, D. (1988) 'New black power lines', *New Statesman and Society*, 15 July.

Jacobs, B. (1986) *Black Politics and the Urban Crisis in Britain*, Cambridge: Cambridge University Press.

Labour Party Black Sections (1985) *Seven Steps to Forming a Black Section*, London: Labour Party Black Sections.

Labour Party Black Sections (1988) *The Black Agenda*, London: Labour Party Black Sections.

Lawrence, D. (1974) *Black Migrants, White Natives*, Cambridge: Cambridge University Press.

Layton-Henry, Z. (1984) *The Politics of Race in Britain*, London: George Allen & Unwin.

Layton-Henry, Z. and Rich, P. (eds) (1986) *Race, Government and Politics in Britain*, Basingstoke: Macmillan.

Miles, Robert and Phizacklea, A. (1980) *Labour and Racism*, London: Routledge & Kegan Paul.

Miller, Fiona (1987) In the *Daily Express*, 9 April: 7.

Morris, Bill (1988) 'Time for new thinking in the Black Section debate', *Tribune*, 8 January, 52 (2).

Omi, M. and Winant, H. (1986) *Racial Formation in the United States from the 1960s to the 1980s*, London: Routledge & Kegan Paul.

Preston, M., and Henderson Jr, L., and Purycar, P. (eds) (1982) *The New Black Politics: The Search for Political Power*, New York, Longman.

Rex, John (1979) 'Black militancy and class conflict', in R. Miles and A. Phizacklea (eds) *Racism and Political Action in Britain*, London: Routledge & Kegan Paul.

Wainwright, H. (1987) *Labour: A Tale of Two Parties*, London: Hogarth Press.

Chapter three

The political construction of class and community

Bangladeshi political leadership in
Tower Hamlets, East London

John Eade

Introduction

Most sociological analyses of class proceed from an implicit assumption of class and community solidarities. Even when classes are recognised as divided into 'fractions' (Hall *et al.* 1978: 345; Miles and Phizacklea 1980) or 'estates' (Rex and Tomlinson 1979), the internal solidarities of these fractions or status groups are regarded as relatively stable, the product of objective material forces. Attention is rarely drawn to the fact that internally opposed ideologies, such as those generated by the rise of the radical left and right within the political arena, may cut *across* such fractions or status groups.

It is equally important to recognise that social and ideological divisions also cut across the solidarities of ethnic groups. Most thoroughly analysed have been the divisions within the Jewish community. An extensive literature has examined early conflicts between German oldtimers and Eastern European newcomers, between the 'alrightniks' who had 'made it' and their socialist counterparts, between Zionists and anti-Zionists, between Reform and Orthodox, or between Jewish employers and employees (see, for example, Wirth 1928; Glazer 1978; Buckman 1983). In Britain, class and ideological divisions within Sikh and Pakistani communities have surfaced in recent years, as Werbner reveals elsewhere in this volume. Ideological conflicts of this type cut across the intra-ethnic solidarities of 'home-boys' or *'landsmann'*, which are usually based on regional associations and which themselves divide ethnic groups internally. Ethnic solidarities, to the extent that they exist, are often situational and impermanent, a response to a particular event, whether social, political, or economic, for example.

Class and ethnic solidarities clearly manifest themselves at the local level (see Gilroy 1987). Yet even at this level 'community' is a constructed solidarity, often situationally evoked. Within a local community different interests emerge in relation to specific policies, so that unity of action is, ultimately, an achievement (see Ward 1978). As Feuchtwang has noted, we need to direct our attention to the organisation and construction of class and ethnic solidarities 'through definite and distinct differentiations' (Feuchtwang 1980: 42).

Consideration of the way in which communities or classes are organised through various differentiations challenges the popular view that political representation entails a process whereby communities or classes speak through their representatives. I have argued elsewhere (Eade 1987, 1989, 1990) that, in some instances, communities and classes were constituted in political institutions and practices. In Tower Hamlets the 'Bangladeshi community' and the 'working class', for example, were differentiated in the context of political struggles and debates over the distribution of scarce resources.

The political construction of community and class was expressed through various ideological constituencies as both community workers and political activists sought to articulate the needs of others. Hence although I focus on particular leaders and organisations, their activities and claims will be located within the general debates and practices operating at various levels of the political system. What will be presented below is an account of the debates concerning the needs of local social collectivities in order to illustrate the ways by which local people were politically constructed and differentiated through various ideological constituencies.[1]

Bangladeshi settlement in Tower Hamlets and political representation

The origins of the Bangladeshi settlement in Tower Hamlets and elsewhere can be found in the arrival of around 5,000 migrant workers between 1954 and 1956.[2] Settlers were drawn from one Bangladeshi district in particular, Sylhet. Initially, the settlers' representatives were the ex-sailors who had established themselves as travel agents and owners of cafés and restaurants (see Adams 1987). In a familiar process of chain migration people came from particular localities within Sylhet itself so that competition between entrepreneurs for control of voluntary organisations and other positions of community responsibility was fought out through kinship and village networks. The intensity of struggles for posts through which an individual could gain access to more powerful agencies, such as the Bangladesh High Commission or the locally dominant Labour Party, was encouraged by the tightly knit character of settlement in the borough's western wards. By 1980 the largest concentration of

Bangladeshis was to be found in Spitalfields while substantial numbers were also established in the neighbouring Weavers, St Mary's, and St Katharine's wards.

By the early 1980s the Bangladeshi population had risen from 5,000 to approximately 24,000, or around 17 per cent of the borough population.[3] Despite the concentrations of Bangladeshi residents in the borough's western wards, families have gradually moved eastwards across the borough, weakening the tightly knit character of the early community. The vast majority of workers among the first and second generation undertake low-paid, unskilled, or semi-skilled jobs, especially in the local garment trade, retail shops, cafés, restaurants, hotels, and hospitals. Many Bangladeshis have not been able to find full-time employment and their weak economic position has been compounded by the restriction of large numbers to the rundown, privately rented housing market and to council housing on dilapidated estates. They have become heavily dependent on state welfare services in competition with members of the white working class, some of whom bitterly resent their settlement in the area.

Bangladeshi businessmen initially provided the community leadership, acting as brokers between their compatriots and local state officials. However, since the late 1970s their leadership has been challenged by a second generation of activists who have found jobs in local government, social and welfare services, or local schools and colleges. The younger leaders emerged from the many youth and community organisations which were established during the late 1970s, partly in response to Bangladeshi pressure for a larger share of local state welfare resources. The growth of Bangladeshi community organisations was also encouraged by central and local government funding, and by the policies of the major political parties, especially the Labour and Social Democratic Parties. The effect of these developments was to encourage community leaders to define and discuss the needs of their compatriots not only in relation to a particular ethnic community but also to what was seen as a local working class.

The second generation's active involvement in local political institutions and policies was encouraged by the events surrounding the 1978 borough election which involved opposition to the National Front and the murder of young Sylheti garment worker, Altab Ali, on the night of the poll. The Labour Party's failure to encourage the involvement of Bangladeshi community leaders in its affairs was cited as a major factor in the emergence of Bangladeshi Independent candidates at the 1982 borough elections. The success of one of these Independents at the expense of one of the Labour Party's representatives in Spitalfields, where Bangladeshis comprised almost half the population, encouraged local Labour Party leaders to introduce a policy of rapid Bangladeshi recruitment. By the next borough election, in 1986, seven Bangladeshi candidates were ready to fight on behalf of the party.

The widening involvement of Bangladeshis in local electoral politics was indicated by the entry of six other Bangladeshi candidates in the 1986 poll – five for the SDP and one for the Conservative Party. Although the Labour Party lost control of the borough council to a Liberal/SDP Alliance after over sixty years of political domination, five Bangladeshi Labour councillors were returned to the council chamber – all from wards with high proportions of Bangladeshi residents, viz. Spitalfields, St Katharine's, and St Dunstan's.

Four Bangladeshi councillors were second generation activists who had recently entered the party. They had established an uneasy alliance with left-wing white party activists, many of whom were also relatively new members of the local ward parties. Both found common cause in their opposition to 'right-wing' party leaders whose power rapidly diminished between 1982 and 1986. White and Bangladeshi activists were able to express their areas of mutual interest through the ideological constituencies of socialism and anti-racism. Yet they were also divided by competition for positions of responsibility within the various levels of the party, as well as by their ties with non-political organisations, such as trade unions, tenants' associations, youth and community groups.

Appeals for political support from residents focused on what were assumed or held to be common interests and social solidarities, despite the considerable differences between local people. The themes of class and community were regularly invoked by both Bangladeshi and white activists as they sought to establish their claims to represent local people within the political arena.

Political campaigns and the language of community and class

The Spitalfields Labour Party

In the ward with the highest proportion of Bangladeshi residents, white Labour Party leaders campaigned for numerous left-wing causes between 1982 and 1986. The rapidly expanding Bangladeshi membership was urged to support the striking miners during the prolonged struggle of 1984, and to protest against central government cuts in local welfare services. The borough council was blamed for failing to prevent the expansion of office building and 'gentrification' in Spitalfields and neighbouring wards. Furthermore, an attempt was made to link these general issues to areas of particular concern to

Table 3.1 Chronology of key events 1978–86

1978	Borough council elections and the beginning of Liberal challenge to Labour Party dominance. Murder of Altab Ali and resultant protests. National Front rampage down Brick Lane. Formation of Liaison Committee involving Bangladeshi community representatives.
1978–82	Growth of Bangladeshi community organisations supported in many cases by central and local government funding.
1979	GLC election leading to left-wing leadership committed to anti-racist policies.
1982	Borough council election: Liberal advance continues and Bangladeshi Independent defeats Labour left-wing candidate in Spitalfields ward, while the first Bangladeshi Labour councillor is returned from St Katharine's.
1982–6	Recruitment of Bangladeshi community activists by Labour Party and growth of white, left-wing influence within local Labour Party institutions.
1986	Termination of GLC. Borough council election: Liberal/SDP Alliance forms new majority group after decades of Labour rule. Five Bangladeshi Labour councillors are elected – four second-generation activists join the St Katharine's councillor elected in 1982. Bangladeshi Independent from Spitalfields defeated as Labour wins back the seat.

Bangladeshis through street protests against National Front activity in the locality.

The ward leaders explained their opposition to the National Front by establishing a relationship between racism and general economic and political processes. In a leaflet which was distributed to local homes they advanced the following argument:

> Racist ideas lead to racist attacks. These ideas breed and take root in people's minds because of the real problems they face – unemployment and poor housing, results of anti-working class policies and neglect by successive councils and now a vicious Tory government.

The leaflet claimed that the ward party needed 'to meet with community groups to discuss these problems. And also how as a community we can organise to stop these attacks. As a ward we welcome and will help organise these meetings'.

The leaflet appeared to imply that racism was a manifestation of false consciousness since the 'real problems' were located in contemporary economic and political developments adversely affecting the working class. An answer could be found in community mobilisation and resistance to racist attacks and the ward party offered its services to the struggle. An implicit assumption appeared to have been made that community groups could represent the general will of the ward as a community. Furthermore, it was suggested that the Spitalfields Labour Party could act as the political representative of the local community through its activities as a political body and through its ward councillors.

'Community' was used here to address all the residents of Spitalfields. Nevertheless, local activists recognised that Bangladeshi community groups and their leaders would be particularly concerned about racist violence since Bangladeshis were the main targets of racial attacks.

The publications of the Spitalfields Labour Party from 1982 to 1986 repeatedly drew attention to the relationship between socialism and anti-racism, even if the exact nature of that relationship was never seriously discussed in public. Socialism was clearly defined in terms of Labour Party opposition to Conservative government policies and the defence of local working-class interests, especially with regard to the provision of council housing, jobs, and welfare services. The special concerns of racial minorities, women and gays, for example, were seen as part of the general socialist struggle against capitalism.

Bangladeshi community activists who joined the ward party used the language of socialism although, like their white party colleagues, they were careful to moderate their language in the context of local electoral struggles. Party electoral appeals had long discussed the electorate in terms which paid little attention to ideological issues. The 'local community' was a popular term of address – a constituency which was as wide as possible and which covered the manifold social and cultural differences among Spitalfields residents.

In the 1985 ward by-election when the ward party entered its first Bangladeshi candidate, the electorate was once more addressed by the left-wing leadership in terms of locality without any explicit references to class or socialism, viz. 'Labour is the only Party that cares for local people and their everyday needs. . . . We need a Labour council that represents the needs of local people. We want Labour councillors who will represent local people rather than themselves'.

The party's commitment to socialist policies was implied rather than openly stated by the references to its campaigns against cuts in local welfare and social services, against 'private development for the benefit of the "better off" people from outside the area', and for more council housing. The relationship between socialism and anti-racism was not discussed.

The selection of Abbas Uddin, a radical young Bangladeshi community worker, was seen by Labour Party activists as a public declaration of their anti-racist credentials. Yet in his English-language address Abbas Uddin also relied on an appeal to localism and the local community. His long experience of the 'problems faced by local people' in the ward enabled him to 'represent the interests of all members of the community on the Council' and he proceeded to describe his involvement in specific local campaigns. The only explicitly ideological reference came in a sentence which was not supported by further elaboration – 'have also taken a prominent role in anti-racist activities and fully support the local Labour Party's socialist policies.' Indeed, the only implicit allusion to particular struggles involving Bangladeshis came in an earlier sentence describing Abbas Uddin's involvement 'with the problems of homeless families, especially those in bed & breakfast accommodation'. A similar approach towards the electorate was adopted in the leaflets distributed by the ward party during the 1986 council elections when Abbas Uddin represented the party together with another Bangladeshi community organiser and a white, left-wing activist.

Variations in the way Labour activists used the terms 'class' and 'community' were primarily caused by the differences between election contests and campaigns between elections. During elections party leaders appeared to be worried about the possibility that an emphasis upon the constituencies of socialism and anti-racism would alienate voters. References were indeed made to those constituencies but attention was focused upon 'local people'. Divergences of interest between white and Bangladeshi residents were ignored in an appeal to the 'local community'.

Voters were presented with a range of specific issues concerning the provision of material resources over which most people could find some common cause. The particular grievances of Bangladeshis were only implicitly recognised during the 1985 by-election, for example, through a passing reference to the issue of homelessness. During attempts to mobilise local support for certain campaigns between elections, however, party leaders clearly believed that they could use more radical language. Yet anti-racist policies and the specific interests of local Bangladeshis were still located within a socialist understanding which placed the struggle of particular groups in the context of class conflict.

Bangladeshi members of the Labour Party who gained positions of responsibility between 1982 and 1986 remained uneasy about the way in which the particular interests of their Bangladeshi supporters were played down. Their alliance with white, left-wing leaders was a 'marriage of convenience' in many respects, which continually threatened to break down under pressure as participants sought to satisfy their different groups of supporters. Bangladeshi party activists were well aware that many of their compatriots were not sympathetic to a number of socialist policies and that votes were mobilised through informal links within the community where the language of socialism and anti-racism had little relevance. If they did not have sufficient regard to the particular needs of their supporters they could be outflanked by Bangladeshi rivals both inside and outside the party. It is to their opponents outside the Labour Party that attention will now turn.

The Labour Party's opponents

The Labour Party's opponents confined their distribution of campaign literature to council elections. In the 1982 council election three white Labour candidates had been challenged by four Bangladeshi Independents and a Bangladeshi community leader representing the SDP (see Table 3.2). English-language leaflets supporting the campaign of two Bangladeshi Independent candidates, Nurul Huque and Syed Nurul Islam, also addressed the electorate in terms of class and race. They claimed to speak on behalf of an exploited working class which, 'whether black or white', had been 'deprived of any access to the decision-making process'.

Nurul Huque defeated one of the Labour Party candidates, a white, left-wing newcomer to the ward, and as a ward councillor presented a continual threat to the Spitalfields Labour Party between 1982 and 1986. When Abbas Uddin was selected by the ward Labour Party to fight the 1985 by-election, Nurul Huque assisted the campaign of Abbas Uddin's most dangerous rival, Abdul Hannan, who stood as an Independent having left the ward Labour Party after a power struggle with its white left-wing and Bangladeshi leaders. Nurul Huque's 1982 electoral address was used as a model for Hannan's English-language appeal while leaflets in standard Bengali described the candidate as the 'militant voice of the oppressed working class and a reliable fighter against racism'.

The language of class was even more striking in the electoral publications used by Nurul Huque and other Bangladeshi Independents than in the ward party's materials. At the same time the distribution of Bengali-language leaflets enabled these Independents to appeal more directly to what were assumed to be the specific interests of Bangladeshi voters. The Bengali leaflets produced by the

Table 3.2 Bangladeshi candidates in borough council elections, 1982–6

1982 Election

Spitalfields

*N. Huque (Indep.)	638	Elected
A.Elboz (Lab.)	560	Elected
S. Carlyle (Lab.)	556	Elected
*S.N. Islam (Indep.)	530	
S. Corbishley (Lab.)	496	
W. Kelly (SDP)	417	
*G. Mustafa (SDP)	407	
G. White (SDP)	401	
*A. Gofur (Indep.)	173	
*S. Huque (Indep.)	157	

St Katharine's

*A. Ali (Lab.)	1,123	Elected
G. Allen (Lab.)	1,096	Elected
J. Ramanoop (Lab.)	940	Elected
M. Borelli (SDP)	740	
D. Mason (SDP)	722	
J. York-Williams (SDP)	699	
R. Cook (Con.)	288	
L. Fisher (Con.)	286	
C. Cook (Con.)	283	
G. Simons (Indep. Lab.)	198	
R. Perkins (Indep.Lab.)	188	
*S. Ahmed (Indep.)	185	
J. Rees (Comm't)	170	
*N. Huque (Indep.)	65	

St.Mary's

R. Ashkettle (Lab.)	877	Elected
B. Saunders (Lab.)	834	Elected
G. Palfrey-Smith (SDP)	241	
*R. Ullah (SDP)	205	
M. Levitas (Comm't)	172	
R. Pearson (Con.)	115	

Weavers

J. Shaw (Lib.)	1,496	Elected
P. Hughes (Lib.)	1,435	Elected
K. Appiah (Lib.)	1,396	
E. Bishop (Lab.)	754	
W. Harris (Lab.)	664	
S. Tyley (Lab.)	612	
R. Dyer (Con.)	267	
*M. Hussain (Indep.)	246	

Spitalfields by-election, 1985

*A. Uddin (Lab.)	784	Elected
*A. Hannan (Indep.)	775	
P. Ainsworth (Con.)	174	

1986 Election

Spitalfields

*A. Uddin (Lab.)	1,246	Elected
*G. Mortuza (Lab.)	1,019	Elected
P. Maxwell (Lab.)	988	Elected
*N. Huque (Indep.)	837	
*A. Rahman (SDP)	590	
W. Kelly (SDP)	444	
*S. Islam (Indep.)	402	
*G. Mustafa (SDP)	387	
J. Emmerson (Con.)	215	
B. Wright (Indep.)	199	

St Katharine's

J. Rowe (Lab.)	1,651	Elected
*A. Ali (Lab.)	1,562	Elected
*M. Ahmed (Lab.)	1,513	Elected
*K. Ali (SDP)	714	
G. Clark (SDP)	695	
*M. Hussain (SDP)	640	
A. George (Con.)	461	
A. Smith (Con.)	410	
S. Folan (Con.)	371	
S. Smith (Indep.)	84	

St Mary's

R. Ashkettle (Lab.)	948	Elected
B. Saunders (Lab.)	861	Elected
*A. Barik (SDP)	316	
P. Mathurin (SDP)	253	
*M. Ali (Con.)	218	

St Dunstan's

S. Carlyle (Lab.)	1,227	Elected
T. Sullivan (Lab.)	1,191	Elected
*J. Alam (Lab.)	1,142	Elected
J. Brett-Freeman (Lib.)	1,058	
L. Morpurgo (Lib.)	924	
P. Truscott (Lib.)	911	
R. Evans (NF)	256	
M. Bashford (Con.)	241	
K. Collins (Con.)	214	

Blackwall

C. Shawcroft (Lab.)	834	Elected
J. Mathews (SDP)	788	Elected
*S. Ali (Lab.)	661	
R. Neale (SDP)	657	
R. Hughes (Con.)	129	

Note: * denotes Bangladeshi candidate

Labour Party were careful translations of English-language originals whereas, during the 1985 by-election, the English and Bengali appeals supporting the Independent, Abdul Hannan, looked towards substantially different audiences. The Bengali posters combined the acknowledgement of class with reference to the Bangladeshi community and community organisations as well as to Hannan's educational attainments and community experience with such groups as the East London Divided Families' Campaign.

Although the Labour Party did not appeal formally to a Bangladeshi audience in its literary appeals to local voters during the 1985 by-election, Bangladeshi party members became involved in a lively informal debate among Bangladeshi voters as to the respective merits of the two Sylheti candidates. These debates were concerned with the value of kinship and village ties, the 'respectability' of the two second-generation candidates and their acceptability to the older community leaders from the first generation.

The ideological constituencies of socialism and anti-racism were drawn into these debates through claims that the interests of different Bangladeshi groups would be more effectively served by supporting Abbas Uddin as their advocate within the locally dominant Labour Party. The strength of Abbas Uddin's position was that a socialist Labour Party would be more likely than any other political institution to advance the interests of different groups of Bangladeshis through its anti-racist policies. In the local competition for scarce resources the party would be able to use its political power to ensure a more equitable deal for Bangladeshi residents.

What the debates, both formal and informal, left unresolved was the question of whether Bangladeshis in council housing, privately rented accommodation, or bed and breakfast hotels, for example, shared a common interest. Appeals to a united community, defined in terms of class, ethnic minority, or locality, went hand in hand with vigorous disputes within the political arena between Bangladeshi activists – disputes which were not simply reflections of social conflicts and divisions. The struggles were to be understood principally in the context of electoral practices and political debates among particular voluntary organisations and residential networks where the categories of community and class were used to establish as broad an appeal as possible.

In the 1982 council election the SDP had entered two Bangladeshi candidates, in the Spitalfields and St Mary's wards respectively. Four years later five Bangladeshis represented the party in Spitalfields, St Mary's, and St Katharine's (see Table 3.2). Like Abdul Hannan, several of these Bangladeshi contestants had recently left the Labour Party after disputes with ward party leaders. They had publicly explained their reasons for leaving the party and entering the SDP by referring to the socialist convictions of Labour activists. Socialist hostility towards the Islamic needs of the Bangladeshi population was alleged in a reference to left-wing opposition to the establishment of a mosque on a GLC council estate in St Dunstan's ward.

The electoral address produced by the SDP for Spitalfields and the neighbouring St Katharine's wards returned to the issue of Islamic religious provision in a list of proposals which ended with a denunciation of the Labour borough council, left-wingers, and Bangladeshi Independents: 'The forthcoming local election . . . gives you a chance to change the Labour Council that has let you down. TOWER HAMLETS cannot afford four years of hard labour neither can the voters afford to be messed around again by so-called Independents.'

The electorate was defined in terms of multi-racialism and community rather than class. The SDP's programme began with the call: '1. To create a truly multi-racial community here in TOWER HAMLETS. All of us must unite to build a better community for our families and for future generations.' The party's anti-racist credentials were established by a denunciation of racism 'in any form' and, indirectly, by a call for equal opportunities in jobs and housing. Like the English-language appeals distributed by the Labour Party and Bengali Independents, Bangladeshi residents were not explicitly mentioned but the demand for the construction of '5 bedroom family houses in the E1 area' recognised an issue particularly associated with pressure groups representing Bangladeshi housing interests.

The SDP document looked towards the construction of a better and 'truly multi-racial community' based upon the unity of local residents. In another SDP leaflet produced by Bill Kelly, one of the Spitalfields contestants, voters were invited to restore a lost unity. After blaming the Labour Party for the ward's manifold problems and claiming that 'the PEOPLE of SPITALFIELDS are fed up with being told what to do by OUTSIDERS', Bill Kelly concluded his statement by exhorting voters to come 'back to the HARMONIOUS COMMUNITY IT ONCE WAS'. The cause of this disharmony appeared to be the Labour Party and outsiders (presumably community workers) who called themselves 'the SAVIOURS of SPITALFIELDS'.

Although the electoral appeals of the major political adversaries in Spitalfields sometimes referred to class solidarities, they preferred to define the electorate in terms of a 'local community', and particular sectoral interests among residents were only obliquely established. The left-wing leadership of the ward Labour Party played down the constituency of socialism in its election campaigns and, surprisingly perhaps, Bangladeshi Independents made more explicit reference to class and race.

In English-language leaflets community was never defined exclusively in terms of Bangladeshi origins. However, the publication of Bengali-language addresses allowed a more direct approach to a Bangladeshi audience which informally discussed a range of issues which found no formal expression in English political debates. All the contestants alluded to the constituency of anti-racism, often combining it with references to the multi-racial character of society. The SDP tried to make electoral capital from an attack on the ideological commitments of 'hard labour' and the issue of religious provision, thereby driving a wedge between socialism and anti-racism. Socialist 'extremists' and 'outsiders' could be blamed for destroying the harmony of the local community and the electorate could be urged to restore a united community which was 'truly multi-racial'.

Political socialisation, the political translation of issues, and factional conflict

What has been described so far can be seen as further evidence of the way in which Britain's ethnic minorities were being socialised into the country's dominant political culture. Community activists, in particular, had become involved in the local political campaigns of national organisations, i.e. the Labour and Social Democratic Parties, and in the process Bangladeshi voters had been encouraged to support mainstream political institutions and policies rather than locally popular individuals who stood as Independents.

The articulation of local interests played a vital role within this process of political socialisation. Particular concerns of specific groups had to be translated into a language that was acceptable both to party leaders and to a wide range of local residents. Local interests were articulated within the political arena through ideological constituencies developed by political activists. During elections the electorate was predominantly defined in terms of localism, but between elections Labour Party leaders, in particular, tried to involve members and local residents in issues concerned with the constituencies of socialism and anti-racism.

Yet the election campaigns indicated that the translation of particular interests of specific groups into the language of party politics was more complicated than the formal discussions of socialism and anti-racism implied. Bangladeshi voters were interested in issues which were not formally recognised in English-language political appeals. Electoral addresses by Labour Party opponents in standard Bengali attempted to bring some of these issues into the political arena, but the Labour Party's Bangladeshi campaigners had to discuss such considerations as the reputation, education, and Sylheti background of the candidates or the need for more mosques through informal avenues.

Political addresses assumed that the particular party which was delivering the address was united in its representation of an electorate whose common interests were expressed through the party's language. Clearly such an assumption was well wide of the mark since both political parties and electorates were riven by internal differences. A distinction was frequently drawn between Bangladeshi and white voters, but other categories were widely used by residents to refine this twofold classification. Loyalties based on district, village, kinship, and religious affiliations differentiated members of the 'Bangladeshi community', while the ethnic and religious traditions of Jews, Irish Catholics, Maltese, and Cypriots divided 'whites' from each other and from other 'whites' such as the 'Cockneys' who sometimes claimed to be the 'real' locals.

The complex overlap of different social solidarities was overlaid by the language used in the political arena to address the electorate. Even so, the varying interests of particular local social networks and organisations were obliquely recognised in political appeals as candidates put forward their policies over issues of local concern. References to the ideological constituency of 'anti-racism' and to particular issues, such as homelessness and five-bedroom council flats, could apply to all black people, to the homeless, or to those with large families. Nevertheless, in the context of Tower Hamlets such references were primarily directed towards Bangladeshi voters and revealed the influence of Bangladeshi pressure groups in the borough.

Between 1982 and 1986 vigorous rivalry among prominent figures within Bangladeshi pressure groups influenced certain struggles in the political arena. Older businessmen, predominantly from Sylhet, who held posts in the largest and oldest community group, the Bangladesh Welfare Association (BWA), encountered stiff opposition from Sylheti second generation activists who were mostly linked to the various youth and recreational groups. These younger leaders had established a national platform through the Federation of Bangladeshi Youth Organisations (FBYD).

The limited influence of the BWA in local electoral politics was demonstrated during the 1982 council election when none of the prominent BWA businessmen received much support. Significantly, the two Bangladeshis, Nural Huque and Ashik Ali, who became councillors, were neither businessmen nor Sylhetis. Both pursued white-collar careers in local authority agencies. Nurul Huque had become involved with local Bangladeshi grievances through his participation in a Spitalfields squatting campaign and his Bengali-language community school, while Ashik Ali had played a leading role in a St Katharine's tenants' association.

The only Sylheti activist who did receive substantial electoral support in 1982 was a second generation GLC housing officer, S.N. Islam. Like Nurul Huque part of his success was due to the backing he received from a campaign front, the People's Democratic Alliance (PDA), which was established before the election through the efforts of the FBYO and older activists who operated outside the BWA. The PDA attempted to draw up a list of candidates who would fight in wards with substantial Bangladeshi settlements, but the attempt failed because of the refusal by certain community activists to accept the selections for the plum ward, Spitalfields. Even so, the two Bangladeshi Independents who challenged Nurul Huque and S.N. Islam in the ward and who were not backed by the PDA fared very badly in the election. Furthermore, the only Bangladeshi to represent a national party, the SDP, in Spitalfields still gained fewer votes than the two PDA-sponsored contestants.

The use of different languages to appeal in some cases to separate audiences has already been noted. The PDA's English-language address referred to eleven specific issues and gave priority to public housing, rents, rates, and amenities. The election appeal in standard Bengali covered roughly the same ground but gave higher priority to education and training and the 'anti-racist movement'. Furthermore, the last of the nine Bengali-language demands referred to an issue which was exclusively a Bangladeshi concern championed by certain second generation activists, viz. the provision of Bengali television programmes.

The political discussion of local needs in terms of class and community was supported, therefore, by references to specific issues which had been raised by local community organisations and their leaders. The Labour Party and SDP also attended to the specific interests of Bangladeshi pressure groups in 1982 but, since their Bengali-language leaflets were close translations of English originals, they did not give as much priority to particular Bangladeshi grievances as the PDA documents.

Between 1982 and 1986 local Labour ward parties became more open to Bangladeshi pressure groups as they embarked on Bangladeshi recruitment drives. Certain Bangladeshi community leaders played a crucial role in the recruitment process and their advancement to positions of responsibility within the party caused much resentment among their rivals who also joined the party. The second generation activists were keenly involved in these disputes during a period when their community organisations and their own careers were encouraged by grants from the borough council, GLC, ILEA, and central government.

The 1985 Spitalfields by-election provided the first test of the uneasy alliance which had been established between the two sets of newcomers to local Labour Party wards – white left-wingers and young Bangladeshi community workers. The party's choice, Abbas Uddin, had been closely associated with the FBYO and local youth groups. He had taken part in homelessness campaigns and was employed as a youth adviser by ILEA. His Bangladeshi rival, Abdul Hannan, who had resigned from the Spitalfields Labour Party, was nominated as a 'People's Alliance Supported Independent Candidate' – a clear reference to the 1982 campaign front. This time, however, youth groups associated with the FBYO leadership refused to support Hannan, who relied largely on his links with the leaders of the BWA for whom he worked in a central government funded post.

There was an even greater gap between the English- and Bengali-language addresses published on behalf of the Independent candidate in 1985. The English document was modelled on the 1982 appeal, whereas the Bengali version concentrated on describing Hannan's educational, community, and professional achievements. Since both Abbas Uddin and Abdul Hannan came from Sylheti backgrounds, the implication of Hannan's Bengali electoral appeal appeared to be that the Independent candidate could be trusted to fight for Bengali interests because of his extensive experience in specific campaigns concerning homelessness, for example, and his educational achievements in Sylhet, Dacca, and England.

The selection of six Bangladeshis to represent the Labour Party in the 1986 council election resulted in more Bangladeshi resignations. Although these defections can be explained in terms of rivalries between community activists, the reasons given for resigning had to be taken seriously. White left-wing leaders had come to rely on a small coterie of Bangladeshi activists who recruited party members through their networks of supporters. Furthermore, left-wing leaders were very uneasy about demands for the provision of Islamic facilities, as were many young Bangladeshi activists. The latter preferred to concentrate on secular issues and tried to prevent religious leaders from influencing the political arena.

The SDP provided those dissatisfied with socialist policies with a forum for their grievances but, as in 1982, the nomination of Bangladeshi candidates still failed to bring success for the SDP. Ironically, the only seat which the SDP did win resulted from the defeat of a Bangladeshi Labour nominee in Blackwall ward. The young Bangladeshi candidate was closely associated with the FBYO leadership and his selection appeared to spark off the 'white back-lash' which many white party workers feared, since he received far fewer votes than his white colleague (see Table 3.2).

General references to the ideological constituencies of socialism, anti-racism, and localism went hand in hand, therefore, with the consideration of particular issues which interested certain local pressure groups. Political representatives were presented in campaign literature as articulating the needs of unitary social entities such as the working class or the local community. Nevertheless, the documents also revealed – through the lists of specific demands – the considerable influence of certain pressure groups upon political organisations. The debate about the provision of material resources for a population heavily dependent on state support was expressed in terms of vague assertions about socialism, anti-racism, and locality, but attention was also paid both formally and informally to specific issues concerned with the implementation of socialist and anti-racist policies. It is to debates about those policies involving Bangladeshi pressure groups outside the arena of party politics that attention will now turn.

Bangladeshi community workers and debates concerning socialism and anti-racism

When the Labour Party lost the borough council election in 1986 its internal dissensions intensified as the uneasy alliance between white left-wingers and Bangladeshi leaders threatened to collapse. Personal rivalries among white and Bangladeshi leaders were closely intertwined with debates about socialism and anti-racism. These rivalries have to be seen not only in the context of internal party factionalism and ideological debates but also, as regards Bangladeshi party members, in terms of the criticisms of the Labour Party advanced by local Bangladeshi community organisations. For many community workers the socialism of white, left-wing leaders was a veil drawn over their 'racist' refusal to share power with Bangladeshi community representatives.

Political policies and practices were discussed by Bangladeshi community workers in numerous community publications outside of the periodical electoral contests. Attention was directed mainly to the 'Bangladeshi community' and to racist attitudes and practices which discriminated against the members of that community. Although most Bangladeshi residents had come from Sylhet or were descended from Sylheti migrant workers, the community was constructed in terms of the ideological constituency of nationalism and the national language – standard Bengali – which differed substantially from the Sylheti dialects used in everyday conversation. The 'Bangladeshi community' was also defined in terms of the constituencies of racism and anti-racism with the result that discussions sometimes extended to a consideration of the common plight experienced by all racial minorities in the borough and further afield.

Just before the May 1986 council elections an article in the FBYO monthly newspaper, *Jubo Barta* (Youth Voice), illustrated the way in which community was discussed in the context of local politics. The election was hailed as 'a major milestone in the political development of the Bengali community' because of the large number of Bengali contestants. The article then proceeded to express the hope that 'the participation of Bengali councillors in political decision making will make a major impact on what has hitherto been a bastion of racist policies and practices' (*Jubo Barta*, April 1986: 1). The community was constructed here in terms of language (Bengali) and, indirectly, a country of origin (Bangladesh), while the constituency of racism was introduced in the political context of a racist, Labour dominated, local council.

The community was seen as suffering more intensely than others from 'a racist and inegalitarian system' and the 'crucial task' confronting Bengali councillors would be 'fighting for change within their parties and within institutions across the board'. Class was introduced in the following sentence: 'The worst thing will be if any Bengali candidates/councillors soft-peddle [*sic*] the fundamental issue of racism and fail to see also the class context within which racism thrives.' With regard to the electoral addresses examined above, given the SDP's failure to make any explicit references to class, this article could be seen as endorsing Bangladeshi Independents like Nurul Huque and, probably even more likely, the second generation Labour candidates, some of whom had been prominent figures within the FBYO.

Although youth workers shared a certain sympathy towards the Labour Party, an adjoining article in the same edition expressed its concern about the party's 'performance on race issues'. In a discussion of the Bethnal Green and Stepney Constituency Labour Party Ethnic Minorities Group (an officially approved organ of 'black' party members, unlike 'Black Sections'), the article explained: 'The Group believes that the only way to achieve a voice within the Party is to have a separatist approach, which promotes the interests of ethnic minorities in terms of rights and representation within the Party.' The article proceeded to contrast this strategy with '"the colour blind" system of socialism' which had failed to raise issues 'which affect the lives of Black people in this country'.

The writer of the article raised once again the complicated relationship between anti-racism and socialism. White socialists had failed to take seriously the issue of racism within the party. An anti-racist strategy within the party depended upon the separate organisation of Ethnic Minority Groups where the particular interests of the black population could be articulated and promoted. Here the Bangladeshi community was placed in the wider context of Britain's 'black' population.

The FBYO, like other community groups, was principally concerned with issues affecting its particular community. After the election it joined other community organisations and Labour Party activists in denouncing the decision of the new Liberal/SDP Alliance Majority Group to define as 'intentionally homeless' families waiting to enter council housing in Tower Hamlets. In *Jubo Barta*'s April/May 1987 edition the move was condemned as 'inhuman and racist' and as having 'immense' implications for 'all working class Black people across the nation' (*Jubo Barta*, April/May 1987: 1). A particular issue involving homeless families (mostly Bangladeshi) was related to a general struggle involving 'working class Black people' against racism – a striking example of the attempt to establish a connection between a section of an ethnic minority, anti-racism, and class.

The Bangladeshi Labour councillors, who entered the council chamber after the May 1986 elections, were given here a clear indication as to what the representatives of a well-known Bangladeshi community group thought about a political struggle concerning housing. The *Jubo Barta* article, like its counterparts in other editions of the publication, used terms such as working class, black people, and racism in ways which have already become familiar in the account of political debates surrounding local elections. Party politics and Bangladeshi community activism had become intimately related. Although there was a tendency among second generation Bangladeshi community workers to look favourably on the Labour Party where a number of community leaders had found a niche, they insisted that the interests of the Bangladeshi population received priority through the constituency of anti-racism. Consequently, they were well aware of the problems involved in the complicated relationship between anti-racism and socialism within a party which was wary of providing 'black' members with a separate representative system.

Bangladeshi activists repeatedly assessed the commitment of white Labour Party leaders to anti-racist practices in terms of the promotion of Bangladeshi members within the party structure. Some Bangladeshi activists, both inside and outside the party, argued that

when the local veteran MP, Peter Shore, retired, the selection of a
Bangladeshi candidate would be the clearest expression of the party's
anti-racist commitment. Consequently, when one of the major
Bangladeshi contestants for the future prize failed to be chosen to
fight a 1988 by-election in St Katharine's ward – a by-election which
had been caused by the death of a Bangladeshi Labour councillor –
the anti-racist credentials of white colleagues were quickly
challenged.

An article in the *Asian Herald* during September 1988 offered a
review of the political developments involving local Bangladeshis
down to the current dispute over the St Katharine's nomination. The
author challenged the socialist pretensions of white left-wing leaders
arguing that:

> The left . . . were not seriously interested in understanding . . . the
> Bengalis. Nor were they keen to open a debate on the whole area
> of Socialist theory and practice and how that related to the Ben-
> gali community. In a very patronising fashion, a section of the left
> began to hand-pick Bengalis on whom they conferred the title
> 'Socialist'. It was colonialism writ large. Instead of opening up for
> discussion the strategic issues, alliances were built around per-
> sonalities.
>
> (*Asian Herald*, 14–20 September 1988: 6)

The Ethnic Minorities Group (EMG) had been 'in the forefront of
influencing the party to adopt an anti-racist programme' while white
left-wing leaders had 'failed to initiate, debate or adopt any strategic
policy on anti-racism'.

The writer saw the recent nomination struggle in St Katharine's as
further evidence of a refusal by white left-wing leaders to share power
with Bangladeshi party members. They had opposed the nomination
of the EMG chairman on the grounds that he was part of a 'Bengali
Mafia' which sought to control Bangladeshi access to party posts and
to the party itself.

The article concluded with a number of recommendations for 'a
creative amalgam of anti-racism and Socialism'. The blueprint
included an appeal to white leaders who were genuinely anti-racist
and socialist to realise 'that ordinary Tower Hamlets voters see the
Labour Party as being led by middle class whites bent more on
rhetoric than the actualisation of policies for the people'. These
leaders should support 'genuine Socialists within the Bengali community who take an independent stand and are prepared to talk
strategy'. The practice of picking Bangladeshi 'stooges' had to be
abandoned because

such a practice will ensure that they end up with people who are neither Socialists nor any longer linked with the specific concerns of the community. True Socialism *a priori* demands the development of organic links with the masses.

(Asian Herald, 14–20 September 1988: 6)

Anti-racism was not explicitly defined in this article but the author seemed to imply that an important aspect of any anti-racist strategy involved the sharing of power between white and Bangladeshi members within the Labour Party. White leaders had allegedly refused to share power with independent-minded Bangladeshi members of the EMG, preferring to establish personal alliances with certain individuals who were not genuine socialists. According to the author, white left-wingers had replied in kind by arguing that the EMG constituted a 'Bengali Mafia' using personal links to advance the political interests of EMG members and their supporters.

The article revealed the limitations of formal ideological debates concerning political representation. Although the author referred, like many socialists, to building links with 'the masses', in the event political support was mobilised partly through appeals to personal networks. Struggles within and between political parties involved personalities and assessments of their 'respectability', 'integrity', political experience, and class background. Bangladeshi candidates were also judged, at least in part, according to their reputation as trustworthy members of the Bangladeshi community, as well as by their links to particular localities and kinship groups within Bangladesh.

At the same time formal discussions of 'working-class' needs and statements about political policies were not empty rhetoric. Voters were interested in the policies and issues for which individual candidates stood; the appeals produced by the Labour Party and its opponents were discussed and carefully assessed by Bangladeshis as well as by white residents. Debates about anti-racism and socialism had to be understood in the context of internal struggles for power within the Labour Party, but the debates were also for a public audience and the problems encountered by members of that audience.

After the 1986 borough election a small group of young Bangladeshi activists decided to debate the issues of anti-racism and socialism outside the institutional framework of local party politics. They formed the Bangladeshi Socialist Society (BSS) and held a series of meetings in the Spitalfields and St Mary's wards throughout 1987 and 1988. The members were generally concerned about the careerism of Bangladeshi councillors and others in powerful positions within the Labour Party and to what extent they represented the interests of Bangladeshi members within the local working class. They

Table 3.3 Political debates and local politics

During elections		
Labour Party	*Bangladeshi Independents*	*SDP*
General emphasis on 'local community' and improvement in the provision of state welfare resources: debates at the formal level of politics coexist with informal debates concerning social and cultural issues among Bangladeshis.		
Few references to socialism; oblique references to the interests of certain Bangladeshi groups (e.g. homeless families) in English and standard Bengali addresses.	Slightly greater notice taken of class and race; use of different languages to address separate audiences; specific interests of Bangladeshi groups addressed through standard Bengali.	Criticism of socialism; anti-racism replaced by multi-racial community; oblique references to the interests of certain Bangladeshi groups (e.g. mosque provision).
Between elections		
Labour Party	*Second generation community organisers in EMG, voluntary groups and other political parties*	
Attempts to launch campaigns linking local grievances to wider class struggle; anti-racism is bound up with recruitment and promotion of Bangladeshi members who are encouraged to relate their specific interests to the general needs of the local working class.	Emphasis on anti-racism and suspicion of white left-wingers; those outside the Labour Party warn of incorporation of Bangladeshi colleagues into the middle class and local state agencies; BSS awareness of the relationship between socialist struggles in Britain and in Bangladesh.	

were also uneasily aware of the way in which Bangladeshi businessmen and, more recently, their own friends in professional jobs were becoming absorbed into middle-class lifestyles and local state agencies.

Yet these meetings also provided an insight into an issue which was not explicitly raised in debates about the representation of Bangladeshi interests – the way in which those deliberations related to political developments within Bangladesh itself.

A major attraction of being elected to positions of responsibility in the Bangladesh Welfare Association, the largest and longest established community organisation in the borough, was the access gained thereby to Bangladeshi government officials both in Britain and in the country of origin. The growth of youth organisations had established a power base for second generation community activists which effectively rivalled the older businessmen who usually controlled the BWA. The younger community workers had encouraged their compatriots to concentrate their energies on British politics and had criticised the older generation's preoccupation with Bangladeshi political struggles. However, the debates of the BSS had clear implications for those thinking about a Bangladeshi régime which was denounced by Bengali radicals as a right-wing dictatorship. One of the best attended meetings of this group was a talk given by a renowned Marxist politician from Bangladesh which led to a lively debate in the British Bengali press. What these meetings exposed was the sensitivity which surrounded the constituency of socialism in terms of discussions about both Britain's class structure and Bangladeshi politics.

The differences between political debates during elections and those which emerged between electoral contests can be summarised as in Table 3.3.

Conclusion

My analysis has focused on the political construction of class and community through the ideological constituencies of socialism and anti-racism. Yet it has become clear that other constituencies, especially localism, have also to be considered: political contestants sought to appeal to the widest possible range of voters during elections. Moreover, the formal level of political debate and electoral practices was linked to an informal level involving networks of support surrounding candidates, local pressure groups, and ideological considerations. Factional disputes within the Labour Party also overlapped with conflicts between Bangladeshi leaders of certain community organisations, and these in turn had consequences for the kinds of issues raised by both the Labour Party and its SDP and Independent rivals.

Political addresses presented candidates and their political organisations as representatives of unitary groups, i.e. the 'working class', the 'Bangladeshi community', or 'local people'. Political representatives claimed to be expressing the needs of their electors, whereas in practice those needs were, in part, constructed according to the political activists' perception of local needs and, relatedly, according to certain ideological constituencies.

Even at the formal level, issues could be articulated which were informally considered by Bangladeshis during elections. Bangladeshi Independents used standard Bengali electoral addresses to appeal to a substantially different audience from the one which was hailed in their English-language documents. During the 1986 election the SDP introduced an issue which had been debated for some time outside the political arena – that of Islam, in general, and the provision of religious facilities, in particular.

The introduction of demands, which were, at first, discussed principally by Bangladeshi residents and certain community organisations, into formal political debates was still undertaken with reference to the political policies and ideological constituencies prevailing within the political arena. However, some considerations, such as the respectability and educational attainments of Bangladeshi contestants, were still dealt with through informal encounters and gossip. The informal level of campaigning enabled residents and activists to discuss grievances which bore only a tangential relationship to such ideological constituencies as socialism, anti-racism, multi-culturalism, and localism.

Just as it was far too simple to present local politics in terms of unitary groups articulating their needs through their political representatives, so it was dangerous to assume that the political arena was easily accessible to all pressure groups (see Saunders 1979). Left-wing activists encouraged the careers of certain Bangladeshi community workers from particular pressure groups. Most of the Bangladeshi community organisations which have developed since the late 1970s had been concerned with secular issues, and the voice of religious leaders was seldom heard in the political arena until the 1986 election. Even then the demands for mosque provision came from second generation Bangladeshi activists who had worked in youth and secular community groups and had become disillusioned with the Labour Party.

When the constituencies of socialism and anti-racism were introduced there was little attempt to explain their implications for political practices. The delivery of anti-racist policies was usually translated into a readiness to select certain Bangladeshi activists for positions of political responsibility. As a result the overlap between party political and community factionalism led to accusations of patronage and the promotion of 'pseudo-socialists' who were not really representative of local social groups, i.e. the 'working class', the 'Bangladeshi community', or 'black people'.

Second generation secular activists from community organisations outside the party political arena were involved in the debates about the socialist and anti-racist credentials of the Labour Party, especially leading members of the FBYO. They continued to charge the Labour Party with racism and encouraged Bangladeshi party members to realise the danger of being manipulated by a party which failed to implement anti-racist policies. Once more, however, the general debate about the relationship between socialism and anti-racism which was raised by Bangladeshi activists outside the Labour Party revolved around the promotion of certain individuals and factional conflicts.

The deliberations of Bangladeshis outside party organisations served to remind activists about the wider pressures bearing upon them. Although this account has focused on particular parties, community organisations, and individuals, the influence of state agencies within Britain and developments in Bangladesh have to be borne in mind.

Despite the differences between political opponents, they all concentrated on the delivery of material resources by state agencies. Furthermore, between the late 1970s and 1986 the expansion of Bangladeshi community groups was encouraged by local and central government funding and Bangladeshi activists were drawn into an intimate relationship with government officials as well as with politicians. Although Bangladeshi community workers made an impact on local politics, some noted the danger of individuals being absorbed by party political and administrative institutions. There was a fear of 'token' gestures towards anti-racism and the specific grievances of Bangladeshi residents. Ever since the entry of Bangladeshi Independents in the 1982 election, the necessity for some degree of autonomy was publicly expressed so that Bangladeshi interests were not compromised by those who claimed to represent 'their community'.

Campaigns on behalf of homeless Bangladeshi families living in bed and breakfast accommodation outside Tower Hamlets, those threatened with deportation, or those who wanted a new mosque suggested the wider dimensions of local struggles. The language of class and community, as well as references to socialism, anti-racism, multi-racial community, and Islam, linked local issues to national and international processes. At the same time the wider dimensions of politics and culture were juxtaposed with appeals to local people and local needs at both the formal and the informal levels of political campaigning.

It is this complex interplay of levels and debates which the foregoing account has explored in an examination of the political representation of a particular locality. Connections between levels and debates have been perceived as well as gaps between them. Behind the language of representation, in which the interests of local collectivities are presented by political representatives, a more complicated process can be perceived involving various levels and debates through which people's needs were politically constructed.

© 1991 John Eade

Notes

1 I am indebted to Pnina Werbner for her helpful suggestions concerning the revision of this chapter.
2 Sylhetis were associated with the locality long before the 1950s. The presence of Indian lascars in the East End was recorded in the late eighteenth century (Adams 1987: 17) and those recruited through Calcutta during the nineteenth century may have come from Sylhet as well as from other East Bengal districts. Some of the Sylheti seamen whom Adams interviewed jumped ship during the 1930s and 1940s. They found work outside London – in Midlands factories, for example – as well as in the metropolis.
3 A borough council survey, 'A short report on the Asian population of Tower Hamlets, Feb. 1984', put the Bangladeshi population at between 14,800 and 18,000 while community workers claimed much higher totals, i.e. up to 40,000. The figure which I have given is a 'guesstimate' which leans towards the lower numbers given in the 1984 survey but allows for the rapid rise in Bangladeshi numbers which has continued since 1984 (see Home Affairs Committee 1986–7: vi).

References

Adams, Caroline (1987) *Across Seven Seas and Thirteen Rivers*, London: Tower Hamlets Arts Project Books.

Buckman, Joseph (1983) *Immigrants and the Class Struggle: The Jewish Immigrants in Leeds, 1880–1914*, Manchester: Manchester University Press.

Eade, John (1987) 'The political representation of a South Asian minority in a working class area', *South Asia Research* 7: 55–70.

Eade, John (1989) *The Politics of Community: The Bangladeshi Community in East London*, Aldershot: Gower.

Eade, John (1990) 'Bangladeshi community organisation and leadership in Tower Hamlets, East London', in Colin Clarke, Ceri Peach, and Steven Vertovec (eds) *South Asians Overseas: Migration and Ethnicity*, Cambridge: Cambridge University Press.

Feuchtwang, Stephan (1980) 'Socialist, feminist and anti-racist struggles', *M/F* 4.

Gilroy, Paul (1987) *There Ain't No Black in the Union Jack*, London: Hutchinson.

Glazer, Nathan (1978) 'The Jews', in John Higham (ed.) *Ethnic Leadership in America*, Baltimore, Md, and London: Johns Hopkins University Press.

Hall, Stuart, Critcher, Chas, Jefferson, Tony, Clarke, John and Roberts, Brian (1978) *Policing the Crisis: Mugging, the State and Law and Order*, London: Macmillan Education.

Home Affairs Committee (1986–7) House of Commons, First Report from the Home Affairs Committee, *Bangladeshis in Britain*, vol. 1, London: HMSO.

Miles, Robert and Phizacklea, Annie (1980) *Labour and Racism*, London: Routledge & Kegan Paul.

Rex, John and Tomlinson, Sally (1979) *Colonial Immigrants in a British City: A Class Analysis*, London: Routledge & Kegan Paul.

Saunders, P. (1979) *Urban Politics: A Sociological Interpretation*, London: Hutchinson.

Ward, Robin (1978) 'Where race didn't divide: some reflections on slum clearance in Moss Side', in Robert Miles and Annie Phizacklea (eds) *Racism and Political Action in Britain*, London: Routledge & Kegan Paul.

Wirth, Louis (1928) *The Ghetto*, Chicago: Chicago University Press.

Part two

Culture Politicised: Protest and Autonomy

Chapter four

The fiction of unity in ethnic politics
Aspects of representation and the state among British Pakistanis[1]

Pnina Werbner

Community as fiction or reality

In an early article on Pakistanis in Britain, Verity Saifullah Khan opened a debate about the nature of Pakistani 'ethnicity' in the British context, and whether or not we may legitimately talk of a Pakistani 'community'. She takes issue with Badr Dahya's account of Pakistanis in Bradford which, in her view, smoothes over 'the internal differentiation of the Pakistani community' (Saifullah Khan 1976: 228). In particular, she questions an assumption she attributes to him, that 'cohesion results from considered deliberate organisations'. She argues that

> although Pakistanis in Britain do not perceive the population of their fellow naturals as a community (in the sense of a group of people with common identification, values, and perspective who interact with each other and have common associations and leaders) they become aware over time of how outsiders see them.
>
> (Saifullah Khan 1976: 227)

This *external definition* is, she feels, false, but it is perpetuated by the media, in the field of community relations, and, significantly, by academics. In similar vein Buckman (1983) argues for the Jewish community that the image of ethnic unity obscures internal class conflicts which radically divide the group from within.

Anwar, in his study of Pakistanis in Rochdale, argues strongly, *pace* Saifullah Khan, that Pakistanis may be regarded as a community 'because they share a common background, have common interests, some form of social structure, hold a common religious belief and a value system and also have a territorial nucleus in parts of Rochdale and in other areas of Britain' (Anwar 1979: 12, also 26, 96, 220). He stresses in particular the dense networks of friendship, kinship, and acquaintance that criss-cross the community, and the fact that they 'share a great many cultural items – religion, language, moral and

113

aesthetic values and other behavioural norms . . . [and] are likely to recognise a common allegiance' (ibid.: 220).

More recently still, in a pathbreaking volume challenging simplistic 'culturalist' approaches to the study of ethnic groups, Paul Gilroy argues that the concept of community is central to the analysis of minority groups: 'It links cultural and political traditions with a territorial dimension, to collective actions and consciousness within the relation of economic patterns, political authority and uses of space' (Gilroy 1982: 286). In Gilroy's view the community is the locus of cultural resistance to the domination of the wider society (ibid.: 285). He thus endorses Dahya's view that the 'whole complex of ethnic institutions manifests the community's wish not merely to express but also to defend and perpetuate their traditional social forms . . . [its] refusal to surrender its ethnic identity' (Dahya 1974: 94–5). Gilroy is, of course, questioning the 'pathological' interpretation of ethnic, 'autonomy' as being simply a reflection of ethnic marginality or 'internal colonialism' (see Williams 1985). In doing so, however, he presents a somewhat utopian picture of a unified 'community'.

This 'romanticising' of community by Gilroy obscures the very issues Saifullah Khan raised in her original critique: namely, the distrust of 'community' leaders which ordinary Pakistanis feel, the parochial alliances they continue to uphold, and the fallacy of identifying outcomes with their imputed 'intention' (i.e. popular resistance). Moreover, the questions raised by Saifullah Khan regarding the complex relation between communal leadership, associational activity, and culturally defined divisions within the British Pakistani population have not yet, I feel, been adequately addressed. In this chapter I propose to develop and amplify these issues by examining in some detail two cases, both of which illustrate the internal divisions – and the transcendent unity – of overseas Pakistanis.

I suggest, *pace* Gilroy, that hegemonic struggles *within* an ethnic community are as endemic as they are between the minority population and the wider society. The character of ethnic 'cultural resistance' is thus as much an outcome of internal hegemonic struggles as it is a response to outside domination. In carrying the debate forward into the 1980s, however, I go beyond Saifullah Khan's stress on ethnic brokerage as a feature of communication, and address more fully the economic and political context in which relations between ethnic minorities and the majority are played out. I thus stress the nature of resource allocation and state intervention in communal affairs.

Ethnicity and the state

Glazer and Moynihan argue that the state is a key to an understanding of contemporary ethnicity:

> the *state* becomes a crucial and direct arbiter of economic well-being, as well as of political status and whatever flows from that. In such a situation . . . as a matter of strategic efficacy, it becomes necessary to disaggregate, to make claims for a group small enough to make significant concessions possible, and, equally, small enough to produce some gain from the concessions made.
>
> (Glazer and Moynihan 1975: 8–9)

According to this view, a group's access to jobs, concessions, and special allocations is directly influenced by its bargaining with the state or para-state organisations. The definition of ethnic boundaries may itself alter in response to such negotiations, as different strategies are assumed in the fight for equal rights or privileged concessions.

In Britain the state is identified with, and thus embodies, the dominant host society; it does so, however, in a specialised capacity in which it becomes both oppressor and benefactor, exploiter and judge. Conflicting trends manifest themselves in opposing state policies and internally opposed state bodies. The speeches of politicians and the draconian immigration regulations of the last decade appear to condone expressions of racism in the wider society. There is public evidence of police bias and unjustified brutality, of the humiliating treatment meted out by immigration officers, of neglect and indifference to the plight of the inner cities. On the other hand the state, as a welfare state, sponsors statutory organisations and advocates policies aimed at supporting communal projects within the notional framework of a 'multi-cultural' society (for a similar argument regarding the contradictory roles of the state, see Solomos *et al.* 1982: 17).

The central theme of my chapter surrounds the conflicts generated by the state's administrative disposition or constraint to define the immigrant group as a corporate unity. Bitter experience has taught administrators and bureaucrats that immigrants are divided by factional alliances and internal competition. Yet administratively, ethnic groups are defined as a fictive unity, analogous in many respects to a territorial community.

There are two key contexts in which this corporate unity is decreed. The first context is that of state funding provided for communal ethnic projects. Notions of administrative equity dictate that there can be only one community centre, one service for the aged, or one battered wives' refuge for each specified ethnic group. The second context is that of representation on multi-ethnic boards and committees. Here too administrative efficiency dictates that each ethnic group can have a limited, specified number of 'representatives' who are henceforth presumed to represent and protect the interests of their group, seen as a corporate unity.

To illustrate my argument I present two case studies. The first concerns the funding of a Pakistani community centre and the battle within the community for the control of the allocation. The second case examines the problem of ethnic representation in a para-state organisation set up to fight racial discrimination. Here too internal divisions within the community surface and must be resolved for the sake of administrative efficacy.

The cases thus highlight the problematic role of ethnic 'brokers' and their inability to enlist a broad consensus. It is a familiar theme in which the stress has often been on the manipulative, maximising, or self-seeking aspects of this role. Ethnic leaders act as 'buffers' between the dominant society and the minority (see Katznelson 1970; Lawrence 1974); they do not represent the true interests of the local population. The buffering institutions they participate in deflect potential protest and create an illusion that problems of racism or economic subordination are being dealt with by the state. In a seminal paper on ethnic leadership Kurt Lewin, it will be recalled, argued that 'leaders from the periphery' were apologists for their ethnic group, ashamed of its distinctive culture (Lewin 1948). In similar vein, Saifullah Khan says that British Pakistani 'leaders are likely to stress their similarities to the host population or at least the sophistication of their eastern ways in a way which overtly or covertly reflects a dissociation from "the backward, uncultured, peasants"' (Saifullah Khan 1976: 226).

This negative construction of leadership strategies, and an exclusive attention to the motivations of specific leaders, tend, however, to obscure the fact that the issues at stake are much broader, expressed both in styles of leadership and in perceived goals. They relate to the basic tendency British Pakistanis have towards expansion, on the one hand, and consolidation, on the other. This tendency is expressed in contrasting symbolic orientations, so that 'political ethnicity' is essentially two faceted, it has a *dual* orientation (see Werbner 1985, 1990a). It involves, as Cohen has argued, a tendency to foster particularistic cultural symbols, excluding outsiders, defining group boundaries, and protecting perceived group assets; but it also involves simultaneously the tendency to emphasise universalistic, inclusive symbols shared with the wider society, and on this basis to demand equal rights and thus seek a foothold in economic or political domains hitherto beyond the group's reach.

The most effective and mobile immigrant groups appear to be those retaining a viable link between cultural 'centre' and entrepreneurial periphery. Immigrant entrepreneurs, whether professionals, artists, businessmen, or politicians, have manifestly mastered some aspects of the wider culture. Despite this, however, most continue to foster viable links within the community. Processes of social mobility, encroachment and predatory expansion do not appear thus to contradict the continuing revitalisation or efflorescence of exclusive values and institutions. Whereas most members of the immigrant group may well remain encapsulated and marginal, its entrepreneurs have forged contacts across group boundaries. In accord with Granovetter's (1973) argument that 'weak' ties represent points of potential change and growth, the entrepreneurial 'periphery', while small, is of key significance.

Clearly, then, the distinction between ethnic 'centre' and 'periphery' is central to my analysis (see Lewin 1948; Higham 1978: 2). Without it, in my view, analyses of ethnic groups or communities become bogged down in the imponderable conundrum of what constitutes ethnic 'interest'. For if ethnic groups are divided by class and parochial loyalties, how can they be said to have 'interests' in common, beyond those of situational antagonism?

Centre, periphery, and the nature of ethnic divisions

A crucial feature of ethnic groups is their ability to perpetuate themselves (see Nagata 1981). Ethnicity as process is thus located in a primary sense in the domestic and inter-domestic domain which determines the social reproduction of a group over time. It is also expressed in the reproduction of culturally specific group institutions. A group's culture must therefore be regarded as constantly evolving in response both to changing circumstances and to the move between generations, as new meanings and practices are negotiated, and as new associations are founded.

'Ethnicity' has become, perhaps, an overworked concept, and it may well have outlived its theoretical usefulness. In *The Empire Strikes Back* the contributors argue forcefully against theorists 'who reduce race to custom or ethnicity' (Gilroy 1982: 284). Rather than 'ethnicity', 'the politics of black liberation is necessarily a cultural politics' (ibid.: 289). I would argue, however, that, as used by anthropologists, ethnicity has always been a holistic concept, addressing itself to the historically specific 'effects of economic, political, ideological and cultural processes' (Solomos *et al.* 1982: 11). Thus, for example, a recent anthropological collection examines inter-ethnic relations as embedded within broader political and economic processes (Keyes 1981). It may be added that, as I illustrate below, both 'political ethnicity' and 'cultural politics' are in a sense expressions of a single phenomenon: the 'politicisation of culture' in the modern state.

Ethnicity as process is only partly related to the situational definition of ethnic groups. Ethnic groups are essentially segmentary, nesting within rising orders of inclusiveness, and they emerge oppositionally and contextually. This segmentary tendency has long been recognised (see Mitchell 1956; Epstein 1958). Properly speaking, we should speak of ethnic 'segments' rather than groups. In utopian terms, an ethnic group is defined by a cluster of cognate features: a common territory, nationality, language, descent, religion, culture, and history. Yet each of these 'ethnic-type' features often appears independently, and discrepancies in the cluster of features have multiplied with the emergence of pluralistic states and world migrations. These continuously 'mix' and 'scramble' disparate features. Each 'ethnic-type' feature remains, however, 'primordial' or 'axiomatic', calling for unquestioning loyalty (see Keyes 1981).

The full complexity of Pakistani 'ethnic' identifications is best driven home through a series of diagrams (see Figures 4.1, 4.2, 4.3, and 4.4).

It is significant for the argument presented here that it is these axiomatic or primordial segmentary divisions which are tangibly elaborated in lasting communal institutions – mosques, cultural societies, and national associations. Of these, national and religious divisions are the most highly elaborated among Pakistanis, lending credence to the view that there is, in some sense, a Pakistani 'community'.

Such *vertical* divisions are cut across by *horizontal* divisions – by caste (*zat*) and class, although it should be noted here that the caste system is, of course, also a segmentary system (Beteille 1964; Parry 1979). While there is no neat correspondence between caste and class, the majority of the Pakistani elite in Manchester originate from the higher 'landowning' castes. The pervasive concern with hierarchy, which Pakistanis share with other South Asians, makes class (defined by wealth, education, and occupation) an underlying factor in political struggles. Yet status within the community is fluid and ambiguous, and the rise or fall in individuals' fortunes sudden and precipitate. Thus class is more a matter of rhetoric and political recrimination than of clearly identifiable strata. I prefer here to use the notion of an 'elite' to refer to those Pakistanis active in communal affairs, most of whom make some claims to wealth, education, or high status.

In recent years the relation between class and ethnicity has received a great deal of scholarly attention (for discussions see, for example, Hall *et al.* 1978; Rex and Tomlinson 1979; Thompson 1983; Lipton 1986; Solomos 1986; Gilroy 1987). Elsewhere I discuss the dynamics of class and ethnic association (Werbner 1985). My primary focus here, however, is on the relation between leadership and centre–periphery relations.

An ethnic group has several 'centres': residential, economic, cultural, religious. I define the 'centre' as the locus of high economic or cultural value and of dense networks of intense interaction. Centres of this kind provide both a social base and a cultural *raison d'être* for political struggles. Moreover, specific ethnic 'interests' are located or identified with these different 'centres'. Such interests are a basis for internal political mobilisation. The relation between centre and periphery is, it must be stressed, an evolving one as immigrant settlement shifts, as new economic enclaves are 'captured', etc. British Pakistanis who were ethnic pioneers and renegades at one time – and thus part of the periphery – have become pillars of the local 'establishment' as others have joined them. The clothing and garment industry in Manchester is a case in point: set up by ethnic pioneers it may now be regarded as the economic 'centre' of the community. Its leading businessmen – large wholesalers with high turnovers – are at the heart of communal activity (see Werbner 1990a). At any one time the 'periphery' is composed of those who have forged social and cultural links across the ethnic boundary.

The evolving trend towards state-sponsored professionalism in immigrant affairs exemplifies this shifting relationship. Fully paid professionals are gradually displacing voluntary ethnic leaders and representatives in many western democracies (see Barton 1978; Eade, this volume). In one sense such professionals epitomise the 'leadership from the periphery' discussed by Lewin. Yet paradoxically, they are better able than voluntary representatives to use 'protest' tactics and styles of leadership.

The two case studies presented here concern conflicts of representation: in the first case, over the allocation of state funding, and, in the second, over ethnic representation in an intercommunal organisation.

Culture, community and state funding

One of the special features of modern welfare states is their provision, not only of individual social benefits, but also of special funds for underprivileged minorities. Such funds were tapped by a committee set up by a local Pakistani Cultural Literary Society

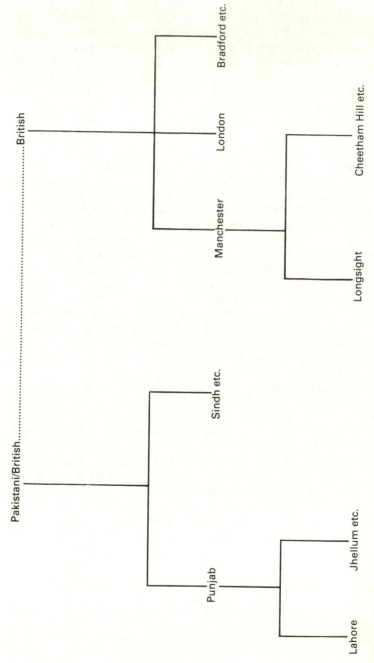

Figure 4.1 The multiple identities of British Pakistanis: nationality/domicile

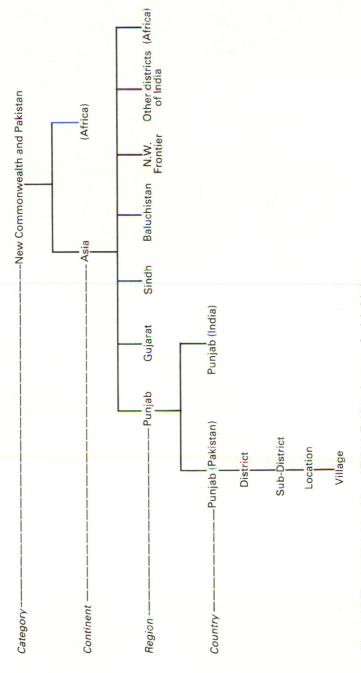

Figure 4.2 The multiple identities of British Pakistanis: area of origin/birth

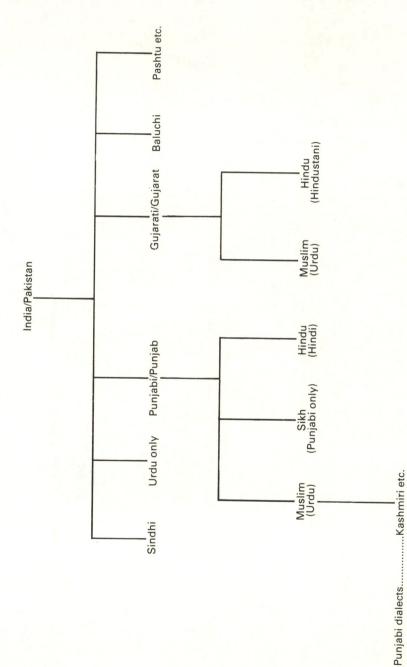

Figure 4.3 The multiple identities of British Pakistanis: mother tongue/religion

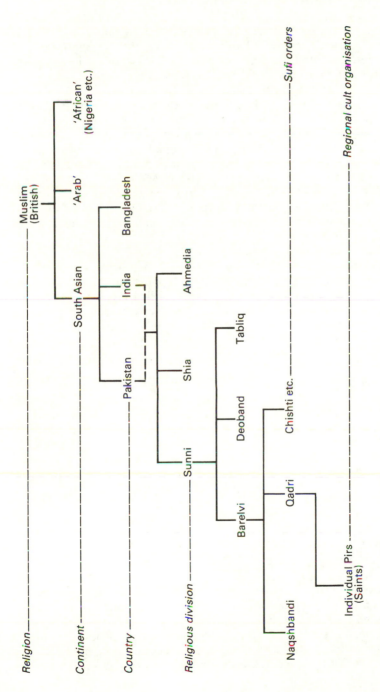

Figure 4.4 The multiple identities of British Pakistanis: religion/nationality/ country of origin

(*bazam-e-adab*). Although the society's membership was restricted, it was granted over £200,000 from the state, through the Inner City Partnership Fund, for the construction of a Pakistani community centre (the final allocation was increased to about £275,000).

The Literary Society claimed in its dealings with the local authority to be run by, and for, the majority 'working-class' Pakistanis. Pakistani businessmen, it was argued, were remote from the needs of working people. the society was founded by a small cadre of Urdu poets and poetry lovers who worked together on the night shift in McVitie's, a factory producing biscuits and cookies which has a large Pakistani workforce. The meal breaks in McVitie's became nightly poetry sessions as local poets (*shaira*) presented their latest work to a keen audience. The McVitie's workers formed the core of the literary society founded in 1970 which held regular poetry reading sessions (*mushaira*).

Mushairas are by no means the select, silent equivalent of western poetry readings. Audience participation is signalled throughout the readings with shouts of appreciation, clapping, and intense involvement. Poets are called upon to repeat felicitous lines or stanzas. Poetry, as the only permitted form of artistic expression among Muslims, encapsulates current experiences and formulates the cultural response to racism or the yearning for home. Much of the poetry also focuses on romantic love. At a large reading more than thirty poets may participate. One of the most esteemed local poets was (he died prematurely in 1987) a factory worker on night-shift work, an urbane, thoughtful, and soft-spoken man with an intense commitment to his cultural heritage. Poets, like their audience, are drawn, however, from all sections of the society, including even women in their ranks. Distinguished visiting poets from elsewhere in Britain or from Pakistan draw large audiences. The organisers, however, represent a small cadre of committed intellectuals.

The McVitie's worker-founders of the society were the group who, in the words of one member, 'cooked up' (or more accurately, 'baked') the idea of applying for funds for a community centre. One long-term member told me: 'The success of our project was our background. We were employees and we were poor.'

Yet to say that these men were just representatives of the Pakistani working class is too simple. Most overseas Pakistanis, both factory workers and businessmen, are of peasant origin. Almost all, rich and poor, employees and employers, have been factory workers at some time during their migratory careers. The men who formed the core of the society were, by contrast, *urban* people, politically conscious intellectuals, who had been teachers, clerks, or students in Pakistan. They constituted a true working-class 'elite' with broader, more varied and more secular interests than those of most first generation overseas Pakistanis. Many of the core members were politically radical and their criticism was directed not merely at the local business elite, but at Pakistani politics at home as well. Many were Urdu speakers, former *mahajir* (refugees), although the most distinguished local poet was a Punjabi. Nevertheless, quite a few of the society's officers originated from Delhi and United Province in India. The audience, however, like the local population, was composed mainly of Punjabis.

In putting through the application for funds, the society enlisted the help of local like-minded English supporters of their cause. Two school teachers, a left-wing solicitor, a librarian, and a historian with a radical outlook and a special interest in ethnic minorities all put a great deal of work into the project. They worked in full co-operation with the society's executive. In a sense, however, the project was 'baked' surreptitiously. None of the Pakistanis beyond the core membership knew about it. None of the recognised 'community leaders' had an inkling of what the ovens held. The society did not attempt, at this stage, to test its popularity through public appeals, nor did it try to elicit widespread support for the envisaged project.

When the grant was made public it did, however, evoke a response which indicated that the community centre was perceived as a threat to the established order and hierarchy of the community. Opposition was signalled by the submission of a rival application, and a consequent series of challenges to the society's sole prerogative. The projected community centre was evidently recognised as an alternative, and secular, territorial focus which could rival the central mosque, and would, moreover, provide credence to its organisers' claims to be legitimate communal representatives.

Opposition came from all the leaders of the various Pakistani welfare associations (including one based, like the society's members, in the immigrant residential enclave and claiming also to represent the poorer members of the community). It also came indirectly from the Central Jamia Mosque and the oldtimer business establishment that still controlled it. A public meeting called at the Town Hall to debate the matter almost erupted into violence and was described by an outsider who attended it as 'really quite terrifying'. The passionate feelings demonstrated against this virtually unknown group of political upstarts were almost impossible to contain.

To appreciate the full significance of the grant and the passions it generated, it needs to be seen in the light of other communal achievements. Thus, the central focus of Pakistani communal efforts in Manchester during the decade between 1970 and 1980 was the building of a new central Mosque. This project cost a total of £250,000 and the entire sum was raised from within the community, much of it donated by wealthy Pakistani businessmen. Elsewhere I argue that the competitive 'giving' to the Mosque project codified relations of hierarchy within the community. In particular, it enabled the affluent business elite to assert its hegemony and influence in communal affairs (Werbner 1985). The Mosque Association (*Jamiat el Muslimin*) has over the years invariably been controlled by a coalition of donor businessmen, mostly large wholesalers or manufacturers in the garment industry, supported by a group of professionals – mainly accountants, lawyers, and doctors. The Mosque constitutes the central arena for internal communal 'politics' with its associated factional alliances and ideological disagreements. It is thus a focus of intense competition and passionate disputing.

In many respects the Mosque represents the highest locus of value and communal involvement. It is the centre of religious debate and learning (and intense disagreement). It is controlled by the Punjabi Sunni majority within the Pakistani community. It is run by businessmen who are members of this majority, mainly oldtimers and early settlers, who have succeeded in carving out an economic enclave within the local garment industry (see Werbner 1984, 1987, 1990a). It is located between the central Pakistani residential enclave and the main Asian shopping area. In other words, it represents the ideological, regional, denominational, economic, and social-cum-residential 'core' or centre of the community. It constitutes the highest level of ethnic incorporation (see Handelman 1977), the peak of communal joint efforts.

It is perhaps not surprising, therefore, that both businessmen and religious dignitaries felt their position to be potentially undermined by the community centre project; and undermined, moreover, by a small cadre of independent intellectuals, many of them non-Punjabis, over whom they could exert little influence.

The granting of such a large sum indicated, perhaps for the first time, both the potential of extra-communal funding and the need to control it. Until then, Manchester Pakistanis tended on the whole to be suspicious and uneasy about accepting funds from outside sources; they perceived, rightly, that outside funding implies increasing external influence on what should be internal communal affairs.

The release of the grant was delayed for several years as the funding bodies insisted that internal consensus and broad public support for the project be mobilised. The Literary Society did finally triumph and become the sole grant recipients. The reasons for this triumph are significant. Most importantly, the Labour Council accepted as valid the society's claims that it represented the working class. Its members lived within the predominantly working-class immigrant enclave and they were employees; indeed the majority were manual labourers. Moreover, the society's grant application was said to be by far the most detailed and professional. The society's executive utilised successfully the invaluable experience of its co-opted English members in dealing with the bureaucratic intricacies involved in state fund-raising. It had also prepared the groundwork by fostering a network of local contacts with school teachers, librarians, and local councillors. All these played a major role in overcoming the united opposition of most other communal organisations to the society's fund application. While these other societies could object vociferously, they appeared unable to validate their claims either to be communal representatives or to be in need of state largesse. Indeed, the Council appeared to feel that Pakistani businessmen had enough resources to pay for whatever project they wished to set up.

Nevertheless, pressure was put on the society to broaden its base, which it did over time. Although this takes us beyond the present discussion, it is interesting to note that as the Centre became a reality, it came to form a new arena where local politics were played out (see Werbner 1990b). As a result, its membership *on paper* increased dramatically. There is evidence, however, that the society never had an independent constituency within the community. Its members were, and remained, an exclusive intellectual core.

The grant to the Literary Society was finally released in 1984 after a complex set of negotiations between the various representative bodies appeared to reach a satisfactory conclusion. Before the long delayed building of the community centre could start, however, a new development occurred which was to dwarf for a time the significance of the Centre while reinstating the unquestioned hegemony of the community's 'establishment'. A large building directly opposite the Mosque in an equally prime location was purchased. The building was vast, and had extensive grounds. Like the Mosque, the deposit on the building was paid for entirely with funds raised through internal communal contributions. Indeed, its purchase was initiated and negotiated by members of the Mosque Association and its board of trustees. Together they set up a new temporary board of trustees to handle the financial aspects of the purchase, whilst the purpose to which the building would be put was hotly debated.

The moving force in the debate was the same communal leader who, some years previously, put in a rival application for a community centre, thus effectively stalling the release of the grant for several years. A highly educated and articulate man, he embodies some of the apparently contradictory characteristics which typify ethnic leaders.

An early settler and businessman in the clothing trade, he is, without doubt, a man of the 'centre', closely linked into the business and professional elite of the early settlers like himself. Originating from an elite Muslim family in India, he was the founder of the first Pakistan Student Association and a founding member of the Pakistan Society in Manchester. As a radical believer in socialist doctrines, however, and as a non-Punjabi and non-Sunni he is an outsider, a 'leader from the periphery'. In his own words, he considers himself one of the few people able 'to see both sides', to bridge the gap between the more conservative Punjabi business community and the more radical members of the cultural society. He sees himself as a voluntary 'social worker', a recognised role often assumed by Punjabi ethnic leaders (see Helweg 1979: 81). He declares his support for the activities of inter-ethnic organisations concerned specifically to combat racism such as the 'Black Solidarity Front', and for the left wing of the Labour Party.

Although this leader may appear to be unique in his placement on the periphery, a brief portrayal of other leaders points to a more complex picture. Hence, one of the most influential leaders in the community was for many years a local wholesaler whose business contacts outside the community were extensive and who lived in a large house in one of Manchester's most exclusive suburbs. Elegant and urbane, this leader dealt with members of the wider society with authority and assurance. He was, nevertheless, truly of the centre – in his kinship, regional, and caste ties, and particularly in his economic prominence; as the largest wholesaler in the community his economic enterprise was embedded in an extensive network of credit and obligation with both manufacturers and market traders (see Werbner 1990a).

Like this leader, the moving force behind the building of the mosque during the 1970s was in some respects located 'on the periphery'. He was a consultant in one of the leading hospitals of its kind in Britain, and he lived, once again, in an exclusive suburb. Yet it was above all his energy, commitment, and enormous administrative skills which lifted the mosque project out of the doldrums, as almost single handed he dealt with planners, architects, builders, and banks, while co-ordinating fund-raising activities and attempting to steer the Mosque Committee through its traditionally stormy sessions. An extremely religious Muslim, he was among the few leaders who combined religious devotion with basic tolerance and a deep belief in the need to transcend religious and communal divisions.

How are we to typify this leader? Like the large wholesaler, he is in some respects a man of the centre, an early settler, a Punjabi with a vast network of local friends and relatives. At the same time he is also a professional of some achievement, highly educated, well versed in the manners and customs of the wider society. Like the wholesaler, his commitment is, however, primarily to the building up of internal communal institutions and he makes little effort to involve himself in negotiations with statutory bodies and cross-ethnic associations.

Generally speaking, the most distinguished local leaders – even those concerned primarily with internal affairs – appear to have mastered some features of the dominant society more successfully than their fellow migrants. This sometimes generates apparently incongruous objectives: thus the radical leader portrayed above was involved during the early 1980s in a major thrust to found a Muslim school (later he was to drop this objective as his involvement in council politics grew, only to reassert it in the late 1980s). In his conversation with me he argued that the salient identity he thought Pakistanis should stress was that of 'British Muslims'. The new building purchased, it was agreed, would serve some kind of educational purpose. The long-term aim of several community leaders appears to be, however, the establishment of a voluntary aided, state-supported Muslim school.

Why, then, was state funding sought for a community centre, whereas the setting up of an educational institution was internally funded – even though the ultimate aim may have been to extract state funding on a large scale? The reasons for the difference are transparent. Both projects were based on precedents of state funding. In the case of the community centre, however, the Inner City Partnership Fund which funded the centre had in recent years funded Afro-Caribbean, Indian, Bangladeshi, and Chinese community centres. It was almost a case of a fund looking for a satisfactory application. The setting up of a Muslim school was, however, a more controversial project, although Catholic and Jewish schools had been funded by the city, and run successfully for many years.

In the eyes of those Pakistanis committed to the project, the local authority is placing unnecessary obstacles in its way. I was told, for example, that the authority's Education Department was concerned that a Muslim school would further deplete numbers in the inner-city schools, or that radical members of the council were simply against any form of religious education. Whatever the case may be, an earlier bid to purchase a vacated school building in the inner city had failed, despite the fact, I was told, that the Pakistani bid was the highest submitted. Hence the view within the community was that such a project could only succeed in the long run through internal communal effort, and this explains the internal mobilisation of funds for the purchase of a suitable building.

The movement to establish Muslim schools has taken on increasing momentum throughout Britain, and given the determination shown by certain sections of the various Muslim communities (the desire for such schools is by no means universal), it seems only a matter of time before they become widely established. This movement, as well as the widespread construction of state-supported community centres, the completion of costly mosque projects (and even large national Muslim religious colleges), and the multiplication of state-funded voluntary welfare services, points towards a single trend which the case presented here highlights: it is a trend which defines with increasing sharpness the cultural-cum-organisational boundaries of the ethnic community.

Institutional completeness and state funding

In an obvious way, the case of the community centre illustrates the impact of internal divisions on inter-ethnic negotiations. Several – corresponding – divisions were brought to the fore: culturally, the divide was between devotees of indigenous Asian Muslim 'high culture' and supporters of religious institutions. Such an opposition is characteristic of ethnic-cum-religious groups. It often corresponds to a further divide between the politically conservative and social radicals. The latter align themselves more explicitly with underprivileged members of the group while stressing universal values. They use the rhetoric of class and class conflict and stress the opposition between the wealthy business community and its less affluent 'working-class' members. Seen from alternative points of view, the wealthy are regarded then as either exploiters or chief benefactors.

I have indicated, however, that the conflict that emerged could not be explained entirely in class terms. Officers of the Cultural Society originated, after all, from educated, middle-class backgrounds. The ideological divide was to some extent buttressed by a regional one between the Punjabi majority, and particularly the early settlers, and a peripheral minority of Urdu speakers.

The image of a community oppressed by a wealthy dominant class provided the Cultural Society with a justification for its claims to representative status. Yet because of the extensive influence of the business faction within the community it preferred to avoid mobilizing large-scale internal public support for the project. The state colluded with this definition without any probing until internal conflicts surfaced. It then demanded further consultations, on the grounds that public funding was involved.

It is striking that for a while the 'establishment' did reassert its hegemony, despite state intervention. Yet without the genuine commitment and efforts of members of the Cultural Society, the Community Centre may never have been funded (funds for the inner city have been ruthlessly cut). Thus 'centre' and 'periphery' interact in dynamic opposition to each other, creating an impetus towards change.

The purchase of the second building ended in a stalemate. The building was sold and the donors' money invested in it lost. Internecine fighting within the established elite put an end to the project and, indeed, to internal fund-raising (on some aspects of the dispute see *Arabia* 1985). The project thus failed. Why? The disputes surrounding the new building are viewed by protagonists very much in personal terms, and they can also be related to a major shift in the balance of power within the business establishment itself, which occurred during the 1980s. Yet it seems to me that the ultimate loss of the building has more profound reasons, linked to broader historical social processes within ethnic groups. Whereas the Cultural Society, like the various mosques, had clear-cut objectives, supported by a cadre of committed enthusiasts, the new building was too closely linked to the Mosque and thus its educational objectives remained ambiguous. It was linked to the Mosque, yet it was not a mosque. There was no agreement about the purpose to which it should be put. A state-supported school would probably have been more effectively set up by a group of parents and educationalists. Without a distinctive group of committed experts the project was unable to transcend factional disputing. The case would seem to illustrate, then, that the emergence of ethnic institutions stems ultimately from the interests of different 'centres' and groups, each with its own cultural or political commitments; analytically, ideology is prior to power, and transcends the vagaries of internal power struggles; cultural diversity not only reflects, but ultimately also *determines* the evolution of an ethnic community in which factional disputes are endemic and yet ephemeral. Lasting communal institutions are an achievement motivated by cultural and social trends which transcend these factions. Ultimately, the building had to be sold, a sad loss to the community as a whole.

Beyond communal divisions, the case reveals a basic thrust to develop and elaborate British Pakistanis' cultural uniqueness, whether as Muslims or as South Asians with distinct cultural traditions. It would appear that, increasingly, much Pakistani voluntary activity has as its aim the achievement of greater and more elaborate 'institutional completeness', as Dahya, following Breton, has argued.

Immigrant groups have always had their specialised food shops and restaurants, burial societies, places of worship, visiting artists, and local cultural societies. The institutional completeness achieved by Asian immigrants to Britain is, however, quite remarkable; indeed, it is on a scale hitherto achieved only by *European* colonial settlers in the developing world. Now Britain has become the destination of reversed cultural imports by its former subjects. Particularly striking is the importation of 'canned' commercial culture: video and record shops supply local Asians with the latest Indian and Pakistani film releases and hit songs; fabric stores display the latest fashions in silks and saris; Asian jewellers import and make 'traditional' jewellery in the latest styles; Asian journals and newspapers are widely distributed through Asian grocery stores, as are books and magazines. A daily newspaper in Urdu, *Jang*, reporting primarily on events in Pakistan, is widely sold (and is, apparently, the only daily in Britain appearing in a foreign language); musical instruments and specialised household utensils are imported or manufactured locally. All these technologically complex products supplement the usual specialised food shops and restaurants selling South Asian foods and spices, either packaged locally or imported, and the special Asian sweet shops and restaurants.

In addition, commercial branches of Asian or Arab based firms provide professional services locally. Muslim banks, insurance companies, national airlines, and travel agencies all have local branches. The commercial nature of all these services is marked, reflecting the sophisticated cultural-cum-commercial base of the immigrants' societies of origin, the enterprise shown by local immigrants, and the sizeable local market available for the goods and services provided.

In Manchester, there is much evidence of further support by the state and local authorities for this thrust towards cultural autonomy. Local authorities provide libraries of South Asian imported books in Urdu and Punjabi as well as Urdu or Punjabi language classes or courses, while 'multi-cultural' education units produce specialised 'ethnic' materials for schools. The Arts Council and Cultural Services fund minority art activities and multi-cultural festivals. The Manpower Services Commission and DHSS fund welfare and communal activities, together with the local Social Services. There are, in addition, special radio and television programmes for minority listeners and viewers. Indeed, the expansion of specialised services for minority groups appears to have taken on a momentum of its own, with important long-term implications which I discuss in detail below.

This wealth of commercial and state-supported services is supplemented by communal voluntary activities. A multitude of cultural, religious, and political organisations cater to the special interests of small groups of enthusiasts. There are sports and youth associations, women's groups, rotating credit associations, burial societies, etc. Most striking, perhaps, is the growing religious elaboration, as each stream or religious organisation sets up its local branches. By now, virtually all the religious divisions prominent in Pakistan have their local institutional expression.

How are we, as anthropologists, to interpret this apparently growing stress on ethnic boundaries, increasingly underpinned by long-term commercial and organisational structures? Is the apparent 'self-autonomy' implied merely an illusory 'smoke-screen', masking the harsh reality of exclusion from jobs and adequate housing? Does it, in a sense, serve to perpetuate the marginal status of minority immigrant groups?

Before attempting to answer this question, I present the second case which, once again, focuses on conflicts of representation stemming from the administrative fiction of an ethnic group as a corporate unity.

Ethnic brokers and the limits of 'Big Man' influence

The second dispute took place during the 1970s and for local people it is by now probably as insignificant as it is unmemorable. It nevertheless highlights some of the broader implications of state involvement in communal affairs. The dispute was precipitated by the formation of a new Pakistani Welfare Association. It focused on the selection of communal representatives by the Manchester Council for Community Relations (MCCR), a co-ordinating organisation set up with the assistance of the Commission for Racial Equality in order to combat discriminatory practices at the local level. In doing so the MCCR relies on an advisory body of representatives from the various ethnic minorities and religious communities, as well as from trade unions, political parties, the police, local authorities, etc. The MCCR employs several full-time officers responsible, respectively, for education, employment, social welfare, youth, and several specific projects, and advised by sub-committees composed of the communal representatives.

At the time of the dispute, Pakistanis were officially allocated two associational places on the MCCR, supplemented by an additional place for a representative of the Muslim community. The two associational places were filled, until this point, by the two existing formal 'bridging' associations which were controlled by sections of the business community and early settlers in the city, and which functioned, respectively, in north and south Manchester. The new association challenged the right of these associations to represent the community.

In order to resolve the issue, the MCCR decided to call a public meeting in which elections were to be held. The meeting was not, by all accounts, a success. As speakers rose to put their cases, they were shouted down, and the gathering threatened to erupt into violence. The Senior Community Relations Officer was hastily ushered out, and the meeting had to be dispersed without a conclusive vote, each association later claiming a victory for itself.

In the end, the issue was decided upon administratively, during the absence of the new association's chairman. It was said that the vote had clearly favoured the two established associations, although some doubt was cast on the composition of attenders at the meeting (it was alleged, for example, that many may have been brought in from a neighbouring town). In any event, the two more established associations co-ordinated their approach, and at a subsequent small meeting with the Senior Community Relations Officer it was agreed they should continue to represent the community on the MCCR. The decision could be seen as a victory for the more wealthy and established business community. As in the first case, they re-established their hegemony in communal affairs. The victory was something of a pyrrhic one, however: in later years the MCCR allocated three and then four seats for Pakistani associations, thus allowing for the incorporation of the challenging association. Yet the disputes continue. Most recently, I was told, eight (!) candidates were put forward to fill the four allocated seats.

Given the intensity of feeling the dispute provoked, it is interesting that members of the MCCR once elected, are not very active. Thus the Mosque Association, which has a permanent seat on the MCCR, has selected at different times three different representatives. Yet each in turn rarely attended meetings. One of them told me: 'B said to me – there are so many people who would like to be representatives and you don't even attend!' But, he added, 'C and D also never used to attend.' He explained, in self-justification, that the minutes and agendas of meetings were often presented without anyone knowing how they had been decided upon,or by whom. It would appear that representation on the MCCR is primarily emblematic (see Huggins 1978). Much of the sub-committees' role is validatory and symbolic, since the bulk of the work is handled by full-time professional community relations officers.

Why is it, then, that Pakistani bridging associations seek outside recognition for their representative status? To answer this question, it is necessary to appreciate the common organisational dilemma which leaders of Pakistani ethnic bridging associations face. The moving force in each association is usually a prominent person within a restricted circle, a Big Man who relies on a narrow base of supporters to finance the activities of his association, sometimes supplemented by state funding. Any attempt to expand this base is fraught with problems as internal divisions within the wider community surface, challenging his claims to leadership and the representative status of his organisation. The dilemma leaders face is a familiar one – the initiatives they take and the liaison services which they provide hinge on an ability to act decisively and efficiently. Yet any attempt to broaden their base of support beyond a narrow circle would, in their own view, simply paralyse the association. Their ability to act would be limited by internal leadership squabbles. At the same time, however, their entitlement to act depends on their status as community spokesmen and representatives. Hence the appeal for outside legitimation.

The ability of the outside, in this case a para-statal organisation, to intervene or enshrine leaders may be seen as another instance of the 'structural position of Asians in British society today [which] is virtually identical to that of any colonised group' (Aldrich *et al.* 1984: 190).[3] To argue thus, however, is to miss the fact that the activities of bridging associations represent a *phase* in a long-term, ongoing trend towards integration into broader political and administrative structures. I shall return to this point below.

The services provided by such associations are in any case quite considerable. All three Welfare Societies active in Manchester in the 1970s, as well as the association most active during the 1980s, fostered their ties outside the community. Two were extremely active in campaigning in the Asian community for Labour Party candidates, strongly condemning attempts by some Pakistani leaders to discredit the local MP (Gerald Kaufman) because of his Jewish origins and (somewhat ambivalent) support for Israel. Although the local community had not yet, in 1975–6, fielded an internal candidate for council elections successfully, there was evidence of increasing attempts to acquire influence and expertise in British politics. The leader of the third association provided his house, located within the central residential cluster, as the base of the local MP's monthly surgeries and himself attempted, unsuccessfully, to gain candidacy in a safe ward (later, the same person stood as an MP candidate for the SDLP). In the recent council elections, a Pakistani councillor was finally elected in the central residential cluster.

The escalation of National Front activities and the counter-mobilisation, mainly through the Anti-Nazi League, of anti-fascist groups created in the 1970s a further arena of political activity in which the societies joined with various other organisations and bodies. From time to time the societies organised and financed busloads of demonstrators sent to support demonstrations against the National Front in other cities.

Apart from activities in the political arena proper, leaders or workers of the Welfare Societies also liaised between individual Pakistanis and statutory bodies on a variety of personal problems. The societies were founded mainly in response to the perceived need for a formal representation of the community in its negotiations with official British bodies and with the government of Pakistan. They processed applications for British citizenship and liaised with the Home Office, the police, social welfare agencies, and educational or housing authorities. These usually turn to the societies for advice and help in problems they encounter which concern Pakistanis. In addition, the societies give advice on means of obtaining mortgages and grants from the local authorities, and arrange for internal mediation of conflicts occurring within the community.

A distinctive feature of the societies' endeavour is the formal dinners they convene, in which they entertain Pakistani or British dignitaries at large and expensive meals, usually at top-class hotels. The dinners are occasions on which the various problems encountered by the immigrant community are publicly debated. Since the societies are run, on the whole, as rich men's clubs, the dinners are funded by leaders and their circles. When I asked if those excluded complain, I was told jokingly that, on the contrary, they say to themselves: 'Well, I've saved ten pounds.' My informant thus implied that participation in such dinners was a duty rather than a privilege. There is, however, also a general view that holding office in such associations (and in internal communal organisations such as the Mosque Association) is the basis for useful contacts with visiting Pakistani officials and dignitaries. The stress in the community is thus on the valuable *links with Pakistan* that leadership in such societies facilitates. The basic attitude of organisers remains, nevertheless, one of benevolent paternalism – it is the duty of the rich to represent the community and to carry themselves the cost in time, money, and effort. In return they expect a measure of prestige and personal kudos.

In many respects the formal dinners epitomise the style of leadership and strategic action adopted by Pakistanis in their battle against racism. Like cultural revitalisation, the style represents a basic orientation, the sign of an ongoing process; and like cultural revitalisation, the orientation is of broader significance than the underlying rivalries or personal ambitions of individual leaders.

Protest, accommodation and reform[4]

The fact that Asian immigrant brokers are often 'middle-class', educated, wealthy, or anglicised is generally regarded as a key aspect of their non-representative status (see Scott 1972: 95–6, 490–5; also Ballard and Ballard 1977: 39). The implicit critique of this apparent 'leadership from the periphery' tends, however, to miss the essentially dualistic orientation of immigrant groups, their tendency to stress, in certain contexts, the values they *share* with the wider society. It is partly because the organisers of the Welfare Societies have mastered some aspects of the wider culture that they are concerned to extend their contacts beyond communal boundaries, to bridge the gap between the community and the society as a whole. They do so by attempting to increase their influence among local politicians and other representatives of the state. In their negotiations with them the emphasis is placed on shared symbols and values, and this dictates the style and choice of leadership in the associations. Whether these organisers are more peripheral in some sense than other leaders is difficult to judge. Of those most active in Manchester, the majority (but not all) tended to be somewhat less religious, and to have certain exceptional attributes (of regional origin or denominational affiliation) which set them apart from the Punjabi Sunni majority. In other respects, however, they were very much of the 'centre'.

Most 'welfare' leaders are early migrants and successful businessmen with a good command of English and the fine arts of British etiquette. The image they present is of sophisticated and enlightened people; they convey a sense that their community is moving towards greater cultural integration into British society. This is important, given the weak political status of the Asian community in Britain. The dominant political ethos is against aggressive ethnic separatism, and thus such separatism would seem to be politically inexpedient.[5] It could only exacerbate what are spoken of as 'race relations', and weaken the position of the community. Behind-the-scenes negotiations, appeals to MPs and other politicians, and mild public protest thus appear to be the main strategies adopted by the bridging associations and their leaders.

Perhaps a brief portrait of one leader may illustrate the point. A man of sharp intelligence and outstanding organisational skills, he and his wife were the moving force behind the most effective, reputable, and efficiently run Welfare Society during the 1970s. He had arrived in Manchester in the 1950s to study textiles and he regards himself as a self-made man. He now heads a large and multi-faceted international business. He and his wife, who is English, live in the Cheshire Green Belt in a beautiful large mansion. Like one of the

137

leaders portrayed earlier, he is non-Punjabi and non-observant. To outsiders he conveys a sense of authority and sophistication, of being at home in the most exclusive surroundings. In his representative capacity he believes in negotiation and co-operation with the police and statutory bodies, and in co-ordinated action with sympathetic groups (the Labour Party, trade unions, anti-fascist groups, etc.).

Although this leader may superficially appear to be beyond the community, the contrary is in some respects true. His contacts with Pakistan are extensive and frequent. He maintains a home in Karachi and visits the country several times a year. As one member of his family told me: 'We know about the events in Karachi almost as soon as they happen; someone always telephones. There is constant phoning back and forth.' Locally, he is regarded as something of an 'outsider'; nevertheless his contacts are extensive, and at various times he has been active in the internal politics of the community. He is undoubtedly prominent and widely respected, particularly for his business acumen. The accommodationist style he adopts is not apologist; it is strategic and political.

It is probably true to say, however, that the role of leaders of this type is being superseded all over Britain by the current trend towards a specialisation and professionalisation of the battle against racism. Just as 'formal' leaders replaced 'traditional' leaders (see Anwar 1979: 174, 183; Aurora 1967: 97, 102), so too the former are no longer at the forefront of the battle. Duly elected Asian councillors have in many towns, although only recently in Manchester, taken over the representative role. 'Black' or 'overseas' associations and 'sections' of doctors, lawyers, trade unionists, or political party activists push for greater parity in their respective fields. The Commission for Racial Equality and the United Kingdom Immigrants Advisory Service, para-statal bureaucracies both financed by central government, utilise legal means as well as public protest to contend with discriminatory practices. Local MPs fight increasingly bitter battles against deportations on behalf of their constituents, supported by community relations councils and local activist groups.

Moreover, a new generation of mainly young, British trained professionals is emerging as local authorities, community relations councils, and a variety of voluntary organisations, indirectly funded by the state and local authorities, employ increasing numbers of community workers, social workers, housing officers, co-ordinators of cultural and arts activities, language teachers, etc. While earlier such posts were often filled by non-immigrants, the pressure is increasingly to appoint qualified members of minority groups to fill these posts (see Kalka in this volume). The cadre of experts which is emerging meet one another in a variety of administrative contexts;

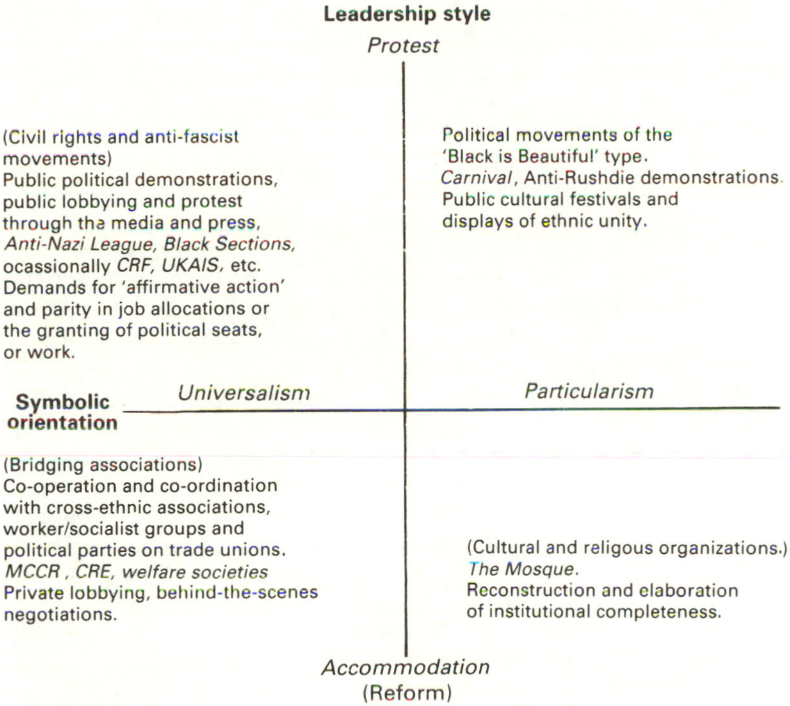

Leadership style

Protest

| (Civil rights and anti-fascist movements) Public political demonstrations, public lobbying and protest through the media and press, *Anti-Nazi League, Black Sections,* ocassionally *CRF, UKAIS,* etc. Demands for 'affirmative action' and parity in job allocations or the granting of political seats, or work. | Political movements of the 'Black is Beautiful' type. *Carnival*, Anti-Rushdie demonstrations. Public cultural festivals and displays of ethnic unity. |

Symbolic orientation   *Universalism*   *Particularism*

| (Bridging associations) Co-operation and co-ordination with cross-ethnic associations, worker/socialist groups and political parties on trade unions. *MCCR , CRE,* welfare societies Private lobbying, behind-the-scenes negotiations. | (Cultural and religous organizations.) *The Mosque.* Reconstruction and elaboration of institutional completeness. |

Accommodation
(Reform)

Figure 4.5 The dual orientation of ethnic minority groups

they represent a new and expert force to be contended with, and many of their battles are fought against the very authorities which employ or indirectly fund them (see Jeffers, Eade, Kalka, and Westwood, this volume).

Such professionals, although in some respects peripheral members of their communities, speak with an authority which derives from detailed knowledge of the social problems affecting community members. They are thus more able to protest or push for fundamental reforms. They represent a new style of leadership. It may be argued, perhaps, that, like the 'salariat' in colonial India and elsewhere who spearheaded the battle for independence (cf. Alavi 1988), this new salariat is acutely aware both of its rights and claims and of the barriers to its full advancement in the society.

At the same time a Muslim radical religious leadership has also emerged, demanding religious parity in education and willing, as the recent Rushdie affair shows, to mobilise for a highly visible, public, and militant protest politics. Many British Pakistanis see their religion not only as a source of all true values and morality, but as their only real protection from racism and racial abuse. A perceived attack on these values thus threatens to undermine the group's self-respect and ultimate shield from racial stigmatisation. The extremity of their response reflects the violence which Pakistanis and other British Muslims feel threatens their integrity and moral worth.

The political picture which has emerged in the 1980s is thus a complex one in which different styles of protest, reform, and accommodation interplay (see Figure 4.5). In a significant contribution to the study of ethnic minorities in Britain, Cohen (this volume (1980)) analyses the Notting Hill Carnival as a form of cultural protest. He links the increase in unemployment and racism with the Carnival's evolving exclusiveness in relation to the majority population, and its heightened revitalisation of traditional forms of cultural protest. For Pakistanis, the cultural reproduction of their indigenous institutions represents, most fundamentally, the value they place on reconstruction, consolidation, and self-reliance. It is, in a sense, also a muted, implicit protest, but the stress on cultural independence is not a permanent barrier to participation in the outside world; most significantly, it constitutes a protection from stigma and external domination.

It is this too which explains the continued hegemony of the business community. Whether liked or disliked, this community enables Pakistanis to make independent decisions, to move swiftly (as in the attempt to purchase the new building opposite the mosque), even to reject state largesse. Encapsulation is not a feature of marginality but of independence. So too, in my view, the accommodationist style adopted by some leaders is strategic rather than apologist. British Pakistanis have an essentially expansionist attitude; the entry of some into administrative and professional jobs in statutory and voluntary organisations is a further feature of their encroachment into wider societal structures.

Conclusion

The cases presented here seem on the surface to confirm the tendency of the wider society to marginalise and encapsulate immigrant or ethnic minorities. In particular, group relations with the state are predicated, we saw, on negotiations with ethnic 'representatives' who usually lack widespread internal legitimation and do not consult group members regarding policy questions. Yet such a simplistic interpretation misses the full complexity of ethnic group relations in the public domain. This is a context in which a plurality of ethnic associations and state organisations attempt to negotiate common definitions. Ethnic relations here are as much a game of images and definitions as they are a matter of tangible results. The process of bargaining increasingly exposes the diversity within the group and the need to resolve the variety of special problems its members encounter. The evident inadequacy of voluntary group leadership itself creates a momentum towards a professionalisation of the services provided by the state. At the same time, state funding provides further impetus for the diversification of internal communal institutions. The general trend is thus away from marginality and towards integral involvement in administrative and political structures.

The portrayal of British Pakistanis as a permanently marginalised 'colonised' minority would thus appear to be essentially misconceived. The one-way deterministic approach which defines immigrants as 'victims' is unable to account for the dialectic process which interaction between the immigrant group and the state generates. This process results in increasing integration into wider structures while, simultaneously, it fosters a separate cultural institutional identity.

There is a broader theoretical implication to the data presented here. Boundary interaction, we have seen, continually reflects or highlights internal divisions, both within the state and within the immigrant group itself. Thus Barth's well-known dictum that 'The critical focus of investigations . . . [should be] the ethnic *boundary* that defines the group, not the cultural stuff that it encloses' (Barth 1969: 15, his emphasis) is, if my analysis is correct, simplistic and, indeed, theoretically misguided (see also Handelman 1977).

Ethnic groups are divided by class, axiomatic categorical loyalties (of region, nationality, religion, and language), and centre–periphery orientations. All these divisions surface in their interaction as 'purposive groups' (see Vincent 1974) with external groups and organisations. Which salient ethnic identity will be stressed is itself, we saw, a matter for negotiation. The state too is divided between local and central government which both fund, in addition, a variety of para-statal and voluntary organisations. The struggle for hegemonic control within the community underlines the fact that it is, indeed, a community. Yet representation is essentially pluralistic, reflecting, as it does, internal divisions. A study of the wider context in which immigrant groups interact must necessarily examine, not only the interface between different groups but the internal structures that motivate their interaction.

Notes

1 The research on which this chapter is based was conducted between 1975 and 1986 and was partly supported by a project from the ESRC, UK. I also rely on knowledge gained during my work as a co-ordinator of a voluntary agency supported by the North West Arts Association. Earlier versions of the chapter were presented at an ASA meeting in 1983 and at the Oxford Conference on South Asian Overseas Communities in 1986. I would like to thank Richard Werbner and Hamza Alavi for their comments on an earlier draft of the chapter.

2 In three separate studies Cohen shows that culturally exclusive symbols evolve: (a) In response to the need to protect an economic enclave from outside competition (Cohen 1969); in this case the stress on cultural exclusiveness was both overt and total. (b) In order to protect an occupational niche where the *overt* stress is on universal symbols (Cohen 1981). (c) In order to protest against exclusion, e.g. where the group lacks economic assets of any significance (Cohen 1980). Here I examine, by contrast, the *overt* but situational assertion of *both* culturally unique *and* shared symbols, in conditions of predatory expansion where exclusion is not total.

3 Anthropologists have discussed extensively the tendency of colonial regimes to enshrine leaders in egalitarian societies (cf. for example Marx 1967; Cunnison 1966), and to intervene chiefly in succession disputes (Richard Werbner 1969; Comaroff 1978).

4 Gunnar Myrdal (1944), in his definitive study of the black American community, first makes the distinction between 'protest' and 'accommodation' as opposing styles of ethnic leadership. Recently, Huggins (1978) suggests a further important distinction between 'emblematic' and 'reform' leaders. Glazer (1978) suggests that American Jews combine protest and accommodation styles successfully and I would argue that British Pakistanis pursue a similar mixed strategy.

5 For an early discussion of the political utility of these contrasting styles, see Beetham (1970).

References

Alavi, Hamza (1988) 'Pakistan and Islam: ethnicity and ideology', in Fred Halliday and Hamza Alavi (eds) *State and Ideology in the Middle East and Pakistan*, London: Macmillan.

Aldrich, Howard, Jones, T. and McEvoy, David (1984) 'Ethnic advantage and minority business development', in Robin Ward and Richard Jenkins (eds) *Ethnic Communities in Business*, Cambridge: Cambridge University Press.

Anwar, Muhammad (1979) *The Myth of Return: Pakistanis in Britain*, London: Heinemann.

Arabia (1985) 'Old differences make a new start in Eid violence', *Arabia* 5: 50.

Aurora, G.S. (1967) *The New Frontiersmen*, Bombay: Popular Prakashan.

Ballard, R. and Ballard, C. (1977) 'The Sikhs', in James L. Watson (ed.) *Between Two Cultures*, Oxford: Basil Blackwell.

Barth, Frederik (1969) 'Introduction', in Frederik Barth (ed.) *Ethnic Groups and Boundaries*, London: George Allen & Unwin.

Barton, Joseph J. (1978) 'Eastern and Southern Europeans', in John Higham (ed.) *Ethnic Leadership in America*, Baltimore, Md: Johns Hopkins University Press.

Beetham, David (1970) *Transport and Turbans*, Oxford: Oxford University Press.

Beteille, A. (1964) 'A note on the referents of caste', *European Journal of Sociology* V: 130–44.

Breton, Raymond (1964) 'Institutional completeness', *American Journal of Sociology* 70: 193–205.

Buckman, Joseph (1983) *Immigrants and the Class Struggle: The Jewish Immigrants in Leeds, 1880–1914*, Manchester: Manchester University Press.

Centre for Contemporary Cultural Studies (1982) *The Empire Strikes Back: Race and Racism in 70s Britain*, London: Hutchinson.

Cohen, Abner (1969) *Custom and Politics in Urban Africa*, London: Routledge & Kegan Paul.

Cohen, Abner (1980) 'Drama and politics in the development of a London carnival', *Man* (NS) 15 (1): 65–87.

Cohen, Abner (1981) *The Politics of Elite Culture*, Berkeley, Calif.: University of California Press.

Comaroff, J.L. (1978) 'Rules and rulers: political processes in a Tswana chiefdom', *Man* (NS) 13: 1–20.

Cunnison, Ian (1966) *Baggara Arabs*, Oxford: Clarendon Press.

Dahya, Badr (1974) 'The nature of Pakistani ethnicity in industrial cities in Britain', in Abner Cohen (ed.) *Urban Ethnicity*, ASA Monographs 12, London: Tavistock.

Epstein, A.L. (1958) *Politics in an Urban African Community*, Manchester: Manchester University Press.

Gilroy, Paul (1982) 'Steppin' out of Babylon – race, class and autonomy', in Centre for Contemporary Cultural Studies, *The Empire Strikes Back: Race and Racism in 70s Britain*, London: Hutchinson.

Gilroy, Paul (1987) *There Ain't No Black in the Union Jack: The Cultural Politics of Race and Nation*, London: Hutchinson.

Glazer, Nathan (1978) 'The Jews', in John Higham (ed.) *Ethnic Leadership in America*, Baltimore, Md: Johns Hopkins University Press.

Glazer, Nathan and Moynihan, Daniel P. (1975) 'Introduction', in Nathan Glazer and Daniel P. Moynihan (eds) *Ethnicity: Theory and Experience*, Cambridge, Mass.: Harvard University Press.

Granovetter, Mark S. (1973) 'The strength of weak ties', *American Journal of Sociology* 78 (6): 1360–80.

Hall, Stuart, Critcher, C. Jefferson, T., Clarke, J. and Roberts, B. (1978) *Policing the Crisis: Mugging, the State and Law and Order*, London: Macmillan.

Handelman, Don (1977) 'The organisation of ethnicity', *Ethnic Groups* 1 (3): 187–200.

Helweg, A.W. (1979) *Sikhs in England: The Development of a Migrant Community*, Delhi: Oxford University Press.

Higham, John (ed.) (1978) *Ethnic Leadership in America*, Baltimore, Md: Johns Hopkins University Press.

Huggins, Nathan I. (1978) 'Afro-Americans', in John Higham (ed.) *Ethnic Leadership in America*, Baltimore, Md: Johns Hopkins University Press.

Katznelson, Ira (1970) 'The politics of racial buffering in Nottingham, 1954–68', *Race* 11 (4).

Keyes, Charles F. (ed.) (1981) *Ethnic Change*, Seattle, Wash.: University of Washington Press.

Lawrence, Daniel (1974) *Black Migrants: White Natives*, Cambridge: Cambridge University Press.

Lewin, Kurt (1965) [1948] 'The problem of minority leadership', in Alwin W. Gouldner (ed.) *Studies in Leadership: Leadership and Democratic Action*, New York: Russell & Russell. (Reprinted from Kurt Lewin, *Resolving Social Conflicts*, Harper Brothers, 1948).

Lipton, Merle (1986) *Capitalism and Apartheid: South Africa, 1910–1986*, Hants: Wildwood House.

Marx, Emanuel (1967) *Bedouin of the Negev*, Manchester: Manchester University Press.

Mitchell, J.C. (1956) *The Kalela Dance*, Rhodes-Livingstone Paper no. 27, Manchester: Manchester University Press for the Rhodes-Livingstone Institute.

Myrdal, Gunnar (1944) *An American Dilemma: The Negro Problem and Modern Democracy*, New York: Harper Brothers.

Nagata, Judith (1981) 'In defence of ethnic boundaries: the changing myths and charters of Malay identity', in Charles F. Keyes (ed.) *Ethnic Change*, Seattle, Wash.: University of Washington Press.

Parry, Jonathan P. (1979) *Caste and Kinship in Kangra*, London: Routledge & Kegan Paul.

Rex, John and Tomlinson, Sally (1979) *Colonial Immigrants in a British City: A Class Analysis*, London: Routledge & Kegan Paul.

Saifullah Khan, Verity (1976) 'Pakistanis in Britain: perceptions of a population', *New Community* 5: 222–30.

Scott, Duncan (1972) 'A political sociology of minorities', unpublished Ph.D. dissertation, University of Bristol.

Solomos, John (1986) 'Varieties of Marxist conceptions of 'race', class and the state: a critical analysis', in John Rex and David Mason (eds) *Theories of Race and Ethnic Relations*, Cambridge: Cambridge University Press.

Solomos, J. *et al.* (1982) 'The organic crisis of British capitalism and race: the experience of the seventies', in Centre for Contemporary Cultural Studies, *The Empire Strikes Back: Race and Racism in 70s Britain*, London: Hutchinson.

Thompson, John L.P. (1983) 'The plural society approach to class and ethnic political mobilisation', *Ethnic and Racial Studies* 6 (2): 127–53.

Vincent, Joan (1974) 'The structure of ethnicity', *Human Organisation* 33: 375–9.

Werbner, Pnina (1979) 'Avoiding the ghetto: Pakistani migrants and settlement shifts in Manchester', *New Community* 7: 376–89.

Werbner, Pnina (1984) 'Business on trust: Pakistani entrepreneurship in the Manchester garment trade', in Robin Ward and Richard Jenkins (eds) *Ethnic Communities in Business*, Cambridge: Cambridge University Press.

Werbner, Pnina (1985) 'The organisation of giving and ethnic elites', *Ethnic and Racial Studies* 8 (3): 368–88.

Werbner, Pnina (1987) 'Manchester Pakistanis: economic enclaves and family firms', in Jeremy Eades (ed.) *Migration, Labour and the Social Order*, ASA Monograph 25, London: Tavistock.

Werbner, Pnina (1990a) *The Migration Process: Capital, Gifts and Offerings among British Pakistanis*, Explorations in Anthropology Series, Oxford: Berg.

Werbner, Pnina (1990b) 'Factionalism and violence in the communal politics of British Pakistanis', in Hastings Donnan and Pnina Werbner (eds) *Economy and Culture in Pakistan: Migrants and Cities in a Muslim Society*, London: Macmillan.

Werbner, Richard P. (1969) 'Constitutional ambiguities and the British administration of royal careers among the Bemba of Zambia', in Laura Nader (ed.) *Law, Culture and Society*, Chicago: Aldine.

Williams, Jenny (1985) 'Redefining institutional racism', *Ethnic and Racial Studies* 8 (3): 323–48.

Chapter five

Red Star over Leicester

Racism, the politics of identity, and black youth in Britain[1]

Sallie Westwood

Introduction

This chapter foregrounds the politics of black youth in Britain and one specific moment within that – the Red Star Youth Project. I did not set out to research the politics of black youth or to tell the story of the Red Star project; the latter grew out of my involvement with an inner-city access course which included a group of young Asian men. It was clear from our discussions of racism, the role of the state, and politics in Britain that their involvement with the Red Star project had generated a political understanding rooted in their experiences, but which clearly provided them with a political language that took them outside the particular and into the national and international context. Red Star had constructed a politics which was innovative, exciting, filled with drama, and alive with heroes. From this initial encounter I was drawn into the drama. The account of Red Star presented here is not, therefore, a neutral account. It has been generated over the last year from the narratives that I have been given by those involved, and by the leader of Red Star. For those involved it is a precious history, one recorded with a sense of pride it is not always easy to convey, but it is essential to record. My role, however, is not only to record and give voice to a specific moment, although many of those with whom I have talked in the last year do see this as my primary task, but to provide an analytical account which, through theorisation, is better able to grasp the complexities of the politics of young black men in 1980s Britain and to deconstruct the stereotypes and myths that surround 'black youth'. It is a challenging task, first, because of my responsibilities towards the members of Red Star; second, because there is no adequate conceptual framework that comes ready-made for the analysis; and third, because I am conscious that to research and write about political struggle can have the effect of domesticating and de-politicising that struggle, leaving out the excitement and the very processes through which political identities are forged.

The Red Star project is part of a long history of organised black struggle in Britain – I use 'black' to denote a political identity, not as a descriptive term, a point to which I will return later in this chapter. The struggle is evidenced in the work of Sivanandan (1982), Fryer (1984), Bryan *et al.* (1985), and Ramdin (1987). It is a struggle in which both community and class politics have figures and in which individual black people from William Cuffay to Mrs Desai have been foregrounded. Equally, there is a history of youth movements in Britain, some independent of party or organisation like the cultural politics of Rock Against Racism. Gilroy and Lawrence (1988) have emphasised that the importance of these independent movements, some committed to socialist ideas and others organised by fascist and racist parties, should not be underestimated. The 1970s and early 1980s brought a resurgence by the ever present, but sometimes dormant, racist organisations like the National Front. These organisations tied their activities to the energies and lifestyles of young white working-class men. In response, black people called up their own organisational resources to confront the National Front, and in the centre of these struggles were young black men of Asian descent. The issues of gender and generation were articulated with racism. Gender is not here understood simply to denote men/male in opposition to women/female but to signal masculinity and its social and ideological construction within the conditions of a racist Britain and the post-war migrations. Equally, the issue of generation is not understood simply in terms of age but in terms of its socio-historical setting. The voices of Asian protest in Southall, Bradford, Newham, and Leicester brought together the ideologies and practices of a specific generation of men and women which have been formed in Britain as black/Asian British. Drawing upon a great variety of discourses and generating critiques of political givens, they forged a new politics – graphically described in Mehmood's *Hand on the Sun* (1986). It was a politics in opposition, not only to racism and class exploitation but to patriarchal relations, the power of older men challenged by young men (although, as Bains (1988) points out, this does not necessarily challenge patriarchal attitudes towards women). It was necessarily a masculinity redolent with the power of young men, ideologically constructed in the media as the power of 'the mob'. It is a common theme with a long history in Britain (see Pearson 1983) whereby young working-class men are presented as dangerous. The development of the youth service, for example, is predicated upon the need to constrain and control young men, and the moral panics that surround them have been well documented (Pearson 1983). But black youth has been racialised in particular ways: these range from the issues surrounding mugging explored by

Hall *et al.* (1978) and Gilroy (1987) to the recent accounts of the riots in Britain. The latter, it has been argued, articulate a moral panic with the crises in British society and the state (Benyon and Solomos 1987).

The crises and restructuring of the capital and the state are the contexts in which our discussion of Red Star takes place – crises of money, profitability, and migratory labour, alongside the crises of consent. Both have generated conflict and coercion and have placed the cities, and young people especially, in the front line. The shift to-wards coercive pressures, exemplified in the changes in forms of policing, have impacted very specifically upon young people, and most clearly on young black men. The moves in the state structure are arguably part of the generation of a new consensus around law and order issues which is being orchestrated from and by the organs of the state and the mass media (see Hall *et al.* 1978). This has major implications for the forms of struggle at both local and national level. The issues raised by the story of Red Star lead directly to a considera-tion of the articulation between racism, power, and the state, especially at the local level, and to the ways in which this articulation has changed in relation to the legitimation crisis. The change has been from a period in which the challenge to the local state involved confrontation and negotiation, to the rise of coercive strategies backed by legal sanctions.

In Britain, crises in the state and of legitimation have historically been bound to colonial adventures and wars (the 1980s saw the Falk-lands war) which have forged new conceptions of state, nation, and citizenship, and new accounts of who is 'alien', 'the other', and out-side the nation (Gilroy 1987; Cohen 1988). These changing ideo-logical configurations have an important bearing upon the nature of black struggles in Britain and the rights of black people to be British, part of the nation, and fully citizens. Reeves in his analysis of racial discourse in Britain highlights this in the following manner:

> It is quite apparent from a study of British political ideology of the last thirty years, for example, that black people have only recently come to be accepted as part of the political audience and as poten-tial voters. Previously, and with a clear dehumanising effect on the discourse used to refer to them, they were treated as political 'objects' rather than as agents in the political process.
>
> (Reeves 1986: 65)

That black people have been excluded and marginalised from the political process through specific racial discourses has a particular resonance in relation to young black people who are too often por-trayed as marginalised elements outside the body politic. Instead, organised black struggle has insisted on black people's rights to be political agents, and Red Star is one specific moment in this attempt to forge a new construction of the nation and the citizen. As the leader of Red Star made clear, one of the aims of Red Star was 'to take politics out of being a spectator sport'.

Thus, my concerns in this chapter and the ways in which I conceptualise them are at some distance from the simple voluntarism or naturalism evidenced in some writing. Jacobs (1988), for example, concentrates on the exercise of power by individuals in relation to the articulated political goals of minority ethnic groups. This focuses attention upon individuals and their relationships with group members, mediated by organisational forms that in turn articulate relations between 'minorities' and the dominant society. Instead, I am seeking to provide an account which – while it recognises interests and individuals -- theorises these as power relations contexted by the state, racism, class relations, and gender relations. The case of Red Star demonstrates that all of these are implicated in calling forth specific subjects within specific contexts. As a way into the discussion I start the chapter with a short note on the Leicester context and a narrative account of the Red Star project. I then go on to discuss the politics and leadership of Red Star.

Red Leicester

Leicester was dubbed 'Red Leicester' (was it a pun on the name of the local cheese?) in 1979 when, despite the national swing to the Conservatives, the city returned three Labour Members of Parliament, not least because many Asian people voted Labour in Leicester South. But in 1983, after the SDP split away from Labour, changes in the electoral boundaries, and the consolidation of the Thatcher Government, this number was reduced to one. Instead, Leicester South became the most marginal seat in the country with a Tory majority of seven votes, and Leicester East returned the notorious Peter Bruinvels, famous for his right-wing views on hanging, Arthur Scargill, and women priests – he was definitely for the first and diametrically and publicly opposed to the latter. However, in 1987 Leicester again became 'Red Leicester' when Leicester South returned to Labour and Keith Vaz unseated Mr Bruinvels, and increased the Labour turnout despite some opposition to his candidacy from within the local party.

The population of the city is now over 280,000, and at the time of *The Leicester Survey* in 1983 (Leicester City Council 1983) 22.1 per cent of the population were of Asian origin, many from East Africa, with 1.8 per cent of Afro-Caribbean descent. Also, there are people of Chinese, Polish, Latvian, Italian, Irish, and Jewish descent in

Leicester. The people who have come to Leicester since the turn of the century have come to work or as political refugees, but the economic power of Leicester, founded on hosiery and the boot and shoe industry, has suffered major decline and restructuring in the post-war period, and especially in the last decade. A well-known hosiery factory I studied in the early 1980s, for example, has had major redundancies in the last year and is currently selling off factory space, following an Australian takeover (Westwood 1984). *The Leicester Survey* (Leicester City Council 1983) reported a city-wide unemployment rate of 14.9 per cent. For black people, and young black people in particular, the situation was markedly worse, as Table 5.1 shows.

Table 5.1 Unemployment in Leicester, 1983

	Overall %	16–19 years %
White	12.9	23.6
Asian	21.7	38.5
West Indian	23.7	45.5

Source: Leicester City Council 1983: 3

Coupled with the high rates of unemployment in Leicester in the early and mid 1980s, was the fact that the East Midlands generally has always been a low-wage area. Consequently, the Leicester City Low Pay Unit estimated in 1985 that 40 per cent of the workforce were low paid, that is, earning below £117 per week, and that an estimated 78 per cent of working women in Leicester were low paid. Leicester, when it can work, is a working town, and when it is not working it is a deeply impoverished city. By 1987 one in five of the Leicester workforce was unemployed (Sills *et al.* 1988).

Avtar Brah's research with young Asian people in Leicester both expresses and analyses the ways in which racism and unemployment are articulated in 1980s Britain with the consequence that 'The young people felt that their future was bleak' (Brah 1986: 67).

It was clear that many of those interviewed had vigorously pursued jobs and further training, and that while the situation was, indeed, depressing, their responses were active and resistant. Avtar Brah concludes:

The experience of unemployment for young Asians is mediated through racial, class and gender divisions in contemporary Britain, but they are not passive victims of structural determinations. They question, resist, challenge and repudiate structures and processes which serve to produce and maintain their subordination. Their political consciousness about the destiny of their labour power derives predominantly from their first hand experience of white dominated institutions but their political ideologies and responses are developed and elaborated within Asian communities and Asian peer groups and, increasingly, in discourse with young blacks and anti-racist young whites.

(Brah 1986: 78)

The Red Star project was itself an example of this political consciousness and the refusal of young black men of Asian and Afro-Caribbean descent to be cast as victims in the system, but, instead, to act upon and shape their world and the world of Leicester politics.

Spatially, like other cities, Leicester has an inner-city core which includes the area where Red Star developed, middle-class suburbs, and a ring of working-class estates on the periphery of the city. Politically the inner city has been, and continues to be, a Labour stronghold, but the county of Leicestershire is less certain for Labour. It has been, and is, a Tory power base. The city council likes to be seen as a 'left of Labour' council but it has engaged much less with municipal socialism than, say, Sheffield or the GLC. The ruling Labour group includes, currently, seven Asian councillors and one Afro-Caribbean councillor. Although there has been, and is, widespread support for the Labour council, the late 1970s also saw an active National Front on the streets of Leicester, coming close to election victories in a couple of city wards, and drawing support from both young and old white working-class sections of the city, on a largely racist platform. Beyond the ballot box there were some noteworthy confrontations between the National Front, the police, black people, and anti-racist activists. Black Leicester particularly is mindful of this history and the earlier history of Asian women's struggles at Imperial Typewriters and Mansfield Hosiery, two local factories. It is wary of the view of Leicester as a sleepy, peaceful, provincial city that has, through mutual tolerance, generated racial harmony, a harmony demonstrated by the election of an Asian mayor in 1987/8. Racism was not, and is not, the monopoly of the National Front. As Cohen has commented: 'racism is not something "tacked on" to English history by virtue of its imperialist phase, one of its aberrant moments; it is *constitutive* of what has come to be known as "the British Way of Life"'(Cohen 1988: 63), and Leicester is no exception to this.

The riots of 1981, as in other parts of Britain, demonstrated the feelings of young people, black and white, in relation to the police. Consistent with the situation in Newham, Bradford, or Southall, a new generation of young black people were growing up in Leicester, living together in the city, attending the same schools, and trying to

151

defend the streets of their locality. Red Star was born out of the demands that this generation made for space and resources within the context of racism and black working-class life in Britain.

At the local level the party political context for the development of Red Star was a Labour city, but one dominated by the labourism of a Labour Party nationally in defeat. Leicester city Labour group celebrates its ability to respond to the needs of ethnic minorities and a recent Association of District Councils report comments: 'few authorities seem to have adopted policies as effective as Leicester, especially on monitoring' (*Leicester Link* 1989). Similarly, in the area of mobilising money under the central government Inner Area Programme, Leicester is generally commended. 'Leicester City Council is widely held to be the programme authority that has done most for the voluntary sector through IAP, both in terms of involvement in the decision making process and in the allocation of resources to voluntary groups' (Sills *at al.* 1988: 150). Leicester is, in effect, taken as a model of good practice. In fact, what municipal socialism there was in Leicester was crucially bound up with the development of the IAP monies; the city council, as the local state, dispensed funds to voluntary projects across the spectrum, including those for ethnic minorities. Critics suggest that this was one way in which the black struggle was deflected into inter-ethnic rivalries for the state's resources, and in which the 'professionalisation of ethnicity' (Bains 1988) was called forth by the state. In this process the state looked – drawing, perhaps, on a colonial model – for leaders with whom to negotiate. But, as the story of Red Star shows, the outcomes of this policy were deeply contradictory because the state and its brokers, in this case the ruling Labour group, could itself generate and galvanise collective action against its politics and its policies. These arguments are especially important now because at one level the infrastructure of black politics outside the political parties – that is, the material base of one important section of the new social movements – is crucially bound to the local state through IAP and other urban programmes. These are currently being restructured and many of the projects that were funded in this way are now in jeopardy. It was within this political context that Red Star would do battle over the years of the project. As I write new battles have begun in Leicester over the future of certain voluntary projects funded through the city council and IAP, including a number of Asian youth projects which are threatened. The response has been a public protest spearheading a campaign that again places young black people up against the state and in conflict with city councillors. To those involved with Red Star it is a familiar tale – one to which we now turn.

The Story of Red Star

Red Star, a redolent sign, took its name and had its roots in a football team, and it has remained closely tied to football up to the present time. The Red Star football team satisfied a demand for sports made by local black youth, but resources were limited, and after the 1981 riots the organiser of the football team started to negotiate with the city council for a youth club. The space that was offered was, however, at some distance from the main areas where the young people lived. At the same time, due to reorganisation, a local boys' secondary school became vacant. It was the school that most young black men in the area had attended. A struggle ensued between local groups for use of the building because it was a prime site and a major resource. Red Star transformed itself from a football team into a youth project and was able to negotiate use of the first floor of the building. This allowed it a material base from which to develop. Access to the school was negotiated with the county council who had responsibility for education and school buildings. With Red Star's entry into the school in 1982 also came project money from the Inner Area Programme and the city council, who voted a grant of £56,500 in 1982/3 and £32,800 in 1983/4 with a projected £67,000 for 1984/5. A management committee and a growing membership followed. Workers were employed on the community programme scheme to organise and develop recreational facilities. Money was spent on promoting football teams, supplying pitch fees, organising fixtures, and paying fines where necessary. There were a number of football teams including, within a youth project, a youth team for younger boys.

At this point the project was concerned with the politics of resources, supplying sports and leisure activities in the sports hall and a space that young black men could own. Seven to eight hundred young people were using the facilities, mainly Asian youth with some Afro-Caribbean and a few white lads. The chief negotiator for the project then became project manager and during 1982 the project continued with some changes in the management committee, including the first Afro-Caribbean member. By 1983 the city council had decided to review the relative autonomy of all voluntary projects, and in 1984 Red Star had its accounts frozen because it was late in returning audited accounts. At the same time the County Council, who were Red Star's landlords, decided to move on the school building and to convert it to a community centre. Red Star were told to move out as a temporary measure, but they were not offered another base in the immediate locality and negotiations between management committee representatives and the council began and continued for months. It was clear that the County Council wanted the project out of the building, and Red Star responded in January 1984 by occupying it on a twenty-four-hour basis so as to secure their licence. But their problems were not over; the City Council now refused to continue funding the project, and by November 1984 the County Council had applied to the High Court for a possession order, following a notice to quit which had prompted a second sit-in. Red Star went to court and successfully fought off the notice to quit, but the County Council was granted a possession order through the courts, one which was never invoked. At the same time the project moved into a political strategy, discussed in the next section of this chapter, by taking on the city Labour Party and by trying to generate public support. But without funds for the project it was difficult to sustain the level of work required. Initially, workers continued on a voluntary basis and the project continued to negotiate and call for funding, which was not forthcoming.

The school that houses the Red Star project now has a new manager, a local black councillor, and the building is due for refurbishing and multi-occupation by a wide variety of groups in the locality. Red Star's legal position remains ambiguous but the hostel that was a development from the project continues, and the Law Centre which the leader of Red Star was instrumental in founding is now entering a new phase following a troubled period. The local newspaper, commenting on the history of Red Star, called it 'a diary of disaster' (*Leicester Mercury*, 4 December 1987). To the members and supporters of Red Star this history looks very different.

The politics of Red Star

As the introduction to this essay suggests, the politics of Red Star is a complex one rooted in the lives of inner-city black youth in the early 1980s. This was the post-riots period when limited resources were directed by the national and local states towards young black people especially. It is a politics of gender and generation within the context of 1980s city life in Britain, and against the racism of a white society: a society that the young black men who were the members of Red Star had encountered as hostile and discriminatory through school, unemployment, the police, and racist groups on the streets.

The national background to Red Star includes the rise of the Asian Youth Movement and the development of the Southall Youth Movement. The latter was galvanised by the death, at the hands of white youth, of Gurdip Singh Chaggar in 1976. But, as the authors of *Southall: Birth of a Black Community*, comment: 'The death of Chaggar may have been the incident that spurred the Asian youth into organising themselves, but the basis of their militancy was the racism they experienced at school, in the streets and in the search for jobs' (Campaign Against Racism and Fascism/Southall Rights 1981: 54).

The year 1982 saw the famous cases of the Bradford Twelve cleared on charges of conspiracy and of the Newham Eight who had been similarly charged. The charges were dropped and four of the defendants were convicted of 'causing an affray'. In both cases the defence campaigns were organised around the rights of Asian people to defend themselves from racist attacks.

To invoke the Southall Youth Movement, the Bradford Twelve, or the Newham Eight is not simply to record the history of black struggles in Britain. There are important ways in which Red Star is both connected to and apart from these struggles. In analysing the politics of Red Star, I am thus conscious of both the similarities and the specificities of the project, and made more mindful of these by two recent but very different accounts of the Southall Youth Movement, by Tuku Mukherjee and Harwant Bains. The first of these is a celebratory account, whereas in the latter – somewhat more distanced – both masculinity and the relations between the Southall Youth Movement and the wider Southall 'community' are problematised. There are strong resonances with my own reading of Red Star in both these accounts, pointing to the complexities of political action and the need for a multi-textured analysis. I will return to these accounts as I develop my own.

Like the Southall Youth Movement, the Red Star project has been both acclaimed and heavily criticised, celebrated as the vanguard of the black struggle and criticised as a lumpen element, a noisy ragbag of disaffected black youth. What I hope to be able to develop is a more complex analysis which concentrates upon two key fields; the first is related to the development of political identities, both individual and collective, without which there can be no political action, and the second, to the issues surrounding state, nation, and citizenship. It should be clear that this analysis is itself an interpretation, a way in which I have analytically reorganised the 'thick description' which constitutes my account of Red Star. It is a reading, but one which is rooted in members' understanding of themselves as political actors and, most importantly, as strategists.

Forging political identities

The politics of Red Star was, as I have suggested, rooted in the lived experiences of young black people; but 'experience' does not by some automatic reaction politicise – it must first be reconstructed through the discourses that are brought to bear upon it. Political subjects must be called forth and it is here that leadership often provides a crucial intervention. Red Star and its leader is a study in these processes. The reason that Red Star was able to place a collective identity 'Red Star' so firmly on the political agenda in Leicester was because an identity had been forged both through the politicisation of the project as members came to know themselves through struggle, but also through the simultaneous and prior processes of subject formation. The dynamic and multi-faceted nature of these processes makes them difficult to grasp and set down, and what follows is a tentative attempt to make sense of them.

The Red Star Youth Project brought together a very wide diversity of young people with a great variety of backgrounds. This was the 'raw material' with which the leadership worked. Here was a project in which ethnic jokes were rife. The jokes used and highlighted stereotypical dimensions of the ethnicities represented in the project. There were Muslims, both Sunnis and Sh'ias, Hindus as well as Sikhs – both Jats and Ramgharias – from the Indian sub-continent and East Africa. Similarly, there were both Hindu and Muslim Gujaratis with their roots in India and East Africa, so that national, regional, language, and religious diversities among Asians cut across each other. There were Punjabis, Pakistanis, and Bangledeshis alongside Afro-Caribbeans with parents whose origins lay in different islands, from Jamaica and Antigua to Barbados and St Kitts. Ethnic jokes and name-calling were one way in which this diversity was managed, and one group gave back as good as it got. Thus, within the project difference was clearly acknowledged and played upon but the results were not always comic. Some members were hurt by the name-calling and its effects could have been very divisive. Ultimately, however, they were not, because set against difference was commonality, and this commonality, in all its complexity, was constantly called up by the leader of Red Star. Alongside it was a shared pride in the ability of Red Star members to defeat ethnic rivalries. It is one of the enduring facets of the Red Star politicisation that out of diversity the members were able to call forth a political identity which, while it recognised difference, acknowledged commonality. The membership had an active part in this, but the leader was crucial in cementing a public, collective identity because he was able to represent the collective identity of the membership to themselves, but in ways that secured their active participation.

Although there were prominent members of Red Star and a management committee, the driving force behind Red Star was a young Sikh, a man who had a degree in politics and history, and had some experience of both student politics and shop-floor organising. He was a socialist and member of the International Marxist Group

(IMG). But what he clearly understood was that the politics of the university, the shop-floor, and the left was not a politics that included young black people, nor was it founded on the streets and in opposition to racism. Nevertheless, the discourses of class relations, workers' struggles, and relations between civil society and the state were called up by him to position the Red Star struggle in relation to class and community politics in the city. He was a charismatic leader who had gone to the same schools, lived in the same streets, and shared the life experiences of the membership – in a Gramscian sense he was truly an organic intellectual who, while he was able to organise the experiences of others, always spoke with, not for, the membership. As members like Raj, Paul, and Jitu expressed this: 'He showed us we had rights', or 'He put the issue to us and then let us make up our minds', and 'He understood where we were coming from'. The leader of Red Star was never challenged as leader and he was, and is, known affectionately as 'Bigger', which might relate to his stature but more importantly relates to his 'big brain'. The members I have spoken to take great pride in the leader, most especially in his 'brain power'. He was acknowledged as a skilled negotiator and orator capable of being 'four jumps ahead' and of giving 'brilliant speeches' that fired the membership. He was an impressive figure, an adept leader as much at home on the football pitch as in a committee room. His flair for bringing together the heterogeneity of the membership and its ideology was expressed as much in the Nehru jacket that he wore as in his own account of the project: he linked struggles against the state to the importance of empowerment for black youth through IZZAT, 'a big word suggesting honour and dignity' in a situation of racism and lack of opportunities for black youth in the inner city. It was a brilliant eclecticism which, as we shall see, showed often in the speeches he made. Harwant Bains's (1988: 237) account of the Southall Youth Movement points to the transformation that turned 'the Sikh warrior into the modern street fighting man', and it is possible to see the leader of Red Star in this way. It would, however, be a caricature of him and would not evoke the strategic sense or imaginative flair which marked his politics and made him an organic intellectual.

In forging a sense of political identity among Red Star members, how and in what sense were members transformed into political actors? What ideas or experiences did they draw upon? They began with their immediate life experiences. Members shared a common locality, they lived and went to school in the area. They were neighbours and friends from working-class black families, some of them very poor families, and although their families contributed to their specific religious and ethnic identities, they could recognise the social and economic commonalities of their lives in Britain. What they could also recognise was their position as a generation which was not simply an age cohort, but was marked apart by special features: a schooling which, through its defeats and humiliations, had also generated a particular view of white authority, and an attitude to the police in the local area, especially sharpened following the riots. Drawing on these specific perceptions and experiences, members of Red Star could mark themselves out as a group with shared needs around which they could organise, and for which they could struggle. Similarly, as a generation they were marked apart by gender. Red Star was never a place where young women and girls could go. It was not considered appropriate. Its members were 'youth', a category of young men, and this was turned into a collectivism through the adoption of machismo styles of politics. Again, Harwant Bains comments upon this in relation to the Southall Youth Movement, and it has many resonances with the street style of Red Star members. But, while it is vital to problematise this style, it nevertheless requires further comment in relation to the forging of political identities. This is especially true in relation to the early 1980s when machismo was on the streets in the form of white racist gangs and black youth had to defend their neighbourhood against racist attack. It is also true in relation to the police, who have their own powerful version of machismo. It is an important call, by all means an essential one, to a shared understanding among young black men beyond their ethnic differences and their individual capacities. It also speaks to the understanding that for working-class black men the basis of their labour power is their physical strength. Thus, the body, as Gilroy notes, is an important site for street style, and is not only given emphasis by the threats it receives on the streets, but is reclaimed as a site for the expression of individuality and collectivity (Gilroy 1987). Red Star members came to understand this very clearly when they intervened in the Labour Party by packing meetings in an exuberant and, to some white people, intimidatory fashion, and also when they occupied their building – defending their space with their physical presence.

The power and dexterity of physical strength were displayed through football which was, after all, where Red Star began, and which was, and is, a passion for many of the Red Star members. There were heroes of the soccer pitch, both Asian and Afro-Caribbean, and it was clear that football brought everyone together, whether on the pitch or the sidelines. For the public schools sports and character-building may go together; Red Star politicised this, demonstrating the power of Red Star through its teams and its ability to carry away trophies, especially in knock-out competitions or leagues that included white teams. Red Star teams and supporters were notorious for the excitement they generated and it is not surprising, given what was at stake, that sometimes the games produced fights and disarray, not necessarily because Red Star started the aggro; they were up against white teams and white refs who were far from sympathetic. The football teams were one very public face of Red Star which was manifest whenever Red Star members moved outside their own locality and took on the wider and often hostile world of white Britain. It meant that to the outside world, Red Star members were sometimes characterised as 'the mob': but the members were undeterred by this. On the contrary, they reappropriated the label, using it to reinforce a collective identity and referring to themselves as 'the Red Star mob' with much merriment.

The football teams emphasised masculine strength and abilities, and also their position as 'black' teams. The term itself underscored the collective appeal to a black identity. This was the early 1980s when the language of black struggle referred to a black struggle which was not yet fractured as it is today, and will be, in the 1990s. The importance of marking out a black identity and coupling that with youth was crucial to the success of Red Star, just as it was, Tuku Mukherjee of the Southall Youth Movement suggests, to the success of the Southall Youth Movement. He quotes Balraj, a member who says: 'Our only security is our understanding and acknowledgement of what it means to be Black' (Mukherjee 1988: 222). Or, as one Red Star member, Aziz, put it: 'We come from all kinds of families but when it comes to our rights we are black.' Black was, and is, a political category, so Red Star members were quite clear that identities were not and are not frozen; no one from Red Star believes that being black denies an ethnic, religious, or class identity. There is a simultaneous lived experience of difference and commonality expressed in the way in which Red Star members discuss their political identity as black youth. It was the terrain on which they chose to struggle; not the category constructed by the police, the schools, or official discourse (see Solomos 1988, for example). It was a black identity forged not just against racism but from diversity, for themselves. It did not, of course, go unchallenged, but this opposition itself helped to emphasise the collective.

From the moment that the project was given access to the school building there was opposition to Red Star. A petition signed by residents in the immediate area received some publicity – publicity out of proportion to its support because the numbers involved were small. At the same time older men in the black communities used the Red Star accommodation during the day to smoke and talk and play cards. More serious opposition to the project came later from the local state and the city Labour Party who drew on the contradictions presented by the political identities of the Red Star members. There were sections of the Muslim community who never accepted that their sons were part of a 'black youth'; they preferred a religious identity, and some of the young Muslim men used their membership of Red Star to mark their rebellion against a Muslim identity as their *only* identity. They wanted both because they recognised the need for both, and they lived with the contradictions, playing football but not drinking, going to the mosque but also being part of the occupations of the building, and taking on a black identity as a felt solidarity with other Red Star members.

The occupations, especially the first, were themselves an education in political action when political identities took on a more active and exciting dimension. Several hundred young black men were involved in a round-the-clock sit-in which meant they had space and freedom through the night to talk, watch videos, eat huge quantities of curry prepared by the leader of Red Star, and engage in strategy and political debate. The excitement of these times still remains, as Mehboob recalled: 'there we were in this huge building with the run of the place, talking all night, playing pool, eating and living it up, and the police they never came, they never dared because they thought they might have a riot on their hands. We had real power then – nobody could touch us'. It was a heady time of political certainties when the leadership and the members made a political calculation in relation to the police and the authorities, a calculation related to their power as an organised collective. That Red Star were organised was evidenced by the length of the occupation, which continued over several months. It required, in fact, a level of discipline and organisation that is often passed over in the memories of the excitement of occupation. The occupations were not the only strategy employed by the management committee. The leader had to enter into a legal battle over the tenancy of the building, a battle which forms part of the discussion that follows. What the occupation forged for the members and their leaders was the agency of politics in which members and leaders were actively engaged in a struggle with the local state and the city Labour Party. It is to this terrain that I now turn.

Nation, state, and citizenship

The second part of my analysis concentrates on nation, state, and citizenship – the stage onto which the individual and collective political identities of the Red Star membership moved. The argument here is that in the generation of their politics Red Star members not only moved into a confrontation with the local state and the city

Labour Party, but that in widening the terrain of struggle they sought to lay claim to their part in the nation as citizens. Thus, the struggles within the Labour Party and through the courts were not just strategic battles over resources and in relation to political interests; at a deeper symbolic level the Red Star struggle was an entry into the nation and to citizenship, a claim to a place in the body politic which sought at the same time to reconstruct the language of 'nation' and 'citizen'.

To invoke the nation is to highlight not the commonly assumed geography of state boundaries but a terrain of struggle and one that has been fought over throughout Britain's history. To speak of nations is to invoke 'imagined communities' (Anderson 1983) that nevertheless are powerful, 'and not a bit less real because they are symbolic' (Hall 1987: 45). Gramsci's analysis of ideological hegemony helps us to understand the ways in which 'the nation' is constructed through a consensus around 'the people'. In Britain this has been underpinned more recently by the rise of an authoritarian populism which promotes a 'little Englander' mentality and by so doing emphasises homogeneity in British culture. It is an exclusionary account which presents those outside as 'others'. History is rewritten to promote homogeneity and to ignore the diversity and heterogeneity which has marked British culture throughout its history. Thus the black presence in British society has had to be recovered, as in the work of Fryer (1984) and Ramdin (1987), for example, and black people have had to fight to be part of the nation, none more so than black youth who in official discourses have often been ideologically constructed as a central part of the 'alien wedge' and 'the enemy within' Britain. Red Star's entry into the political arena fractured both the ideological construction of black youth as a marginal group, and therefore not truly part of the nation, and the invisibility of black people in the hegemonic account of Britishness.

That the Red Star membership should make this shift relates in part to their understanding of the 'nationalism of the neighbourhood' (Cohen 1988) in which they had secured a political identity and a degree of power located with a specific urban space, a territory marked out and defended. But as Reeves (1986: 108) comments: 'As Winston Churchill recognised, a continuum exists between the lofty defence of the abstraction of the nation and the mundane defence of the neighbourhood street.' The Churchillian reference is to the exclusionary nationalism of white Britain at the time of the Second World War, but young black men in 1980s Britain also sought to engage with 'the abstraction of the nation' and claim some part of it as their own. How did they seek to do this, symbolically and strategically?

161

On the ground Red Star was not immediately confronted by 'the nation' but by the local state and the Labour Party politicians who were the gatekeepers to the resources they needed. Yet the project also understood that resource politics required public support. Here again the similarities and specificities of Red Star in relation to the Southall Youth Movement are clear. Mukherjee (1988: 222) writes: 'The "hooligans" of 1976 have come a long way and are the protectors of the whole community today.' Whereas Bains (1988: 237) notes that 'The success of the SYM is due to what it has come to symbolise – the resistance of the Asian community to racism – rather than any ability to organise or educate local youth', and he continues, noting that the SYM was able 'to establish itself with a mystique of popular grassroots appeal and subsequently to gain major financial support from the state'. What Bains is objecting to is the suggestion that the SYM speaks for Southall because he is crucially aware of the number of different voices that exist. Mukherjee has no such problems and his account reinforces the view of the SYM as defenders and voices for the community. Red Star members, on the other hand, spoke for themselves and as a voice for black youth. The Red Star leader was clear in his purposes and the aims of the project, and continued to speak for that section of the black working-class community who were the members, black youth in the inner city.

Red Star never suggested that it was speaking for and on behalf of 'black people' because the leader and members were alive to the contradictions within the communities and between the various interests that existed. This had, in fact, major implications for the political career of the Red Star leader, who was identified with black youth, an identification which was crucial to his strength and his success, but which proved to be a limitation when he sought to move further into the Labour Party and seek selection as a Labour councillor. The political identities of the Red Star members generated a fierce loyalty to the project and to their own demands. When interviewed at the time of the occupations one member said 'We will fight to stay here because we are needed' (*Leicester Mercury*, 14 November 1984), a direct appeal to the fact that Red Star satisfied a need for youth provision in the inner city.

Red Star members had shown that they had power and that they could defend a building, but they were painfully aware that the terrain of struggle was broader, that decisions about their future lay elsewhere. Having engaged with direct action in relation to the building, they then decided to take their collective strength directly to the local state by a mass visit to the City Council offices where they demanded access to the City Council leader. It was an exuberant and witty show of strength which placed the Red Star collective physically in the heart of the local state, much to the surprise and annoyance of both officers and local councillors. Young black men crowded into the building, jammed the lifts and refused to budge until they had seen the leader of the council. Ultimately, access was denied and in protest someone let off the fire alarm and waited for people to start rushing out of the building. It was the public face of Red Star – rowdy and as outrageous as possible, bringing street style into the anonymous corridors of power because that is its symbolic importance, bringing the margin to the centre with Dadaist humour and marking at the same time an escalation in the struggle within the Labour Party. This public defiance of official practices expressed the collective view that we, too, are citizens and have rights which include making politicians accountable.

But Red Star's relations with the state were public in other ways as well that also marked them as citizens with rights in law – Red Star went to court, or rather the leader of Red Star went to court, to defend the rights of the project to a tenancy within the school. Again, the move into a legal battle signalled not simply the defence of the project but a claim to be part of the nation and therefore to protection under the law. The case was a complex one in which Red Star's tenancy was upheld, but the rights of the County Council to a possession order were similarly supported and confirmed in the county court. The legal battle was politicised through the sit-ins, and it was the politics of Red Star that confirmed the tenancy, but recourse to the law demonstrated to the local state and local politicians that Red Star was something more than a bunch of rowdies, that there was a willingness to fight on terrain not chosen and perhaps not initially understood. This new terrain was, in the course of the legal battle, made intelligible, and the success of the Red Star leader in this sphere confirmed the view among the membership that with such a leader Red Star could fight on any ground! Red Star was jubilant; it had the building not only by occupation but by some measure of legal protection. Red Star members too would be counted as citizens under the protection of the law. Strategically it was an important battle, but elsewhere the struggle continued.

'Elsewhere' was, of course, the city Labour Party, and entry by Red Star into this arena was strategic in relation to lobbying support and shaming councillors, but equally, I am suggesting, entry into the Labour Party was a symbolic entry into the nation and the political life of the nation. It represented a move away from the sidelines, the streets, and the football pitch, and into the arena of representational politics, the meetings of ward Labour Parties, the constitutional rule book, and individual manipulations and alliances. There was no reason as far as Red Star members were concerned not to bring a little life to this arena, with some street style and some fun at the expense of their adversaries. Red Star members joined the Labour Party through the local ward: but it was not any old ward, it was a crucial city ward where the leader of the council was a councillor, alongside the chair of the powerful 'manpower' committee; the perfect place to put the case for Red Star. Members lived locally and so joined up in an organised campaign and soon managed to ensure that the leader of Red Star became the ward secretary. Red Star members packed the monthly ward meetings in an attempt to secure a resolution in support of the project, and they raised it at the annual meeting of the ward where more than forty members turned up and insisted on a debate on the issue, fired by a speech from the leader. The Labour leaders wanted the Red Star supporters to leave but they refused, and the debate became more heated, to the point where tempers frayed and fists flew, but there was no vote on the resolution in support of Red Star. The members had tried to galvanise the left in the ward, and they did have some support which they mobilised as they moved further into the local Labour Party, producing a censure motion on the two ward councillors after the money to Red Star was cut off. The leader of the council and the other councillors were accused by the leader of Red Star of working against the interests of young black people, and in a charged atmosphere the leader of Red Star likened the machinations in the Labour Party to those of Macbeth, invoking Shakespearian tragedy and politics as a way of highlighting the roles played by prominent Labour councillors in the troubles of Red Star. It was a dramatic speech and one which, of course, called up an icon of English culture and nationhood in the service of black youth. It was powerful both in this and in the way that it dramatised, through Shakespeare, the treachery of the councillors as this was viewed by Red Star members.

The Red Star issue had serious repercussions for the cohesion of the Labour group in the city, which culminated in members of the left wing of the group picketing the Labour group meeting. This was, in part, the outcome of a much more public campaign by Red Star to discredit the Labour councillors, especially the leader and those in their ward. Red Star's challenge presented the Labour group with a dilemma: on the one hand, it claimed to govern a city with a large black population and with youth unemployment definitely on the agenda at this juncture; on the other, its leadership was engaged in a very public row about resources for young black people in one of the most deprived sections of the city. Needless to say, the party leadership fought back both within the ward and in the city more generally. It did so by concentrating on discrediting the Red Star project, and most especially its leadership because by this stage the interventions in the Labour Party had become more than the lobbying or disrupting of ward meetings.

Faced with a Labour Party that did not seem to be on their side (as one member, Manjit, put it, 'We joined the Labour party and they sold us out'), the members decided to seize the opportunity to bring their own councillor into the Labour group. Within the city ward a battle ensued over re-selection of the city councillors in which the leader of Red Star was put forward as a candidate. It was a political calculation that nearly paid off when on the crucial night of the re-selection meeting the members packed the meeting; but, as Dinesh said, 'I thought we had got it right; then I tried to calculate who was for us and who was against us and it didn't quite add up.' The reason 'it didn't quite add up' was that the leader of the Labour group had also made some political calculations and had called up a section of the Muslim community, alongside his own white support in the ward party, to defeat the challenge by the leader of Red Star. The Labour leader and others in the Labour group had used the divisions between generations and between political identities, emphasising a Muslim identity at the expense of a black one. They used, in effect, the politics of difference, finding a Muslim candidate, in fact a Welsh convert, when an initial strategy to involve an Asian Muslim lecturer from the university failed because he refused to stand. Although the Labour councillors did their sums the vote was not easily won; there was considerable uncertainty, and the case was referred to the National Executive of the Labour Party, which supported the vote against the leader of Red Star. It was a blow, and despite other attempts in other wards to secure selection for him Red Star did not succeed in this. The Labour Party closed ranks and, in fact, did more than this. Relations between the leader of the council, the leader of the Recreation and Arts Committee, and Red Star collectively, and in the person of the leader, deteriorated further.

As a move to highlight their case and generate public support Red Star produced, through the ward party, a leaflet pointing to the needs of black youth and the undemocratic and racist ways in which city councillors were responding to these needs. In addition, they tried to secure support from other voluntary sector groups and the communities adjacent to the project. The Labour Party and the local newspaper had, however, been quite successful in identifying Red Star with rowdiness and anti-social behaviour, and this did little to enhance the reputation of the project in the city. The image was reinforced by the way in which the leader of the City Council took the case of the leader of Red Star to the regional party for investigation on the charge of 'bringing the party into disrepute'. The leader of Red Star threatened to sue for libel. Eventually, both leaders backed off, but the rumblings of the Red Star row continue and are open to reactivation at any time.

Despite the spirited defence of Red Star, and the strategic acumen of the leader, Red Star did not have its grant reinstated. What Red Star members had succeeded in doing was creating political turmoil in the city because they had not simply organised around a set of demands for resources; instead, they had taken on the Labour Party agenda and tried to shift the ideological terrain of Labour Party politics. They had foregrounded the needs of black youth and exposed the machinations of Labour Party councillors, while highlighting racism in the party. Red Star members had tried to engage with the labourism of white politics and had demanded that they too be on the agenda, not as a problem but as citizens with rights within a nation of which they were a part.

Not yet concluded

Labour councillors in Leicester, faced with diminishing budgets and the poll tax, looked decidedly unnerved by a picket of the council meeting in February 1989 which protested about cuts to voluntary sector projects, most of which were black youth projects. Among the protesters and those mandated to speak on their behalf was the leader of Red Star who, like the project, won't go away. Red Star, with its ambiguous tenancy, still occupies space in the school building and the football teams, although they are no longer known officially as Red Star teams, are unofficially still named in this way. Similarly, the hostel for young black men, although it, too, has another name, is known as the Red Star Hostel. This is an ongoing concern, like the reactivated Law Centre in which the leadership of Red Star had a defining hand. The histories of these projects also speak of the relationship between the state and the local black communities. The hostel, as the home of young black men, is regularly raided by the police in a way that the original Red Star project was not, and this underlines the changes in relations between the police, the local state, and young black men. The hostel and the Law Centre are centrally bound to the politics that marked Red Star, a politics both of resources and of rights, while the broader legacy of Red Star lives in the hearts and minds of the black men who were politicised through their membership of the project. They may read the *Sun* but the events at Red Star showed them that the media and the newspapers have also to be read. Similarly, the lessons of Red Star – that politics is about engagement – have remained, and some of the men are active in local community groups. They have stayed away from the Labour Party, regarding its structure and politicians with suspicion, offering an alternative analysis rooted in their own experiences of politics and the political identities that they forged as black youth.

Red Star activities gave the membership a collective language; crucial to that language was an identity as black youth which did not obliterate ethnic and religious identities but used this as the terrain of struggle. It did so by forging a political identity located with collective action, and the commonalities among young black men in the inner city. A black identity was positioned by an analysis of racism and the means whereby an anti-racist politics could be created. For those involved, the militancy of Red Star and the engagement with collective action has endured as the standard by which politics is measured, generating a commitment to direct action. The sense of empowerment has stayed with those involved, even in the hostile conditions of the late 1980s.

Red Star's interventions in the Labour Party meant that the local media, the local state, and the party had to take them seriously and include them in their discourses and their deliberations. It is in this sense that Red Star members entered the nation and claimed a place on the agenda. They claimed this place not as objects of political discourse but as subjects and as active citizens. As the leader of Red Star made clear, one of the objects of his politics was 'to take politics out of being a spectator sport' which is, of course, a wider problem for liberal democracy. The issue facing the new social movements is that in order to get *on* the agenda, they have to *disrupt* the institutional arrangements that exclude individuals and collectivities, because parliamentary politics is exclusionary in relation to the active citizen; this is an endemic part of western democracies. Red Star members demonstrated that they could disrupt the ideological terrain by insisting that the Labour Party took 'race' seriously. In doing so they demonstrated that the Labour Party was not capable of integrating a politics of black youth. It is not possible, therefore, to speak simply of success or lack of success in relation to the politics of Red Star. Instead, it is rather that, as Melucci comments,

> concrete concepts such as efficacy or success could be considered unimportant. This is because conflict takes place principally on symbolic ground, by means of challenging and upsetting dominant codes upon which social relationships are founded. . . . The mere existence of a symbolic challenge is in itself a method of unmasking the dominant codes, a different way of perceiving and naming the world.
>
> (Melucci 1988: 248)

© 1991 Sallie Westwood

Notes

1 This chapter would not have been possible without the warm, generous support and interest of Red Star members to whom I owe an enormous debt. I owe very special thanks to the leader of Red Star who has read and commented on the paper and to 'Scratch' – the original Daw-Tana. Equally, my thanks to Ali Rattansi for reading and commenting on earlier drafts of the chapter.

References

Anderson, Benedict (1983) *Imagined Communities: Reflections on the Origin and Spread of Nationalism*, London: Verso.

Bains, H. (1988) 'Southall youth: an old-fashioned story', in P. Cohen and H. Bains (eds) *Multi-Racist Britain*, London: Macmillan.

Benyon, J. and Solomos, J. (ed) (1987) *The Roots of Urban Unrest*, London: Pergamon Press.

Brah, A. (1986) 'Unemployment and racism: Asian youth on the dole', in S. Allen *et al.* (eds) *The Experience of Unemployment*, London: BSA/Macmillan.

Bryan, B., Dadzie, S. and Scafe, S. (1985) *The Heart of the Race: Black Women's Lives in Britain*, London: Virago.

Campaign Against Racism and Fascism/Southall Rights (1981) *Southall: Birth of a Black Community*, London: Institute of Race Relations/ Southall Rights.

Cohen, P. (1988) 'The perversions of inheritance: studies in the making of multi-racist Britain', in P. Cohen and H. Bains (eds) *Multi-Racist Britain*, London: Macmillan.

Cohen, P. and Bains, H. (eds) (1988) *Multi-Racist Britain*, London: Macmillan.

Fryer, P. (1984) *Staying Power: The History of Black People in Britain*, London: Pluto Press.

Gilroy, P. (1987) *There Ain't No Black in the Union Jack: The Cultural Politics of Race and Racism*, London: Hutchinson.

Gilroy, P. and Lawrence, E. (1988) 'Two-tone Britain: white and black youth and the politics of anti-racism', in P. Cohen and H. Bains (eds) *Multi-Racist Britain*, London: Macmillan.

Hall, S. (1987) 'Minimal selves', ICA Document 6, Identity, London: Institute of Contemporary Arts.

Hall, S., Critcher, C., Jefferson, T., Clarke, J., and Roberts, B. (1978) *Policing the Crisis: Mugging, the State and Law and Order*, London: Macmillan.

Jacobs, B. (1988) *Black Politics and Urban Crisis in Britain*, Cambridge: Cambridge University Press.

Leicester City Council (1983) *The Leicester Survey*, Leicester: Leicester City Council.

Leicester Link (1989) Leicester: Leicester City Council, March.

Mehmood, T. (1986) *Hand on the Sun*, Harmondsworth: Penguin.

Melucci, A. (1988) 'Social movements and the democratization of everyday life', in J. Keane (ed.) *Civil Society and the State*, London: Verso, pp. 245–60.

Mukherjee, T. (1988) 'The journey back', in P. Cohen and H. Bains (eds) *Multi-Racist Britain*, London: Macmillan.

Pearson, G. (1983) *Hooligan: A History of Respectable Fears*, London: Macmillan.

Ramdin, R. (1987) *The Making of the Black Working Class in Britain*, New York: Wildwood House.

Reeves, F. (1986) *British Racial Discourse: A Study of British Political Discourse about Race and Race-related Matters*, Cambridge: Cambridge University Press.

Sills, A., Taylor, G. and Golding, P. (1988) *The Politics of the Urban Crisis*, London: Hutchinson.

Sivanandan, A. (1982) *A Different Hunger*, London: Pluto Press.

Solomos, J. (1988) *Black Youth, Racism and the State: The Politics of Ideology and Policy*, Cambridge: Cambridge University Press.

Westwood, S. (1984) *All Day, Every Day: Factory and Family in the Making of Women's Lives*, London: Pluto Press.

Chapter six

Drama and politics in the development of a London Carnival[1]

Abner Cohen

Introduction

Analysis of the relations between cultural forms and social formations, which is the principal aim of social anthropology, has been
formulated largely in terms of correlations. We often juxtapose the
cultural and the social and say the two are causally related. But two
processes may operate epiphenomenally, without any necessary causal connection between them. To establish such a connection it is
essential to find how the two variables in question here – which differ
so fundamentally in many respects – affect each other.

One way of doing this is to explore the dramatic process underlying the rituals, ceremonies, and other types of symbolic activities
that pervade social life. With this approach the study of socio-
cultural causation and change becomes the analysis of the creation
or transformation of dramatic forms, their production, direction,
authentication, the techniques they employ; and the transformation
they bring about in the relationships between the men and women
they involve.

The sociological importance of analysing the drama of ritual and
ceremonials has been stressed within social anthropology by a number of writers, among them Gluckman (1942), Mitchell (1956),
Peters (1963), Frankenberg (1957, 1966), and Peacock (1968).
Turner (1957, 1974) in particular has evolved dramatic analysis into
a method for the study of the relations between politics and ritual
action.

The work of the anthropologist in such analysis is similar to that
of the dramatist in the Brechtian tradition, whose play would take a
familiar, everyday event out of its ordinary ideological sequence and
'throw it into crisis' by showing it in the context of power struggle in
society. In a recent monograph (Cohen 1981), I attempted to do this
consistently by demonstrating how such ordinary symbolic performances as a ball, a university graduation ceremony, a funeral service, or

a wedding festivity repetitively reproduce or modify power relationships, and how they combine in a culture that functions instrumentally to transform a category of senior civil servants and professionals in a West African nation-state into a cohesive power elite.

But most of these studies, including my own, suffer from insufficient longitudinal data to permit validation of the analysis in terms of interrelated historical movements. It is principally to overcome this methodological difficulty that I have recently concentrated on the study of a current London annual carnival, which has developed, both culturally and politically, in the full light of recorded publicity.

The Carnival is staged on August Bank Holiday in the narrow streets of Notting Hill in North Kensington. Its basic mobile unit consists of a steel band providing a loud and heavy beat, a colourful masquerading section enacting a massive theatrical theme, a number of revellers who 'jump up' in dancing, and a larger number of followers and supporters.

The loud beat, the music of the calypsonian, and the vigorous dancing – all accompanied by heavy drinking and smoking – go on for hours and induce an intense state of ecstasy and mirth among the participants, who become so carried away by the spirit of the occasion that they lose track of the prescribed route and wander around the narrow streets until well into the night.

The two-day event is the culmination of months of preparation by various artistic groups, which over the years have become permanent cliques of friends, interacting in primary relationships that are not necessarily connected with the Carnival. In time, these relationships become associated with a body of values and norms and, with the spread of Rastafarianism, are also invested with ritual beliefs and practices. The preparations for Carnival are punctuated by massive gatherings in fêtes, launching balls, seminars, exhibitions, calypso tents, gala performances, and educational sessions for the young.

The Carnival was first held in 1965. It was then local and polyethnic and attended by a few hundred men, women, and children, about half of them West Indian.[2] By 1975, Carnival had become national, exclusively West Indian, and was attended by a quarter of a million people.[3] In 1976 Carnival made the headlines when it occasioned a bloody confrontation between West Indian youth and the police, with hundreds being injured and taken to hospital. Over the next three years Carnival became a major issue for manipulation by internal factions and external interest groups.

In this chapter Carnival is discussed as a two-dimensional *movement*, involving a continual interplay between cultural forms and political relations. Cultural forms are evolved to express the sentiments and identity of people who come together as a result of specific economico-political conditions and at the same time they serve to mobilise other people as well. These in turn develop more elaborate cultural forms, which mobilise still more people, The nature of mediation between cultural forms and political formations is considered. The various cultural elements in Carnival are shown to be linked together in political action, but the event itself is an artistic form *sui generis* and cannot be explained in terms of politics alone. The issue is explored in the course of discussing a serious rift in the Carnival leadership over the question of whether Carnival ought to be a cultural event or a political demonstration.[4]

For the purpose of the present discussion the history of Carnival is divided into three distinct periods: 1966–70, characterised by poly-ethnic participation and heterogeneous cultural expression; 1971–5, characterised by the domination of the Trinidadian tradition of steel band music, calypso, and masquerading; and 1976–9, dominated by the appearance of British-born West Indian youth and the introduction of reggae pop music, with its associated Rastafarian symbols and ideologies. Each period is marked by new political developments and new cultural forms.

Underlying these developments is the process by which a group engaged in political confrontation mobilises its culture and its communal relationships to co-ordinate its corporate action in the struggle for power.[5]

Working-class poly-ethnic amity (1966–70)

The first period saw a small-scale, local carnival, which was a working-class, poly-ethnic event, with a variety of cultural themes derived from different traditions. That was a period of full employment (or, as some economists claimed, overemployment) resulting from a boom in the British economy, which led to a mood of public optimism aptly captured by the slogan of Harold Macmillan, the Prime Minister of the day: 'You've never had it so good'. Those were the years of 'Swinging London', the Beatles, Mary Quant, Twiggy, the miniskirt and a variety of youth movements of the 'Make love, not war' type.

Carnival was organised by a remarkable woman, Rhaunee Laslett, who had been born in London to an American Indian mother from North Carolina and a Russian father. When she grew up she decided to identify with her mother's culture. 'We are a spiritual people', she explained. In the early 1960s she founded a Community Neighbourhood Service in the area, taking immigrant youth released from prison and helping them readjust to life in Britain. In May 1966, in between sleep and wakefulness, she had a vision suggesting that she gather people from different ethnic groups in the area in a joyful procession. Many people emphasise that Notting Hill was at the time grim, grey, and dull, with a population that included immigrants from different lands, and self-proclaimed drug addicts, homosexuals, radical students, and drop-out children from middle-class families.[6]

For three months following her vision, Laslett threw herself energetically into mobilising local talents for the Carnival. When it was finally staged on August Bank Holiday, it offered a medley of bright colours, artistry, and ethnic heterogeneity. There were dancers from the Ukraine, Cyprus, and India, and a variety of musical groups including a small West Indian band that had been formed in a pub at Earls Court by Russell Henderson. The procession was led by an Englishman who rode in a stage-coach, masquerading as Queen Victoria. Many people helped organise the event: local shopkeepers, community leaders. The picture that emerges from statements by a few participants and from documents, including hundreds of photographs, is of a happy, humorous procession, with about half of the participants being local, working-class Britons.

In the following three years greater sophistication in organisation and in the artistic activities was introduced into Carnival, with the enterprising Mrs Laslett mobilising more volunteers and contributors and ever more varied talents. Local West Indian residents played an increasingly significant part.

In 1970, towards the end of this period, because of growing tension in the area, Laslett cancelled the event only two weeks before it was to take place. But the movement had acquired a momentum of its own; other local leaders took over and staged the procession on time. A local newspaper gave the following account:

> By 2.30 p.m. about 800 colourfully dressed families left Powis Square either on foot, in lorries, or in various prams and pushchairs and marched for about 3 miles led by Ginger Johnston and his African Drummers and witchdoctor. For over two hours the Carnival weaved through the streets and finally arrived back at the square, by which time Sacatash, an American rock and roll band, had set up and started to play. Music continued nonstop until midnight with Mataya Stackhouse, James Metzner and various local musicians playing on the stage. By 11.15 Ginger Johnston who had held the whole event together returned to end the Carnival with a dance round the square until midnight.
>
> (*Friends*, 2 October 1970)

Thus the 1966–70 period is characterised by co-operation across ethnic lines, notably between West Indian immigrants and British working-class natives. West Indians who came to Britain had already been brought up as Christians, spoke English as a mother tongue, and were British-orientated in their education and culture generally. Many of the men, and certainly a number of the Carnival leaders, initially married or lived with native British women. In Notting Hill there was clear working-class solidarity between immigrants and natives, struggling with the local authorities over housing, schools, and neighbourhood amenities. Carnival was an expression, as well as an instrument, of that class solidarity. But in the next few years the situation was drastically transformed.

Search for identity and the Trinidadian tradition (1971–5)

The second period saw a dramatic change in the character of Carnival. Within only two years Carnival became almost exclusively West Indian in its leadership and arts and nearly so in attendance. In particular the period saw the dramatic development of steel-band music in the heart of inner London as the major musical basis for Carnival and as a powerful symbol of the movement associated with it. The tradition of the Trinidad Carnival was systematically studied by the Notting Hill leadership and adapted to the British situation.

These developments were closely connected with economic and political upheavals that enveloped the West Indians in Britain generally and those who lived in Notting Hill in particular. With the ending of the economic boom of the 1960s, unemployment became rife. West Indians were particularly hard hit, in part because they were relative newcomers, in part because many were semi-skilled, and in large part because they were the victims of racial discrimination. The relationships of amity that had existed between them and native working-class Londoners gave way to tension over employment, tension whipped up and heightened by Enoch Powell's prophecies of imminent racial violence and rivers of blood (Powell 1969: 281–314). The National Front, an extreme right-wing anti-black and anti-Jewish party, gained an increasing following among native inner-city dwellers.[7] Immigration regulations were tightened severely, which further contributed to the uneasy situation.

The impact of these developments in Notting Hill was particularly strong. It was here that the early wave of West Indian immigrants, especially those from Trinidad, first settled. And it was here that in 1958 the worst racial violence in Britain's history occurred, when in a series of incidents scores of white youths attacked black residents. The government and the courts took severe measures, and the trade unions and various church denominations condemned the attacks. That determined response, together with economic prosperity and full employment during the 1960s, inhibited the development of a negative reaction among the West Indians. But now, in the 1970s, all the bitter fears of the West Indian residents were revived. They were exacerbated in 1970 by a violent confrontation between police and West Indian demonstrators in an incident that came to be known as 'the Mangrove Restaurant Case'. The incident led to a protracted court case against nine West Indian leaders, some of whom later became deeply involved in the organisation and staging of Carnival. Among them was Darcus Howe, since 1974 editor of the periodical *Race Today* which has consistently championed the Carnival, and who in the last four years has also been Chairman of the Carnival Development Committee. The restaurant in question became the Carnival centre, where artistic judges stand to select the best bands and masquerading groups and distribute prizes contributed by the proprietor.[8] At the same time, the solidary white–black community formed during the previous decade on the basis of neighbourliness, and of joint struggle for improved housing conditions and public amenities, was shattered by the building of a monstrous motorway fly-over, the A40, which dissected the area, causing massive disloca-tion, dispersal, and the rehousing of many inhabitants in different locations outside the area.

The West Indians' reaction to these conditions took different forms. Their trust in joint white–black organisations, such as trade unions and political parties, was shaken. Leaders began to advocate the development of exclusively West Indian formal organisations. The ideologies, methods, and policies of Black Power groupings in the USA were studied and, when possible, applied. On the whole, however, the development of a single all-West Indian formal organi-sation has been thwarted by a number of factors, and the various associations have so far been fragmentary and some rather ephem-eral.[9]

These circumstances prompted a strong movement towards an increasingly homogenised cultural identity which would serve to in-fuse West Indian consciousness, facilitate communication between various sections of the community, and foster viable leadership in several fields. Where formal, associative organisation proved diffi-cult or inadequate, communal mechanisms were called upon. A widespread, active, and at times conscious search for a homogeneous West Indian culture began in art, literature, drama, music, dancing, and religion. A great deal has been achieved but, apart from pop music, these cultural forms have so far involved only relatively small audiences. The Carnival, on the other hand, has proved over the years to have immense possibilities for cultural expression and hence indirectly for mass political mobilisation. Carnival can absorb and integrate a variety of artistic traditions and other cultural forms and can involve different types of groupings within a symbolic unity in sustained activities almost throughout the year.

The 1971 and 1972 Carnivals were rather poorly staged and attended affairs. Racial tension dampened neighbourhood enthusiasm. With the withdrawal of Mrs Laslett as organiser, with the rehousing of many residents away from the area, and also with the waning of hippy and other nonconformist movements in Notting Hill, there was less white participation and interest in Carnival. Those whites who continued to participate had no clear concept of the event or a grasp of the arts and conventions involved. The West Indians on the other hand, initially under predominantly Trinidadian leadership, knew what Carnival was, and had the tradition, the experience, the artistry, and, increasingly, the motivation to seize on the event, revitalise it, and make it exclusively their own. What they lacked was organisation and leadership. A gifted young Trinidadian, Leslie Palmer, fitted the role; within four years he had completely revolutionised the event, transforming its structure and content almost beyond recognition. He himself was too young to have mastered the Carnival tradition before emigrating to Britain many years earlier. He subsequently went back to Trinidad, looked closely at the organisation and artistic forms of the celebration, and came back to London to work on the Carnival. In particular, he concentrated on the mobilisation of steel bands and masque[10] groups.

Quite apart from its content, the tradition of Carnival is itself of great symbolic significance to the Trinidadians. In Trinidad it was originally celebrated by white plantocrats in the island. After emancipation in the 1830s, former slave islanders joined in large numbers and within a short time came to dominate Carnival and drove the masters away from its street processions. During the following decades they changed the character of Carnival with the introduction of new musical forms, new dances, and new forms of masquerading, infusing into the celebration African artistic patterns. They consistently used it to criticise and ridicule the ruling classes and their culture and over the years had frequent clashes with the police. The authorities attempted to impose restrictions on it and occasionally even to abolish it. At times they passed legislation prohibiting the use of drums, on the grounds that they were disturbingly noisy and incited rowdiness. They also banned the wearing of masks, on the grounds that some men committed crimes while thus disguised. But the black population often managed to get round these prohibitions by inventing replacements for drums and masks, and over the years Carnival became an organising mechanism for protest and opposition. With the independence of Trinidad, the political situation changed and the celebration today is a national, government co-ordinated, middle-class dominated, tourist oriented affair, in which men and women from different ethnic, religious, and other social groups participate. Thus to the Trinidadians in Britain, Carnival was the symbol of emancipation, resistance, protest, and triumph.[11]

The steel band, which has so far formed the backbone of Carnival, is also a Trinidadian invention. When the colonial establishment banned the beating of drums, the black carnivalists began to experiment with various means of producing rhythm for dancing. At different times they tried the African shac-shac,[12] bamboo sticks, spoons in bottles, biscuit tins, dustbins. In the 1940s they eventually discovered the musical possibilities of the 44 and 55 litre oil drums. By heating the base of the drum, carefully beating and lowering it, then raising sections, they could alter its frequency of vibrations to produce a limited range of notes. With the drums cut in varying lengths, a full range of notes and tones could be produced. A steel band thus consists of low-tenor pans, double pans, high-tenor pans, cello pans, guitar pans, tenor-bass pans, and bass pans.[13]

Like Carnival, the steel band has acquired a powerful symbolic significance, well beyond the making of loud rhythms; and like dominant symbols generally, it has acquired different, sometimes contradictory, meanings. In the first place, there is a feeling of pride and elation at its invention, and many Carnival leaders emphasise that the pan[14] is the only musical instrument invented in the twentieth century. Indeed, there are currently attempts in both Trinidad and Britain to play classical music on it.[15] At the same time, with its rust, rough edges, and clumsy appearance, the pan is a symbol of poverty and social disadvantage, a protest that in lands of plenty, endowed with so many sophisticated musical instruments, a people should be forced to pick up abandoned shells to express their artistic feelings.[16] This symbolic value of the pan is manifest when one considers that the simple pan is today more expensive than many ordinary musical instruments. The oil drum itself costs only a few pounds, but heating, beating, grooving, cutting, and tuning it has become a highly specialised, labour-intensive profession practised by a few West Indian families in London. The final product today costs well over a hundred pounds. With a steel band consisting of about twenty pans, costs can be substantial.

The steel band transforms the people who play in it and dance to it, and fosters links between them. One leading steel band man said that 'the steel band was born in violence and it expresses violence'. In Trinidad the bands were initially formed by neighbourhood gangs of unemployed youth, who staged night raids on industrial premises to obtain the oil drums. When no empty drums could be found, they simply emptied full ones, moved them into a hiding place, and painted them immediately to hide their identifying marks. The pans served as 'military' drums when attacks were staged on rival gangs from different neighbourhoods. This is why parents, church, school, and police had always opposed bands.[17] Between band members, a deep life-long bond is formed.

Panmen literally hammer the steel furiously to express their built-up outrage against past oppression and indignities as well as against discrimination and injustice. (Darcus Howe (1976: 175) writes that, infuriated by the police raid on the Mangrove Restaurant during the 1976 Carnival, he had to join one of the bands and spend two or three hours 'knocking hell out of steel' in order to regain composure.) Theirs is the sound of protest, the loud reverberating sound of twenty strong men together beating 'the iron' in the heart of densely populated London. The impact cannot fail to be eloquent, the more so as it almost invariably leads to complaints by neighbours, no matter how well-meaning the players are. The effect of the pan beat on the followers who 'jump' to the rhythm is electrifying. Like a football team, every band has its supporters who follow its performance during the year and who jump behind it on Carnival day. They support it financially, physically, and morally.

The nature of steel band involvement in Carnival during this period can be seen in the development and organisation of Zulu,[18] one of the foremost steel bands in Britain, prize-winner in successive Carnivals. Its founder and musical arranger, known as its Captain, is John Baker. Baker emigrated to London from Trinidad in 1968 and soon was shocked by the extent of discrimination; he sought to re-establish his identity as Trinidadian. He set out to organise a band, and in 1973 was approached by Leslie Palmer, who invited him to participate in Carnival that year. He got about twenty panmen together, trained them, and eventually participated in Carnival, his band linking with a masque group. The next year Zulu established its own masque section.

Zulu's general organiser has been Malcolm Thomas. He came from Trinidad in 1973. There, in deference to his middle-class parents' wishes, he had no contact with steel bands or Carnival. Nor had he himself felt any strong inclination to join. But when he came to Britain his attitudes began to change. His brother-in-law was a member of Zulu, and Thomas, being a newcomer, followed the band as supporter. Then, he explains, he felt that in order to assert his Trinidad identity he had to become active in the band. 'Here in Britain we need the steel band more than in Trinidad', he argues. He learned to play the pan and filled in for absent members. When one member eventually dropped out, he took his place. The band

discovered his organisational abilities and entrusted him with organising the masque section. Two separate committees were set up, one
for the pan section and one for the masque section. In 1978, the two
committees merged and Thomas became chairman. He set up five
masque sectors, in five different Greater London neighbourhoods,
each sector having its own leader. In the preparation for Carnival
Thomas visited the different sectors and met with local West Indian
groups, seeking suggestions for the masque theme for the forthcoming Carnival. He then presented the various suggestions to the band's
central committee, which eventually decided on the specific theme to
be adopted, taking into consideration such factors as costs, weight of
mask, and colour. After a professional artist drew up the sketches
and designs, an all-night fête was held in a Kensington club, where
designs of the various costumes were displayed so that followers
could decide which costume each would choose. While the band
played and slides of previous Carnivals were screened for a large
audience in an adjoining room, people registered orders for the
costumes and paid a deposit towards the cost.

Further down the Zulu hierarchy, one of the five sector leaders is
Andrew Davis. He came to London from Trinidad in 1960, and
joined Zulu as supporter in 1973. He does not play pan, preferring to
lead in masquing and dancing. He said, 'Carnival is inside our blood.
It is ours and cannot be taken from us. There is nothing degrading
about it. Yes, it began in slavery, but that is part of history.'

With steel bands, Palmer also mobilised enterprising artists to
design and make costumes and masks in keeping with Trinidadian
traditions. One artist who has since participated in every Carnival,
winning a prize almost every time, is Lawrence Noel. Like Malcolm
Thomas and others, he had little to do with Carnival in Trinidad. He
had been a school teacher since he came to Britain in the early 1960s;
in 1973 Palmer, who was his friend, pressed him to work for Carnival.
His wife urged him to participate and he himself was feeling the need
to establish a West Indian identity within British society. He
accepted the challenge and applied himself to the art of wire-bending
for making head masks. Today he regrets not having started this
artistic activity earlier. He runs an art club for West Indian youth
called the Trinbago, with a membership of about 200. A few weeks
before Carnival 1978, I visited him at his house in East London. The
entire household – all members of the family, including Noel's wife –
were busy making masks and costumes for the scores of mas players
who had registered for Carnival. Coils of wire, cloth, brightly coloured feathers, steel-cutters, finished masks, and masks from
previous Carnivals filled every room and corridor. In the 1973 Carnival Noel joined with a steel band which had no masque section and

he has been with them ever since. He emphasises the educational character of his work, hoping to impart his techniques and art to as many young West Indians as possible. He works with his family and pupils all the year round, not just for the Notting Hill Carnival but for other appearances. His club has been featured in many other festivals and has appeared on television. In choosing a masque theme for Carnival, he is guided by the potential for colourfulness, exoticism, within reasonable costs, as well as motif. In 1977 his theme was 'Red Indians', his choice being inspired by admiration for the American Indians who had fought so bitterly and valiantly against foreign domination.

A different type of artist is Larry Forde, sometime Mas Officer of the Carnival Development Committee and now its secretary, as well as the leader of a masque band called Sukuya. He came to Britain in 1954. He is widely read in mythology, symbolism, costumes, African art generally and African masks in particular, and is a full-time artist. He develops a theme for Carnival after a great deal of thinking, then draws designs for the various costumes and masks, subsequently employing art students to cut the cloth and execute them. His themes are elaborate and complex. His subject for 1977 – the Jubilee year of the coronation of the Queen of England – was 'Mansa's Guests in Regina's Feast', a subtle artistic composition combining African, British, and Caribbean elements.

Thus the 1971–5 period saw the introduction to Britain of the Trinidadian carnival tradition, developed over some 150 stormy years, with its concepts, techniques, arts, conventions, and symbolism. These have been adapted to serve the new interests of a West Indian population, most of whom came from Caribbean islands that had no carnival tradition.

Youth and the Jamaican connection (1976–9)

The next period witnessed new developments in the structure of Carnival, both political and cultural. On the political side, it saw the sudden appearance on Notting Hill streets of a new generation of West Indian teenagers, born and educated in Britain. It is a generation of alienated, disillusioned, demoralised, and rebellious youth, whose plight has affected their parents, souring their relation to British society. Many of these teenagers have been underachievers in school. A working party of the Black People's Progressive Association and Redbridge Community Relations Council, including both teachers and parents, investigated the reasons for this poor educational performance and concluded that the development of a negative self-image in a hostile society was the central cause of West Indian underachievement. British society portrays black people in a negative fashion, and this attitude is internalised by some West Indian children. The resultant poor self-identity, can lead to a lack of confidence and a reduction in motivation which in turn can affect schoolwork.

(BPPA/RCRC 1978: 11)

A scarcity of jobs compounded by discrimination results in a large proportion of West Indian school leavers being unemployed.[19] Many of them spend their time hanging around the streets in neighbourhood youth gangs. Inevitably some end up in trouble with the police. Even those who do not actually commit an offence are sometimes suspected by the police and arrested because of mistaken identity or simply for behaving 'suspiciously'.[20]

The youth made their first massive and sudden appearance in Carnival in 1975. Palmer had introduced stationary discos under the motorway fly-over to attract them. A commercial radio station, Capital Radio, which broadcasts pop music most of the time and to which most of them used to listen, became a Carnival patron that year and urged its listeners to attend. On Carnival day, a mobile broadcasting relay unit was placed on a double-decker bus, and the station's disc jockeys went on the air for four hours, reporting live the developments of the festival. The station also donated prizes for the best artists. That was the first Notting Hill Carnival to be attended by about a quarter of a million people. Inevitably in such a crowded gathering there were hundreds of cases of pickpocketing, camera snatching, illicit sale of alcohol, damage to gardens in the residential area. Only a few policemen were present and they could do little.

For the next Carnival, in 1976, over 1,500 policemen were on hand, and, judging from many eyewitness and newspaper reports, they were highhanded and severe.[21] The youth reacted violently. Some of them, loosely organised in gangs, staged lightning attacks on the police with bottles and stones and dispersed rapidly among the crowds to regroup later. Hundreds of policemen and some civilians were injured and taken to hospital.

That confrontation had serious and wide-ranging repercussions. For the present discussion, our concern is with the effect on Carnival. It was argued by many of the leaders and some outside observers that the youth resorted to violence because they had no means of active artistic participation.[22]

Carnival had until then been organised principally by Trinidadians along traditional Trinidadian lines. But the majority of the West Indian immigrants in Britain are from other Caribbean islands, particularly Jamaica, that have no tradition of carnival or steel band music. In Britain the young in particular, including the children of Trinidadian parents, had had little interest in Trinidad's carnival traditions. Their 'counter-culture' is expressed and dramatised through the lyrics and rhythm of reggae, and through the concepts, beliefs, symbols, and practices of Rastafarianism, with both cultural forms tending to be linked, particularly in the songs of Bob Marley and his band, the Wailers.[23]

Reggae songs speak of violence, blood, fire, police, oppression; but also of love and Jah Rastafari, the Black God who would redeem the Black People and take them back to the Promised Land, Africa.[24] Both reggae and Rastafarianism developed dramatically during the 1960s in the slums of Kingston, Jamaica, whence they soon spread throughout the rest of the black diaspora. In Britain, both movements have been embraced by the British-born West Indian youth. Certain conditions in Jamaica resembled those in Britain, and the new cultural forms could thus be easily transplanted to Britain. During the last three years, a British-based reggae has emerged in the music and songs of such West Indian groups as Aswad, the Cimarons, and Steel Pulse. Some of this music reflects the black experience in Britain. But because these groups have to cater also for other British audiences, their sounds and lyrics are seen to be 'adulterated', and the youth's attention thus remains fixed on Jamaica, whence the latest 'sounds' are eagerly awaited.

Reggae and Rastafarianism gave British-born West Indian youth a world view, political philosophy, an exclusive language, rituals, special forms of appearance and lifestyle, and ecstasy through music, dancing, and marijuana smoking. More significantly, together they have become articulating principles for the formation of primary neighbourhood groups, who move in the slums of the inner city to attend one sound system or another.[25]

Thus for the young West Indians, who today form a large proportion of Britain's West Indian population, reggae is the idiom of cultural and social expression. This fact was not lost on the Trinidadian leadership of the Carnival, who sought means to accommodate the new music. After the 1975 Carnival, sound systems playing reggae records were installed along the route of the procession, as well as under the motorway fly-over. But these arrangements proved unsuccessful because they split the event into an active, mobile procession, and passive, fragmented, stationary, record-playing discos. The young were restless to do something rather than just listen on the spot.[26] The issue became serious in the wake of the 1976 violence. Two questions arose: whether reggae would blend with steel band music in creating carnival revelry, and whether sound systems could be made mobile.

Most Carnival leaders and steel band organisers were emphatic that reggae records were not suitable for a mobile carnival. The steel band plays continuously for a long stretch of time, and thus provides the basis of uninterrupted rhythm for dancing and marching. Reggae records, by contrast, are short, lasting only a few minutes and thus lack continuity. Revelry involves jumping, and this fits pan rather than reggae which, some people believe, contains a melancholic element. Further, there is the ideological argument that reggae sound systems provide 'consumerist music', not live music, in contrast with steel bands. Instruments used in reggae are manufactured, European-invented instruments, while the pan is West Indian through and through.

There are also technical difficulties. Music for revelry on the road requires powerful sounds, and this is provided naturally by the steel band. In sound systems, too, there is emphasis on the power of sound provided by strong amplifiers; many of the hundreds of sound systems operating in West Indian neighbourhoods in Greater London boast of having up to 1,000 watt amplifiers. But on the road, where high volume is even more necessary than indoors, it is difficult to provide sufficient battery strength for such powerful amplifiers. There is also the difficulty that mobility would disturb the needle on the record, though this has proved to be the easiest of the technical problems to resolve, through cassettes instead of records.

In Carnivals 1977, 1978, and 1979 there was great progress towards resolving some of these artistic and technical problems. In the first place, there were sustained efforts to bring steel band and reggae music into some kind of accommodation in the taste of the West Indian population generally. Young people are being educated in steel band music and many schools with large numbers of West Indian children now have steel bands.[27] In parties organised by the Carnival committees for the young, steel band and calypso regularly alternate with reggae. The BBC daily radio programme *Black Londoners*, under the artistic direction of West Indians, provides the two kinds of music. In recent years there has also been a tendency for some reggae bands to include among their instruments one or two pans; on the other hand, some steel bands employ one or more of the more conventional musical instruments. In all pre-Carnival dances, fêtes, launching parties, gala performances, afternoon parties for children, both types of music are performed. Some ingenious devices have also been developed to make the record-playing sound systems more like live music and more adaptable to local conditions in their tunes and lyrics. West Indian sound systems in Britain today employ expensive, highly elaborate electronic equipment that enables the operators to 'intervene' in the recorded sound, raising some sound elements and lowering others. More significantly, many systems now employ, in addition to the disc jockey, a toaster, i.e. an artist who, against the background of recorded reggae rhythm, improvises songs, poetry, current affairs comment, or conveys political messages; his function in this respect thus resembles that of the traditional Trinidadian calypsonian accompanying the steel band. Finally, elaborate devices have increasingly overcome the technical problems of putting sound systems on mobile platforms and providing enough battery power to produce loud music. Thus, in the 1978 and 1979 Carnivals there were some mobile sound systems on the streets of Notting Hill followed by groups of dancers.

As an indicator of these developments in the cultural forms and politics of Carnival, I turn to a brief account of a small masque group called Lion Youth. The group was first organised in 1977 by two young women, from Jamaica and Guyana. Both women were graduates of an arts college in North London; both had worked behind the scenes in previous Carnivals as designers of costumes, working anonymously for leading Carnival men.

Early in 1977 they decided to form their own masque group. They resented the domination of Carnival by males, when, they argued, most of the preparation and work were done by females. Indeed, one of them said that women were the pillars of the whole West Indian community in Britain. The two women also resented the domination of Carnival by Trinidadians, when the majority of West Indians were from other islands. They were both in continual contact with black teenagers and thus well aware of the problems, thoughts, and sentiments of the new, British-born generation of West Indians. They wanted to capture the mood of the youth and thus chose for their first masquerading theme Rastafarian representations. One of them explained that she herself had always been interested in African messianic movements and was full of awe and admiration for the Lenshina prophetic movement.[28]

They approached for support the church of a section of the Rastafarian movement known as the Twelve Tribes of Israel. Church members responded favourably and provided the group with space for a workshop and with food during the weeks of preparation. The two women also elicited financial support from different sources; the black bookshop New Beacon, the masque band Sukuya, the Carnival Development Committee, and the Race Today Collective. Twenty-five girls and two boys appeared in the masquerade in colourful procession, the girls wearing costumes in gold, red, and green, a combination representing the Ethiopian flag and also the colours of the

Rastafarian movement. They carried umbrellas bearing the Lion of Judah and the Star of David, and a banner commemorating Marcus Garvey, regarded as the galvanising spirit of the black liberation movement of the 1920s and 1930s and in effect the founder of Rastafarianism.[29]

Lion Youth's appearance in the 1977 Carnival was acclaimed as a significant success. One of the two leaders returned to the West Indies immediately afterwards, but the other worked energetically for a whole year to organise a bigger masque band for the next Carnival. About ninety girls and boys aged between 15 and 18 registered to take part. The theme chosen was 'Yut War' (Youth War). In view of the group's success in the previous year, the Arts Council granted her about £900 in aid for the preparations. About fifty local West Indian men and women, many of them parents of the participants, helped. The leader contacted a well-known sound system called People's War, run by two brothers, to provide reggae music for the street procession on Carnival day. Half the Arts Council grant was spent on equipment to render the sound system mobile. The masquers paid £8 each for their costumes. The leader of the group aimed to involve as many people in preparations for Carnival as possible and hoped to establish her band as a training framework, teaching the young to make their own costumes and masks, decide on their own themes, provide their own music and develop their own consciousness of the problems affecting the lives of the West Indians.

What the story of Lion Youth indicates is that a new generation of British-born youth appeared during the 1976-9 period on the streets of Notting Hill to participate in Carnival and to develop new themes and new artistic forms, and thereby to change the structure of the event. Carnival is thus being continuously transformed, within certain cultural and social conventions, into an expression of and an instrument for the development of a new homogeneous West Indian culture, transcending affiliations with islands of origin in confrontation with the economic and political realities for the West Indians in contemporary Britain.

Carnival as a politico-cultural movement

The division of the history of Carnival into three distinct periods is to some extent arbitrary, for we are dealing with a large-scale, ongoing, politico-cultural movement within a dynamic and complex post-industrial society. In this movement political issues and artistic forms are intimately related.

On the political side there has been over the years a continual mobilisation of West Indians from different islands of origin, from different localities of residence within Britain, from different age groups, and from the two sexes. If these immigrants were integrated economically and socially within British society they would not need such an exclusive gathering. This was to some extent evident during the 1960s which witnessed co-operation across ethnic lines over common class issues. But unemployment and discrimination in various fields drove them to seek co-ordination of political action. However, no formal all-West Indian association has so far evolved. The West Indian Standing Conference, an affiliation of more than twenty different organisations, has so far been a loosely knit group, which has yet to win the confidence, support, and loyalty of the majority of people.[30] Effort is being made to establish functional, specific, formal associations, such as the Black Parents' Association which is concerned with the schooling of black children. On the whole, however, the development of associative organisations has so far been inhibited by a variety of factors that cannot be analysed here.[31] One is a deep suspicion among West Indian working-class people of all organisations, a suspicion probably born of past experience. They simply fear that any organisation they join will enable 'the system' to control them. This is probably the reason why, for example, such a deep-rooted spiritual movement as Rastafarianism remains very largely unorganised. The Rastas simply carry God with them wherever they go. Thus, apart from two numerically insignificant organisations – the Twelve Tribes of Israel and the Ethiopian Orthodox Church – the masses of Rastas in both Jamaica and Britain have not evolved an established church with an established ritual hierarchy and a clearly recorded doctrine. The movement, massive as it is, is completely acephalous, decentralised, mercurial, and elusive, leaving the police and the authorities in both countries completely in the dark. This may be its strength, though also its weakness, in that the movement is lacking in corporate co-ordinating mechanisms.

But organisation need not be associative, for it can be informally articulated through communal relationships and cultural forms. The organisational functions of group boundaries, communication, and authority can be articulated in terms of symbolic forms. Carnival, as suggested earlier, is one of these forms, and because of its immense political and cultural potentialities has proved efficacious in many respects. It has infused collective consciousness among West Indians and has continually drawn public attention to the plight of West Indian youth. It has fostered numerous overlapping groupings whose members interact continually, exchanging information and talking over shared problems. Carnival itself is the occasion for reunion among friends and acquaintances who would not otherwise meet.

Many men and women say they go to Carnival to meet people whom they have not seen for a long time.

These political–organisational functions of Carnival are in a dialectical relation with the cultural, artistic forms of Carnival. They continually impinge on carnival music, masquerading themes, and calypso lyrics. The cultural is structured by the political, though it is not determined by it. There is a great deal of continuity of cultural forms, but this is not the result of regression into the past. The Trinidad carnival traditions have been developed in the course of a century and a half of experience and of trial and error. Three distinct media of artistic expression have been developed to highly sophisticated conventions: music for the road, masquerading themes and techniques, and lyrics of social comment and political satire. These conventions are now formulated in terms of elaborate rules maintained in each of these fields by panels of judges, who every year regulate competitions between various groups and individuals. Many African traditions have been built into these conventions: African drumming, mask-making and masquerading, the West African institution of praise and satire-singing. Artistic conventions are being continuously refined and developed in both Trinidad and Britain. In Britain, the artistic traditions of Jamaica are now being brought to bear on these arts – a significant process of cultural homogenisation, similar to that of 'supertribalisation' reported for Africa – to express as well as to bring about unity across islands of origin.

Some Carnival leaders believe that Britain offers greater potential for developing carnival arts than Trinidad. Materials for masks and costumes are more readily available in Britain, as are college-trained West Indian designers and artists.

As time goes on, a significant new dimension is added to carnival culture. The movement becomes more deeply rooted in people's psyches as it inevitably fosters the formation of special groupings whose members interact with one another in primary relationships. There are now countless overlapping networks of stable relationships of amity among thousands of people who are active for most of the year in Carnival preparations, to say nothing of the masses of supporters. Among the West Indians generally, extended kinship ties are limited, and people establish close primary relationships with friends.[32] The bonds of friendship are indeed deep and strong. Most men and women spend all their spare time in small, intimate groupings. Thus, the bonds between members and supporters of a steel band, for instance, are powerful and long-standing. To take one example, Darcus Howe was a member of Renegade Steelband in Trinidad, and although he has lived in London for many years he regularly visits the band, of which he is a 'life member'; in the 1978

Notting Hill Carnival he arranged for the band to come to London to participate in the event, along with a band he had formed in Brixton. Again, a public seminar scheduled by the Carnival Development Committee in preparation for Carnival 1978 was cancelled when a young member of an affiliated steel band suddenly died. The various masque groups, calypsonians, and steel bandsmen have considered one another intimate friends for many years. These overlapping networks of friendship have come about in the course of the struggle and preparation for Carnival, and interaction within them often goes beyond Carnival affairs. If we superimpose on these networks those of the numerous primary neighbourhood groupings of Rastafarians and sound systems' supporters who, increasingly, are hooking into the networks of Carnival artists and leaders, we find that what has evolved is a gigantic network for communication, the infusion of consciousness, and the co-ordination of action. These primary relationships are governed by a whole set of values and norms, and sometimes also of ritual beliefs and practices, and thus become related to existential issues. In this way the culture of interpersonal relationships of amity becomes involved in the artistic activities of Carnival.

The dialectic between political and cultural variables involved in Carnival operates on different levels: on the level of the whole collectivity of West Indians in Britain, on the levels of island groupings, neighbourhoods, artistic groups, age groups, and on the level of leadership. The collectivity becomes aware of its current problems, deliberates on them, and probes for solutions. As its members differ in age, sex, experience, and other characteristics, they stimulate one another, and in the process some prove more particularly creative in tackling one or another of the corporate issues, and thus assume crucial roles in the mediation between cultural and political issues. In the process, they manipulate traditional symbols, modify others, or create new ones. Leslie Palmer perceived the plight of the West Indians in Britain in the early 1970s and their need for a distinctive and exclusive expression through Carnival. More than others at the time he had the vision, the organisational skills and the determination to mobilise the Trinidad carnival traditions and its arts. Malcolm Thomas, who had nothing to do with carnival back in Trinidad, experienced after only one year in Britain a compelling urge to express his identity in steel band music, and later to help others by applying his organisational skills to mobilise talents, ideas, and personnel for the Zulu steel and masque band. The two leaders of Lion Youth were in their own way even more inventive, for they went beyond the traditional symbols to express and guide the mood of the West Indian youth generally in the late 1970s in terms of a new artistic–political synthesis.

Some leaders combine artistic and political organisational abilities in equal measure; others are inclined more to the one sphere than the other. Darcus Howe is a leading political activist and is at the same time a committed carnivalist, playing mas, beating steel, organising new bands. His role in bringing art and politics together is paramount. By contrast Selwyn Baptiste, Director of the Carnival Development Committee, though partly concerned with political issues is essentially an artist providing leadership for other artists. He has close primary relationships with many bands and his influence on them is significant. Similarly, Larry Forde specialises in masque-designing and is in close contact with masque bands. Others are more politically inclined. Thus leadership is a collective process in which all members of the collectivity are involved, each contributing to the corporation their specialised effort, all the time bringing political and cultural factors to bear on one another.

The irreducible in culture

Politics and culture are dynamically related in the development and structure of Carnival. But Carnival, like all other symbolic forms, is not exhaustively reducible to either of these variables. It is a bivocal form, an ambiguous unity of cultural and political significance.

Despite the crucial part played by politics in shaping the structure of the cultural event, it would be futile to try to explain, or rather explain away, the cultural in terms of the political. On the contrary, cultural symbols and the communal relationships they generate and sustain are so powerful in their hold on people that political groups everywhere, including the state, always attempt to manipulate them in their own interests.[33] This is a fundamental theoretical issue, but instead of discussing it in abstract terms, I shall deal with it here by examining a serious rift in Carnival leadership that followed the 1976 violence – a rift that resulted in the formation of two rival Carnival committees, the CDC (Carnival Development Committee) and the CAC (Carnival and Arts Committee). Many issues were involved in this split – financial, personal, loyalty to island of origin, neighbourhood – but by far the most basic was whether Carnival was essentially a political or a cultural movement.[34]

The CAC combined two streams of thought whose general orientation can be described as utilitarian. The first is represented by Louis Chase, CAC's chairman until he resigned in the middle of 1978. He is a Barbadian and had had no experience of any kind in carnival or the related arts. He is simply a politician. He argued (Chase

189

1978) that Carnival was essentially a political event and should be used as a political lever to press for reforms and concessions. When his critics charged that he knew nothing about carnival traditions, he retorted that the coal miners' leaders in Britain are not always coal miners themselves. His stance was generally supported by four local black organisations on the committee. The second stream of thought in the CAC was commercially inclined, arguing that Carnival held immense economic possibilities for West Indians, that it could be promoted as a tourist attraction and a base of related industries, producing, for example, special T-shirts, costumes, and masks, thereby providing employment and income for many West Indians.

Until 1976, these leaders were part of one unified Carnival committee. Their views, however, were rejected by other members of the original committee, most particularly by the leading artists in the steel bands and mas bands and by the calypsonians, who eventually quit the committee and re-established themselves without the others as the Carnival Development Committee, proclaiming that *they* were the Carnival, that there could be no Carnival without them.

The CDC artists and organisers were no less politically or financially conscious than the CAC, but they argued that Carnival was essentially an artistic, creative event *sui generis*, of value in its own right, and that any overt, instrumental exploitation of it would destroy it altogether, would in fact destroy its political impact. They implied that only if it were overtly non-political could it be politically efficacious. The journal *Race Today* (July–August 1977: 115) published a long letter to the editor signed by a Rastaman, Dread Ray, in which he argued that turning Carnival into a political protest was a sure way to destroy it, that he did not go to Carnival to demonstrate, but to 'enjoy I self in love and unity with I people'. Larry Forde, at one time Mas Officer and currently secretary of the CDC, expressed sorrow when in the 1977 Carnival a radical political party entered a float bedecked with placards saying: 'The Police are the Muggers'; he himself was probably no less antagonised by the police, but he argued that this kind of sloganeering did not fit the nature of the event, that the same message could in fact have been conveyed indirectly in an artistic form, probably with much greater effect. The CDC chairman, Darcus Howe, has been one of the most radical political activists among the West Indians in Britain, but he maintained that, without any overt political message, the very fact that a quarter of a million people came to Notting Hill to attend Carnival in the face of opposition from the police, the local council, and some local residents, and in the face of internal factionalism, alone was a political event of the first order. The CDC were not unaware of the importance of finance, but maintained that once they commercialised Carnival their arts would become pecuniary arts and various carnival groups would end up becoming instrumental parts of the hegemony of the established system. The committee did seek financial aid from public institutions, particularly from the Arts Council, but insisted on having no strings attached. They said they were not begging but demanding aid by right, as tax-paying citizens. They have at the same time been attempting to raise money from the proceeds of pre-Carnival public performances by various bands so as not to rely on 'the handouts of the state and other charitable trusts' (*Westindian World*, 18 May 1979). Thus the general view of artists and leaders in the CDC is that Carnival is first and foremost a cultural event and that once it is directly politicised its nature will change and the masses will cease to participate, leaving on the road only political activists who would inevitably transform it into a political demonstration.

This cleavage between the two committees should not be exaggerated. The CDC have a few politicians, the CAC a few artists, and the same men often combine concern with both pursuits. The controversy is very much a manifestation of the growth and increasing complexity of the Carnival movement. A similar debate can be found within the Rastafarian movement and also within the Black Power movement in the USA. The issue has been paramount, for example, in the work of the black American poet and dramatist Amiri Baraka, who points out that all writers have their political line, but that the question is how to express this artistically without descending to propaganda (Sollors 1978: 251–3). The black British poet and writer Linton Kwesi Johnson puts the problem differently:

> If politics creeps into art unconsciously, without the writer trying, that is often the most powerful political expression; but when artists try to be political in their art, it usually ends up badly, whether in poetry or in a novel or other art forms. People do not like to be preached at.

> (Johnson 1977)

The same issue was raised by the Marxian dramatist Bertolt Brecht, who directed a polemic against so-called socialist realism which, during Stalin's reign in the USSR, ended up in crude glorification of the Revolution, the Party, and its leaders; that was why the Soviet theatre at the time ended up playing to nearly empty houses (Esslin 1977). Brecht maintained that a truly Marxist theatre should aim at making the audience think for themselves actively and creatively. Another Marxist writer, Herbert Marcuse (1979), has recently reverted to 'two-dimensionality' by attributing autonomy to art, in relation to politics. Along the same line of thought, Irving Howe concludes his argument in *Politics and the Novel* by stating 'At its best, the political

191

novel generates such intense heat that the political ideas it appropriates are melted into its movement and fused with the emotions of its characters' (Howe 1957: 21).

This issue of the nature of the relation between art and politics is part of the broader question of the relation between culture and power relationships, the central theoretical concern of social anthropology.[35] Culture generally is expressed in terms of symbolic forms and performances that are by definition *ambiguous*, having reference to both political and existential issues simultaneously. It is only because of this ambiguity that the symbols of kinship and ritual have been so effective in the articulation of political interests and organisations in both pre-industrial and industrial societies. Once the symbols are reduced to either politics or existential issues alone, they become unidimensional signs, lose their potency and hence their social significance.

Carnivals are irreducible cultural forms, but, like all other cultural forms, are seldom free of political significance. They range in their political functions from the maintenance of the established order, serving as 'rituals of rebellion' (Gluckman 1954), to the articulation of protest, resistance, and violence against that order. The same carnival may vary in its politics over time. Thus, in its pre-emancipation years, carnival in Trinidad was staged principally by the white plantocracy of the island as one way of expressing and maintaining their status and domination; after the slaves' emancipation, it became the expression of protest and resistance by the black population; in recent years it has become a festival of poly-ethnic, inter-class, national integration, fully controlled and supervised by the government (Wood 1968; Hill 1972). Similar changes of function have been observed in the histories of other carnivals.[36]

It is obvious that the dynamic relation between culture and politics is complex and needs further analysis based on the study of different situations, on different levels, under different cultural traditions, using different methodological approaches. I have attempted to probe the potentialities of the dramaturgical approach in applying it to the analysis of a carnival movement in different historical stages within a complex industrial society, focusing in particular on the processes of mediation, or rather the causal interconnections, between political factors and cultural symbols. The part played by various individuals and groups in this mediation was analysed. Leadership was seen as the process by which a collectivity mobilised, revived, modified, created, and integrated various cultural symbolic forms, sometimes derived from different artistic traditions, in reaction to changing economic–political conditions that necessitated communal organisation for the co-ordination of political action.

Towards the end I tried to show how political strategies are – to use Irving Howe's words – melted into a cultural movement, fused with the activities and emotions of people, to produce potent symbols that exist in their own right and are irreducible.

Postscript (1981–90)

Since this article was first published in 1980 there has been an even sharper rise in unemployment, more particularly so among black youth. Yet during the 1980s the Carnival became 'peaceful', thriving artistically and culturally, with its attendance almost hitting the two million mark!

When it had become clear that the event could not be stopped or geographically dispersed, the authorities sought to contain it and co-opt it. Different strategies were set in motion to achieve that, with subtle, loose co-ordination of policy by different public institutions. The radical leaders of the 1970s were skilfully marginalised and duly replaced by moderate men, with emphasis on professionalism. More public money was given to the bands and later to the organisers, totalling £300,000 a year towards the end of the decade. The now annual glossy magazine *Notting Hill Carnival* published greetings and good wishes messages from prominent figures, including the Prince of Wales, the Prime Minister, leaders of the opposition parties, the Archbishop of Westminster, and the Commissioner of the Metropolitan Police. In 1983 a permanent office for the now 'united' Carnival and Arts Committee (CAC) was inaugurated and the first full-time salaried secretary was appointed. The 1980s also witnessed the setting up of the Carnival Development Project, taking about thirty youth at a time and training them in leathercraft, silk-screen printing, steel pan making, wire-bending, and costume-making.

The ideal music to accompany the mas (masquerading) bands on the road continued to be that of steel bands. But as these were relatively few in number, excessively expensive to hire, and complex in their organisation and performance, an increasing number of mas bands hired sound systems to accompany them on the road. These had in the meantime surmounted the technical problems of power for the sound and transportation for the equipment and personnel, and were much cheaper. They also played more suitable music for the occasion, particularly 'Soca', a combination of soul, calypso, funk, and reggae.

But the worst fears of the organisers of the 1970s about the basic structure of the Carnival materialised in the 1980s in that the event was irretrievably split into the mobile mas bands and the stationary sound systems. For although many sound systems accompanied mobile mas bands on the street, many more installed themselves along the Carnival route throughout the area. In 1987 there were 160 of these, with deafening sounds powered by mains electricity taken from private houses. Almost every one of these systems was the centre of a large crowd, with many stalls, selling Caribbean foods, records, books, paintings, T-shirts, and handicrafts. The crowds ate, drank, and danced, often oblivious to the mas bands that passed by. The organisers appealed to the sound system operators to lower the volume of their sound when a mas band passed, reminding them of the effort and expense that had gone into the preparation of mas and of how unfair it was to spoil their performance. The systems' operators promised but rarely obliged. Under pressure from the CAC the sound systems formed their own 'British Association of Sound Systems' in the hope of introducing order and responsibility, but that too had very little effect.

This split in Carnival structure would not by itself have been problematic were it not for the continued concentration of vast and demographically ever increasing numbers of volatile youth, restlessly milling around the sound systems, drinking, smoking marijuana, and generally raring for action. Some of them were organised in 'steaming' gangs, who had perfected strategies and tactics for forceful bag and jewellery snatching. Above all, Carnival gave the youth the opportunity of the year – challenging and outwitting the police, secure in their large numbers and in their perfect anonymity within the crowd.

The Carnival leadership were fully aware of all that and had consistently asked the police not to provoke the youth by their massive presence. Two young members of the CAC wrote in the magazine *Carnival 1981*:

> We as youth cannot really begin to enjoy ourselves at Carnival when we see the State's Army constantly surrounding us in numbers. The same people who within the next year will forget our three days of cultural fun and harmony and turn back on us with their truncheons, handcuffs and vans. Seeing all this builds up tension and frustration within us.
>
> *(Notting Hill Carnival 1981)*

The police were aware of the rage and uneasiness their presence stirred among the young black carnivalists and also of the severe criticism sometimes meted out to them by the national press for their 'high-handedness'. They did their best to present a friendly image. They sought to understand the ideology and traditions of the Carnival. They sent police officers to attend the Trinidad carnival in order to learn more about its organisation and problems. In Notting Hill, police officers met regularly with the Carnival organisers to seek

194

their advice. They even gave *orders* to members of the force to smile. Sometimes a police band played for the carnivalists in the streets, and it played in Westminster Cathedral, where a thanksgiving service took place on the eve of Carnival. Policemen were seen dancing with the carnivalists and were extensively photographed being kissed by revelling black women. At one time they distributed badges with the inscription 'Mets are Magic' ('Mets' referring to the Metropolitan Police). Often, they also tried to abide by the request of the organisers and adopted a 'low profile', turning a blind eye to some arrestable offences.

But they could not afford to under-police the Carnival. It was necessary to control crowd movements for safety, to protect the local residents and shops as well as the large number of tourists and onlookers, and although marijuana smoking was ignored, it was necessary to prevent the sale and consumption of heavier drugs. Thus, as the years went by, greater numbers of police, with ever more sophisticated strategies and techniques of policing, were mobilised for the event. Between 7,000 and 9,000 were in attendance during the two days of Carnival. They were divided into two sections, one of which was kept as reserve around the area, ready with transport and fully equipped with riot gear, while the others were interspersed in twos among the crowd, continually communicating by walkie-talkie through the hierarchy of command with the Control Room. With further surveillance through strategically placed video cameras, the command in the Control Room monitored the situation all the time. As an unpublicised policy, they ignored individual crimes, but up to a limit, said to be about thirty crimes an hour. When that limit was exceeded the riot squads were rushed in to control the situation. This actually occurred on Carnival Monday, 29 August 1987, when towards the evening the rate jumped to nearly 100 crimes an hour, eventually leading to a violent battle between the youth and the police.

In the meantime, the value of housing properties, particularly in London, had soared and a large number of old houses in the Notting Hill area were brought by developers and converted into luxury flats which attracted many 'yuppies' (young upwardly mobile professional men and women who epitomised 'Thatcherite Britain'). These were highly articulate and vociferous residents and were able to agitate against the Carnival. The festival figured as a major issue in the July 1988 Kensington parliamentary by-election. That was followed by a vigorous and sustained national media campaign against the Carnival and its leadership when the *Independent* published (1 August 1988) a summary of a leaked report that had been prepared by management consultants, Coopers & Lybrand, about the organisation of the Carnival. It contained a devastating criticism of the seven members of the governing body of the CAC, describing them as unprofessional, laid back, feeble, and who represented neither the residents nor the performers. The report recommended the replacement of the CAC by fifteen trustees drawn from performers, local residents, and the providers of funds. In editorials, articles, and news features the national press dwelt on the mugging, robbing, and violence that characterised Carnival 1987 and for a while it looked as if Carnival 1988 would not take place. However, the organisers fought back and last-minute negotiations and compromises made it possible to stage the Carnival which, partly thanks to bad weather, passed peacefully.

A few months later the CAC went into liquidation, because of a deficit of over £100,000 in its accounts, and was immediately replace by the CEC (Carnival Enterprise Committee) which emphasised the commercialisation of the festival, amidst mounting accusations of a 'sell-out' by some community groups.

It is evident from the above discussion that during the 1980s the state used its various institutions – financial, ideological, social, political – as well as sheer physical force, to co-opt the Carnival. Except for the 1987 brief riot, that effort seems to have been successful. The leadership was moderate and so were many of the artists and band organisers. The masquerading bands seldom staged political themes and they became concerned mainly with 'pretty mas', with emphasis on the exotic, the colourful, the glittering, the imaginative.

But the Carnival remained nevertheless a political challenge, its greatest achievement in this respect being that it existed at all, on its own ground, in the face of opposition from some of the residents, the police, the local council, and right-wing organisations. It succeeded in infusing a consciousness of common identity and interests among all working-class West Indians. Despite its apparent 'peacefulness' it remained tense, with violence and political challenge never far from the surface – a sharply contested celebration. The moderate leaders of the 1980s maintained the political structure that had been created by the radical leaders of the 1970s. It is still the only viable all-West Indian articulation of an informal political organisation which, partly because of the dispersal of the community in different electoral constituencies in none of which they are a majority, is politically more significant than any Black Sections within national parties or black Members of Parliament.

Notes

1 The material on which this article is based was gathered with the help of a research grant from the Social Science Research Council (SSRC) of Great Britain. The text was written while I was a Fellow at the Center for Advanced Study in the Behavioural Sciences, Stanford, USA, 1978–9, with financial support from the National Science Foundation (Grant No. BNS 76–22943 A02). I am grateful to these institutions for their assistance. I owe a special debt of gratitude to the leaders and artists of the Notting Hill Carnival for giving me so much of their time in discussion. I would like also to record my thanks to my colleagues who commented on an earlier draft of the chapter: Muriel Bell, James Gibbs, Marilyn Strathern, James Watson; and to Hakim Adi, Karen Gunnel, and Colin Bennett for assistance in the research.

2 In 1971 there were about 543,000 West Indians in Britain (SCRRI 1977). Over 55 per cent of them lived in Greater London. They were mostly young, with 62 per cent aged 24 or under. About four-fifths of the men were manual workers – skilled, semi-skilled, or unskilled. In contrast, two-thirds of the employed women were in non-manual, personal service, managerial, and professional categories. West Indians in Britain come from various Caribbean islands, particularly Jamaica. Most of those islands have ethnically heterogeneous populations, with those of African origin forming the majority. In some islands, e.g. Trinidad, about half of the population are Asians, mainly from India. In this chapter the term 'West Indians' refers only to those of African origin. Under the influence of the Black Power movement in the USA, they prefer being called 'black' and calling most of the rest of the native population in Britain 'white'. These two terms are now extensively used in the literature, by both West Indians and others.

3 Inevitably the numbers attending such occasions can only be estimated. This is generally done by newspaper or radio correspondents, and by the police. The figures mentioned in the text are arrived at by collating various estimates. That most frequently given for the Carnivals of 1975 to 1978 is a quarter of a million. Some sources went even to as high as half a million for one Carnival, probably assuming an attendance of a quarter of a million for each of the two Carnival days. The figures given for the 1979 Carnival were smaller.

4 *Culture* is a notoriously ambiguous term used in different senses by different people, including anthropologists. Carnival leaders and artists use it to refer mainly to literature, music, and the other arts. I use it in a wider sense to refer, in addition, to the values, norms, beliefs, and symbolic practices governing interpersonal and group relationships (such as kinship and friendship), or concerning existential issues (such as religion). I use the term *political* in an extended sense referring to the distribution, exercise of, and struggle for economic–political power. Most Carnival leaders use it in a similar sense.

5 The process is discussed at length in Cohen 1969, 1974a, 1974b, 1981.

6 See also Austin 1979.

7 For the history, organisation, ideology, and activities of the National Front, see Walker 1977.
8 There are now plans to turn the Mangrove Restaurant into a community centre. See Gould 1979.
9 For a brief discussion of this problem see Pearson 1977.
10 The term *masque* refers to the representation of a theatrical theme by a band; it is thus different from 'mask' which refers to the covering of the face and/or head. These two terms are discussed by Crowley (1956: 194) who points out that in Trinidad both are 'mas', though they are distinguished clearly in the masquers' minds.
11 This is a very compressed account based on historical literature. See in particular Pearse 1956; Wood 1968: 8–9, 242–7; Hill 1972. Further details are given in Crowley 1956; Powrie 1956.
12 The shac-shac is a dried and hollowed gourd, loosely dressed with a net threaded with beads; when gripped and shaken by hand it produces a high sound which can serve as a rhythm for dancing.
13 For details see Hill 1972; Noel 1978.
14 'Pan' is the steel drum when finished as a musical instrument.
15 See Hill 1972; Noel 1978; also newsletters and leaflets of the Steelband Association of Great Britain.
16 Experimenting with the musical potentialities of the oil drum was initially carried out on empty drums abandoned in Trinidad by the US forces during the Second World War.
17 For a detailed discussion of these points see the interview with Selwyn Baptiste published in *Race Today* 1977: 137–42.
18 This is a pseudonym; so are the names of the band leaders.
19 See Stadlen 1976.
20 A great deal of bitterness and agitation among West Indians in Britain is caused by the continued existence of a law, referred to as 'Sus', enabling the police to arrest people suspected of perpetrating a crime. See Phillips 1976.
21 See, for example, Pilger 1976 writing for the *Daily Mirror*.
22 See Wintour 1977.
23 There is a colossal volume of literature on reggae music, principally in popular music journals such as the weekly *Melody Maker*, *Black Echoes*, and *New Musical Express*, as well as the monthly *Black Music* and *Jazz Review*. West Indian journals in Britain such as the *Westindian World*, *Jamaican Gleaner*, *Afro-Caribbean Post*, publish regular articles on the latest reggae bands and records. For some discussion of the social and political significance of reggae, see Hebdige 1975, 1979; Johnson 1976, 1977a; Troyna 1977; Pryce 1979. Most of this literature deals also with the links between reggae and Rastafarianism. For a more direct discussion of Rastafarianism, see Smith *et al.* 1960; Kitzinger 1969; Nettleford 1970; Wilson 1973: 63–9; Barrett 1977; Cashmore 1977, 1979; Owens 1978.
24 Hakim Adi carried out for me a survey of 420 reggae records produced in 1977 and 1978. Of the total, 23 per cent dealt with political issues, 41

per cent with Rastafarianism, 27 per cent with love, and 9 per cent with a variety of other topics.

25 See Stellman 1974; Phillips 1976; Troyna 1977; Dodd 1978; Hebdige 1979; Pryce 1979. A sound system is a West Indian disco, operated by one or more men, sometimes in one club, but more often visiting different halls. Sound systems vary in the sophistication of their equipment, the collection of records they play, and the originality of their disc jockeys. A 'big' sound system tends to have a core of loyal supporters who follow it wherever it plays and who vote for it in contests with other systems. (For a brief discussion of such contests, see *New Society*, 23 March 1978: 655.)

26 See Wintour 1977.

27 Some school steel bands are organised within the Steelband Association of Great Britain which holds annual festivals during which prizes are given to the best bands and artists.

28 For an account of the Lenshina movement, see Rotberg 1961.

29 For further details about this group, see *Race Today*, 1977: 143.

30 In June 1978 the conference advised West Indians to keep away from the forthcoming Notting Hill Carnival because of the division of the Carnival leadership into two committees (see *Westindian World*, 23 June 1978). But there was no indication that many people followed that advice.

31 For a discussion of some of these factors, see Pearson 1977.

32 For a detailed discussion of West Indian family structure, see MacDonald and MacDonald 1978.

33 For a general discussion of this point, see Cohen 1979. It is interesting that, in the last fifteen years or so, the Soviet Union has concentrated on developing new ceremonial traditions providing politically approved rites of passage that are charged with socialist values. See Binns 1978; Lane 1979.

34 The split into the two committees has been discussed extensively in the mass media. See *Westindian World* 11, 18, 25 February 1977; D. Howe 1977; Chase 1978.

35 For discussion of this issue, see Cohen 1974a, 1979.

36 See Edmonson 1956 for the New Orleans carnival; Gilmore 1975 for the Fuenmayor carnival; Bezucha 1975 for carnival in rural France; Da Matta 1977 for the Rio carnival; Manning 1977, 1978 for the Antigua carnival.

References

Austin, H. (1979) 'Carnival: reflections on a community', *New Community* 7: 114–17.

Barrett, L.E. (1977) *Rastafarianism*, London: Heinemann.

Bezucha, J.B. (1975) 'Masks of revolution: a study of popular culture during the second French republic', in Roger Price (ed.) *Revolution and reaction*, London: Croom Helm.

Binns, C. (1978) 'The development and significance of the Soviet festal and ritual system', paper presented at the Annual Conference of the National Association for Soviet and East European Studies, Fitzwilliam College, Cambridge, 8–10 April 1978.

BPPA/RCRC (Black People's Progressive Association and Redbridge Community Relations Council) (1978) *Cause for Concern: West Indian Pupils in Redbridge*, Ilford: Black People's Progressive Association and Redbridge Community Relations Council.

Cashmore, E. (1977) 'The Rastaman cometh', *New Society* 25 August: 382–4.

Cashmore, E. (1979) *Rastaman: The Rastafarian Movement in England*, London: George Allen & Unwin.

Chase, L. (1978) *Notting Hill Carnival – Street Festival*, London: privately published.

Cohen, A. (1969) *Custom and Politics in Urban Africa*, London: Routledge & Kegan Paul.

Cohen, A. (1974a) *Two-dimensional Man*, London: Routledge & Kegan Paul.

Cohen, A. (1974b) 'Introduction: the lesson of ethnicity', in Abner Cohen (ed.) *Urban Ethnicity*, London: Tavistock Publications.

Cohen, A. (1979) 'Political symbolism', *Ann. Rev. Anthrop.* 7: 87–113.

Cohen, A. (1980) 'Variables in ethnicity', in Charles Keyes (ed.) *Ethnic Change*, Seattle, Wash.: University of Washington Press.

Cohen, A. (1981) *The Politics of Elite Culture: Explorations in the Dramaturgy of Power in a Modern African Society*, Berkeley, Calif.: University of California Press.

Crowley, D.J. (1956) 'The traditional masques of Carnival', *Caribbean Quarterly* 3 and 4: 194–223.

Da Matta, R. (1977) 'Constraint and license', in S.F. Moore and B.G. Myerhoff (eds) *Secular Ritual*, Assen/Amsterdam: Van Gorcum & Co.

Dodd, D. (1978) 'Police and thieves on the street of Brixton', *New Society* 16 March: 598–600.

Edmonson, M.S. (1956) 'Carnival in New Orleans', *Caribbean Quarterly* 3 and 4: 233–45.

Esslin, M. (1977) *Brecht: A Choice of Evils*, London: Heinemann.

Frankenberg, R. (1957) *Village on the Border*, London: Cohen & West.

Frankenberg, R. (1966) 'British community studies: problems of synthesis', in M. Banton (ed.) *The Social Anthropology of Complex Societies*, London: Tavistock Publications.

Gilmore, D. (1975) 'Carnival in Fuenmayor', *Journal of Anthropological Research* 31: 331–49.

Gluckman, M. (1942) *Analysis of a Social Situation in Modern Zululand*, Manchester: Manchester University Press.

Gluckman, M. (1954) *Rituals of Rebellion in South-east Africa*, Manchester: Manchester University Press.

Gould, T. (1979) 'The Mangrove seven', *New Society* 4 January: 5–6.

Hebdige, D. (1975) 'Reggae, rastas and rudies', in S. Hall and T. Jefferson (eds) *Resistance through Rituals*, London: Hutchinson.

Hebdige, D. (1979) *Subculture: The Meaning of Style*, London: Methuen.

Hill, E. (1972) *The Trinidad Carnival: Mandate for a National Theatre*, Austin, Tex.: University of Texas Press.

Howe, D. (1976) 'Is a police Carnival', *Race Today* 8 (9): 173–5.

Howe, D. (1977) *The Road Make to Walk on Carnival Day*, London: Race Today Publications.

Howe, I. (1957) *Politics and the Novel*, Cleveland, Ohio and New York: Meridan Books.

Johnson, L.K. (1976) 'The Reggae rebellion', *New Society*, 10 June: 589.

Johnson, L.K. (1977) 'Jamaican rebel music', *Race and Class*, 397–412.

Kitzinger, S. (1969) 'Protest and mysticism', *Journal of the Scientific Study of Religion* 8: 240–62.

Lane, C. (1979) 'Ritual and ceremony in contemporary Soviet society', *Sociological Review*: 253–78.

MacDonald, J.S. and MacDonald, L. (1978) 'The black family in the Americas: a review of the literature', *Sage Race Relations Abstracts* 3, 1–42.

Manning, F.E. (1977) 'Cup match and Carnival', in S.F. Moore and B.G. Myerhoff (eds) *Secular Ritual*, Assen/Amsterdam: Van Gorcum & Co.

Manning, F.E. (1978) 'Carnival in Antigua', *Anthropos* 73: 191–204.

Marcuse, H. (1979) *The Aesthetic Dimension*, London: Macmillan.

Mitchell, C. (1956) *The Kalela Dance*, Rhodes-Livingstone Paper 7, Manchester: Manchester University for the Rhodes-Livingstone Institute.

Nettleford, R.M. (1970) *Mirror, Mirror*, Kingston, Jamaica: William Collins & Sangster.

Noel, T. (1978) *The Steelband*, London: Commonwealth Institute.

Owens, J.V. (1978) 'Literature on the Rastafari: 1955–1974', *New Community* 64: 150–64.

Peacock, J.L. (1968) *Rites of Modernisation*, Chicago: Chicago University Press.

Pearse, A. (1956) 'Carnival in nineteenth century Trinidad', *Caribbean Quarterly* 3 and 4: 175–93.

Pearson, D.G. (1977) 'West Indian communal association in Britain', *New Community* 5.

Peters, E.L. (1963) 'Aspects of rank and status among Muslims in a Lebanese village', in J. Pitt-Rivers (ed.) *Mediterranean Countrymen*, Paris: Mouton.

Phillips, M. (1976) 'Brixton and crime', *New Society* 8 July: 65–8.

Pilger, J. (1976) 'Behind the frontline', *Daily Mirror*, 1 September.

Powell, E. (1969) *Freedom and Reality*, Kingswood: Elliot Right Way Books.

Powrie, B.E. (1956) 'The changing attitude of coloured middle class towards Carnival', *Caribbean Quarterly* 3 and 4: 224–32.

Pryce, K. (1979) *Endless Pressure*, Harmondsworth: Penguin Books.

Rotberg, R. (1961) 'The Lenshina movement of Northern Rhodesia', *Rhodes-Livingstone Journal* 29: 63–78.

SCRRI (Select Committee on Race Relations and Immigration) (1977) *Report on the West Indian Community*, London: HMSO.

Smith, M.G., Augier, R. and Nettleford, R. (1960) *The Ras Tafari Movement in Kingston, Jamaica*. Mona: University College of the West Indies.

Sollors, W. (1978) *Amiri Baraka/Le roi Jones*, New York: Columbia University Press.

Stadlen, F. (1976) 'The Carnival is over', *Times Educational Supplement*, 26 November.

Stellman, M. (1974) 'Sitting here in limbo', *Time Out* 234: 11–13.

Troyna, B. (1977) 'The Reggae war', *New Society*, 10 March: 491–2.

Turner, V.W. (1957) *Schism and Continuity in an African Society*, Manchester: Manchester University Press.

Turner, V.W. (1974) *Dramas, Fields and Metaphors*, Ithaca, NY, and London: Cornell University Press.

Walker, M. (1977) *The National Front*, London: Fontana/Collins.

Weber, M. (1947) *The Theory of Social and Economic Organisation*, New York: Free Press.

Wilson, B. (1973) *Magic and the Millennium*, London: Paladin.

Wintour, P. (1977) 'Bored enough to riot', *New Statesman*, September: 291–2.

Wood, D. (1968) *Trinidad in Transition*, London: Oxford University Press.

Chapter seven

Striking a bargain

Political radicalism in a middle-class London borough[1]

Iris Kalka

The idea that the modern welfare state, with its growing intrusion into community institutions on one hand, and its increasing bureaucratisation on the other, encourages what has come to be known as 'new ethnicity', has by now been extensively explored (see Glazer and Moynihan 1975; Fox *et al.* 1982; Walzer 1982). The term 'ethnic group', indicate Glazer and Moynihan, is no longer associated with marginal groups at the edges of society, destined to disappear or barely survive. Rather, it denotes groups which are 'major elements of a society' (Glazer and Moynihan 1975: 5). Novak proceeds from this observation to suggest that technology and modernism lie behind the resurgence of ethnicity. Whereas technology 'liberates certain energies for more intense self-consciousness' (Novak 1982: 32), the secular, pragmatic nature of modernism drives people to seek for their 'roots'. Yet even in one and the same place, the upsurge of ethnicity is not uniformly spread. In line with Cohen's (1969, 1974) earlier proposition that interest is a major force in the making and maintenance of ethnic groups, Glazer and Moynihan contend that it is the struggle for power that is ultimately responsible for this new type of ethnicity. It is a matter of 'strategic efficacy', they add, which leads states to pursue the support of groups which are large enough to produce some gains, but smaller than the 'loosely aggregated' social classes.

Given that the state provides incentives for ethnic claims to be made, the question still remains as to *how* precisely these are put forward, and *what* kind of ethnic allegiances emerge in *which* circumstances. These are the questions which this chapter addresses.

There are several reasons for examining a geographical area defined by administrative boundaries. Local authorities in Britain are responsible for administering schemes under which resources are allocated. Hence, they act as mediators between their ethnic population and central government.

Two main schemes have been administered by local authorities since the late 1960s. Both were designed to make services more responsive to the needs of ethnic minorities. In both schemes central government's contribution amounts to 75 per cent of the grants, the rest being financed by the local authority. In Harrow, the staff employed under these schemes are not necessarily members of ethnic minorities. This is particularly true in the case of the scheme known as Section 11, based on the 1966 Local Government Act, which empowers the Home Office to reimburse spending on 'special provision . . . in consequence of the presence within their [local authorities] areas of substantial numbers of immigrants from the Commonwealth whose language or customs differ from those of the host community'. Nearly all Section 11 funding in Harrow was used for English tuition, and mostly white people were employed. Ethnic minority members were more likely to be employed in projects which they themselves initiated, and these were funded by the second scheme, known as Urban Aid.[2]

Although the resources allocated to these schemes increased throughout the 1970s, they were always marginal to mainstream funding. And, as Young has succinctly observed, 'there is a notable lack of agreement on the legitimacy of using either scheme to the *specific* benefit of black populations' (Young 1983: 288).[3]

It should be noted, in this context, that local authorities support a wide variety of voluntary organisations and also aid Community Relations Councils (CRCs), which are the local branches attached to the Commission for Racial Equality. A local authority, though responsible for implementing government's policies, exercises its own discretion in various services which it provides, all of which affect its ethnic population. Considering that local authorities are the main service-providers, their influence is paramount. This situation leads to considerable variation in the amount of resources allocated to, and the nature of, these services in different localities (see Kirp 1979: 44). Finally, local authorities influence public opinion by statements made by Members of Parliament belonging to their constituencies and, indirectly, through their policies and their resource allocation.

The chapter begins with an outline of the background against which the current debate between Harrow Council and its ethnic, mainly Asian, population has emerged. It then proceeds to delineate the 'race relations scene' in the borough, with specific reference to the relevant events and developments that took place in the 1980s. In particular it expands on the various forums created by Harrow Council in which to consult the ethnic community, on the council's influence on the organisation of ethnic minorities in the borough, and on the ideological premises to which both sides resorted in the course of the debate which evolved during this period.

The Gujarati settlement in the London Borough of Harrow

About 1,500 expellees[4] who left Uganda in the autumn of 1972 arrived in Harrow (CRC 1974), a borough which previously had a small Asian population. In 1971 the number of all New Commonwealth citizens in Harrow was about 8,000, or 4 per cent of the borough's population. Ten years later the proportion of the New Commonwealth citizens in the borough's population had increased fourfold.

More than 40 per cent of Harrow's Asian population in 1984 had settled in the borough in the three years that followed the Ugandan expulsion (HEAP 1985). This sharp rise was clearly due to the arrival of the expellees; whereas in 1971 the numbers of those born in India or East Africa were 2,775 and 1,490 respectively (CRC 1976), in 1981 Indian-born residents in Harrow counted 6,407 and East African-born counted 9,914.

In the 1970s there were Asians who aspired and could afford to live in a suburban middle-class area such as Harrow. This was, as Bhachu (1985: 31) indicated in her study of East African Sikhs, a rather attractive option. The neighbouring area to the south of Harrow, the borough of Brent, already had – in the early 1970s – a substantial Asian population. In 1972 it received a large number of Ugandan expellees and Asians settling in Harrow could thus use the services provided in the neighbouring area. Hence, the proximity to a large Asian settlement encouraged the expellees and other Asians to make their homes in Harrow.

Within a short space of time, less than a decade, Harrow was established as an area of substantial Asian population, attracting mainly the better-off Asians. These were Asians who were able to purchase the more up-market property, mostly two- or three-bedroom semi-detached houses built between the wars. Like the majority of the borough's inhabitants, most Asians in Harrow were owner-occupiers.[5]

This said, it should be added that Asians have not been equally dispersed throughout the borough, but have concentrated in its southern, less prestigious wards, where the prices of property have been lower, and the quality of housing poorer. It was not because of the large neighbouring Asian population that Asians concentrated in these wards. The fact that only a small proportion of the incoming Asians lived during the 1970s in Harrow-on-the-Hill, one of the southern, more lucrative parts of the borough, indicates that they were unable to purchase houses in certain parts of the borough. By the 1980s, however, many had begun to move to the northern wards and to Harrow-on-the-Hill.

A comment should also be made on the fact that about 70 per cent of Asian residents in Harrow were of Gujarati origin. The majority of Asians in East Africa came from Gujarat (Bharati 1972) but the movement of Asians following the expulsion was selective. Ismailis, for example, were attracted to Canada because they could join their already settled relatives (Adams *et al.* 1983). It is common knowledge among Ugandan Gujaratis that many Ismailis were settled in Canada, a result, so they say, of the relationship between their leader, Aga Khan, and the then Canadian Prime Minister, Pierre Trudeau (see Wood 1983: 15).

A somewhat similar selection process took place in Britain. Punjabis, the second largest Asian minority in East Africa, preferred to settle in the Greater London area in and around Southall, which was a well-established Punjabi area. Following the initial stage of Gujarati settlement in Harrow, internal migration increased the flow of Gujarati entrants. By 1984, about 4 per cent of the Asian residents in Harrow were Sikh and 12 per cent were Muslim (HEAP 1985).

The arrival of Asians entailed a certain measure of adjustment to a new and unfamiliar environment. Employment and secure tenure were evidently the two main concerns of the new arrivals. The local authority, being the major service-provider, represents the institutional and bureaucratic side of this adjustment, and Asians who were not proficient in English encountered difficulties which led to a poor use of the existing services and facilities. This was already evident in 1972, soon after the expellees arrived. The local authority was aware that the expellees tried, as much as was possible under the prevailing circumstances, to be self-sufficient (see Cunningham 1973). English tuition was available, and the number of English classes grew throughout the 1970s. Yet the council was slow to provide information in Asian languages, or to employ interpreters so as to make services more accessible.

The formation of voluntary associations

During this period Gujaratis, as well as other Asians, began to form a variety of voluntary associations, some of which were branches of already established national organisations. Gujaratis founded caste, religious, educational, and other associations. Caste and religious associations were the most enduring, commanding large resources which were raised, mainly, from their respective members. These resources enabled the associations to set up community centres (in the case of caste associations) and temples or other places of worship (in the case of religious associations). Religious meetings, called *satsangs*, were also held in community centres and private homes (see Michaelson 1987: 41–6).

By the end of the 1970s, plays, lectures, poetry readings, and even alternative medicine sessions and cookery demonstrations, were conducted in the Gujarati language in various venues in the borough. Gujaratis also commuted to neighbouring areas to participate in similar activities.

Official dignitaries were often invited to functions organised by Gujaratis, and the hosts praised the (by now) well-known entrepreneurial spirit of the newcomers and their rich cultural heritage. On one occasion, for example, a caste association invited the Mayor of Harrow to a wine and cheese party. One member described at great length the caste's history, thus conveying the message that his caste members were not to be confused with other Asians (see Cohen 1984/5). The mayor, for his part, addressed the hosts as 'British citizens of Asian origin' (*Harrow Observer*, 14 February 1978), thus failing (intentionally or unintentionally) to grasp the message which they had tried to deliver. As on similar occasions, a donation for charity was made, this time for the mayor's own charity, so the Gujaratis were more successful in conveying the message that they did not – as was often believed – keep their resources to themselves. Events such as this – which showed that Gujaratis relied on their own resources – were designed to demonstrate that Gujaratis were an asset, rather than a liability, to the wider society. In addition, Gujaratis presumably entertained the hope that this generosity towards the wider society would eventually be reciprocated, and not necessarily in kind.

Money was also sometimes donated by individual Gujaratis. For example, a chemist who had a chain of pharmacies organised a charity event to raise money so as to send a sick white child and his family for a holiday. The event began with a Gujarati meal and continued with a programme of Gujarati dance and music. All the guests were Gujarati, apart from the Mayor of Edgware who was the honorary guest.

Individual Gujaratis who donated money, for whatever purposes, were highly praised by fellow Gujaratis. In addition to raising their status within their own social networks, acts of charity were also means of advertising their businesses to a potential clientele. These contributions could also legitimise claims for positions of power, that is, within their associations, but this could be obtained only when substantial contributions were made (see Werbner 1985: 369). In any case, these activities show that already in the 1970s status-seeking Gujaratis tried to broaden their power base, and that new avenues of access to the host society were contemplated.

The most active Gujarati association in Harrow during the 1970s, the Anglo-Indian Art Circle, was founded to – amongst other things – 'promote Anglo-Indian culture and social integration' (*Harrow Midweek*, 7 May 1974). It organised social and cultural events, raised money for local charities, and its founder member often protested against various discriminatory practices. Grievances were expressed, for example, regarding discriminatory practices in the borough's Housing Department. This was not a somewhat belated response to the unwelcoming reception of the expellees in 1972, but rather an expression of the growing power and self-assurance of Gujaratis in general, and this founder member in particular. Eventually, his contacts with council officials were rewarded, and he became the manager of an Asian community centre (see p. 218).

The agitation expressed by Asian associations during the 1970s was sporadic, and there were no associations which acted permanently as pressure groups, i.e. whose main purpose was to influence the local authority or other state institutions. This sporadic response was, on the whole, matched by indifference on the part of the local authority. As the council later admitted, the newcomers of the 1970s were expected to integrate into 'the community' (see pp. 211–12).

Bearing in mind this kind of involvement it seems unjustified to speak of relationships that existed between the local council and the Gujarati community during the 1970s. If there was any ongoing dialogue, it was mediated by the local CRC. The Anglo-Indian Art Circle co-operated with Harrow CRC, and at least to this extent contributed to the consensus that existed at the time. According to this consensus the state, or, for that matter, the local authority, were expected to make minor adjustments to accommodate the ethnic population, mainly by making services more adept at meeting the needs of the newcomers.

The fragile consensus which existed in the 1970s was soon to be shattered.

Race relations on the agenda

Once the borough of Harrow adopted an equal opportunities policy, in March 1980, expectations began to mount that some 'action' would follow, for instance, in the form of carrying out ethnic monitoring. It was widely believed amongst Gujaratis that there were no Asians holding posts in the higher echelons of the council's workforce. Ethnic monitoring[6] was therefore pursued by Gujaratis mainly

to confirm this conviction, in the hope that this would be an intermediary stage that would pave the way to further action.

Several events that took place in Britain during the 1970s made it
difficult for Harrow to remain aloof and stick to the old status quo.
In 1976 the Race Relations Act which was passed in Parliament
imposed on local authorities the obligation to 'eliminate unlawful
racial discrimination' and 'promote equality of opportunity, and
good relations, between persons of different racial groups'. The
Commission for Racial Equality followed with guidelines which all
local authorities were advised to pursue (CRE 1982), and later with
guidelines for London authorities (CRE 1985). It also produced a
Code of Practice to be implemented by all employers in Britain. The
Home Office, for its part, responded to the Race Relations Act with
suggestions to facilitate the acceptance of members of ethnic
minorities to Section 11 posts.

Various local authorities followed the 1976 Race Relations Act
with policy statements, each declaring its intention to remove discriminatory practices in the selection of personnel for its workforce.
Ethnic monitoring, designed to expose these discriminatory practices, was the next step and some local authorities (including the one
adjacent to Harrow, the borough of Brent) set up Race Relations Units.

The equal opportunities policy in Harrow was also intended to
eliminate sex discrimination, in accordance with the Sex Discrimination Act 1975. Yet neither the council nor the ethnic population held
sex discrimination to be a major issue to reckon with. The fact that
the brief of the equal opportunities adviser, subsequently appointed
by Harrow's council, was 'to develop positive initiatives . . . with
particular emphasis on employment practices in relation to the
minority communities' further certified that this statement was effectively addressed to the ethnic population.

This policy statement legitimised concerns with regard not only to
equal access to jobs, but also to equal access to services. The two were
apparently linked, for it was perceived that the appointment of
ethnic personnel, e.g. in the Social Services Department, would
improve the services rendered to ethnic clients. Furthermore, there
was concern over the very nature of some of the services, and
demands were made in the name of 'special needs', e.g. in the case of
Asian elderly people.

The council had to obtain resources to appoint personnel from
the ethnic population, whether from inside or outside the borough.
It probably envisaged that a few posts would satisfy those who began
to advocate that an equal opportunities policy would be meaningless
without redressing the imbalance in employment practices. A
decision to conduct ethnic monitoring in Harrow was taken in 1982.

209

The survey took three years to complete, and the council's reluctance to act kept the issue on the agenda. As a result of the growing awareness that some 'action' was, in any case, necessary, new posts were created. Three Asian social workers were appointed in 1982, and their posts were funded by the Section 11 scheme. These posts were, for the first time, created outside the field of education. They could have hitherto been classified as attempts at making services more responsive. Asian activists, however, now claimed that these new employees constituted a form of cheap labour, because only 25 per cent of their wages were paid by the council. If additional staff were 'really needed', it was argued, their wages should have been paid for from mainstream allocation.

These arguments need to be understood in the context of the overall employment situation in the borough and the fact that the local authority was the largest employer in the area, employing a total of about 8,000 persons (including part-time employees).[7] An implementation of equal opportunities policy had, therefore, far-reaching implications, particularly in areas such as Harrow with large ethnic populations (see *Labour Research* 1986). In addition to the fact that Asians were under-represented in the council's workforce and virtually absent from its higher grades (a fact that was established by the ethnic monitoring survey), unemployment rates were much higher amongst Asians and almost double those of the local indigenous population (HRC 1985). Creating a few jobs under Section 11 could not, of course, reduce unemployment, but this could have diverted the efforts to recruit more ethnic employees to the borough's workforce.

As will soon become evident, this and other matters relating to ethnic minorities became a focus of a continuing debate between the council and representatives of the ethnic minorities.

Consulting ethnic minorities

Several consultation forums were created by the borough of Harrow during the early 1980s, in which ethnic residents were expected to put forward their views on matters that were of concern, presumably, to the entire ethnic population.

The establishment of a Police and Community Consultative Committee (PCCC) in 1982 followed a recommendation made earlier by Lord Scarman, in the aftermath of the Brixton riots.[8] The committee which was established had no executive power. It was administered by the council, but its running costs were reimbursed by the Metropolitan Police Fund (Home Office Guidelines, 16 June 1982).[9] It is interesting to note that the official guidelines of the

Home Office did not specify that consultation should be confined to the ethnic residents only, although the whole exercise was intended to reduce the probability of riot recurrence, and facilitate collaboration between the police and ethnic minorities.

The discussions that preceded the creation of the PCCC were undertaken by the Working Party on Racial Assaults (WPRA), a committee established earlier in 1982 to combat racial attacks in the borough. Hence, it was perceived that the setting up of the PCCC was primarily in relation to the ethnic population. The WPRA, nevertheless, held that 'it would be impractical to seek to achieve exactly equal representation for each individual minority group on the PCCC'. Eventually, when the terms of reference of the PCCC were drawn up, there was hardly any reference to ethnic minorities.

The setting up of this committee illustrates the ambiguity that persisted throughout the early 1980s, and the reluctance to address directly issues that were of concern to ethnic residents. Even the name of this committee makes it blatantly clear that the ethnic population as a whole was expected to remain within the fold of 'the community', as if the borough's inhabitants were bound by no ties other than those implied from sharing the same physical space. The fact that another committee, the Community Liaison Working Party (CLWP), which replaced the WPRA after the 1982 local elections, did not incorporate in its name a reference to the ethnic population is yet another example of this kind.

At this stage Asian activists did not have much influence, and the council usually approached Harrow CRC to obtain the opinion of ethnic residents, e.g. in matters relating to racial assaults.

A somewhat similar procedural problem that arose in 1985 demonstrates that by then ethnic minorities in Harrow had gained much more influence. The issue concerned was the setting up and the terms of reference of a consultative committee, affiliated to the CLWP, which would become a platform for the ethnic residents to present their views to the council. As on previous occasions, councillors were hesitant to set up a forum that would be addressed solely to problems of ethnic minorities in the borough. Suggestions on the nature of this committee were sought and letters from residents' associations soon followed. These associations argued that such a forum would lead ethnic minorities to expect 'an excessively high level of support'. It was also suggested that ethnic minorities should improve their ability to speak English, so as not to remain 'isolated in *the community*' (letters of residents' associations: CWLP minutes, 20 May 1985 (Agenda item No. 7); emphasis mine).

These associations evidently wished to maintain a status quo according to which ethnic minorities would not receive more resources than they had already gained. For this end they were prepared to adjust the concept of community which had been used previously, one which suggested that the borough's inhabitants were socially homogenous; they began to refer to 'the community at large', or, alternatively, to 'all sections' of the community.

The establishment of a consultative committee was eventually approved, with the intention of revising its brief after one year (this was the normal procedure in similar cases). Though no resources were involved, the access of ethnic residents to the council and the influence which they would have gained as a result were sufficient for indigenous residents to raise objections. It is apparent, nevertheless, not only that the residents' associations did not achieve their aim, but also that their appeal on behalf of the 'community at large' met with diminishing success. In other words, attempts made by the veteran local power elite to represent the not-so-new newcomers proved of little effect. In 1986 another consultative committee was established, to review the equal opportunities policy of the borough.

The council, in this process, sought the middle way, for its leading party wished to attract voters on all sides. In 1985, voting became a sensitive issue since local elections were due soon (in 1986), a fact that Asian delegates kept reminding councillors of in the meetings described below.

The hidden agenda – the council

In the course of consultation, councillors became acquainted with delegates, mainly Asians who were involved in one (and often more than one) of Harrow's ethnic associations. This, of course, was a two-way process. However, beyond this apparently trivial fact, which points to the informal aspects of these contacts, the forums had an intrinsic value for the 'race relations agenda' in general, and for the internal leadership of the Asian community in particular.

Asian delegates gradually became familiar with the manner in which council committees conducted their affairs, and decisions resolved and executed. An agenda for each meeting of the CLWP was drawn up by the committee members and was circulated amongst councillors and delegates. At times, information required for a certain discussion, together with the agenda and minutes of previous meetings, were sent only a day or two before a meeting. Ethnic delegates commented on this procedure and also disapproved of the inadequacy of the information provided. Disapproval was expressed in the strongest terms. 'We feel dismayed and humiliated', said one activist, 'by the way you treat us.' Delegates also resented the fact that all meetings were conducted on council premises. 'You should come to us', they said, adding that councillors were isolated and knew little about Asians in the borough.

No sooner had a meeting opened when accusations were made by delegates on the one hand, and 'clarifications' offered by the chairman on the other.[10] When delegates repeatedly enquired about certain items of information, the chairman either apologised for not having them, or said that such information, e.g. on the number of New Commonwealth children in schools, could not be obtained. Complaints and accusations immediately followed. At times, a few months elapsed before information became available. Alternatively, the chairman commented that a certain argument put forward by delegates was of no relevance to the meeting, that it would be discussed at a later date, or that the speaker's opinion was not shared by other delegates. In short, the chairman had a repertoire of stock answers at his disposal. A comment was not 'relevant' when it did not serve the purpose of these meetings as he conceived it. Yet at the same meetings some items which were not listed on the agenda were discussed, often at length.

'We are here to consult you', the chairman often retorted, 'so that you tell us what to do.' This tactic assisted council representatives to assume the role of 'listeners', one which was designed to be passive. Hence, the council rarely came forward in these meetings with suggestions of its own. Meanwhile, delegates began to debate amongst themselves. So, the discussion often became an internal debate in which council representatives could act as 'pacifiers'.

The minutes of the meetings did not reveal fully these proceedings. They did not reflect all the complaints and comments made by delegates, nor did they delineate comprehensively their requests and queries. They were mainly intended to record resolutions, and delegates complained that the minutes were therefore inaccurate. To remedy this situation, delegates later requested that their remarks would be minuted.

It became evident in these meetings that although the CLWP was on the defensive, the formula of response allowed it to avoid responding to many issues raised by Asian delegates, or agreed earlier by both sides to be written down on the agenda.

Eventually, a delegate of one small pressure group spelt out this state of affairs, and pointed to the fact that the chairperson allowed each debate to drift till it became a series of accusations and apologies. 'We are all wasting our time', he concluded. His comment, made at one of these meetings, gained little attention.

In fact, it appears that accusations gradually lost their impact. When councillors were blamed for being racist, they said that they were not and did not like to be called racists. They themselves, it was admitted, were not free of prejudice, but they could be helped by such means as Racism Awareness Training.[11] This was probably designed to complement a self-portrayal of people seeking mutual under-standing, but in the eyes of the activists the lack of initiative did not compensate for what at least some of them saw as sheer racism.

With the passing of time, then, activists became less inhibited about expressing accusations and directing them personally to coun-cil members. No attempts (except on a few occasions) were made to 'calm down' the activists who made them, and the onus of the debate thus shifted from 'action' to questions of morality and social justice.

The debate was couched in terms derived from the institutional interpretation of racism. Some delegates, for example, cited the for-mula according to which prejudice combined with power produced institutional racism (see Sivanandan 1985). This form of racism, it was argued, was embedded in the very ethos of the British estab-lishment and was perpetuated in virtually all British institutions (see Rex 1986: 108–14). The people who had once suffered from colonial-ism were now exploited by more subtle means. Their suffering, which was the prerogative of people whose complexion was dark, turned them all into 'blacks', people who were oppressed and deprived of rights to which they were entitled. Hence, Asian activists who identi-fied themselves as 'black' expected councillors to address them accordingly. It is on these ideological premises that a clear distinction was made between Harrow's 'white' and 'black' residents. This ideology also gave Asian activists the assurance that they were in the right and, to a lesser extent, was utilised as a cohesive force to draw members to several pressure groups that were established dur-ing this period. Nevertheless, the activists who advocated solidarity with all deprived and disadvantaged minorities, were also members of caste and religious associations and at times presented themselves as their delegates. Hence, the benefits which they expected to gain were not always in accordance with those implied from the ideo-logical premises explained above.

Beyond general agreement on these premises, however, activists varied in their opinions as to measures that the council should take. They also differed as to the extent to which a 'conspiracy' existed in the white establishment, i.e. the extent to which co-ordinated attempts were made to bar 'blacks' from positions of power. It is clear, though, that neither side in Harrow entertained a notion of the unity of the other. Asian activists were conscious of personal rivalries between councillors and of differences of opinion within the council workforce. The councillors, on their part, were aware of the attempts of Asian activists to present a united front, in spite of their rivalries (see Werbner, this volume). They were also aware that delegates tried to present themselves as 'leaders of the Asian community', and openly expressed doubts as to the authenticity of this depiction. Such doubts were designed to discredit the authority of the delegates, some of whom represented small pressure groups who counted fewer than fifty members.[12]

Activists of one small pressure group were the most vociferous, often clashing both with councillors and other activists. The last part of this chapter expands on the nature of these rivalries, and explains the various factors involved in their emergence.

The hidden agenda – Gujaratis and Pakistanis

One of the most striking features to emerge from observing the CLWP meetings was the difference in the respective strategies employed by Pakistanis and Gujaratis. Although Pakistanis were very active, Gujarati activists, by comparison, were much more militant. The number of Pakistanis in the borough was small, probably no more than 5 per cent of the Asian population in Harrow. Yet they were over-represented not only in the CLWP but also in the local CRC. The strategies which they adopted, described below, should be explained against the overall composition of the ethnic population in Harrow and its broader implications.

Pakistanis felt that Gujaratis were being favoured by the council, and reiterated the complaint that they were being deprived of using a community centre which was intended to cater for the 'Asian community'. On these occasions it was suggested that the council should compensate them, a suggestion which made plain the competition which existed between the two minorities.

Competition, as the following illustrates, also existed between Pakistani associations. When delegates of two Pakistani associations presented Urban Aid applications, one was asked whether his association could not have applied jointly with the other association. This representative, who was put in a difficult position, argued that the applications concerned different provisions. Both projects, he continued, could benefit Pakistanis in Harrow, but his own was – considering the needs of Pakistanis – more urgent. The delegate perhaps entertained the hope that both projects would be approved. This would have reduced the probability of other Asian associations receiving a grant the same year.

It is worth noting in this context that a rivalry such as existed between Gujaratis and Pakistanis was absent from their relationships with the Afro-Caribbeans who, according to the 1981 census, constituted around 7 per cent of Harrow's ethnic population. Three or four Afro-Caribbeans attended each of the meetings, and their comments did not, on the whole, antagonise the other participants. They were considered as one ethnic minority, but so were Pakistanis and Gujaratis. The fact that the council established a community centre to cater for all Asians shows clearly that Pakistanis and Gujaratis were expected to use resources allocated jointly to the 'Asian community'. Hence, Pakistanis needed to struggle to achieve the kind of recognition which Afro-Caribbeans automatically enjoyed. In short, Pakistanis not only needed to become 'visible' but also had to demonstrate that they were a rival group to the Gujaratis.

This helps to explain their intensive activity, e.g. why almost half of those present at some of the meetings were Pakistanis. It also explains why Pakistanis were more inclined to participate in Harrow CRC and become office bearers. Their 'visibility' was in this case reflected in the number of associations registered with the CRC. The Pakistani associations were more numerous than Gujarati associations, and in 1984–5 the chairperson of the CRC was a Pakistani. Though this was a convenient way to become 'visible', participation did not carry immediate benefits apart from the opportunity of being updated on race relations issues and informed on available funds.

Gujaratis, however, spoke of Harrow CRC as a 'Pakistani stronghold', pointing out that owing to the Pakistanis' influence one of its three employees was a Pakistani (the other two employees were white). They would then add that the CRC was racist like all other government-aided organisations. Hence, activists who were at one time voluntary office holders withdrew their participation from the various committees of the CRC.

There were some circumstances, however, in which unity rather than rivalry seemed to be a more effective way of achieving aims, and the following debate demonstrates this.

In the early 1980s, Harrow Council turned to the CRC for advice and at times made it an arbitrator in matters relating to ethnic minorities. Section 11 grants, for example, were made to Harrow on the basis of consultation with the CRC, although the Home Office regulations demanded that applications should be preceded by consultation with the ethnic population.[13] By 1985 Harrow was forced to consult its Commonwealth population concerning the continuation of Section 11 posts; otherwise, the Home Office warned, this funding might be withdrawn. This meant that Harrow was in danger of losing resources.

In the ensuing debate some Gujaratis voiced the opinion that all delegates and other participants should vote against Section 11 funding. Conversely, the Pakistanis argued that continuation of funding necessitated that the council be more responsive to the needs of all ethnic minorities in the borough, and that it had the responsibility to ensure that no minority would be favoured. They were thus prepared to put suggestions that would enable the council to demonstrate its 'good will'. The 'Gujarati block' was nevertheless adamant that no 'blacks' should be allocated posts initiated under this scheme. In any case, Gujarati delegates maintained, mostly 'white' people were employed under Section 11. They also raised doubts as to the benefits that Asian children would gain from the continuation of these posts. Most Asian children born in Britain, they explained, did not require additional English tuition, and since most of Section 11 money was spent on education,[14] this money was not well spent.

Finally, when the matter was put to the vote, the Pakistanis voted against the suggestion put forward by the Gujaratis. Yet when the Pakistanis found that they had been outvoted, they agreed that another resolution be put to the vote. This time there was a unanimous decision against using Section 11 money.

Although Gujaratis voted unanimously on the issue of Section 11, they were not a united lobby. There were rifts amongst them, some of which came to the fore in council forums. In the Section 11 debate, those who debated against it were at first in the minority. Yet they were able to mobilize their contemporaries and, later, the remainder of activists, to vote against using Section 11. The Pakistanis, it seems, lagged behind as far as their subscription to a 'black' identity and what flows from it was concerned, but they too began to consider and to endorse ideas subscribed to initially by Gujaratis.

The answer to the question why Gujaratis should be more 'militant' than other minorities has to be measured not only against the various collective benefits at stake but also in relation to personal interest.

The most 'militant' Gujaratis were also those who had a vested interest in posts related to the 'race relations industry', e.g. that of equal opportunities adviser. A few had already been employed in similar posts outside the borough, and one was unemployed and had applied for the post of equal opportunities adviser, and also for a post in the CRC. Others sought a political career, wishing to become councillors, and a few stood as candidates in the 1986 local elections. Conversely, none of the Pakistanis held a similar post, though there were a few who became candidates in local elections.

It is therefore patent that some Pakistanis and Gujaratis perceived their participation in these forums as a step towards improving either their individual employment prospects or their positions as representatives and leaders. Hence, even those who advocated that they were 'black' spoke at the same time of the 'Asian community', implicitly or explicitly suggesting that there was an Asian vote with which councillors should reckon. Once Gujaratis began to realise that the CRC's influence was diminishing, it became a target of verbal attacks. Yet for the Pakistanis, whose number in the borough was much smaller, the CRC still had something to offer. The CRC could not advance the interests of those who sought a fully fledged political career, but a position in the CRC could still enhance individuals' status in their own associations.

The fact that Gujaratis were the largest minority in the borough meant that they were given priority when it came to employing additional staff under the government schemes. Hence, all social workers appointed in 1982 were Gujarati, and so was the manager of the community centre. Also, if the council was to implement its equal opportunities policy, the Gujaratis would benefit more than other minorities as a result of their numerical advantage. This priority was not automatically granted and at times Pakistanis challenged it. In any case, changes were incremental, and new priorities could not – in a short period of time – change the overall makeup of the Section 11 workforce, let alone that of the council.

Gujaratis appeared to be correct in their observation that the continuing acceptance of these schemes would have legitimised the council's position and would not be, in the long run, in the interests of the Asians. Clearly, they wished to de-legitimise the council's position, and put forward their own suggestions as to how the minorities should be integrated in Harrow. It is for these reasons that the Gujaratis had a vested interest in promoting the message of institutional racism, rather than demonstrating allegiances that would portray them as people who pursue nothing but their narrow interests. This was beneficial in the long run, for pressing that the council implement its equal opportunities policy, and also to cement a coalition with other Asians. In the short run, however, it was beneficial to make claims in the name of 'special needs'. Two of the more 'militant' associations, for example, applied for funds from the Greater London Council, and received money to cater for the needs of Asian disabled and elderly people, needs which fit well the rubric of 'special needs'. It is evident thus that claims for 'special needs' coincided with claims for equal opportunities.

Conclusions: the politicisation of ethnicity

The establishment of ethnic groups in Harrow during the 1980s, it has been shown, was directly connected with the equal opportunities policy issued by the borough of Harrow, and subsequently with the creation of forums, i.e. committees, for debating ethnic minority issues. These forums can in turn be likened to an infrastructure that facilitated the presentation of claims and demands. Or, in other words, the very existence of such platforms legitimised at least some of the claims which were made, e.g. that ethnic minorities deserved special treatment. Meetings thus became a focus in interaction between people who previously had not been engaged in an ongoing discussion, one that could potentially result in the formulation of policies and involvement in their implementation.

The developments which this chapter has described were not divorced from those that took place in Britain as a whole. It is unlikely that the needs of the people concerned were fundamentally different during the 1970s from during the 1980s. It therefore cannot be said that demands arose entirely as a result of new needs. Rather, during the 1970s, Asians established numerous associations, of which only one was active in raising issues that concerned Asians as residents of the borough of Harrow. This was also the period when these newly arrived Asians were establishing themselves financially, and this partly accounts for what appeared to be their lack of interest in the local political arena.

It is now possible to return to the questions posed at the beginning of this chapter, and summarise its conclusions. It was indicated that there was some discontent during the 1980s amongst ethnic residents in the locality under study, discontent which did not find an outlet until the local authority, due mainly to external pressures, decided to incorporate members of ethnic minorities in a consultation process. Once this step was taken, it became increasingly difficult for the local authority to set the pace and dictate the issues that would be discussed.

Activists who previously had had to articulate their own tactics on how to approach the council, now had direct access to both the council and its employees. Moreover, since committee meetings were open to the public, people who were not involved in the locally based ethnic associations could now put forward their own opinions. They were not impelled first to become 'internal leaders', though this was a safer way to exert influence. That is, only participants who were delegates could claim to represent at least a certain segment of the Asian population. Nevertheless, since the majority of Asian residents in the borough were totally unaware of the struggle conducted presumably on their behalf, activists did not wish to risk their authority as representatives being challenged from within. Delegates of small associations could thus act with the same amount of assertiveness as of those of larger ones. The only threat to the legitimation of their authority as leaders was brought about, as shown earlier, by the councillors themselves.

Whereas the above argument complements the answer as to the circumstances in which ethnic claims are being made, the nature of ethnic alliances that emerged has yet to be summarised. In Harrow, alliances between various Asian groups were fragile because they did not carry with them any substantial benefits for a considerable length of time. It was not obvious that unity would be rewarding. Hence, the pressure lobby was more transient in character, and much less stable, than the long-established associations,.

Whilst alliances tended to be fragile, the claims that were being made tried to compensate for this weakness. By endorsing themselves to a specific ideology, delegates attempted to achieve greater unity and at the same time press more effectively for action. These attempts were at times jeopardised, since this ideology did not provide, as expected, clear, easily acceptable guidelines. The people concerned had a 'stock' of overlapping ethnic allegiances at their disposal, to reinforce various claims. They evidently entertained multiple ethnic identities, oscillating between those arising from regional loyalties, those connected with the Indian sub-continent, and those which emerged as a result of their disadvantageous position in British society. Though this in itself was not a weakening element, the multiplicity of identities was bound to come, at least on some occasions, to the fore.

The segmentary nature of roles, the multiplicity of ethnic identities an individual may claim, all these seem to have permeated the public arena, regularly leading to seemingly contradictory claims of ethnic affiliation and conflicting demands.

Some Gujarati delegates in Harrow, for example, who advocate solidarity with all deprived and disadvantaged minorities, represent highly ranked (i.e. of higher castes) associations, although this form of organisation does not suggest the broader unity which they claim. In their capacity as delegates, they also put pressure on the council to assist their respective associations with the teaching of their mother tongue or with other projects. It is evident, therefore, that sectarian interests exist in parallel with wider ones.

What has been described is a result of the *politicisation* of ethnicity, a process where the state elicits certain claims from social categories which could previously be loosely described as cultural or religious enclaves. Various cultural traits have been fostered by the state, in the form of provision of 'ethnic' food in schools or hospitals, building places of worship, or mother-tongue tuition. They have become a focus for competition between contenders for resources. The politics of minorities must be couched in ethnic terms.[15]

This politicisation gathered momentum once the minorities concerned discovered that they were entitled to certain benefits. In Harrow, this process was slow to start since the borough was never a high-priority area, particularly in the case of Urban Aid. By 1986 Harrow was no longer entitled to benefit from this scheme. Though these benefits have always been marginal to mainstream funding, they nevertheless gave rise to numerous organisations and political manoeuvres.

In Harrow the scarcity of state funding can be exemplified by the fact that whereas one community centre for the entire Asian community was financed by Urban Aid, two community centres were run by Gujarati caste associations. Yet caste and other Gujarati associations do not have unlimited resources at their disposal. The resources which they can potentially command, in a situation where state funding is scarce, depend ultimately on the aggregate income of their members. Hence, the fact that Asians (in this case) are barred from equal access to posts, and the influence which can be achieved by means of being part of the local establishment, affect their overall socio-economic position and must in the long run weaken their capacity for voluntary activity.

As I have indicated in passing, the emergence of loyalties on new ideological grounds does not in any way hinder the existence of thriving Gujarati networks. Most Gujaratis are unaware of the ongoing debate in the town hall, and activists often complained about the apathy and the difficulties involved in 'organising' Gujaratis. Perhaps this very apathy has allowed a new ethnic elite to emerge in such a short space of time. This elite is composed of well-educated people who have taken it upon themselves to study subjects related to racism, colonialism, and so on. They hold numerous conferences and repeatedly debate these issues. The same people who now write speeches, manifestos, and pamphlets were only a few years back, to use their own phrase, 'collaborators' with the establishment.

In such a situation the rewards offered by the state in exchange for relegating people to 'minority' status will always be insufficient in two respects: they will never satisfy individual ambitions and will never contribute adequately either to welfare provisions or to institutions which are managed by ethnic residents. Presumably, if more funding became available, more contenders for power would come forward. Though this portrays, to some extent, the situation in Harrow, it still seems that the shortage of resources and the absence of control which accompanies state provision, eventually lead also to greater self-reliance and political activism than would otherwise have developed in that period. Activists who are incorporated into the so-called white establishment are being 'neutralised' in this process, only to be replaced by new activists. New activists are careful not to accuse their ex-colleagues for their low-key militancy.

Finally, most of the new activists, unlike the old ones, are either British born or have been educated in Britain. The new generation of Asians is better versed in English and is generally more familiar with

British institutions. It therefore seems that the political activism that characterises Harrow's ethnic residents will continue to thrive. And, though the first ethnic candidate to represent Harrow – in the 1987 general election – failed to achieve a majority, it seems that political activism will not remain within the realms of local politics.

© 1991 Iris Kalka

Notes

1 The analysis here is based on a study of Gujaratis in the London borough of Harrow, conducted between 1983 and 1986.
2 Initially Urban Aid was limited to nursery provision and children's homes, but it was later extended to take on a wide range of other social and, eventually, industrial and commercial projects (Young 1983: 289–90).
3 Some researchers use the term 'black' to describe minorities of non-white complexion. This has, as explained below, resulted from minorities' own self-identification as 'black', and it could therefore be misleading to describe similarly all Asians and other non-whites. Although some Asians in Harrow resent the term 'ethnic', this term is the least confusing and is therefore used in the text.
4 The dispossessed Ugandan Asians, according to the UN Convention on the Status of Refugees, were not 'refugees' and are therefore described here as 'expellees'. Only a small minority of expellees, those who held Ugandan citizenship, qualified as refugees.
5 According to data produced by the Harrow Ethnic Action Project (HEAP 1985) a project funded under a Community Programme contract with the Manpower Services Commission, the proportion of Asians owning their own flats or homes was 89.1 per cent. This figure was based on a sample of the entire Asian population in Harrow.
6 Ethnic monitoring is generally based on the collection and analysis of records of the ethnic origin of employees and job applicants. The Commission for Racial Equality provides guidance for local authorities as to the categories of ethnic origin to be used and recognises that these 'may well differ according to particular circumstances and community preferences' (CRE 1983).
7 A survey, based on the 1981 census on employment policies of local authorities, conducted by *Labour Research*, reveals that 6.0 per cent (1981 census) of Harrow's white workforce was ethnic, while the proportion of white ethnic residents was almost double, 11.2 per cent. It adds that all the local authorities with higher than average ethnic population (except two) had adopted an equal opportunities policy (*Labour Research* 1986).
8 In his report Lord Scarman recommended that 'a statutory framework be developed to require local consultation between the Metropolitan Police and the community at the borough or Police District level' (Scarman 1981: 130).

9 It was only in July 1985 that the police agreed to pay the administrative expenses of the PCCC and reimburse the running costs of the committee (from November 1982 to July 1985). According to the borough officials, Harrow was one of the first local authorities to set up a PCCC without any promise that funding would be available.

10 Meetings which I myself attended were held in 1985–6. The description of these meetings, as opposed to information obtained from minutes and other documents, refers only to this period.

11 Racism Awareness Training, based on the American model of Katz, as described in her book *White Awareness Handbook for Anti-Racism Training* (Katz 1978), became popular in Britain towards the end of the 1970s. According to the Commission for Racial Equality this form of training is designed 'to produce in participants a heightened awareness of racism . . . reinforced by both fact and feeling, sufficient to ferment a determination to resist and actively confront racism both personally and institutionally and in the wider society' (from a report on a seminar on Racism Awareness Training held by the Commission for Racial Equality on 31 October 1984).

12 The names of the small pressure groups are not given in the text, since their delegates could then be easily identified. As a result of the acrimonious relationships, particularly between Gujaratis, I have decided not to provide any identifying details.

13 In guidelines to local authorities regarding Section 11 applications, the Home Office specified that 'Consultation should in the main be with those who represent the intended beneficiaries of the post'. These could either be the local Commonwealth immigrant community *or* the local CRC (Home Office Circular No. 97/1982). A year later the Home Office suggested that a review of Section 11 posts should be undertaken. It then specified that 'Local authorities are strongly encouraged to consult their Commonwealth immigrant community *and* [emphasis mine] the local community relations councils about this provision during the review process' (Home Office Circular 94/1983). Immigrants from countries other than the Commonwealth did not therefore qualify for the Section 11 scheme.

14 In 1984/5, out of £559,080 spent under Section 11, £65,000 was spent by the Social Services Department and another £10,173 was spent on an equal opportunities adviser. The remainder of the sum was spent on education (around 87 per cent).

15 The impossibility of drawing permanent boundaries defining an 'ethnic group' is apparent here, and does not contradict the existence of cultural symbols as a force in the preservation and reproduction of ethnic groups.

References

Adams, B.N., Pereira, C. and Bristow, M. (1983) 'Ugandan Asians in exile: household and kinship in the resettlement crisis', in G. Kurian and R.P. Srivastava (eds) *Overseas Indians – A Study in Adaptation*, Delhi: Vikas.

Bhachu, Parminder (1985) *Twice Migrants – East African Sikh Settlers in Britain*, London: Tavistock.

Cohen, Abner (1969) *Custom and Politics in Urban Africa*, London: Routledge & Kegan Paul.

Cohen, Abner (1974) *Two-dimensional Man*, Berkeley and Los Angeles: University of California Press.

Cohen, Gaynor (1984/5) 'Ethnicity in a middle-class suburb', *New Community* 12 (1): 89–99.

Commission for Racial Equality (1982) *Equal Opportunity and Local Government*, London: Commission for Racial Equality.

Commission for Racial Equality (1983) *Implementing Equal Employment Opportunity Policies*, London: Commission for Racial Equality.

Commission for Racial Equality (1985) *Racial Equality and Social Policy in London*, London: Commission for Racial Equality.

Community Relations Commission (1974) *One Year On*, London: Community Relations Commission.

Community Relations Commission (1976) *Ethnic Minorities in Britain: Statistical Background*, London: Community Relations Commission.

Cunningham, C. (1973) 'The work of the Uganda Settlement Board', *New Community* 2 (2): 261–7.

Fox, R.G., Aull, C.H. and Cimino, L.F. (1982) 'Ethnic nationalism and the welfare state', in Charles F. Keyes (ed.) *Ethnic Change*, Seattle, Wash.: University of Washington Press.

Glazer, N. and Moynihan, D.P. (1975) *Ethnicity*, Cambridge, Mass.: Harvard University Press.

HEAP (Harrow Ethnic Action Project) (1985) 'Final Report', Harrow: unpublished report.

Harrow Resource Centre (1985) 'Harrow's declining economy', Harrow: unpublished report.

Katz, J.H. (1978) *White Awareness Handbook for Anti-racism Training*, Norman, Okla.: University of Oklahoma Press.

Kirp, D.L. (1979) *Doing Good by Doing Little*, Berkeley, Calif.: University of California Press.

Labour Research (1986) 'How well are councils tackling job race bias', *Labour Research* 75 (5): 11–13.

Michaelson, M. (1987) 'Domestic Hinduism in a Gujarati trading caste', in R. Burghart (ed.) *Hinduism in Great Britain*, London: Tavistock.

Novak, M. (1982) 'Concepts of ethnicity', in W. Peterson, M. Novak and P. Gleason *Concepts of Ethnicity*, Cambridge, Mass.: Harvard University Press.

Rex, John (1986) *Race and Ethnicity*, Milton Keynes: Open University Press.

Scarman, Lord (1981) *The Brixton disorders – 10–12 April 1981*, London: HMSO.

Sivanandan, A. (1985) 'RAT and the degradation of the black struggle', *Race and Class* 26 (4): 1–33.

Walzer, M. (1982) 'Pluralism in political perspective', in M. Walzer, E.T. Kontowicz, J. Higham and M. Harrington (eds) *The Politics of Ethnicity*, Cambridge, Mass.: Harvard University Press.

Werbner, P. (1985) 'The organisation of giving and ethnic elites', *Ethnic and Racial Studies* 8 (3): 368–88.

Wood, J.R. (1983) 'East Indians and Canada's new immigration policy', in G. Kurian and R.P. Srivastava (eds) *Overseas Indians – A Study in Adaptation*, Delhi: Vikas.

Young, K. (1983) 'Ethnic pluralism and the policy agenda in Britain', in N. Glazer and K. Young (eds) *Ethnic Pluralism and Public Policy*, Toronto and London: Lexington and Heinemann.

Chapter eight

Competing to give, competing to get
Gujarati Jains in Britain

Marcus Banks

A mystery of the east

An intriguing puzzle for students of Jainism is to explain why Jainism
survived in India while Buddhism, similar in both origin and teach-
ings, died out. Of the theories advanced, most take into account a
significant organisational difference between Jainism and Buddhism
– the Jain 'professional ascetics' (to use a phrase of Weber's), the *sādhu*s and *sādhvī*s[1] ('monks' and 'nuns'), actively incorporated the laity
into the organisational structure of the religion, while the Buddhist
ascetics did not. The Jain *sādhu*s, and to a much lesser extent *sadhvi*s,
became in some sense leaders.

This difference between the two traditions manifests itself during
the medieval period (fifth to thirteenth centuries AD) with the
appearance of the Jain *śrāvakācāra*s, or texts on lay discipline – a
millennium after the deaths of Mahavira (the founder of Jainism)
and Gotama Buddha. During this first millennium, it seems that lay
affiliation to the Jain and Buddhist creeds was of minor importance
to the ascetics, who were more concerned with the patronage of various royal houses. But after the first wave of Hindu reformism in the
sixth century AD, the Jain ascetics started to look increasingly to their
wealthy lay devotees for patronage. This process was consolidated in
the twelfth century with a further Hindu renaissance and the Moghul
invasions. Both religions lost their royal patronage, and while Jainism effectively 'Hinduised' in order to survive, Buddhism died out.
The ascetics thus shifted their allegiance from power to wealth, a
move which protected the corpus of tradition but which ensured that
Jainism never again played a major role in Indian history. While
individual Jains held prominent economic and political roles during
the following centuries – as they do today – Jainism, as a religious
system, ceased to fill a dominant cultural role.[2]

In this chapter I discuss some of the fund-raising activities of a
modern-day, overseas Jain organisation (where there are no ascetics)

and conclude by examining again this balance, or tension, between patrons and clients and the position of leader-figures between the two. The crux of my argument is that the leaders of any religious group which seeks to expand its activities within a secular state system must be able to appeal to a variety of different financial supporters. I argue that a diversity of objectives will be presented to the various groups of supporters and that, in the particular case I examine, this has resulted in the initial supporters becoming increasingly marginalised as higher stakes are sought elsewhere. For a leader in such an organisation to be successful he must do more than present a number of public faces, he must be able to create and sustain a moral community of givers.

Some time later, back in England

In 1982 there were about 1,200 Jains of East African Gujarati origin living in Leicester, divided about equally into two *jāt*s or castes – the Halari Visa Oswals and the Visa Srimalis (henceforth, Oswals and Srimalis). I have discussed elsewhere the political and religious structure of the Leicester Jain 'community' (Banks in press) and a brief outline should suffice here.[3]

In 1978 the Srimali Jains, together with a few Oswals, organised under the title 'Jain Samaj', purchased a disused Congregational chapel in the centre of Leicester's business district for around £40,000. By 1982 some £90,000 had been channelled into and through this building by the Srimali Jains and others, and further expenditure of some half a million pounds was estimated. Where did this money come from? And who decided how it was spent?

The Jain Samaj was founded in Leicester in 1973. It started as an organisation to meet the social and religious needs of Leicester Jains, Oswal and Srimali. By 1982 the Leicester Oswals had withdrawn from the organisation; additionally, the hundred or so member households of Leicester Srimalis had been joined by a further hundred or so member households, mostly Srimali, from elsewhere in the UK and about fifty households living abroad, in western Europe and the USA (it is difficult to say how many of these are Srimali).[4] By 1982 the organisation had also changed its name from 'Jain Samaj' to 'Jain Samaj (Europe) Leicester'. I have discussed elsewhere the somewhat strained relations between the Leicester Srimalis and the Leicester Oswals (Banks in press). All that needs to be noted here is that a degree of competition exists between the two *jāt*s.

Thus, while all households of Srimali Jains living in Leicester are, to my knowledge, members of the Jain Samaj, they do not form the majority of members. However, the majority of office holders on the

Jain Samaj's executive committee are Leicester Srimalis, and the property that the Samaj purchased is in Leicester. While I shall discuss fund-raising in detail below, it is important to note that Leicester offered the attraction of employment, not investment, to the incoming East African Asians. It would therefore be wrong to think of the Leicester Srimalis and Oswals as necessarily wealthy.

It is similarly important to realise that, whatever its source, the money raised by the Jain Samaj was not spent by the 'community' as a whole in some mysterious collective fashion, but by committees, bureaucracies, and individuals.[5] Moreover, the items or causes on which the money was spent were not clearly conceptualised. In particular, the status of the building the Samaj purchased has been a source of much ambiguity. During my eleven months of sustained fieldwork, and on subsequent visits, it was presented to me in a variety of different lights and, as it represents the major capital holding of the Samaj as well as a major symbolic focus, it is worthy of further discussion.

The Jain Centre, as this property is now known, is a major achievement and landmark for the Jain Samaj. Leicester has a large Asian population (between 40,000 and 50,000, or some 22.1 per cent of the total population, in 1982) divided by language, regional origin, religion, and a variety of other factors. There are numerous organisations that claim to represent these religious, linguistic, regional, etc., divisions. Among these, the Jain Samaj is just one, jockeying for recognition with the rest (which also includes the Leicester Oswal Association). Many, if not all, of these groups want or need money. Some of them also want or need property. Both, or at least access to both, are within the grant of Leicester City Council and so access to the council and to the ears of (white) bureaucracy generally is a goal for which Asian organisations in Leicester find themselves in competition.

The Leicester Jain Centre differs from most other property owned or used collectively by Asians in Leicester (that is, temples, mosques, community centres) in being located in the city centre, away from residential areas. This means that the usual objections – noise 'pollution' and car-parking facilities – raised by (white) residents and city councillors to the use of buildings as temples, for example, do not really apply. The consequence, however, is that few Jains in Leicester have easy access to the centre – it is certainly not a place where one can just drop in, as with, say, several of the city's Hindu temples.[6]

Owning property focuses the attention of the Jain Samaj and places the Leicester Srimalis in a position of apparent or potential power within the Leicester Asian 'community'. Not only has the Jain Samaj, since 1978, no longer had to compete with other groups for hired properties and facilities at key times of the year (Divali, for example); it is (or was in 1982) able to hire out its own property, when not needed for Samaj functions. At the same time, the way in which the property is managed and the uses to which it is put, become of great interest to the Samaj members and provide a framework for internal factionalism.

The importance of corporate property ownership for Asian groups in Britain cannot be overstressed. For Asian groups, unable to dominate the economic sector of the country as they did in East Africa, and hindered in many ways from pursuing their own political and social organisation, still less from imposing it on the majority population (Jains in Britain would be unlikely to get a whole city's slaughterhouses and butchers' shops closed down for a day as they can in India, for example), the absence or presence of property, and the functions held there, provides an arena for corporate action and competition.

The money to purchase the Jain Centre came from a variety of sources, although, as the heading 'Building Fund' in the accounts of the Samaj covers both the cost of purchase *and* (intended) refurbishment, it is a little difficult to be specific. Certainly, in 1979, a year after the fund was started, Leicester Jains (Oswals and Srimalis, but mostly Srimalis) had contributed a little less than one-third of the total sum in the fund (£12,600 of £43,600). A slightly smaller sum had come from Jains in London (Oswals and Srimalis, but mostly Oswals), and a slightly larger sum from a small but wealthy group of Srimali Jain diamond merchants in the Netherlands. But these sums were trivial compared with what was to come in. As I discuss below, some much larger sums came to the Jain Samaj through central and local government agencies.

But what was everyone giving money for? At various times, the Jain Centre was described to me as a *wāḍī* (in India, a sort of '*jāt-hall*' where members of a *jāt* hold marriage functions, feasts, etc.); a temple (*derāsar*); a 'community centre' complete with crèche, restaurant, and drop-in centre for the unemployed; and an international study and meditation centre for furthering Jainism and world peace. Of these possibilities, the contentious one is the *wāḍī*, for it restricts the building to a very small clientele. (The 'community centre' is probably the most inclusive.) Interestingly, the idea of the centre as *wāḍī* was one I only ever encountered among older Leicester Srimalis who had least to do with the executive committee. Members of this committee, on the other hand, as well as other members of the Samaj associated with them, advocated one or other of the remaining labels.

Through conversations with employees of Leicester City Council, I discovered that the council was, on the whole, somewhat perplexed by the idea of 'castes' (*jāts*). A commitment to multi-cultural policies (the council was Labour) meant that an application to, say, use a private residence as a mosque, or to fund a Gujarati-speaking social worker, was understandable. But why should Gujarati-speaking Lohannas and Gujarati-speaking Patidars, to take a fictional example, *both* want to purchase and use a building as a 'community centre'? Why couldn't they get together and have a joint Gujarati 'community' centre?[7] Religious groups were, however, understandably exclusive, and as long as the Jain Samaj stressed its Jain identity (and concealed the fact that, after 1977, half the Jains in Leicester – the Oswals – were no longer members), it was treated favourably by the council. Again, I write as though the Jain Samaj has some sort of collective rationality: on the contrary, as I mention below, there were sometimes sharp differences of opinion between the members of the committee – who were the public mouthpieces for the Samaj – and the membership they represented.[8]

Raising money

I turn now to look in more detail at the money flowing into and out of the Jain Samaj – especially into it. My information covers a four-year period (1978–82) and comes from two sources: the Samaj's annual balance sheets and notes in the Samaj's magazine (*Jain News/The Jain*). Neither source is fully comprehensive. The balance sheets represent a set of complete but vague data (vague because all sums under particular headings are aggregates), while the notes in the magazine represent a set of specific but probably incomplete data (specific, because sums are mentioned individually; incomplete, because only income in the form of gifts and donations is listed and because not every donation is recorded). I also have information from a variety of less formal sources, however, and I believe I can use the two sets of data to indicate trends, even if the specific sums may not be accurate.[9]

In India, Jains make a distinction between money donated as *devdravya* and money donated as *sādhāraṇa*. *Devdravya* means 'god('s) money' and refers to monies collected or donated in the temple (*derāsar*) which can be used only for the service of the temple and its idols (*mūrti*) – that is, maintaining the fabric and providing materials for worship (*pūjā*) – for clarified butter (*ghee*), camphor (*kapūr*), incense (*dhūp*), etc. *Sādhāraṇa* ('general') funds cover everything else – the upkeep of *upāshrayes* (rest houses for Jain ascetics), *bhojanśhālās* (dining halls), *dharamśhālās* (rest-houses for lay pilgrims), and money given to less specifically Jain causes – animal welfare, medical charities, etc. The distinction between *devdravya* and *sādhāraṇa* is made at the time of giving, not spending, and is determined by the wish of the giver or the circumstances. Hence, money collected during the evening *ārtī* (lamp-waving) ritual in a Jain temple is automatically *devdravya* and the temple authorities cannot decide to spend it on fodder for cattle. However, while *dev-dravya* funds cannot be used for *sādhāraṇa* purposes, the converse does apply – *sādhāraṇa* funds can be 'upgraded' into *devdravya*.

Because money spent in the service of 'god' – on the temple and the idols[10] – is thought to bestow merit (*puṇya*) and possibly even salvation (*moksha*) or enlightenment (*kevaljñāna*), donating money as *devdravya* is more popular than donating money to be used for *sādhāraṇa* purposes. This poses a particular problem in India, where the pan-Indian Jain temple trust which manages many of the famous pilgrimage sites has an abundance of *devdravya* funds, but finds it difficult to raise money for the upkeep of the various rest-houses and other facilities associated with the sites. In Leicester, a conscious distinction between *devdravya* and *sādhāraṇa* was not made – at least officially – although the *ārtī* fund that I discuss below was in some ways a *devdravya* fund.

Before discussing the implications of this and other points raised in the preceding discussion, let me outline some of the grants, donations, and gifts made to the Jain Samaj. These are all gifts of money (cash and cheques) given by Jains (and others) to the Samaj on various occasions and under various headings. All the grants, donations, and gifts eventually find their way to the Samaj's treasurer. The annual totals are listed in the Samaj's balance sheets while many of the sums are also listed individually in the Samaj's magazine. In addition, sums donated are often announced (with the name of their donor) at various functions held in the Jain Centre.[11]

Regular Donations

Membership

Membership fees, although listed separately in the Samaj's accounts, are part of the general pool of money used for the development of the Jain Centre. I include them as a 'donation' in that it would be possible for an individual to attend all the functions of the Samaj without being a member. Although the membership fee is in some ways analogous to fees paid by Jains for *jāt* or *gaccha* (a kind of *jāt* sub-section) membership in India, it confers few tangible benefits. Although Jainism can be presented as an achieved religion, most Jains treat it as ascriptive; therefore, why should one pay to be counted as something one has a right to by birth? Payment of a membership fee thus implies a commitment to or endorsement of the Jain Samaj as a temporally specific organisation. It also implies recognition of the bureaucratisation of Jainism as it is manifested in Britain.

At the formation of the Jain Samaj in 1973, ordinary membership cost 50 pence per annum, life membership was £25, and to become a patron of the Samaj, £50. Patronage automatically confers life membership. In addition, the names of patrons will in due course be prominently displayed in some part of the Jain Centre. After the purchase of the Jain Centre, and the consequent high costs envisaged for the future, ordinary membership increased to £1, life membership to £100, and the cost of becoming a patron to £1,000 minimum. In fact, most of the ordinary members of the Samaj contribute more than the minimum £1, either by making donations during the year on auspicious occasions (personal or public) or by responding to particular appeals. In Table 8.1 I give details for the four-year period (1978–82) for which I have details (details of ordinary membership were not available; however, given that the sums below represent about sixty memberships and the total membership was only about 200 at the time, ordinary membership fees would add no more than £120 to the final total).

Table 8.1 Total sums raised in membership, 1978–82

	Patrons £	Life Members £	Total £
July 1978 – June 1979 (old costs)	200	50	250
July 1979 – June 1980 (new costs)	3,101	2,434	5,535
July 1980 – June 1981	1,000	2,667	3,667
July 1981 – June 1982	2,000	691	2,691
Total	6,301	5,842	12,143

The ārtī fund

Ārtī – the waving of lights before an idol – is a common occasion in both India and England for Jains to make a small financial donation in a communal setting. Most in Leicester give regularly (on a daily, weekly, monthly, or yearly basis), although it is possible to make a single contribution to the *ārtī* fund. Smaller sums are placed in the tray (*thālī*) holding the lamp before it is waved in front of the idol or image, or dropped in the collection box (*dhārmik bhanḍār*) afterwards. Larger sums are handed directly to the treasurer, if he is present, in the form of cash or cheque. While I was living in Leicester, a small amount of money, perhaps 50 pence, was given each weekday by a small group of men who met regularly at the centre for a brief session of worship. A slightly larger sum, perhaps £5 or £6 was given every Sunday by the 10 or 15 men and women who met for a more prolonged session of worship (a *satsangh*). A still larger sum, about £15 on average, was given by the family who sponsored the once-monthly *satsangh* (also held on a Sunday, and attracting anything from 50 to 200 people, depending on how influential the family was and how hard they had campaigned to attract people to 'their' *satsangh*). The largest gifts of all were made during Paryushan, the Jains' annual festival of forgiveness. I discuss these donations separately below.

All told, then, the *ārtī* fund – a direct equivalent of *devdravya* monies in India – can expect to swell by some £400–500 a year, plus any additional sums donated by individuals in response to sudden good fortune. But because of the ambiguity over the status of the Jain Centre that I mentioned above, it is not at all clear whether money spent on refurbishing it is a suitable use of the *ārtī* fund. For example, in 1981 some £3,500 was taken from the *ārtī* fund to refurbish a room in the centre to act as a temple until the (planned) temple elsewhere in the building should be complete.[12] This caused some controversy between the executive committee (who sanctioned this use of the funds) and some other Samaj members who felt that this was not a wholly religious use of the *ārtī* fund, in view of the fact that the room would revert to a secular use (as a library) when the main temple was completed. In fact, over the four-year period 1978–82, the sums donated to the *ārtī* fund were as shown in Table 8.2 (the amount by which the totals are in excess of the estimated £500 baseline income indicates the degree of additional giving).

Table 8.2 Annual income to the *ārtī* fund, 1978–82

	Sums donated £
July 1978 – June 1979	353
July 1979 – June 1980	1,281
July 1980 – June 1981	1,965
July 1981 – June 1982	1,963

Sporadic donations

Jīvadayā

Jains in India are renowned for making large – sometimes huge – donations to further the cause of *ahisṁā* (the desire not to cause harm to living things and a central principle in Jainism), generally in the name of *jīvadayā* (literally, 'compassion (for) life'). This may take many forms, from the support of medical charities and animal shelters (*pīnjrāpoḷ*s) to buying grain to deposit in special rooms (*jīvat khānā*s) where household dust is deposited so that insects caught up in the sweepings can live out their natural lives (see Lodrick 1981 for more information on these activities).

In Leicester, the total sum collected in the name of *jīvadayā* over my four-year sample period was small (£56) and most of this was sent to a flood-relief fund in Gujarat. Jains in England seem to take no collective interest in indigenous animal welfare organisations or charities (the RSPCA for example) although some make contributions to such charities in India.[13] Those with large sums to spend, however, generally choose a more 'social' project (bearing in mind the caste implication of the word 'social' in India, as in 'social worker' – one who expends time and money for his *jāt*'s welfare or political ends), such as endowing or building a school in their Indian town or village of origin.[14] Of course, there is nothing particularly Jain about this.

The Building Fund

This, the largest single fund of the Jain Samaj, was set up shortly before the purchase of the Jain Centre, and by 1979 £44,000 had been raised, over half being donated in the one-year period July 1978 to June 1979. Donations to the fund can be large – £2,000 from one individual in Leicester alone – and by June 1982 the balance stood at over £86,000.

Simultaneously, however, the estimated cost of the centre rose from £100,000 in 1979 to £500,000 early in 1983 (and has since continued to rise). The fund was intended to cover the purchase and renovation of the centre, with enough surplus to meet running costs for some years.

In a way typical of such projects, costs rose more than expected and deadlines were rolled back, leading to some disquiet among the ordinary members of the Samaj: would it ever be finished? Even as late as December 1986 (with an announced completion date six months ahead) another £200,000 was urgently required at the Leicester end and Rs1,100,000 (about £55,000) needed in India to complete the temple being carved there. The majority of these obstacles seem to have been overcome now and the grand opening took place in the summer of 1988. In Table 8.3 I give details of donations made to the building fund, excluding external grants. The third year's sum includes a single donation of £10,000 towards a library. In fact, there has been a steady decline in the giving of smaller sums since the building was purchased. Since 1982, the significant private donations seem to have been large sums from wealthy individuals for specific purposes, while 'donor fatigue' seems to have set in among the ordinary membership, at least in Leicester.

Table 8.3 Building Fund donations (£s), 1978–82

July 1978 – June 1979	22,850
July 1979 – June 1980	17,280
July 1980 – June 1981	18,240
July 1981 – June 1982	2,740

The Happiness Fund

As mentioned above, members of the Samaj make financial donations on personal or public auspicious occasions. (They have also donated items of furniture, etc., or earmarked financial donations for specific purposes; with the exception of the temple itself, the value of these items is not great – monetarily or symbolically – and I have disregarded them for the purposes of this chapter.) These donations are referred to in the Jain Samaj's magazine as being donations to the 'Happiness Fund' (*kushi bhet*).[15] Members will donate in this way on the birth of a child or grandchild, the marriage or engagement of a son or daughter, examination success, the conclusion of a visit or pilgrimage to India, or on any other occasion of personal joy which it is wished to make public.

There are various named causes subsumed within the Happiness Fund which donors may specify – Jain Youth, Jain Bhagini Kendra ('ladies circle'), *Jain News/The Jain* (the Samaj's magazine), and the Jain Samaj itself. The Jain Youth group was in fact moribund at the time of my fieldwork, so the sums donated in its name were frozen in the hopes of its revival. Similarly, the Bhagini Kendra, while not totally moribund, met rarely and did little to entail any expenditure. Again, the money was held in anticipation of future needs – a crèche perhaps? The magazine, on the other hand, especially in its post-1982 format and under a new title (*The Jain*) was seen by its editors and the executive committee as an important publicity tool, and while a large part of its costs were met through selling advertising space, the donations were also helpful.

In Table 8.4 I give details of these various contributions.

Table 8.4 Donations to the Happiness Fund, 1978–82

	Jain Youth (£)	Bhagini Kendra (£)	Jain News (£)	Jain Samaj (£)	Total (£)
1979	8	3	23	300	334
1980	10	5	11	1,036	1,062
1981	28	28	34	448	538
1982	44	67	121	1,103	1,335
Total	90	103	189	2,887	3,269

Note: 1979 figures are for six months only.

Non-Samaj donations and grants

It is useful to consider these in two categories – 'Asian' and 'non-Asian' – although another way of describing them might be 'private' and 'public'. Either way, they represent channels external to the Samaj and its membership through which money has flowed to the Samaj, either spontaneously or on request.

Although most of the Samaj's members have made a donation over and above their membership fees, donations are also made by interested groups and individuals who (presumably) approve of the Samaj's stated aims but are not directly involved. These donations tend to be independent of any personal or public auspicious occasion and are non-recurring. The most significant of these is the donation of a temple by Jains living in India.

This temple was carved in India, shipped over in pieces and is currently being erected within the Jain Centre. A façade for the exterior of the building is also planned. The cost is estimated at some £2–300,000 although the project was only in a planning stage when I was conducting my fieldwork and I have had less access to data since then. Quite who these Jains in India are is less certain, though various members of the Samaj – not least its president, vice-president, and treasurer (in 1982–3) – have important contacts with wealthy Jain businessmen in Bombay and with influential Jain religious leaders (*ācāryas*). It is through these twin channels that the money has been raised. In late 1983, one of the Dutch Jains laid the foundation stone of the centre and made a donation of £25,000.[16] Otherwise, non-Samaj donations have been made by various Asian-owned shops in Leicester, although the sums involved are not large.

Since the acquisition of the centre, the executive committee of the Samaj has made repeated attempts to obtain grants for the centre's refurbishment from local and central government and/or various quangos. By the end of my fieldwork period, three of these applications had been successful: one each from the Manpower Services Commission, the Inner Aid Programme, and Leicester City Council – a total of some £85,000 (£20,500 from the City Council, about £1,100 from the Inner Aid Programme, and £63,000 from the MSC for labour costs). Obviously, strings are attached to these grants (e.g. they have to be used for the purpose for which they were claimed), but the very fact that the Samaj received them is a measure of its obvious success, especially *vis-à-vis* other Asian groups in the city.

Competing to get

Before going on to discuss a final source of fund-raising – one that is perhaps the most interesting, if not very effective in the Leicester context – I should perhaps draw together some of the themes already raised.

The Jain Samaj, as I have already mentioned, has a bureaucracy which, at its simplest, resolves into an executive committee and a membership. Members of the committee are elected every year, although the committee at the time of my fieldwork had been in place for three or four years and continued to be so for a further three or four years (with minor changes). There seems, however, to have been nothing particularly sinister in this – I heard grumbles of discontent from the ordinary membership, but several people also told me that no, they wouldn't consider standing for office, it would involve far too much work. There is also another factor: the Samaj, or rather, the Samaj in relation to the Centre, changed dramatically between about 1979 (a year or so after the Centre was purchased) and the present, and these were changes that were brought about by members of the executive committee, especially the president. We thus have something of a runaway train phenomenon: now that the engine for change was in motion it would be hard for anyone to get off, and even harder for anyone else to take over the controls.

As to where the Samaj was going, that is a harder question to answer. The earliest plan was for a Leicester Jain temple to serve the needs of Leicester Jains – Oswals and Srimalis – as the two *jāt*s were co-operating at this point (around 1975). There were precedents for this in the mosques and Hindu temples that had sprung up in Leicester by this time. Later, after the Oswals and Srimalis had parted company, the leadership – that is, members of the executive committee – realised the virtue of subscribing to a purely religious identity and, when such a large building was purchased to be the Jain Centre (1978), it was realised that it could be something more than just a local temple, especially as it would be the only Jain temple in Britain – indeed, in Europe.[17]

So a dual strategy was embarked upon – money was to be raised by appealing to Jains in India (and elsewhere) who would be willing to finance a temple, and applications were made to non-Jain bodies in Britain who would support refurbishment of the Jain Centre as a 'community' centre.

Hence, although the Jain Youth body and Bhagini Kendra were moribund or at a minimal operative level, applications could be made in their names for grants. For example, a small sum of money was requested from the Inner Aid Programme (IAP) to buy a table-tennis table for the Jain Youth. Similarly, the Bhagini Kendra – being associated with women's domestic activities – was the organisation that would supposedly take charge of the crèche and kitchen facilities for the proposed 'drop-in centre for the unemployed' (for which an application was also made to the IAP).

There is an element of competition in both strands of this strategy. Jains in India have numerous demands made on them, and although (Jain) temple-building is not common in India today, there is always some project under way somewhere. For example, during my field-work in India a year or so later, there were at least three temple-building projects under way within a radius of 200 kilometres of the city where I was based, to which Jains I knew in the city had contributed (or were considering contributing) large sums of money. So when the Leicester Jain Samaj launched its appeal in India it was having to compete with other local projects. Similarly, the coffers of Leicester City Council (and the Manpower Services Commission as well as the Inner Aid Programme) are not bottomless – all money received from them indirectly thwarted the plans of some other organisation.

There is no doubt that the Jain Samaj has been remarkably successful in financial terms. This success stems largely, perhaps solely, from the efforts of members of the executive committee – and especially from the efforts of the president. The members of the committee were, in 1982, all Srimali Jains resident in Leicester (with the exception of the vice-president who lived in London) but they are not particularly representative of the Leicester Srimalis. Of about a hundred Srimali household heads I surveyed in 1982, the majority in work were factory workers and unskilled clerical or shop workers. A smaller number were petty businessmen or shopkeepers. In contrast, the committee at this time was made up of two (medical) doctors, a dentist, a lawyer, a businessman, and an accountant.[18] Although the rest of the committee, like the majority of the Leicester Srimalis, were East African Asians whose fathers or grandfathers had been born in the Saurashtran peninsula of western Gujarat (also known as Kathiawad), the president had come to Britain directly from India and was a native of central Gujarat. Through him, and through the fathers of two of the other members, the committee had access to wealthy and/or powerful lay and ascetic Jains in India, particularly in Bombay, and it was through these channels that money was raised to pay for the temple.

Competing to give

Jains in India, especially those in North India, are 'traditionally' businessmen – shopkeepers, traders, money-lenders, brokers, importers, and exporters. This is their well-known stereotype and one that they are rather proud of. They are also known as gamblers – they would even gamble on two drops of rain rolling down a window-pane, a non-Jain friend told me once. Gambling is a risk, whether in relation to raindrops or futures markets, and it is also competitive – one person (or the house) will win the stakes of all those who take part.

There is a similar element of risk and competition in an auction. The seller invites competitive bids in the hope that the final price will be greater than that determined by conventional market forces (although by placing a reserve price on the item or commodity the sellers can insure themselves against loss and thus reduce or eliminate the loss).

The Jains – uniquely among South Asian groups as far as I can tell[19] – have institutionalised competitive bidding within their ritual corpus and this practice has been brought to Britain with them. In India, bidding (*bolāvāvuṅ* in Gujarati, literally 'calling') is for ritual roles; these are sometimes of a 'theatrical' type, where actors dress as historical or mythological characters, and sometimes are simply in the form of a right to perform a ceremony. 'Winning' either of these types of roles brings honour to the successful bidder (almost always a man, though it may be his wife or another family member who takes the role) and demonstrates his wealth and importance.[20] Competition for both the 'theatrical' and the ritual roles is fierce and can reach thousands, even lakhs, of rupees.

On a more mundane level, however, the performance of the evening *ārtī* (lamp-waving) is routinely auctioned in Jain temples. At large and important temples this will happen daily, and, as the rest of the worshippers (including unsuccessful bidders) will make small offerings anyway, the temple cannot really fail to gain.

Small temples, however, which will probably only auction the *ārtī* on special occasions (the birthday of one of the *tīrthaṅkaras*, for example), might well be 'gambling' on making more money through auctioning than through an equitable donation on the part of all those present, especially if they are in need of money. This is particularly the case at the Jain Centre in Leicester.

Ārtī can be performed in front of any image, consecrated or not, and in Leicester at the time of my fieldwork, auctioned ārtīs took place in the main hall (the ex-church) in front of a painting on canvas of the *tīrthaṅkara* Mahavira, rather than in front of the idol in the small (and temporary) temple room. *Ārtī* was auctioned during the festival of Paryushan, an annual nine-day period of meditation, readings, and minor ceremonies.

Each evening, just before sunset, about a hundred of the Leicester Jains gathered at the Jain Centre for the meditation known as *pratikramaṇa*. After it was over, about an hour later, they assembled in the main hall where they were joined by some hundred others. There then followed a further hour or so of religious songs (*stavanas*), speeches, announcements, homilies, and finally, the bidding for *ārtī*, followed by the *ārtī* itself. The Jains divide the ritual into two parts: *ārtī*, which is performed with a five-flamed lamp while one *stavana* is sung, and *maṅgaldīvo*, which is performed with a single-flamed lamp to the accompaniment of another *stavana*. In Table 8.5, I give details of the eight nights on which *ārtī/maṅgaldīvo* was auctioned (an additional ceremony on the Thursday afternoon meant there were two auctions that day).

Although the successful bidders gave the sums shown in Table 8.5 to the Samaj's treasurer after bidding, they were in fact not bidding in cash but in *maṅs* of *ghee*. (A *maṅ* – or maund – is an Indian unit of weight equivalent to about 38 kilograms.) The idea is that the *ghee* will fuel the *ārtī* flame. In India, at 'auctions' that I attended, one *maṅ* was equal to one or ten rupees. In Leicester, one *maṅ* was equal to

Table 8.5 Ārtī bidding, Paryushan 1982

Day	Ārtī		Maṅgaldīvo	
	Successful bidder	*Sum bid £*	*Successful bidder*	*Sum bid £*
Sun.	Anil Mehta	50	Hari Shah	50
Mon.	Lalji Shah	40	Lalji Shah	35
Tues.	Hari Shah	30	'Jain Samaj'	40
Wed.	Chiman Shah	20	Manu Doshi	30
Thurs.	Velji Mehta	30	Chiman Mehta	15
	Ramnik Mehta	20	Manu Doshi	30
Fri.	Hari Shah	35	Chandu Shah	40
Sat.	Kesu Jain	150	Natu Mehta	100
Sun.	Manu Shah	50	Manu Doshi	50
Total		425		390

ten pence so that, for example, Anil Mehta's winning bid on the first day was five hundred *maṅs*. Of course, everyone knows they will give cash if they win the bid and that this cash will not be used to purchase hundreds of kilos of *ghee*, but they agree to refer to the cash as a commodity instead. By doing this they restrict the uses to which the cash can be put. In fact, there is a dual conversion, as this 'commodity' becomes a gift, losing (symbolically at least) its power as currency altogether. Instead, it must be consumed in flame. But the *ārtī* fund, as *devdravya*, can also be used for the maintenance and upkeep of temples, as well as for items of offering, so money raised during the Leicester *ārtī* bidding went into the *ārtī* fund, which could then be used for expenditure directly related to the temple part of the Jain Centre.

Before moving on, there are some points of interest which arise out of Table 8.5. First, it is obvious that while the winning bids were for sums that the individuals probably considered significant, the total sum raised, less than £1,000, is trivial compared to the half a million pounds estimated then as the total costs of building and equipping the Jain Centre. In fact, bidding during the 1982 Paryushan was very slow (I was told that it was much better in previous years, though I had no way of checking this). Hari Shah, for example, who won the second bid on the first day and two after that, was in fact the auctioneer. He set the sums given as starting bids and then, when no one bid against him, was forced to take them himself. In fact, very rarely was there more than one person bidding – whoever did was simply encouraged to raise their bid by the auctioneer until they refused to go any higher. The exception was the Saturday; here Kesu Jain and Natu Mehta bid against each other and then allowed one another to win one bid each. But there is an artificiality about this too, as Kesu Jain was the Samaj's president and Natu Mehta the vice-president. The sums offered in competition may be considered 'symbolic', in that they were not large and were offered somewhat grudgingly with very little real competition. At the end of this chapter I will argue that this lack of enthusiasm was a result of what one might call a 'moral confusion' as to why the money was being given.[21]

More contentious was the *maṅgaldīvo* winning bid on the Tuesday. The bid was actually won by Kesu Jain, the Samaj's president but, possibly to encourage a feeling of communal solidarity, he took it in the name of the 'Jain Samaj' and the whole committee went up to perform the ceremony. Afterwards, a heated argument took place between Kesu Jain and a non-committee member of the Samaj, Vipin Mehta. Mehta's complaint was that although the ceremony was supposed to have been performed for the entire Samaj it was apparently the committee that had benefited – otherwise, why should they all be physically present behind the flame, why not just a single representative? In other words, while some ordinary members of the Samaj allowed the committee to represent the Samaj's – and hence their – interests in some areas (in dealing with the City Council, for example), there were other areas in which the committee could or should not.

It was noticeable, in fact, that during the post-*pratikramaṇa* sessions, up to the time of *ārtī*, the committee sat aloof, at a table to the side of the stage from where the religious songs and homilies were addressed, and to a large extent ignored the proceedings (which were organised by non-committee members). They concentrated instead on various bureaucratic tasks – sorting out the finances, preparing membership lists, answering letters. This business activity, especially the written parts of it, was carried out almost exclusively in English, in contrast to the exclusively Gujarati dialogue between the stage and the audience/congregation facing the stage (the bidding procedure for *ārtī* was also in Gujarati).

Thus there was effectively a mundane space (the committee table) and a sacred space (the stage) facing the mass of the Samaj members. While the ordinary Samaj members communicated with the mundane space during the course of the evenings (going up to take out membership, or to convert ordinary membership to life membership, etc.), they actually formed the personnel occupying the sacred space (taking turns to go up and sing songs etc.). The one chance that arose for these barriers to be broken down – taking the *maṅgaldīvo* the name of the Jain Samaj – was squandered by the committee moving temporarily *en bloc* from the mundane space into the sacred space and out again, bypassing the rest of the Samaj members.

A man for the times

It is likely that the expression of Asian religions in Britain is as flexible and shifting as in South Asia, although the policies of 'multi-cultural education' may serve to reify, much as westerners in Sri Lanka and elsewhere tried, consciously and unconsciously, to reify a 'pure' Buddhism a century or so earlier. Certainly, there is no monolithic 'Jainism' in either Britain or India, but instead a number of interpretations (interpretations not merely of texts, but of custom, practice, history, experience). Consequently, it should not be assumed that because they were in control of what was apparently a religious organisation, the committee of the Jain Samaj was made up of pious and 'orthodox' men.[22]

In this context, it is worthwhile looking briefly at the Samaj's president, Kesu Jain. He is, in many respects, a true 'ethnic marginal'

– a feature of ethnic leadership discussed by Werbner elsewhere in this volume. As already mentioned, he came to Britain directly from India and is a professional (a solicitor). Like other ethnic leaders (and like most of the rest of the committee) he lives in one of the outer suburbs of the city, away from the main Gujarati and indeed the main 'ethnic' areas. Because of his education and his birth in central, as opposed to western, Gujarat, even his (Gujarati) language use differs from that of the rest of the Leicester Srimalis (although, because of their stay in East Africa, some of them speak a more fluent and less accented English than he); some teenagers told me they found it difficult to follow what he said in Gujarati. He is also an extremely complex man and, at the time of my study, clearly aware that his leadership position isolated him from the rest of the Srimalis, but fired with a vision that he knew would benefit them if only they could realise it.

On one level his leadership was clearly a strategy for personal fulfilment, if not advancement – he told me on various occasions of other organisations he had been involved with (a political party, a Rotary-type association, various mild inter-racial/inter-religious organisations), but for each there was some sorry tale which led to his disillusionment and withdrawal. So he turned to the Jain Samaj, of which he had always been a member. At this time (in the mid-1970s) it seems to have been a small, local, and fairly unambitious organisation but, as Kesu Jain became more interested in the religion of his birth, he came to see the great potential it had. While on one level the story so far could be true of any leader and organisation ('ethnic' or otherwise) it must be said that various aspects of Jainism now begin to play a part. Within the Jain ethos can be found a stress on vegetarianism (Kesu Jain was a member of the Leicester Vegetarian Society), personal morality and inner guidance through meditation (Kesu Jain became a member of the Quaker co-ordinated Leicester Inter-Faith Council) and *ahimsā*, usually mis-translated as 'non-violence' (the 'Gandhi' fad – from the Attenborough film – peaked just after I left Leicester). It was these elements that Kesu Jain stressed, and which were in turn stressed in the Jain Samaj's official statements and publications, while the myriad other facets of Jainism – the worship of idols, the place of the ascetics (*sādhu*s and *sādhvī*s), the cult of attendant deities – the 'exotica' in short, were downplayed or ignored. This stress was pleasing both to Kesu Jain's Indian patrons (as the elements he emphasised transcended sectarian, caste, and regional divisions among Indian Jains) and to (white) representatives of the local and national state (even the most xenophobic of Tory MPs could hardly get upset about vegetarianism and anodyne hopes for world peace).

Kesu Jain's vision – for the Leicester Jain Centre to spread a message of peace throughout Europe – was, to a greater or lesser extent, shared by the other members of the committee. For the most part, however, they immersed themselves in their work. None of them seemed to have any serious designs on his leadership position – the challenge, if anywhere, lay outside among the Oswal Jains – but as the Jain Samaj accumulated successes (a major grant, a spread in the local newspaper, a visiting dignitary) this challenge receded. Instead, the committee formed a cushion of mediation between the ordinary membership and the president. Like him, they were professionals, but they were also of East African and western Gujarat origin and had ties of blood, marriage, and friendship with non-committee members.

But this mediation was not always successful. There was, at the time of my fieldwork, a small, ill-defined but very vocal group among the ordinary membership, who felt that every step the Samaj took under Kesu Jain was a further step in the wrong direction. For example, it was the 'exotica' that they felt to be the most relevant aspects of Jainism, for it was in the various rituals and ceremonies and through contact with groups in India clustered around certain *sādhu*s and *sādhvī*s that they could create some feeling of community, some feeling of togetherness. Vipin Mehta was expressing these sentiments when he attacked the committee for performing *maṅgaldīvo* in the name of the Jain Samaj. Moreover, just as the Jain Centre was necessary to Kesu Jain's vision, it was necessary to those with 'communalist' sentiments. The £40,000 that had initially been raised to buy the building, had largely been raised within the 'community'; they had responsibilities, therefore, only to themselves. But Kesu Jain and the committee had effectively sold off the property, attaching different labels ('community centre', 'only Jain temple in Europe', 'international Jain study centre') and selling it in lots. An auction had been held, at which the Leicester Srimalis, having little money and no clear vision, had tendered a losing bid.

Big Men in competition

'Competitive gifting' of the type described as taking place at the Paryushan *ārtī* ceremonies is not unknown in the ethnographic record, though it is harder to find instances of structured and formalised competition. An example from New Guinea is given by Gregory (1982: 203–9), where competition was introduced to try and intensify capital accumulation. In Poreporena village, church structures duplicated the structures of the traditional clan system and supplied the role of deacon as an alternative to that of the 'Big Man'. The patterns of traditional gift-exchange were duplicated among the deacons in rivalry to raise the maximum amount of money possible for the church in the course of a year. 'The system', says Gregory, 'has been a colossal success' (ibid.: 207), a success which he then contrasts with the failure of a rotating credit scheme, the Hiri Development Corporation.

For Gregory, the failure of the Hiri Development Corporation scheme and the success of the Poreporena church scheme rest on the difference that gift-debt was created in the Hiri case and not in the Poreporena case (Gregory 1982: 208). This is because the Poreporena gifts were alienated from their givers – a feature of 'destructive' gift-exchange systems of the Potlatch type. Following Mauss, Gregory notes that a 'gift to god' is such a 'destructive' strategy but, if the gifts are given to an intermediary acting for the god, then accumulation can take place. In the Poreporena case, however, there is a more or less exact mapping of a new structure onto an old one. The moral community of givers remains the same. In the Paryushan case I have given, the Jains are in competition among themselves, as they would be in India, but they are also competing in a wider arena. It is an arena of which the boundaries are uncertain, where there is a confusion as to what exactly constitutes the moral community.

There are a number of areas where competition is encountered by the Leicester Jains or members of the Jain Samaj, several of which I have outlined in this chapter: they compete with other 'ethnic' groups for money from the state, they compete with Indian Jain groups for funds to build their temple, the Leicester Srimalis are (were) in competition with the Leicester Oswals to be *the* Jain group in Leicester. Within the Srimali group they are competing to give, as well as to get – the Paryushan bidding is one example, another is the competition (again, not really very fierce) to host the monthly *satsaṅgh* or worship session. In the latter example, prestige accrued to the hosting family from the lavishness of the refreshments they provided and the numbers of participants they could attract.

Finally, as outlined above, there has been in some senses a competition for or an auction of the future of the Jain Centre. This is competition *for* something, but expressed partly through competition to *give*. Set against the New Guinea examples, the Jain Centre as an enterprise lies somewhere between the two that Gregory documents. It is a 'failure' for the Leicester Srimalis as they no longer see gifts made to it as Maussian 'gifts to god' and the symbolic capital they accrue by gifting is valueless to them – where is the prestige for a British Telecom worker in being associated with an international meditation centre? But it is a successful enterprise for those outside

Leicester with large sums of money to dispose of – it is a 'modern', European way of making gifts to god; it sanctifies sophistication.

Conclusions: a letter to a king

I started this chapter with a puzzle, which I attempted to solve by making a distinction between the patrons of the medieval Jain ascetics and their followers. Light can be shed on the progress of the Jain Samaj over the last ten years or so by making a similar distinction.

There are no *sādhus* or *sādhvīs* (monks and nuns) in Britain – the group I identified as 'leaders' who were balanced between the pre-medieval Jain patrons and the post-medieval Jain laity. Jain ascetics are prevented by their vows from using any form of transport other than bare feet, and it is only in the last century or so – the tail end of two and a half millennia of Jainism – that this has really become a problem. But during the last four hundred years there have grown up a number of Jain reform movements that have either been critical of the ascetics or that have rejected them altogether.[23] Hence, although Kesu Jain bore a heavy burden of leadership, he lacked the sacred legitimation (and responsibilities) of an ascetic, and so could and did rely on non-ascetic precedents for the style of his leadership.

He was caught in the same balancing act between patrons and followers as the medieval ascetics, but chose to swing the balance in the opposite direction. His followers, as I identify them, were the Leicester Srimalis. They had elected him to leadership in the mid-1970s and continued to support him, although with increasing resignation, over the next ten years. Within a short space of time, the money they had to offer him was running dry, but they remained dependent on him, partly because he could act as a broker to obtain large sums of money from patrons, and partly because he was offering his *seva* – 'service' – which places him in a superior position. In truth, the situation was never presented to me in these terms, but the ambiguity that Mayer (1981) discusses as being an attribute of *seva* was readily discernible in Leicester. To quote Mayer:

> We see, then, that the performance of true *seva*, involving a sacrifice of time, effort and non-attachment, can put public workers in a position superior to those of the public they serve – perhaps in the same way as the performance of austerities and the act of renunciation can bring an individual more spiritual power, and even a superiority over the gods he worships.
>
> (Mayer 1981: 162)

His patrons? They were of two kinds; on the one hand were the rich but distant Jains, the wealthy Dutch diamond merchants and Bombay businessmen, on the other were the newspaper editors who offered publicity, the councillors and even the Lord Mayor who attended functions and offered legitimation and potential protection. Both kinds of patron offered channels for fund-raising, together with legitimation through associating their names with the Jain Centre – spheres in which the Leicester Srimalis could not compete.

It is my argument that it is not simply enough to identify donations as 'gifts to god' or to distinguish between arenas of gift-debt and non-gift-debt in an abstract and neutral way. Instead, leadership strategies (by which I mean strategies that leaders employ to achieve their ends – however defined – and not strategies employed to *become* a leader) can serve to manipulate these categories and in so doing can change the rules of the game. Competitive gifting through the *ārtī* bidding becomes meaningless when a whole new set of prestige stakes is set up for the wealthy, external patrons.

Similarly, by pursuing strategies that change the label attached to the Jain Centre, a more attractive 'god' to give to is set up before these influential patrons. The status of medieval south Indian 'Jain' kingdoms needs clarification through further research (see Dundas 1985: 162), but there were certainly kings who looked favourably on the Jains. In what was surely an unconscious echo of this former royal patronage, Kesu Jain, on behalf of the Jain Samaj, sent a letter to the future King of England and his wife in 1982, congratulating them on the birth of a son. Given Prince Charles's spiritual proclivities – at least as reported by the popular press – who knows what the future may hold?

© 1991 Marcus Banks

Notes

1 The subject matter of my article demands that I use a fair number of Gujarati and other terms. While I have inserted diacritical marks on all such words I have not distinguished between Gujarati, Sanskrit, and Prakrit terms. Similarly, to avoid confusion, I have marked plurals with a simple unitalicised 's' at the end of the word.

2 This short summary is a gross oversimplification of the facts and of the serious work devoted to the problems raised by various scholars. One of the most useful sources is Williams's (1963) study of the *srāvakācāra*s. See also Jaini's (1980) paper on why Jainism 'survived'.

3 For a variety of reasons, mostly to do with the small numbers of Jains in the UK, it is useless for me to try and disguise the fieldwork location. I do, however, feel a reluctance to discuss other people's financial affairs – probably something to do with being English, I imagine – and so I have used pseudonyms where relevant in this chapter and on occasion I have

fudged some of the details. Fieldwork was carried out as part of my doctoral research and was supported by the then Social Science Research Council (SSRC).

4 As among Indian Jain (and other) organisations, membership by household or household head/senior male of joint family is more common than individual membership.

5 I side with Morris in seeing certain individuals as instrumental in the process of 'communal crystallisation' (Morris 1968: 40). The 'communities' thus formed are temporary action sets (or 'part-time' action sets), which is why I prefer to keep the word 'community' in inverted commas while referring to the Leicester Jains.

6 I should perhaps point out now – rather than later in the chapter – that since 1984 the interior of the Jain Centre has been subject to extensive building work which has rendered it largely unusable at times. The rapid changes that have taken place within both the Jain Samaj and the Jain Centre during the fifteen-year period 1973–88 are the reason that I am concerned to tie my observations to particular dates.

7 The use of the word 'community' in India and among Asians elsewhere is particularly interesting. On the one hand it helps create a (misguided) equivalence between Asian groups ('the Muslim community', 'the Gujarati community', 'the Lohanna community'). On the other hand, the term has a potential use in 'sanitising' (see Reeves 1986) caste discourse in a situation such as the modern Indian political arena where caste and caste discrimination have been declared illegal.

8 Actually, even a purely religious identity is not always a guarantee of success. Some years ago, the Leicester Oswals also tried to purchase a disused church in the centre of Leicester to use as a Jain temple. They were blocked, however, by the bishop, who said that the ordinances of this particular church prevented it from being used for non-Christian religious purposes. It later became a carpet warehouse.

9 I am of course faced with another problem, that of ethics. All the published data I have used, however, are publicly available (or were at the time) and I do not believe there is anything particularly contentious about the data I obtained through conversation and observation, though I admit I have been more selective over the use of these.

10 For Jains, 'god' (*bhagvān*) is represented by the twenty-four *jinas* or *tīrthaṅkaras* – (human) beings who achieved enlightenment (*moksha*) and who now reside in perfect bliss in the highest heaven (*īśatprāgbhārābhūmi*). Strictly speaking they cannot grant boons or favours or involve themselves in any way in the affairs of mankind, but many Jains seem unwilling to accept this – see Banks (in press).

11 It was often not possible to separate out the donations and gifts of the Leicester Jains (Oswals and Srimalis) and so all the data given below concern the membership of the Samaj in its entirety. As a general rule, however, sums given by Leicester Jains diminish over time, partly because they had less money to give and partly because they were the first to give.

12 In fact, the Samaj keeps all its finances in one account and the ārtī fund
    has a separate existence only on paper.

13 When I went to India after completing the bulk of my Leicester fieldwork,
    a few individuals gave me small sums – ranging from £2 to £25 – to
    spend on their behalf at various temples and animal welfare shelters.
    But I got the impression that no individual or corporate body in India
    was relying for financial support on the Leicester Jains – whether in the
    form of remittances to family members or donations to a temple or
    other charity. Indeed, as I point out below, the Jain Samaj was crucially
    dependent on money flowing *from* Jains in India and elsewhere overseas.

14 One well-known Halari Oswal, who made his fortune in Kenya, spent
    several lakhs of rupees building a large medical school and commerce
    college, both of which bear his name, in the city near his village in
    Gujarat. He himself had no desire to live in India, however, and retired
    to London, where he died.

15 In India, it is common to give donations on solemn auspicious occasions –
    such as the death anniversary of a relative – as well as on festive
    occasions – weddings, births, etc. In Leicester I only came across one
    such donation (to commemorate a death anniversary).

16 There is, and has been for many centuries, a belief among Jains that
    building a temple – and thus, presumably, contributing to the building of
    a temple – bestows much merit (*punya*) and possibly even salvation
    (*moksha*).

17 Oswals in London had purchased a large house in its own grounds which
    was to have been a temple-cum-'community' centre, but had run into
    planning difficulties.

18 The committee consisted of six office holders and seven ordinary
    members. Here, and throughout this chapter, I am considering only the
    office holders when I refer to 'the committee' as they met at least once
    weekly, were present as a body at almost all functions, and took all
    day-to-day decisions.

19 I consulted all the literature on Hindu ritual that I had to hand while
    writing this chapter and also consulted various friends and colleagues
    who have worked with Hindu groups, but came up with no evidence of
    Hindus doing what I am about to describe. I would welcome further
    information. Pnina Werbner has, however, drawn my attention to a
    Jewish custom of auctioning ritual roles in the synagogue, and I am
    grateful to her for this.

20 Some have also, rather cynically, pointed out that donating vast sums to
    the temples in this way is a useful method of disposing of 'black' money
    (that is, undeclared income) in India.

21 I am grateful to Pnina Werbner for pointing this out.

22 I have argued elsewhere (Banks in press) that the term 'neo-orthodox'
    describes them better.

23 Two major examples would be the Sthanakavasi sect, founded in the
    mid-seventeenth century, which rejected idolatry and was critical of
    ascetic laxity, and the Kanji *panth* (movement) founded by an ex-ascetic
    in the early part of this century. Both sects do have ascetics, but their

role is diminished, especially in the Kanji *panth* which was very successful among Jains in East Africa.

References

Banks, Marcus (in press) 'Orthodoxy and dissent: varieties of religious belief among immigrant Gujarati Jains in Britain', in M. Carrithers and C. Humphrey (eds) *The Assembly of Listeners: Jains in Society*, Cambridge: Cambridge University Press.

Dundas, Paul (1985) 'Food and freedom: the Jaina sectarian debate on the nature of the Kevalin', *Religion* 15: 161–98.

Gregory, Chris (1982) *Gifts and Commodities*, London: Academic Press.

Jaini, Padmanabh S. (1980) 'The disappearance of Buddhism and the survival of Jainism: a study in contrast', in A.K. Narain (ed.) *Studies in the History of Buddhism*, Delhi: BK Publishing Corporation.

Lodrick, D.O. (1981) *Sacred Cows, Sacred Places: Origins and Survivals of Animal Houses in India*, Berkeley, Calif.: University of California Press.

Mayer, Adrian C. (1981) 'Public service and individual merit in a town of central India', in A.C. Mayer (ed.) *Culture and Morality: Essays in Honour of Christoph von Fürer-Haimendorf*, Delhi: Oxford University Press.

Morris, H. Stephen (1968) *The Indians in Uganda: Caste and Sect in a Plural Society*, London: Weidenfeld & Nicolson.

Reeves, David (1986) *British Racial Discourse*, Cambridge: Cambridge University Press.

Williams, R.H.B. (1963) *Jaina Yoga: A Study of the Medieval Sravakacaras*, London: Oxford University Press.

Part three

Community Associations and the National Context

Chapter nine

Organisational splits and political ideology in the Indian Workers Associations

Sasha Josephides

Introduction

The very terms 'ethnic leadership' and 'ethnic politics' imply that what passes for politics among minority groups is qualitatively differ-ent from the politics of 'indigenous' groups. Analysis has often focused on the kin ties, business connections, and other such links in explaining political allegiances among immigrants and their descendants, at the cost of looking at the political issues themselves. In this chapter I argue that certain *political* issues are at the basis of the development of one apparently 'ethnic' organisation – the Indian Workers Association. Existing anthropological writing on the IWA (Desai 1963; John 1969) takes its inspiration from Bailey (e.g. 1969) with his methodological individualism, Mayer (1966) with his 'action sets', or Barth (1966) with his maximisation model. This chapter argues against the non-historical utilitarian approach exemplified in this early work on leadership and factions. This is not to imply that individual men, their networks, and their endeavours were of no sig-nificance in associational politics: in the next section I examine the qualities of these individuals which enabled them to achieve prom-inence within the organisation. The main part of the chapter, however, concentrates on the ideological issues with which the IWA has been concerned. These, rather than individual rivalries, I argue, have been the cause of three major splits within the organisation.

Leaders and followings

Like the associations of all groups, IWAs have provided the frame-work for certain men (and it always is men) to achieve prominence within their communities and beyond them. It could be argued, indeed, that these men were in any case prominent or they would not have been elected to office. In other words, office does not so much confer leadership status as follow from it. Nevertheless, office does, of course, in its own turn serve to consolidate social prominence, validate it, and provide an extra peg on which to hang it. Election to office is therefore both the result of prominence and its cause.

The social bases for prominence or for the creation of a following, and hence for election to office, are numerous. In the case of the IWA the following factors have been cited: village-kin and *ilaqa* (area) ties (Desai 1963: 103–7; John 1969: 48–63); economic prosperity with the attendant ability to provide employment and housing, thereby creating groups of dependants (Desai 1963: 103–7; John 1969: 48–63); the ability to carry out 'social work' (Hiro 1971: 156; John 1969: 48–63), and education (Desai 1963: 103–7). These various qualifications are not mutually exclusive. For example, good 'social workers' are likely to be prosperous or well educated or both. Such factors have contributed to men being elected to IWA office in the past and continue to be important in the present. Once elected, such leaders need to continue as before to consolidate their support. Like men from most associations and, indeed, most politicians, IWA leaders present themselves as taking on the burden of office rather than seeking it. In fact such leaders are very hard working individuals with 'leadership' often meaning little more than filling out forms for people, interceding on their behalf and taking on the various tasks associated with the broker notion of ethnic leadership.

In relation to achieving prominence outside the community, it is sometimes said that an ethnic or community leader is the creation of the media and other agencies. This way of looking at it can also be applied to IWA leaders since statements on the views of 'the Asian community' are regularly elicited from IWA leaders, and they are asked to sit on various committees as representatives of Indians or Asians (different terms have been used at different periods). But other factors intervene: in the case of the IWA there is also the charisma of a particular man. The now legendary Udham Singh appears to have had IWA leadership status conferred upon him posthumously. Udham Singh was an engineer and an active trade unionist who in 1940 shot dead Sir Michael O'Dwyer (the governor of the Pubjab at the time of the massacre of unarmed peasants and workers in Amritsar in 1919) and is widely credited with being a founder of the IWA. Whether or not he was will never be known for sure as there is conflicting evidence on this point.[1] However, the fact that he has been appropriated in this way by and for the IWA is of ideological significance and points to the connections being made between freedom-fighting and the IWA.

In a very different way, Jagmohan Joshi, a leader of the IWA from the early 1960s until his death in 1979, while still a young man, had attributes of a charismatic leader. He is mainly recalled for his ability to clarify political issues, in both writing and his speeches, and his great energy in mobilising people and initiating movements. Many of his written speeches and pamphlets are still available as IWA documents. But he is also remembered for his personal qualities. For example, one man who joined the IWA after attending a number of discussion groups led by Joshi talked of the respect he felt for Joshi's ideas and the impression that Joshi respected him, even when they disagreed. He said it felt as though he had a special relationship with Joshi, and that other people felt the same way about him. They might not see him for a long time and then they would meet again and that special feeling was still there. He also believed that no one has been able to grasp the leadership position since Joshi. Another man talked of Joshi as the backbone and soul of the organisation and said he had a nervous breakdown when Joshi died. A third man who did not know the sequence of events within the IWA (see pp. 261–70) and had not known Joshi felt that had Joshi not died the IWA would have remained united; this reflects the kinds of notions current which stress the ability and qualities of leaders rather than actual events they participated in.

Still another aspect of the charismatic attributes of IWA leaders is the predominance of poets in leadership positions. Joshi himself is known for his poetry and other leaders rose within the organisation because of their poetic abilities. Another IWA leader, Naranjan Noor, was, according to the people who first recruited him to the organisation, a good poet and was therefore able to achieve great prominence because he could move and inspire people. There are other examples of people's ability being judged in relation to their poetry. For example, at a recent IWA celebration I attended, a Punjabi friend who is not sympathetic to the organisation nevertheless admired a poetry recitation by one of the leaders and listened to him with great attention.

However the importance of individual leaders within the IWA should not be overstated. With the exception of Udham Singh who through the agency of martyrdom has become a hero in the Punjab as well as among Punjabis in the UK, IWAs do not subscribe to the cult of the individual. On the contrary, from their biennial reports it would appear that each newly elected secretary of the IWA starts off by criticising the past leadership. In some cases such criticism only involves stating that the previous leadership was inactive or defective in some other way, thereby allowing the association to deteriorate; in others, more serious charges are brought. But the pattern of criticising the past leadership, possibly borrowed from Communist Party practice, suggests that the influence of particular individuals cannot predominate in the IWA in the long term. This brings me to my central point, which is that, looking back at developments within the IWA over the years, the defining forces do not appear to be particular leaders but specific political issues. I therefore want to shift the chapter now from the attributes of particular men to the ideologies of the group. In order to look at these ideologies and the resultant splits in context an account of the formation and the early history of the IWA follows.

IWA history: expansion, federation, and ideological divisions

According to Desai, the IWA was formed in the 1930s by some Sikhs[2] and a few others, mainly from the business, student, and professional categories of Indians, and was confined in activities and membership to London (Desai 1963: 102–3). Most other accounts and the IWAs themselves consider the first IWA to have been created in Coventry in 1938. Its founder members are said to have included Udham Singh. Hiro also names Ujagar Singh and Akbar Ali Khan as co-founders (Hiro 1971: 157). In my own interviews I was given the names of Babook Chima, Kartar Singh Nagra, and Anant Ram among those of the founders.

Other IWAs were also formed around 1938. According to some published sources (John 1969: 45), the bulk of the membership of these early organisations were pedlars,[3] but there is also a mention of a business, student, and professional membership (Desai 1963: 102–3). Some members say that, since most of the early settlers were not workers, the early association could not have been composed of workers.

Most sources consider these early IWAs to have been largely concerned with the independence of India, though there are different degrees of emphasis as to the extent of this concern, and regarding the differences between the IWAs and other Indian associations (cf. Desai 1963: 103 with Hiro 1971: 157).

After 1947, with the independence of India, the IWAs went into decline[4] and were then reactivated in the early 1950s. At this time the Punjabi population had grown in numbers and was continuing to grow. These new IWAs were still concerned with the situation in India because those involved in reactivating them felt the independence was a compromise between the colonisers and the feudal lords (interview with an IWA leader), but they also had a role to play in improving the living conditions of Indians in the UK. For example, the IWA South Staffordshire was formed by some socially active Indians in order to provide a voluntary service for the community (Hiro 1971: 156) while the IWA Birmingham initially concerned itself with the problem of Indians with forged passports (Desai 1963: 105; Aurora 1967: 45).

IWAs were reactivated or newly formed in all locations with Punjabi concentrations. The IWA Coventry, reactivated in 1953 (Hiro 1971: 156, but see note 4), was probably the first. Other local associations mentioned in the literature include the two referred to above, the IWA South Staffordshire (now Wolverhampton) formed in 1956 (Hiro 1971: 156) and the IWA Birmingham formed in 1959 (Desai 1963: 105). In my own interviews I was also told of the following branches formed in the 1950s: London, Nottingham, Leamington, Nuneaton, Bradford, Gravesend, Leeds, and Huddersfield. In 1956 or 1958 the IWA Southall was formed.

The local IWAs were co-ordinated but independent until 1958 when they were centralised to form the IWA (GB). According to most published sources centralisation was advised by Nehru when he visited Britain in 1957. However, IWA members see it much more in terms of how they themselves felt the association should develop.

A leading member of the Communist Party who was involved in the Coventry IWA in the 1950s gave me the following account of the history of that period:

> In the 1950s we [the IWA Coventry] became larger and larger and had to contact people outside Coventry. We sent people from Coventry to different centres to form a political nucleus. They organised politically in small groups. This went on for four to five years and then it became essential to form IWAs. First a branch was formed in central London, then in Nottingham, then Southall branch was formed and so on. In 1959 the IWA was centralised.

With centralisation the local associations became branches of the national association and the office holders of the branches made up the General Council. The national office holders and Central Executive Committee were elected from this General Council. Policies and so on were decided on from the centre and a third of the income of each branch went to the centre.

This picture of a very rigid structure is not shared by all IWA members and indeed some of the branches appear to see themselves as having had more autonomy than the view from the centre would suggest. This perspective is supported by De Witt John who describes the unified IWA (IWA (GB)) as a 'loose federation of the local associations' (John 1969: 45).

The IWAs became the most important Punjabi associations in the immigrant communities and commanded mass participation. John estimates that in some cases more than half the adult male Punjabis may have joined the local IWA (John 1969: 47). By the 1950s there was a broader social spectrum of Indians in Britain and the IWA membership reflected this, except that it continued to be a male organisation. It encompassed a range of political party affiliations, including Akalis, Communists, Congress Party members, and members of the British Labour Party.

Of the different political affiliations operating within the IWA special mention has to be made of the communists as they were the most organised group and able to exert more influence than their numerical strength would suggest. Indian communists in Britain belonged to the Communist Party of Great Britain (CPGB) until 1965 when the majority formed their own association (see below). However, even when CPGB members, they had their own separate Indian branches and their own officers, and could conduct meetings in Punjabi and concentrate on issues and activities of interest to Punjabis (John 1969: 67). One of their concerns was the development of the IWA, and given the proliferation of local IWA groups and its centralisation, they saw the IWA as *the* mass organisation, and were therefore committed to working within existing IWAs and creating new ones where a branch did not exist. Because of the paranoia in Britain regarding communism during the 1950s and 1960s and the tendency to use the charge of communism as a slur in order to dismiss IWA demands and ridicule their positions,[5] the IWA has regularly had to point out that it is *not* a communist party and the vast majority of its membership are not party members. As one communist leader put it, 'if a large section of the membership were members of the party, then the time would be ripe for revolution, but unfortunately that's not the case'. However, the communist members are over-represented on the executive committee of the association, partly because, through their commitment, 'they take the headache' (interview quote), and partly because they have the support of non-communists also. According to one leader 'the reason why their influence is so great is because their cause is the cause of all poor people; they are known as the fighters'. The communists in the IWA did not expect other members to join the party, and recognised that the IWA, as a broader organisation, would not have the same political consciousness as the party. This was acceptable so long as the IWA did not move in a direction the communists considered would, as an organisation, compromise its politics. In that case, according to one of the communist leaders, they would have to let go of the association as it could no longer be the basis for a mass movement.

The existence of a range of people with different views within the IWA meant that there were always different opinions on the role of the IWA, even before centralisation. The most marked tension was that between those who wanted the association to be a welfare/social group and those who wanted to emphasise its political work, of which more will be said below. These tensions came to a head periodically, at the time of IWA elections, which were always hotly contested, particularly in the 1960s. John gives a description of two 'alliances' being formed at election time: the 'communist' group, which consisted of communists and sympathisers, and a second alliance, known by the name of its presidential candidate, which came together temporarily to contest the elections; thus two slates of candidates would contest each election (John 1969: 70–1). The group that lost the election 'formed an "Action Committee" to protest against irregularities in the elections. Occasionally the losers went further and formed their own association' (ibid.: 73).

John, writing of the Southall elections of 1965, states that

> For months before the elections, rival groups manoeuvred and tried to negotiate alliances. . . . Perhaps a hundred men took time off work to visit Indian homes and drum up support. 3,000 Indians voted in the election – 75 per cent of the IWA members and perhaps half of the adult Indian males in Southall and surrounding towns.
>
> (John 1969: 48)

Cyril Dunn (*Observer*, 21 April 1968), writing of the 1968 elections under the headline 'Little India goes to the polls', talks of five parties contesting the twenty-one executive committee posts. The elections were conducted on the local council election model with polling booths being set up in two schools, and symbols were used to identify the different parties. This system has persisted and the slates have been institutionalised to such a degree that only team nominations consisting of twenty-one candidates are now accepted for IWA elections (*Des Perdes*, 25 October 1985).

It is doubtful that electioneering on such a scale ever took place in the IWAs in other parts of the country and some IWA leaders say that if the kinds of 'slates' described by John ever existed they do not at the present time. However, accounts given by several people of the Coventry elections in the 1950s and 1960s certainly fit in with John's two-alliance model.

Besides the work involved in maintaining the organisation the IWAs had full programmes and became involved in a number of initiatives. The most pressing issue to absorb the IWAs in the 1950s, and, indeed, the main reason why some IWA leaders went to see Nehru when he visited Britain in 1957, was the question of the forged passports. In the mid 1950s it was extremely difficult for Indians to be issued with passports to enter Britain as India was trying to curb emigration. Because of this some people asked for passports to go to other countries and then came to Britain, while others fell into the hands of racketeers in India and paid for forged passports. This led to Indians living in Britain not having valid passports, which meant they could not have their passports renewed or visit India,. The IWAs worked both to help individuals facing this problem and to lobby the Indian High Commission so that each Indian in Britain with a forged passport could be issued with a valid one. This was one of the first campaigns which eventually succeeded and brought prestige to the IWAs (Desai 1963: 105; Aurora 1967: 45).

IWAs also fulfilled what has become known as a 'social work' role, with leading members filling out forms for fellow Indians, helping them in their dealings with bureaucracy, and generally giving help and advice where it was needed. The social work role of the IWAs has persisted to the present day although it has changed in form.

Another IWA activity which had both political and social importance was the arranging of public meetings. These meetings usually took place in a town hall and involved speakers, sometimes from India to talk about the situation back home, sometimes from Britain to speak on subjects such as trade unionism and British immigration law. Such meetings often included cultural entertainments. IWAs were also involved in the hiring of cinemas to show Indian films. This has always been a method used by immigrant associations to raise funds, but it became of less and less importance, and in the present day, with the advent of videos, hardly exists at all.

The aspect of the work of the IWA which distinguishes it from the majority of other ethnic associations is its commitment to trade unionism and its political agenda. The disagreements among IWA activists regarding the kinds of political work they should be involved in and the alliances they should be making will become apparent in the discussion of the splits – as, indeed, some of these differences were factors in creating splits. For the time being, suffice it to say that IWAs became involved in all trade union activity and anti-racist and anti-immigration legislation work, and some IWAs were instrumental in forming multi-racial, anti-racist groups which were outside the state system, notably the Co-ordinating Committee Against Racial Discrimination (CCARD) formed in 1960/1 and the Black People's Alliance (BPA) formed in 1968, while others became involved with state bodies such as the Commission for Racial Equality (CRE) and its precursors, and the Campaign Against Racial Discrimination (CARD).[6]

So the history of the IWA is of a number of local associations, some formed independently of one another because of particular needs (such as the South Staffordshire branch discussed by Hiro); others formed by a core of people within an overall design (i.e. the communist formulation) coming together and forming a centralised body. Even before the IWA was centralised there were many differences within local associations, and also from association to association, which led to minor fissions and takeovers. However, after centralisation the call for unity and political consensus became much stronger, and this created the potential for the organisation to break up into its political constituents. The splits described in the next section have been explained both by scholars and by the people themselves in terms of personality conflicts, fights for resources such as cinemas, power-seeking of individual leaders who, it was said, could only be satisfied if they headed their own organisation, and so on. There can be no doubt that all these explanations have some validity and that those individuals who felt they had to leave a group for those sorts of reasons indeed did so. At the same time it cannot be a coincidence that the splits resulted in groups with different political ideologies, and that although there has been some exchange in personnel between the groups, the actual groupings have survived for lengthy periods.

Organisational splits

Moderates and radicals: the 1960–2 split

According to the members of the IWA Southall, the association never became a part of the centralised association which was set up in 1958. The IWA (GB) claims in turn that Southall first affiliated and then withdrew. One IWA (GB) leader gives 1962 as the date when Southall withdrew, and cites the names of two IWA Southall office holders who were also on the IWA (GB) central committee as evidence that Southall had indeed affiliated. Another IWA (GB) leader gives 1960 as the year of Southall's withdrawal. However, whatever the actual details, there is agreement that Southall and the IWA (GB) went their separate ways and there is some agreement regarding why this happened. Vishnu Sharma, a leader of the Southall IWA at the time, considered the centralised group which had been formed to have been initiated by, and dominated by, the Communist Party. He wanted his group to remain non-sectarian and become a mass movement, bringing together Indians of all political persuasions. Although he himself is a communist he did not want to be part of an organisation which was CP controlled. The other IWA leaders from that period agree that this was a reason why Vishnu Sharma wanted the Southall branch to retain its autonomy, but at least one of the people from the IWA (GB) considers this separation to have been a class split and sees the IWA Southall as a bourgeois association.

It is also said by some commentators that the split was a reflection of the split within the Communist Party of India (CPI). To consider this point, an aside is necessary on what was happening within the CPI at this period. It is generally agreed that the CPI split was directly attributable to the breakdown of ideological unity within the international communist movement arising out of the Sino-Soviet dispute (Retzlaff 1969: 330). However, factionalism within the party in India was also connected to a number of internal issues. The CPI analyses of the nature of the ruling Indian Congress Party, attitudes towards the INC's foreign and internal policies (ibid.: 340–1), organisational issues, and, decisively, the border dispute with China, were all matters which deepened the rift between left and right in the party. These differences eventually led to a split in the CPI which was formalised in 1965, from which time there were two Indian communist parties; the rightist CPI and the leftist Communist Party of India – Marxist (CPI–M). The communists in Southall IWA supported the CPI while most of the communists in the IWA (GB) aligned themselves with the new party, the CPI–M. However, the CPGB only recognised the CPI, so those Indians who sympathised with the CPI–M could not work within the CPGB. They therefore left the CPGB and formed their own Association of Indian Communists in Great Britain in 1965. By 1966 the Indian branches of the CPGB had dissolved.

To return to the question at hand, although the communists in IWA Southall stayed in the CPI whereas the IWA (GB) communists aligned themselves with the CPI–M, this did not happen until after 1964 when the party split in India, whereas the IWA Southall/IWA (GB) split took place at least two years before that. It is possible that just as the factions which led to the split existed among Indian communists in India long before the party was formally divided, they also existed among Indian communists here. Nevertheless, the IWA split cannot be seen as a result of the Indian split since it predates it.

Furthermore, it is also said that IWA Southall is dominated by the Congress Party, and certainly, on the basis of the party affiliation of the leadership, there is justification for pointing to both CPI and Congress influence. The executive of the IWA Southall has often included members of the Overseas Congress Party. A general secretary of the IWA Southall, Tarsem Singh Toor, who was assassinated in 1986, was at the same time the secretary of the Indian Overseas Congress (*Asian Times*, 14 February 1986, no. 157). Another piece of evidence informants give for linking IWA Southall with the Congress Party is that Indira Gandhi was invited to speak in Southall in 1979 (she was prevented from doing so by the Midlands IWAs). From reports of past Southall elections it appears that CPI and Congress people have sometimes put up separate slates and sometimes coalitions. Other Indian parties, such as Janata, also regularly put up candidates. It should also be stressed that throughout the period and to the present time, whatever the political sympathies of individual members, the organisation as a whole does not have any formal alignments with parties in either India or Britain.

Given the plethora of parties that have tried to control Southall, it is not possible to sustain the argument that the separation of the IWA Southall and its continuing independence from the IWA (GB) is due to a specific party split in India. Rather, the wider issue, reflected both in the general comment of the IWA (GB) that the split with Southall was a class split, and in the IWA Southall's position that they did not want to be aligned with the Communist Party but to unite all Indians, is a more useful way of looking at the differences in the positions of the two groups. It also indicates the importance of the class versus ethnicity issue. While the IWA Southall wanted to unite all Indians, claiming that all Indians have something significant in common by virtue of being Indian, the IWA (GB) wanted to be an organisation of Indian *workers*, and was concerned with the class interests of that specific group. This has sometimes meant that the IWA (GB) has supported one group of Indians against another, e.g. in strike action where the workforce and the employer have all been Indian (e.g. the case of Raindi textiles). So where there is conflict of interests, the policy of the IWA (GB) would not be to strive for the unity of the ethnic group, but to support the working class within it.

Other major conflicts between the IWA Southall and the IWA (GB) which were relevant in 1962, and continue to be important, are related to the role each grouping saw the IWA fulfilling and the way they perceived race relations in Britain.

To start with the first issue, the IWA Southall was committed to welfare and social work, and to providing entertainment. This last activity meant they were able to make money through showing Indian films at the Dominion cinema. The IWA Southall's welfare role involved carrying out a great deal of case work. In 1962 they opened an advisory centre on a part-time basis, and in 1965 they bought the building they were using and were able to offer the service full time. In 1967 they bought the Dominion cinema in Southall, thus combining all their activities under one roof and acquiring valuable assets. The cinema was later taken over by the Department of the Environment, renovated, and reopened as a community centre housing a number of projects.

None of these activities in itself created conflicts, but the issue of the Dominion cinema was always a contentious one since it meant that Southall became by far the richest branch, as well as being the largest. This led to Southall feeling it had more to give than to receive from the centralised organisation, and therefore refusing to accept the same conditions as the other branches or central committee directives. Also, the central committee did not want Southall to become exclusively a case-work organisation and, according to one person from the IWA (GB), nor did it regard Southall's money-making activities as acceptable. The IWA (GB) felt the organisation should rely on donations from the membership, and not set out to earn money. The issue of the Dominion cinema comes up again and again in interviews, with ex-IWA members saying it was the real reason for the split, and present IWA leaders placing its significance in the context of other differences in outlook.

The second issue had to do with the different perspectives on race relations held by the IWA Southall and the IWA (GB). These hinged on how the two organisations saw immigrants in this country, and the way they related to race relations bodies. The impression given by press reports (e.g. Colin McGlashen, *Observer*, 9 January 1965), De Witt John (1969), and the IWA (GB) leaders, is that the IWA Southall had an assimilationist philosophy and saw their role as being to educate Indians to make themselves acceptable to the British. The IWA (GB), on the other hand, considered the problem to be racism and therefore saw the role of the IWA as one of fighting racism and not of changing Indians.

These differences became more pronounced after the split and after the race relations legislation of the mid-1960s which brought government race relations machinery into existence. The IWA Southall worked with these bodies and also joined CARD.[6] All this was unacceptable to the IWA (GB): their analysis of state racism was such that they refused to become involved with government bodies or with CARD, which they saw as a front organisation for the Labour Party. One IWA Southall principle which was shared with the IWA (GB) was that they should not accept state funding. However, when Vishnu Sharma lost his leadership position this principle was dropped.

At the present time the IWA Southall is an autonomous organisation and has no branches. It has a committee of twenty-six (all men) of which ten are office holders (Report of the General Secretary, IWA Southall, 1985). The composition of the IWA Southall is said by other IWAs to consist mostly of businessmen and certainly the leadership appears to be predominantly middle class.

In 1986, the president, Piarra Khabra, estimated that some five hundred members attended the last general meeting. He says the IWA Southall is more progressive than any other black organisation in the country and that it is the most democratic, with all decisions being taken through voting. The IWA Southall has changed its constitution several times, and P. Khabra believes it is time to change it again. He considers it an important attribute of the organisation that it is able to change to meet the needs of society.

In 1986 the IWA Southall was located at Southall town hall from where it ran three MSC-funded projects – a welfare advice service, Southall community support service, and an IWA environmental project. Thirty-six people were working for these projects including three supervisors and three full-time workers (Report of the General Secretary, IWA Southall, 1985). The association continues its campaigning and representational role and has recently been involved in the campaigns against the nationality laws, racist attacks, and many other issues. It is consulted by the press, the police, and other groups when these bodies want to tap the feeling in Southall. It also has links with a number of other agencies and one press release describes it as an umbrella organisation of Asians in the area (ibid.). Its wider political involvement has included backing the miners' strike, opposing the abolition of the GLC, and taking part in CND marches.

As this account indicates, whether the IWA Southall is seen as a 'bourgeois' association or not, it certainly took a moderate road on most issues when compared with the IWA (GB) and it fits into the pattern of many ethnic associations which are part state-funded, run welfare and social centres, and become involved with CRCs, Race Relations Committees, and so on. The IWA (GB), on the other hand, remained independent of the state and involved itself with trade union issues and black politics. However, neither the parting of the ways of the two IWAs nor the apparent differences between them are absolute. For example, at associational election time it is always possible for the IWA (GB) to win support in Southall and they always try to do so by putting up their own slate. On the trade union front, one of the first important Asian strikes, the dispute at Woolf's over management's attempts to break the union, was led by N.S. Hundal of the IWA Southall. It is nevertheless true to say that the IWA Southall was the more moderate of the two associations at the time of the split and continues to be so.

Militants and communists: the 1967 split

Although the IWA (GB) eventually had branches in Southall and the rest of the country, it was concentrated in the West Midlands. One ex-IWA member talked of a 'dual system', with the IWA Southall under the leadership of Vishnu Sharma in the south, and IWA (GB) under the leadership of Jagmohan Joshi in the Midlands. However, this 'dual system' broke down when a further split took place within the IWA (GB) in 1967.

This split was more clearly related to Indian politics. As already outlined above, the communists within the IWA (GB) aligned themselves with the CPI–M and worked together with the Association of Indian Communists in GB. There were a number of differences both within this association and within the IWA on a variety of issues regarding Britain, India, and the international scene. These differences were brought to a head by the Naxalbari uprising in West Bengal.

The Naxalbari uprising was not supported by the CPI–M. A CPI–M supporter in the UK explained this by saying the CPI–M did not consider the uprising to be revolutionary since the peasants had not seized land from the landlords but from some tea planters who had been given land for their own use. They were not owners but tillers. It was also considered too small to be significant. However, in China it was hailed as a small fire which could spread across India. Those Indian communists who were involved in the uprising or sympathetic to it later broke off from the CPI–M to form the CPI–ML (Marxist–Leninists).

The sequence of events in Britain was complicated and involved a number of meetings both of the Association of Indian Communists in GB and of the IWA (GB), and the participation of two members of the politburo of the CPI–M. There are differing perspectives of what happened at these meetings, but the outcome was a split between Jagmohan Joshi and his group who backed the uprising, and those who were behind the CPI–M.

Although the Naxalbari uprising brought about an open rift, there were many other issues of conflict. The question of whether the IWA should follow the CPI–M line was a major one in the sense of whether they agreed with their politics, and also from an organisational point of view, as some people wanted to develop their own organisation and not to have to take orders from Calcutta. Other differences included the analysis of the global situation and international politics. Also, Joshi's group was linked with China because there were many Marxist–Leninists within the group, and the analysis of the leadership on many issues could be seen as a Marxist–Leninist analysis. Still more important were a number of issues to do with Britain.

The analysis presented by Joshi's supporters regarding racism was that black workers, through their struggle against imperialism in their own countries and their double exploitation in this country, have become more aware. Black workers were therefore the group destined to lead the struggle, but once they were involved in struggle white workers would join with them. The position of the other side was that black workers did not have a special role, and the initiative for the struggle had to come from the whole of the working class. An additional difference arising out of this one was that Joshi's group, because they saw black workers as having a special role, believed in forming alliances with other black groups; the other side in the dispute was against this type of alliance as they considered it to be a kind of inverted racism which would distance them from ordinary white workers who, they felt, were the most important allies of all. The difference in these two positions was fundamental and led to one group becoming concerned with black power issues while the other was committed to a more traditional class analysis. The black power dimension was, and is, a fairly controversial one. The IWA had to tread carefully in defining what it meant by it in order not to lose Indian members. The efforts to create a black alliance met with some success: this IWA forged links with black groups, culminating in the formation of the Black People's Alliance, and later there were limited links with the Black Panthers.

Joshi's group also believed in defence committees (which the other group thought were suicidal), and it took a strong stand against affiliating with CRCs or other government bodies or accepting state funding. The other group was more ambivalent on this issue.

From 1967 there was no longer one IWA (GB) but two. However both are called the IWA (GB). In order to avoid confusion I shall call one IWA (GB) A. Jouhal and the other IWA (GB) P. Singh. The former refers to the group which supported Joshi and the latter the group which supported the CPI–M. Because this split was of the centralised body, it affected all the branches and resulted in two local IWAs existing in most areas.

The two IWAs continued to do similar work and in some cases even worked together, e.g. on bodies such as Campaign Against Racist Laws (CARL) and Campaign Against Racism and Fascism (CARF) and in some trade union activities. However, the two groups were definitely rivals, competing for members and for recognition as the 'real' IWA, both in the eyes of the community and in the eyes of the press. As outlined above, political differences between them were various but for many people their divergent relationships to the Naxalites were the defining characteristics of the two groups, and to the present time one group is referred to as 'Naxalites' and the other as 'communists'. In fact, the notion of Naxalite no longer refers to the uprising in West Bengal but simply means militant. The idea that one IWA was more militant than the other certainly reflects the difference between the two, and is even reflected in their constitutions (see appendix).

The IWA (GB) A. Jouhal (the 'Naxalite') included many non-Punjabis, both in its membership and through its alliances, and was oriented towards Britain and the international scene. The IWA (GB) P. Singh was oriented more towards India. These orientations appear to be partly reflected in the languages used by the two associations. For example, the IWA (GB) A. Jouhal has published many pamphlets in English while the IWA (GB) P. Singh has published extensively in the Punjabi newspaper *Des Perdes*.[7]

The situation in the 1980s is that both the IWA (GB)s are active although not at their previous capacity. Most of the local branches are still in existence, though some are not very active. Youth and women's groups have been set up by both IWAs. Both groups continue with their representational, campaigning, and trade union roles. The IWA (GB) A. Jouhal supports an advice centre in the IWA's building on the Soho Road in Birmingham, which is also the headquarters of the association. The IWA (GB) P. Singh does not appear to have much of a case-work role.

The members of both groups have a number of party affiliations but the leadership continues to be predominantly communist. The IWA (GB) P. Singh has clear links with the CPI–ML through the Association of Indian Communists in GB, and provides a platform for visiting CPI–ML politicians. The IWA (GB) A. Jouhal does not have such links with any party in India. As an organisation neither group supports any British parties but individual members belong to the Labour Party, and a member of each of the IWA (GB)s has recently become a Labour Party councillor.

The overall position regarding the Labour Party of the IWA (GB) P. Singh is that it is no different from the Conservatives, since both are bourgeois parties and neither challenges capitalism. Both IWAs have also put up Independent candidates for a number of local elections.

Most of the other positions of the two IWAs continue as outlined above but the organisations are rethinking some of their strategies. They are also facing a new issue: the question of Khalistan and the rise of Sikh fundamentalism. All IWAs oppose Khalistan, and all have been attacked by Khalistanis – both physically and verbally – while the newspaper of the IWA (GB) A. Jouhal has been publicly burned outside the Gurdwara (Sikh temple) in Birmingham. Both IWA (GB)s admit to having lost membership through their anti-Khalistan stand, but say they are building up again.

Sikhism: the split of 1983

Another split took place within the IWA (GB) P. Singh (the 'communists') in the early 1980s, and resulted in Naranjan Noor, the president at the time, creating his own organisation. The technical issue which created this split had to do with party discipline; the substantive matter was the IWA's position regarding Sikh culture. According to the leadership of the IWA (GB) P. Singh, Mr Noor was checked by the organisation over a number of issues, the main one being the turban case which resulted in Sikhism being accepted as an ethnicity, or even a nationality, in Britain.

The background to this case was that Mr Noor, a teacher in Wolverhampton at the time, issued a statement calling the Wolverhampton headmaster who refused to allow children to wear turbans to school a racist. Two weeks later the IWA called a meeting and his own branch members criticised him; they felt he should have made a different type of statement. He then championed the turban case. On this point I was told by his critics that the IWA supports religious freedom but it cannot be *used* to save the symbols of religion. He was therefore criticised on the grounds that championing the turban case was the duty of religious people, and the IWA, as a secular organisation, should not take it on. Officially the IWA did not support him though, as individuals, some did. Mr Noor next organised a meeting in Leicester for the Gurdwaras in the name of the IWA. This brought about further criticism.

Following this conflict, when the IWA elections came up Mr Noor was directed not to contest any of them. Defying this directive, he still stood for elections (and was elected). He was therefore expelled from the Association of Indian Communists in GB. After the expulsion, according to his opponents, his support in the IWA diminished. He carried some people with him out of the association and organised a new IWA. I shall call this IWA the IWA (GB) N. Noor.

Mr Noor's presentation of the split between himself and his old IWA is that they were taking an 'anti-Indian culture stance'. He does not regard his secession as a split, nor does he accept that he was expelled from the IWA (he was not expelled from the IWA but from the Association of Indian Communists). Instead, he claims that he and his faction ousted the then leadership. His association is, in his view, the 'real' IWA. Hence, there is now also dissent regarding which IWA has the ownership of the IWA building, a matter which appears fraught with legal ambiguities.

This IWA is small and it is not possible to say whether it will survive in the long term. However, the split is significant because it concerns the issue of Sikh ethnicity and Sikh nationalism.

The positions of the IWA (GB) N. Noor on most issues are similar to those of the IWA (GB) P. Singh and they also have a similar relationship to the CPI–M in India (although according to the IWA (GB) P. Singh it is not recognised by the CPI–M). The formal position on India is also the same: both associations oppose the creation of an independent Khalistan. However, because the blame for recent events at Amritsar is attributed by the IWA (GB) N. Noor to the Congress Party (it considers Congress to have 'planted' Bhindrawala in the Akali Party and in the Temple, in order to 'create problems' for Akalis), the Noor IWA does not blame the Akali Party for those events. In the biennial report Mr Noor's IWA calls on the Indian government to accept the ten demands of Akali in order to solve the Punjab problem. Indeed, Mr Noor actually went to talk to Bhindrawala in the Temple and to consult him on the turban case, and is linked to him unfavourably in the eyes of other IWAs.

The main difference between Mr Noor's position and that of the other IWAs relates to his analysis of culture, and the importance he attaches to the symbols of Sikhism. The IWA (GB) P. Singh does not consider Sikhism to be a 'nation' or an 'ethnicity', but a religion. Its members consider the Punjab to be a distinct culture area and therefore want to promote Punjabi culture, but say this culture group includes Hindus and Muslims, not just Sikhs.

Conclusion

The IWA started off as one organisation with specific aims. Today there are four organisations bearing its name and they display a broad range of strategies and political views. The greatest divergence is probably between the IWA Southall and the three other organisations. Over the years, however, other important ideological shifts have occurred, precipitating the schisms between the other three organisations. The kinds of issues the IWAs have split over have been numerous.

A major source of cleavage has always been the allegiances to particular parties in India, and the politics of India. However, it is important to stress that what happens in Britain does not simply mirror what happens in India. Analyses which assume a simple causal relationship between Indian politics and events in the IWAs in Britain are strongly refuted by many members of the IWAs who point to the various specifically local issues in Britain that have concerned them.

The question of what relationship the IWAs should have with the British state and its local representative bodies, comes up again and again in discussions with members of all the IWAs. The issue is fraught with dilemmas, particularly on the question of whether IWAs should accept financial help and whether they should agree to sit on government bodies. So far IWA Southall has been the only IWA association to accede to such institutional incorporation into state-sponsored bodies. Most of the arguments against accepting state funding and participation in government co-optive bodies are well known: it is felt that it is not possible for a group to remain autonomous if it is being funded by the state; that for a group fighting the state to do so using state funds verges on the absurd. On participation on co-optive committees the argument is similar: if a group, in this case black people in Britain, wants to change structures of oppression this cannot be done by participating in the very bodies which have been generated by those oppressive structures. The counter-arguments are more pragmatic: given the limitations of resources and the urgency of the issues affecting black people it is sometimes necessary to accept funding, or sit on co-optive bodies. In fact, most IWAs usually do not refuse to sit on these various bodies in a blanket way, agreeing to sit on them under certain conditions, but it is rare for these conditions to be accepted.

In this context the issue of whether racism could be fought using traditional class analysis and traditional class struggle has been continually debated. In this matter the two IWA (GB)s formed different positions, which led them to look for different types of alliance.

A further issue dividing the IWA membership relates to its bases of unity: should the IWA unite on the basis of ethnicity or class? One of the remarkable features of the IWA (GB)s has been their continued loyalty to their working-class members. This upholding of the workers' cause contrasts sharply with, for example, the shifting allegiance of Cypriot communists in the UK for whom the unity of the ethnic group is given precedence over the fight against exploitation by Cypriot entrepreneurs. Yet IWA Southall has in fact developed as an ethnic – Punjabi – association, and it is doubtful that it can still be referred to unambiguously as a workers' association. So, too, the schisms in the IWA (GB) have had an underlying ethnic dimension. The most recent split was, indeed, explicitly on ethnic nationalist causes, and as such was symptomatic of a greater cleavage within the Punjabi–Sikh community as a whole, both in Britain and in India.

Hence, the most recent issue to confront the IWAs has been the demand for a separate state of Khalistan and the idea that Sikhism is a separate ethnicity and culture. In the 1980s these questions were central to the relationship of the IWAs with other Sikh organisations and were, of course, at the centre of the split with Mr Noor.

I have stressed throughout this chapter that seceding organisations which have emerged from IWA schisms have persisted. This is not to say that the organisations are static. With the changing political situation the IWAs have changed as well and it is conceivable that they could even reunite. Hence, at present the IWA (GB) A. Jouhal and the IWA (GB) P. Singh are working together on a number of campaigns, and people from the IWA (GB) P. Singh have said that, at the present time, racism in Britain and the issue of Khalistan are issues which unite them rather than divide them. The spirit of unity was also working in a different direction. In 1988 the celebrations of the IWA's Golden Jubilee were carried out jointly by the IWA (GB) A. Jouhal and members of the IWA Southall. At the same time attempts were being made in Coventry to create a new branch bringing together all the IWA elements with the exception of the IWA (GB) P. Singh. Also there are suggestions that the IWA (GB) A. Jouhal has reformulated its position regarding a number of issues in Britain. For example, at a public meeting in 1987 Avtar Jouhal said the role of community organisations in the 1980s and 1990s is to work as pressure groups on mainstream political parties. How this statement should be interpreted, and the way IWAs will reconstitute themselves, are open questions.

What can be said is that, in the final analysis, all IWAs share some fundamental premises. Personal rivalries, ideological divisions, organisational schisms, external communal pressures, tend to highlight the historic *divisions* within the broader parent organisation. Yet, like the wider labour movement itself to which the IWA belongs, such divisive issues mask a basic unity of purpose.

Given the publicity attending the periodic factional and ideological struggles, it is easy to brand leaders as self-seeking or manipulative, as 'non-representative' of the whole community. It is, indeed, clear that internal schisms have undermined the representative legitimacy of the IWA which was a feature of its federated unity and strong centralised institutions in its heyday. Other 'Indian' or black organisations have been established, fractionising the common front forged during the initial migratory period.

Yet the very passionate involvement in the IWA which has precipitated the schisms within it, is also the basis of its continued organisational strength. The commitment of leaders and their followers to ideological issues is profoundly rooted both in the struggles within India itself, reflecting the continuing loyalty to the home country, and in the fight against racism and disadvantage in Britain. It is passionate commitment, rather than sheer self-interest, which fuels internal disputes. The ideological and symbolic discourses in which these disputes are articulated reflect the historical moments in which factional conflicts, and the cleavages they generate, occur.

© 1991 Sasha Josephides

Appendix

The aims and objectives of the centralised IWA organisation were as follows:

To organise Indians to:

1 safeguard and improve their conditions of life and work;
2 seek co-operation of the Indian High Commission in the UK towards the fulfilment of its aims and objects;
3 promote co-operation and unity with the trade union and labour movement in Great Britain;
4 strengthen friendship with the British and all other peoples in Great Britain and co-operate with their organisations to this end;
5 fight against all forms of discrimination based on race, colour, creed, or sex for equal human rights and social and economic opportunities, and co-operate with other organisations for the same;
6 promote the cause of friendship, peace, and freedom for all countries and co-operate with other organisations for the same;
7 keep its members in particular, and people in Great Britain generally, informed of political, economic, and social developments in India; and
8 undertake social, welfare, and cultural activities towards the fulfilment of the above aims and objects.

Constitution of IWA (GB) Prem singh

Aims and objects

To organise Indians to:

1 safeguard their interests;
2 fight to improve their conditions of life and work;
3 encourage them to join the trade unions and to promote co-operation and unity with trade union and labour movement in GB;
4 strengthen friendship with the British and all other peoples in GB and co-operate with all progressive organisations to this end;
5 fight against all forms of discrimination based on race, colour, creed or sex, for equal human rights and social and economic opportunities, and co-operate with other organisations for the same;
6 express solidarity with the people fighting for national salvation and promote the cause of friendship, peace and freedom of all countries, and co-operate with other organisations, national and international, striving for the same;
7 keep its members, in particular, and people in GB generally, informed of political, economic and social developments in India; and to strengthen the democratic forces there;

8 undertake social, welfare and cultural activities.

Constitution of IWA (GB) Avtar Jouhal

The Association shall work to organise Indian immigrants and their descendants in Great Britain to:

A
1 Wage militant consistent and uncompromising struggle in every possible way against racialism and fascism in Great Britain in all its forms.
2 Organise safeguards against fascist attacks on life and property.
3 Fight against discrimination based on national origin, creed, sex, religion and equal rights of national minorities in all fields.
4 Unite with other black people, other national minorities and those sections of the indigenous population who uncompromisingly oppose racialism and fascism.
5 Fully participate in the Trade Union movement and in all struggles of the British working class against capitalism and for socialism.

B
1 Support all economic, social and political struggles of the Indian masses against semi-feudal and semi-colonial society in India and for a people's Democratic India.
2 Publicise the political, economic and social situations in India among its members and other people.
3 Seek co-operation and unity in action with other organisations working for the same end.

C
1 Support the National Liberation Struggles of the Asian, African and Latin American peoples and co-operate with other organisations working for the same end.
2 Support all the just struggles of the people of all countries against imperialism of all types.

D
1 Promote welfare services, undertake cultural and social activities for the fulfilment of the above aims and objects.

Notes

1 The IWA (GB) Avtar Jouhal consider him to have been a founder member while the other IWAs give him little prominence. Most

published sources refer to him as a founder or the founder, but a recent article in *India Abroad* claims he was not even in Coventry at the time of the setting up of the IWA.

2 It is often said that the IWA is a predominantly Sikh association. Many people go further and say it is a predominantly Jat Sikh association. IWA members get irritated by these claims and point to the existence of non-Jat Sikh members, non-Sikhs, and non-Punjabis. This is one of those points which can never be satisfactorily resolved. Certainly there are non-Jat Sikhs in the IWA. Jagmohan Joshi and Vishnu Sharma, two of the most central people in the IWA, are Brahman. There are a number of Gujarati and Bengali members, particularly in the London branches. At least two of the people I interviewed were Ramgharia caste, and Dallats (an Asian word meaning 'oppressed' used to refer to the so-called scheduled castes) abound, particularly in Derby and Bedford.

3 It is not always clear whether this category refers to actual itinerant traders or to people of the pedlar (Bhatra) caste. Desai (1963: 4–5) says pedlars were Bhatra Sikhs.

4 Though there is photographic evidence that the IWA Coventry existed throughout these years (see group photographs of an IWA executive committee for each of the years from 1945 to 1953 in *Ingland vasda Panjab* (The Punjab in England), Part iv, published in Coventry around 1988). One informant said there was a revolt and the young people took over the 'old guard' in 1953, so it may be more a question of a transformation than a resurrection.

5 For example, Harry Baker of Birmingham Trades Council withdrew his support of an anti-colour bar statement issued by a group convened by Jagmohan Joshi, because it had communist support (*Evening Despatch*, 10 August 1961). Much of the press coverage on the IWA throughout the 1960s was obsessed with whether or not they were communists. This reached a peak in the late 1960s over the question of IWAs and industrial disputes (see Duffield 1988: 131).

6 The different positions of the IWA Southall and the IWA (GB) in relation to CARD are discussed by Heineman (1972: 95–6 and passim).

7 This is an impressionistic view supported by an analysis of the Punjabi press by Darshan Singh Tatla (personal communication).

References

Books and Articles

Adams, T.W. (1971) *AKEL: The Communist Party of Cyprus*, Hoover Institution Press.
Anthias, (1982) 'Class and ethnic divisions in Cyprus', unpublished Ph.D. thesis, Bedford College, University of London.
Aurora, G.S. (1967) *The New Frontiersman*, Bombay: Popular Prakashan.
Bailey, F. (1969) *Stratagems and Spoils: A Social Anthropology of Politics*, Oxford: Blackwell.

Barth, F. (1966) *Models of Social Organisation*, RAI Occasional Paper no. 23, London: Royal Anthropological Institute of Great Britain and Ireland.

Chandra, Bipan (ed.) (1983) *The Indian Left: Critical Appraisals*, New Delhi: Vikas.

Clark, David (1975) 'Recollections of resistance: Udham Singh and the IWA', *Race and Class* 17 (1): 75–7.

Desai, R. (1963) *Indian Immigrants in Britain*, Oxford: Oxford University Press.

Duffield, Mark (1988) *Black Radicalism and the Politics of De-industrialisation*, Aldershot: Gower.

Heineman, B.W. (1972) *The Politics of the Powerless*, Oxford: Oxford University Press.

Hiro, D. (1971) *Black British, White British*, London: Eyre & Spottiswoode.

Jacobs, Brian (1986) *Black Politics and Urban Crisis in Britain*, Cambridge: Cambridge University Press.

John, De Witt (1969) *Indian Workers Association in Britain*, Oxford: Oxford University Press.

Mayer, A. (1966) 'The significance of quasi-groups in the study of complex societies', in Michael Banton (ed.) *The Social Anthropology of Complex Societies*, London: Tavistock.

NCCL (National Council for Civil Liberties) (1980) 'Southall 23 April 1979', report of the Unofficial Committee of Enquiry.

NCCL (National Council for Civil Liberties) (1980) 'The death of Blair Peach', supplementary report of the Unofficial Committee of Enquiry.

Ramdin, Ron (1987) *The Making of the Black Working Class in Britain*, Aldershot: Gower.

Retzlaff, Ralph (1969) 'Revisionists and sectarians: India's two communist parties', in Robert A. Scalapino (ed.) *The Communist Revolution in Asia*, London: Prentice-Hall.

Sivanandan, S. (1982) *A Different Hunger*, London: Pluto Press.

Southall Rights (1980) '23 April 1979', London: Crest Press.

Documents and Newspapers

Report of the General Secretary, IWA (GB) Avtar Jouhal:
   1967 (Leicester Conference)
   1970 (Nottingham Conference)
Report of the General Secretary, IWA Southall:
   May 1974
   May 1985
'Smash racialism and fascism', IWA (GB) Avtar Jouhal, 1976.
'The victims speak: A comment on the White Paper and the general racial situation in the UK', IWA (GB) Avtar Jouhal, n.d.
Lok Shakti
Lalkar
National and Midlands Press
Des Perdes
India Abroad

Chapter ten

The churches, leadership, and ethnic minorities

Mark R.D. Johnson

Introduction

In any discussion of 'leadership' in society, and especially with regard
to the location of black or ethnic minority communities in Britain,
the role of religious agencies and in particular the churches cannot
be ignored. Leadership, of course, may refer to a number of
attributes or levels. There are political and administrative leaders –
those who speak for specific groups in political and administrative
forums such as local authority councils, Parliament, and the many
consultative bodies which these agencies set up. For political forums,
some degree of popular support or legitimacy may be required –
although certain bishops of the Anglican church sit in the House of
Lords by right of title and may exercise leadership on that account,
having been selected by a relatively 'undemocratic' route: as Fogarty
(1989: 43) observes, 'A Bishop speaks with the weight of his office.'
For consultative bodies, by contrast, it is frequently sufficient merely
to have been 'identified' as a 'community leader', and for that purpose religious leaders are often seen as relatively easily located
spokesmen (less often spokeswomen). But leadership comes in other
forms as well: in campaigning groups where commitment and a degree of articulacy are the prime qualities required, and in spiritual
leadership which may be more important to the members of the religious community than to the wider world. Pastoral leadership is
allied to this, although qualitatively distinct, and in both spheres –
campaigning and spiritual leadership – church members and priests
play an important local role which is not necessarily acknowledged
beyond local arenas.

The central feature of leadership as it is discussed in this volume,
however, has to do with the way black or ethnic groups challenge
British society, and attempt to bring about change in it. In that sense,
too, the churches have played a significant historical role in affecting
the climate of 'race relations' in Britain. While it is undoubtedly

correct to observe that the abolition of slavery owed as much to the struggles of black people themselves, and to the economic factors discussed by Adam Smith, as it did to 'humanitarianism' (Williams 1966: 197), there can be little doubt that at least in the popular mind in Britain the role of the churches was critical in attaining this end. Thus Coupland's words on the 'Memory of Wilberforce' may be echoed: 'The conscience of all England was awakened. That . . . the slave system was abolished . . . not because it was good policy or good business to abolish it . . . but simply because of its iniquity' (Coupland, cited by Williams 1966: 201).

Clearly the 'saints' of the anti-slavery movement did manage to capture the high moral ground, and utilise that argument convincingly, thereby establishing a tradition of involvement in social reform for the religious establishment. Indeed, it was precisely on this basis that the Church Missionary Society commissioned its report, entitled *Act Now* (Hooper 1970), arguing that Wilberforce and his co-campaigners had been instrumental in its foundation, and that church members had played a continuing leading role in all the agencies that had developed to combat racism and prejudice.

More recently the Archbishop of Canterbury's Commission on Urban Priority Areas placed considerable emphasis on issues of 'race relations' in its study of urban blight (ACUPA 1985). That study, released in December 1985, was to provoke an extraordinary debate in the media, lasting for over two months. Even before its release a 'senior Government figure said . . . that parts of the report . . . were "pure marxist theology"' (*Sunday Times*, 1 December 1985) and a *Times* leading article labelled it 'A flawed faith' (*The Times*, 3 December 1985). Initial expectations were that its proposals would be ignored, that the 'political will to fight decay and deprivation is missing' (Longley 1985). Indeed, Paul Johnson wrote: 'the Church of England's report . . . has proved an unrelieved disaster which I fear has done permanent damage not just to the Anglican Church itself but to the cause of organised religion in general' (*Daily Telegraph*, 21 December 1985).

However, subsequent events would appear to indicate that such pessimism was misplaced: the report did turn out to be, in David Donnison's words, 'No mere church charade' (*Observer*, 6 December 1985). For example, in Birmingham a major festival for all Christians in the city was organised in April 1989, led by Archbishop Desmond Tutu: 'How did it come about? – It all started with Faith in the City. . .' (*Celebration News* 1: Easter 1988). Whatever the intentions, this week-long rally was seen by many, as was its twenty-four hour long predecessor, as 'a pastoral visit to black Christians in Birmingham' (Daniel 1988). Those who attended the events at the National

Exhibition Centre and in Birmingham, including many white Christians from surrounding areas who had little knowledge of black congregations, shared with those black fellow Christians in worship, praise, and prayer. Despite the financial failure of the initiative, there can be little doubt that this was for many who attended a significant learning experience.

Nor has the Church of England confined its 'anti-racist' or 'multi-racial' initiatives to the organising of public (and evangelistic) activities, or to the sponsorship of 'urban programme' welfare and economic projects. Most recently, headlines even in relatively secular newspapers have been given to the debate in the church's parliament, Synod, regarding the representation of black people. Such activity is not uncontested. In 1984, for example, Digby Anderson of the Social Affairs Unit contributed a full page in the *Daily Mail* under the heading 'Politics and the Church don't mix'; in this he observed: 'The Church today is not one of benign pastoral bishops, parochial clergy and parish churchgoers, but a highly articulate collection of committees, activists and bureaucratic lobbyists' (*Daily Mail*, 14 April 1984).

More recently, Fogarty, while acknowledging that 'the churches are of all organisations the ones most centrally concerned with the definition and propagation of values', has also queried how far it is proper for them to engage in such debates and participate in political activity (Fogarty 1989: 47).

The question that we need to ask here, however, is to what extent has this activity and lobbying facilitated the expression of some (perhaps indefinable) 'leadership qualities', or indeed generated a cadre of 'leaders', among Britain's black communities? That there are black leaders of churches is indisputable; that church leaders play an important role in society and politics is also a verifiable fact. Whether there is a necessary and visible connection between these two statements may prove more difficult to establish – especially since (in contrast to the more ostensibly secular society of America), recent students of British society appear largely to have neglected the role of the churches in social formation, in favour of other potential explanatory variables.

The churches and leadership

Among the literature which does exist relating to the role of churches and religion in social formation and leadership, certain themes can be discerned. There is, for example, an understanding that the non-conformist churches in particular played a critical role in the development of the Labour party and other movements deriving their support from the working classes. In part this was achieved by the creation or development of a class or elite of (largely) men who could discuss and organise the working class as equals with the capitalist owners and managerial classes, through their experiences of leadership within the churches. Other studies consider the role of religious organisations as 'cultural shelters' for migrants, and thus as buffers against the experience of racism. However, many commentators on the role of 'black-led churches' have argued that their principal function has been religious, and that there is little evidence that they have played until recently a significant role in the development of a political leadership. Indeed, the avoidance of political controversy by some black churches was blamed by the leaders of others for the unexpectedly low attendance at the visit of Bishop Tutu. Given the experience of the campaign for civil rights in the USA, however, where the leadership of the Revd Martin Luther King (Jnr) and other church colleagues was critical in the successes achieved by American blacks (Garrow 1988), it is relevant to ask why or whether the same pattern should not be found in Britain. Equally, of course, it has to be admitted that King was not necessarily seen as the leader of all the American black churches: 'Clearly many black fundamentalists viewed his liberalism and his connections with the "social gospel" of Rauschenbush with great suspicion . . . many thousands of black Christians remained locked within an otherworldly pietism which was alien to King's whole approach' (Leech 1988a).

Evidently the two types of churches can coexist and it would be wrong to expect all black churches to fall simply into the one category – and hence we should not be too surprised if some concentrate upon the production of a 'private' spiritual leadership and appear to ignore the social and political struggle of the 'public' world. As Goulbourne says, discussing West Indian political leadership in Britain, 'Unlike the church in Black America, the denominations in Britain appear to have little or no interest in politics. There may be some sense, of course, in keeping the worlds of Caesar and God rigidly apart' (Goulbourne 1988: 6). It may be argued that the American black churches came late to the public political arena proper, and that there has been more recently a swing against such involvement, but the period of engagement was undoubtedly significant and relevant to the British case.

Black churches: a threat and a blessing

The late Eric Williams, Prime Minister of Trinidad and Tobago for over two decades, selected a telling observation from the work of the historian, Arnold Toynbee, in his *Study of History* (the phraseology is that of the period 1934–54, when the work was originally published):

'It is possible that the Negro slave-immigrants who have found Christianity in America may perform the greater miracle of raising the dead to life . . . they may perhaps be capable of rekindling the cold grey ashes of Christianity' (Toynbee, cited by Williams 1966: 196). As we shall see, such an interpretation recurs in present-day analysis. However, an alternative viewpoint on the growth of black-led churches in Britain has come from the reports of sociologists such as Hill (1971, 1980) and Calley (1965). According to this viewpoint, the growth of black-led churches was a response to the experience of ethnic and status deprivation or 'a magico-religious refuge from the stresses and strains of settling down in a new country' (Calley 1965: 144). Certainly the churches have fulfilled such a role – as Rex and Moore (1967) observed in their study of Sparkbrook – and the growth of which they interpret as a withdrawal from white society. As Gerloff states:

> Many black Christians who were members of the historic churches in their homelands, stayed away from their original denominations and joined independent congregations who provided them precisely with that kind of identity, spiritual belonging and opportunity for sharing which is crucial for a people's sense of dignity. . . .
>
> Under the pressures of social discrimination, black Christian communities have built up their own training programmes . . . members, children and adults alike, in Sunday and Saturday schools, in correspondence courses and in bible colleges . . . which all have as their central concern the development of the potential of their own people. . . . All these manifold forms of voluntary education and encouragement for self-expression have motivated people deprived of 'normal' schooling or who have been discriminated against in the British educational system. Yet they have not been given social, let alone, state, recognition.
>
> (Gerloff 1980: 9, 10)

With recent changes and proposed reforms of the education system, there is, in fact, some evidence that black-led church schools may now take a higher profile and receive a greater degree of state support – although this may not always be an unmixed blessing – once again requiring the poor to subsidise their own escape routes from poverty. Nor are black-led schools always seen as an appropriate response to problems of racism. However, to the community such developments as the Seventh Day Adventist Church secondary school in Tottenham and primary school in Birmingham are seen as fulfilling a need (Maynard 1988). In this, the black churches are indeed providing a channel for the development of leadership and sustaining a role that historically dates back to the days of slavery:

> The black churches . . . have long been places for spiritual, cultural, social, in many cases even political survival. For the slaves, for instance, religious meetings were the fountainhead of black culture . . . the source of resistance and the training ground for black leadership, self-expression and self-determination.
>
> Black-led churches in Britain today are truly functioning organisations of West Indian and African immigrants. They are indeed the only organisations which offer unrestricted leadership to black people emanating from their own communities . . . they have provided crime prevention, court assistance, a fight against addiction, stabilisation of family life and educational facilities, and have increasingly co-operated with community workers, advisory services and the police. The 'host community' in contrast has hardly recognised at all that from which it has benefited.

> (Gerloff 1977: 15, 16)

Even if we accept that in the beginning the black-led (largely pentecostalist) churches accentuated their spiritual rather than social role, there are parallels to be drawn with the Methodist church in the eighteenth century. As Hempton insists, Methodism was in its origins a religious and salvation-oriented movement rather than a political one, which, however, became drawn into political debates such as that over slavery. This in turn meant that

> the anti-slavery agitation had two main consequences for the development of Methodist political attitudes. First, the libertarian rhetoric employed throughout the anti-slavery campaign further eroded the ability of Wesleyan conservatives to keep political control of the connexion. . . . Second, the style and techniques of the anti-slavery agitation served as models for subsequent religio-political crusades.

> (Hempton 1984: 210)

In contrast, Moore and Colls's studies of Methodism in the North East of England

> agree that the most important feature of village methodism in mining communities was not so much the politics of its leaders and members, as its sense of community and reassurance for people experiencing profound social and economic changes. . . . It helped explain and took the sting out of, suffering and death. It provided a moral and religious framework for the education of the young. Its individualistic conversionism and corporate expectancy in prayer meetings added drama and a sense of importance to

otherwise humdrum lives . . . and created a religious alternative to the local (tavern) culture.

(Hempton 1984: 214)

. . . there was within the Methodist structure ample scope for individual self-improvement to find institutional expression. It was through the opportunities afforded by chapel culture that Methodists were able to hold places of influence in local trade unions out of all proportion to their numerical strength.

(Hempton 1984: 215, citing Colls)

Given the role played by Methodism, should we only look for the development of black leadership through 'black-led' churches? For it is said that these structures and opportunities were available in the Methodist Church, as a minority church, from its inception. If this is so, however, it might well be argued that since the practice of Christianity has become – relatively speaking – a minority interest for the white community, and no longer such an integral part of the state establishment, the same could be said today of historic churches. And, in looking at the leadership of black pastors and congregations, neither should we ignore the fact that, in keeping with other projects arising from the Caribbean and Asian communities, 'black-led' does not mean 'black only': significant numbers of white Christians do attend and belong to such churches, providing a rare opportunity (it may be thought) for whites to experience black leadership in British social settings.

Further, there are crises to be noted in the role of black-led churches, whether those which are more common in the West Indies and of syncretist or bricolagist origin (Turner 1980: 49; Werbner 1985, 1986), which might be taken to include the Ethiopian Orthodox Church and Rastafarian groups, as well as the more established churches such as the New Testament Church of God. Indeed, it is true to say that some of this latter group are only 'black-led' in Britain. Churches such as the Seventh Day Adventists (Howard 1987: 37), Wesleyan (and other) Holiness, or Churches of God have headquarters in America that are certainly white-dominated (see Calley 1965: 21, 126 or Leech 1988b: 22). Other pentecostalist churches are emphatically black-led, and have gained in the past (and may do so again in the future) from being perceived as such both by government funders and by disenchanted young people seeking alternative sources of spiritual support (Onwordi 1988). However, it has also been observed that 'young people are leaving the established Pentecostal movement in droves' (Dixon 1989b), and ministers of such churches have to face difficult times in balancing their appeal.

283

Attempts to form or recreate cultural and personal support systems based upon distinct cultural traditions and ways of worshipping are important both to the individual's sense of identity and, in a sense, as a form of resistance or counter-culture (Werbner 1985: 253). However, these may run into resource problems when based upon relatively small communities and congregations. There is bound also to be tension between evangelical notions of personal salvation and the individual social desire to 'belong' and receive recognition in a wider society – especially if that society is a secular one with attractive 'glittering prizes' and an emphasis upon such distractions as personal attractiveness, dress, and display.

Nevertheless, black-led church-sponsored cultural and welfare centres have been developed and have played an important role in service provision and resistance on behalf of the black community. One well-known example of this was the organisation known as Caribbean House, in London, founded by Ashton Gibson, who also played a leading role in the setting up of the Afro–West Indian Council of Churches (Gibson and Lewis 1985). The growing 'gospel music' scene in Britain, regularly reported on in the church pages of the black press and now supported by regular concerts and competitions in the Albert Hall, on television, and by groups such as the British Gospel Songwriters Association, attests to the growing cultural confidence and nation-wide organisation of the black-led churches. Such agencies, through promoting a positive image, may 'provide leadership by concerning themselves with building the confidence of black people . . . by attention to cultural projects' (Goulbourne 1988). One cannot leave this subject, however, without reference to the problems of leaders of such churches and cultural agencies. Gibson himself was never an uncontroversial individual, and much of his work was destroyed as a result of a row about the propriety of his bookkeeping – allegations which have also dogged similar groups elsewhere ('Gibson walks free as fraud charges thrown out', *Voice* newspaper, 18 October 1988). The life of community leaders can be made more difficult when they struggle against what they perceive to be establishment racism and seek to adopt unconventional strategies to achieve their ends in the struggle against racism.

Caring for bodies as well as souls

The social gospel, then, does require 'deeds' as well as words and theology. Indeed, William Booth, founder of the Salvation Army, opened the first Labour Exchange ninety years ago in London, some thirty years before the state adopted such an initiative. The social role of the black-led churches in Britain is not insignificant, even if they have not been seen to take as important a public role as that taken in welfare-supporting activities by some American churches. Many have been instrumental in running educational projects such as 'Saturday schools' (and are, indeed, increasingly supporting the growth of a number of 'regular' schools), and many have programmes for the elderly. This welfare role, together with the development of economic (employment-generating) projects, has been increasing recently, drawing strength from such inner-city programmes as the government-funded Inner City Partnership and Urban Programme, the Community Programme of the Manpower Services Commission, and now the (Anglican) Church Urban Fund. It is important, however, to consider the degree to which these churches have seen their function as being to promote physical as opposed to spiritual welfare. Certainly most black pastors engaged in such 'social' projects would not wish to consider them to be divorced from their spiritual work, seeing them not only as a means of outreach or evangelism, but also as essentially part of their ministry to both black and white.

Utilising precedents such as the work of Booth and the arguments of the Archbishop of Canterbury's commission, and the resources of 'legitimacy' and membership which the established church commands, the present-day churches, most notably those from the evangelical tradition, have set in motion a series of initiatives. In this activity they have received enthusiastic backing from government sources:

> Black church leaders and the Government are joining forces to fight unemployment and decay in the inner cities . . . described by Employment Minister Kenneth Clarke as a unique partnership between church and government, a project named Evangelical Enterprise . . . will set up a network of inner-city taskforce teams (beginning in North Kensington and North Peckham) where Government will match pound for pound the money raised by church congregations.
>
> ('Churches fight the good fight', *London Evening News*, 1 April 1987)

What this report did not state was that 'Evangelical Enterprise' is also innovative in that it represents a further partnership between the (white-led) Evangelical Alliance and the West-Indian Evangelical Alliance. Within twelve months, the churches involved had exceeded by £10,000 the target they had set themselves (and set up nine successful projects).

Examples of such projects include the *Handsworth Connection* – a community newspaper under the auspices of twenty-three local churches, which provides journalistic training and employment (paid for out of the MSC's Community Programme) while also supplying information on job opportunities and welfare support – and a £400,000 project in Highfields, Leicester. The latter scheme represents a triple partnership, in which, with Task Force support and with training supplied through a 'pairing' arrangement by McAlpine's, the New Testament Church of God is refurbishing the church's accommodation to create a purpose-built community centre, business agency, and training centre. Similarly, under this initiative, fourteen churches in Chapeltown, Leeds, have combined to refurbish a church as a community business consultancy; six evangelical churches have formed a limited company to establish a launderette and coffee-shop centre in Peckham; and another consortium in Tower Hamlets is

> aiming to create a 'Christian Training Centre' with outreach support for Asian community workers and a unique Compact arrangement with Christian businessmen in the City of London to guarantee interviews to those passing through the courses of the Training Centre that will focus on the most demoralised and least skilled of local people who could gain meaningful employment in the City next door.
>
> (*Evangelical Enterprise* information sheet, Spring 1988)

These developments have been welcomed by government and drawn inexorably into the publicity surrounding its Action for Cities initiative. Clearly the role played by black church leaders and Christians has been seen as critical, exemplified, for instance, in the part played by one such leader, Leonard Johnson, both in the development of the Stonebridge Depot project and in apparently preventing the development of a riot in that part of Brent during the disturbances of July 1981 (Roberts 1988). Projects such as that, the New Testament Church of God centre in Leicester and others supported by the Evangelical Alliance have all raised the profile of 'black churches' and their pastors, bringing them into partnership with government ministers and officials and giving them greater legitimacy as 'community leaders' which should prove of value in their future dealings with the British establishment.

Those organising such projects clearly have the ability to mobilise substantial resources in addition to the funds provided by government. However, equally, they could not function without the backing given by the Task Force offices, most notably in facilitating their contacts with other sources of support such as the MSC – backing that has hitherto been hard to obtain. To this they are able to add their in-depth local knowledge and 'street credibility', resources which many of the local Task Forces seem to lack ('Who's up to the task', *Voice*, 29 March 1988: 16–17). Thus at a 'community consultation' in

a black-led church organised by the Coventry-based Churches
Initiative in Training, Employment and Enterprise (CITEE), attended
by more than forty local people (the Task Force's best attendance
previously at such meetings had been nine), it was stated that the proposed project would

> release the skills, facilities and strengths of the network of
> Coventry churches . . . use indigenous churches and existing street-
> level contacts to target recruitment at the most needy groups,
> rather than the groups which are easiest to recruit; especially eth-
> nic minorities, the young . . . and the long-term unemployed . . .
> fully involve local people in the operation and management of the
> project and build upon entrepreneurial skills already evident in
> the target area (by establishing a database of such skills through
> local church pastors) . . . as far as possible enable the project to
> become independent of outside support and funding.
>
> (Marshall 1988)

In the last point lies the rub – for while most of these projects have
generated substantial funding from members to match the statutory
sector input, few of them have been able to continue (or indeed
begin) without that core funding. Indeed, it might legitimately be
asked whether it is right that the poorest members of society should
be expected to finance their own regeneration: it is one thing to pull
oneself up by one's bootstraps, but another thing to have to supply
the bootstraps in the first place!

Black leadership in the 'established' churches

As Goulbourne (this volume) remarks, those of West Indian origin
in Britain have not in general sought to confine their struggles to an
'ethnic communal arena'. Therefore the study of church involvement
in race-related issues cannot be restricted to the 'black-led' churches.
Nor, indeed, should it be confined to 'West Indian' Christians – in
Britain as in America (Williams 1988) there are substantial numbers
of Christians of Asian origin. The report of a commission set up
by the Bishop's Council of the Diocese of Birmingham specifically
comments on this point, observing that

> The black Christians' sense of rejection in Britain is a very signifi-
> cant part of their history . . . (one Asian minister remarking) 'It is
> very sad, white churches want to spend most time talking to Sikhs,
> Hindus and Muslims. They do not want to talk to us or care for us
> at all'.
>
> (O'Brien 1988: 27)

All the major British denominations have now issued reports considering their relationship with black people in Britain. In general they have concluded that they have to an extent failed in their mission to include black people in their activities and to let (or encourage) black Christians play a full role in these and in their own leadership. Much of the churches' involvement in the anti-racist struggle has sprung from liberal-minded whites – but this too is important, especially in so far as it has in some sense revitalised the churches or given them a new mission (Johnson 1988a, 1988b).

Of course, as stated above, it has been observed that the black-led churches in recent years have been growing fast in numbers. For this reason, it is not to be wondered at that the churches have sponsored such enquires as those of the Methodist and Catholic churches (Walton *et al.* 1985; CHAG 1986), and have responded with such concern to the reports and the evidence they contained that the churches were failing to build on potential strengths that lay within the inner cities. Clear evidence of the under-representation of black members of congregations in leadership roles was demonstrated by Walton *et al.*'s study of the Methodist Connexion; and repeated in a study of the Anglican Diocese of Southwark which observed that, while over one-seventh of the 167 congregations participating were from ethnic minorities, only one-twentieth of lay church officers were black (or Asian). Even smaller proportions of minority church attenders were representatives of their church at deanery or diocesan synod, despite contributing more than proportionately to church growth in terms of baptism, confirmation, and Sunday school attendance. The authors of the report observed that many churches failed to reply to their survey or reported that 'racism was not an urgent issue' for them. This mismatch between the expressed anti-racism and the commitment displayed by the churches' leaderships and the day-to-day development of their memberships will clearly prove to be a major stumbling-block in their work.

There is now possibly increased sensitivity in theological college training, and in congregations who follow the anti-racist training courses which have been prepared (such as those run by EURAP and MELRAW, and the study pack 'Members One of Another', 1986). These may lead to growth in the numbers of black adherents of British churches, but, as Wilkinson and colleagues observed (Wilkinson *et al.* 1985), there are considerable barriers to be overcome. Despite the slowly growing numbers of black churchpeople in the hierarchies, such as Bishop Wilfred Wood of Croydon, the eight black members of the 520-strong Anglican Synod, or the election of a black Vice-President of the Methodist Conference (Leon Murray, in 1985), there is a considerable imbalance in the power relationship, and low representation of black worshippers in active positions in the churches. This is true both for the involvement of the laity and, as shown by the WISP study in the Catholic Church, in terms of recruitment to the priesthood (although that study, confined as it was to Westminster diocese, did overlook the presence of a black Catholic bishop, the Right Revd Patrick Kalilombe, at the Selly Oak Colleges, Birmingham). Among the Baptist churches of Birmingham, further, Parkinson found that 'those churches who are now strong in numbers are those who have welcomed and integrated black people into the fellowship; those who are now weak numerically have failed to do this' (Parkinson 1988: 25). Efforts to ensure black representation in the Church of England Synod, however, and despite earlier support (Petre 1988a, 1988b), were rejected by a vote in the House of Laity after a painful and, at times, patronising debate (news reports and letters, *Church Times*, 10 February 1989 and 17 February 1989). In the churches, as in other fields of endeavour, such imbalances perpetuate the existence of 'institutional racism' and militate against greater acceptance of these churches by black people as legitimate agencies for representation and with which to be involved.

However, steps are being taken to remedy these deficiencies, as some of the examples above may indicate. The Anglican church has set up (amidst some controversy) its Committee on Black Anglican Concerns chaired by Bishop Wood of Croydon; and in Birmingham (again) the Revd Rajinder Daniel was appointed Diocesan Adviser on Black Ministries in March 1987. In this role he has been active in raising awareness and in organising conferences for the parishes of the diocese to meet with leading black (and Asian) Christians including Raj Patel of the campaigning organisation, Evangelical Christians for Racial Justice. The journal of that group, *Racial Justice*, has been a lively source of debate and education and recently noted the important development of the 'surfacing of black self-help/black consolidation groups within the historic white-led denominations [for those who] no longer wish either to leave a white-led church nor continue to be suppressed from taking on leadership roles' (Patel 1989: 14).

The foundation of the Simon of Cyrene Institute (named for the African who according to biblical tradition carried Christ's cross) marks a departure for the Church of England in this respect. The institute, initially set up by the Committee on Black Anglican Concerns, will, while remaining open to both black and white Christians, seek to encourage particularly the recruitment of black ordinands to the priesthood by the provision of a form of 'access' preparatory course, as well as providing a service for other theological colleges in the development of their own 'multi-cultural/multi-racial' policy and curricula. During the course of this proposal's development it broadened its support base, so that it has in fact become an ecumenical venture – again illustrating the benefits to the churches of their involvement in the movement towards equality of opportunity!

It should also be noted that one of the few recent (major denomination) black ordainees was a woman, Eileen Lake (Tyers 1988). Black-led churches have long been accustomed to having female ministers, and Io Smith of the New Testament Assembly in East London (Schwartz 1988b), Pastor Esme Beswick, the first ordained black hospital chaplain in Britain, and Bishop Eunice McClean of the Pilgrims Union Church, have all played a distinguished part in the leadership of black Christians in Britain, both in things spiritual and in the organisation of church members to tackle issues of material welfare. More controversially, the first Anglican woman bishop, Barbara Harris in America, was also black and traced her career through a history of struggle for black rights alongside Martin Luther King and in community groups in Philadelphia (Alemoru 1989; Sandford 1989). It remains to be seen whether the British establishment churches will prove to be so ready to welcome such contributions – but Eileen Lake has proved at least that, as she says,

> There is a place for us as British black people, despite how our parents were treated and abused when they first started attending English churches. I feel I can use my position to encourage other black young people and as a sign that we are not fighting a losing battle in society and the Church.
>
> (quoted in Tyers 1988: 11)

Conclusion

I have argued in this chapter that there are many types of leadership to be found in the churches, and among black Christians of Asian or Afro-Caribbean origins. Further, these types of leadership may be exercised at different levels, whether nationally or regionally in the wider community or for the specific benefit of black communities and congregations interacting with the institutions of white society, and no less significantly also for congregations in their local and parochial settings. Some of these latter leaders may more particularly emerge in smaller 'bricolage' churches whose focus is spiritual and cultural, not seeking to influence the secular world. Yet such leadership may form, as it did in the Methodist church, the seedbed for later developments.

Very recently, in the dispute over the failure of the Labour Party to select a black candidate for the Vauxhall by-election (1989), the Revd Hewie Andrew was proposed as an Independent candidate and seen as a latter-day British Jesse Jackson. As a Methodist minister and trained teacher he has been instrumental in setting up 'supplementary schools' and chairing the London Collective of Black Governors, an initiative designed to increase black leadership utilising the opportunities presented by the increase in school governing body membership under the Education Act 1988. While unsuccessful in the by-election, he polled a respectable number of votes (1 per cent), coming fifth in the poll after the three major parties and the Green Party, and beating the more widely known barrister, Rudy Narayan. In the process he received considerable coverage in the media. Like Bishop Wilfred Wood (Chaudhary 1988b), Dr Robinson Milwood (Milwood 1989; Sanders 1989; Jackson 1985: 47), Canon Ivor Smith-Cameron, and Canon Sebastian Charles, he has succeeded in making use of his position within the established churches to 'go an extra mile', serving the black community by speaking out on black issues or working with groups within the black community while at the same time performing a more traditional role within those churches. The legitimacy associated with that established position, combined (it must be admitted) with a degree of novelty for the media, has proved a distinctive source of influence.

At the same time, the fact that black church leadership is so rare as to constitute a novelty has led the established churches to reconsider their own positions, and to take steps whereby the increasingly recognised under-representation of black Christians within their numbers might be redressed. Such activity has included surveys of parishes, revealing distressing imbalances (Southwark 1986; Walton *et al.* 1985; CHAG 1986), conferences and meetings, bruising public (and political) debate at the Anglican synod (Chaudhary 1988a; Petre 1988a, 1988b), and, more recently, steps towards some form of affirmative action as exemplified by the Simon of Cyrene Institute project.

Clifford Hill, in his survey of the relation between London churches and West Indian migrants, concluded that

> The Church is, without doubt, the largest and most effective organ for racial integration in the country . . . the Church, because of its unique position and standing, must therefore be seen as the key figure in the present situation and as the body upon whom the greatest responsibility for the future lies. There can be no doubt that up to the present the London churches have not been fully alive to their responsibilities.
>
> (Hill 1963: 75–9)

I have argued here that the Church, by which I mean the churches, remains potentially a significant agency for the overcoming of the effects of generations of racial discrimination and racism, even if one would no longer speak of 'racial integration'. As the Seventh Day Adventist Pastor Kennedy observes, 'I see the future of our church as producing leaders' (quoted in Jackson 1985: 115). Hill found 'rays of hope' in the proportions of West Indians who held positions of responsibility in London churches – proportions which have increased only slightly in the intervening decades. This study, and those which it has reviewed, have demonstrated, however, that through such agency there has been a growth of 'leadership', not only within the West Indian or Afro-Caribbean community but also among Asian Christians, which has had its effects upon the situation of the minority community, on their relationships with the white community, and, indeed, upon the perceptions and actions of the white community itself. While slow, such progress is not without value, and it would appear that in the longer term the role of the churches in British 'race relations' will indeed prove to have been very significant. That much depends upon the faith and courage of a few individuals, particularly those black Christians who have suffered and dared to challenge established orders, is indisputable, but perhaps that is the nature of the church and the Christian faith itself – and no one would now dispute the impact of the first disciples and apostles whose leadership laid the foundations of what Christianity has become today.

© 1991 Mark R.D. Johnson

References and sources

ACUPA (Archbishop of Canterbury's Commission on Urban Priority Areas) (1985) *Faith in the City: Report of ACUPA*, London: Church House.

Alemoru, O. (1989) 'One who God's mighty hand has lifted up', *Voice*, 21 February: 17.

Bailey, A. (1989) 'Christianity is for us', *Voice*, 31 January: 45.

Ball, W. and Troyna, B. (1987) 'Resistance rights and rituals; denominational schools and multi-cultural education', *Journal of Education Policy* 2 (1): 15–25.

Calley, M.J.C. (1965) *God's People: West Indian Pentecostal Sects in England*, London: Oxford University Press.

Cardinal Hume's Advisory Group (1986) *With You in Spirit*? London: Roman Catholic Diocese of Westminster.

Charman, P. (1979) *Reflections: Black and White Christians in the City*, London: Zebra Project.

Chaudhary, V. (1988a) 'Black voices in the church must be heard', *Voice*, 25 October: 5.

Chaudhary, V. (1988b) 'I'm a striker in God's soccer team', *Voice*, 15 November: 17.

Colls, R. (1977) *The collier's rant: song and culture in the industrial village*, London: Croom Helm.

Daniel, R. (1988) 'The longest day – Desmond Tutu in Birmingham', *Racial Justice* 9: 24.

Dixon, M. (1988) 'Let Women Lead (Soul Stirrings)', *Voice*, 27 September: 43.

Dixon, M. (1989a) 'Forging links for God (Soul Stirrings)', *Voice*, 21 February: 37.

Dixon, M. (1989b) 'The church in crisis', *Voice*, 30 May: 23.

Dodd, V. (1989) 'Tutu smear campaign slammed', *Voice*, 11 April: 11.

Dummett, A. and McNeal, J. (1981) *Race and Church Schools*, London: Runnymede Trust.

Fogarty, M. (1989) 'The churches and public policy: the case for a review', *Policy Studies* 9 (4): 43–8.

Garrow, D.J. (1988) *Bearing the Cross: Martin Luther King Jnr and the Southern Christian Leadership Conference*, London: Jonathan Cape.

Gates, B.E. (1980) *Afro-Caribbean Religions*, London: Ward Lock.

Gerloff, R. (with others) (1977) *Project in Partnership in Black and White*, Westminster: Methodist Home Mission.

Gerloff, R. (with others) (1980) *Learning in Partnership*, London: British Council of Churches.

Gibson, A. and Lewis, C. (1985) *A Light in the Dark Tunnel: Ten Years of West-Indian Concern and Caribbean House*, London: Centre for Caribbean Studies.

Goulbourne, H. (1988) *West Indian Political Leadership in Britain*, Occasional Paper 4, Coventry: Centre for Research in Ethnic Relations, University of Warwick.

Hansard (1987) 'Inner city problems: report of a debate initiated by Lord Scarman', *House of Lords Official Report*, vol. 484, cols 13–122.

Haslam, D. (1979) 'The Grunwick strike', *Migration Today* 23: 5–6.

Hempton, D. (1984) *Methodism and Politics in British Society 1750–1850*, London: Hutchinson.

Higham, J. (ed.) (1978) *Ethnic Leadership in America*, Baltimore, Md: Johns Hopkins University Press.

Hill, C. (1963) *West Indian Migrants and the London Churches*, London: Oxford University Press for Institute of Race Relations.

Hill, C. (1971) 'Pentecostalist growth – result of racialism', *Race Today* 3 (3): 187–90.

Hill, C. (1980) 'Afro-Caribbean religion in Britain', in B.E. Gates (ed.) *Afro-Caribbean Religions*, London: Ward Lock.

Holden, T. (1985) *People, Churches and Multi-racial Projects*, London: Methodist Church Division for Social Responsibility.

Hooper, R. (1970) *Act Now – Race Relations in Britain: The Churches and CMS*, London: Church Missionary Society.

Howard, V. (1987) *A Report on Afro-Caribbean Christianity in Britain*, Leeds: Community Religions Project, Department of Theology and Religious Studies, Leeds University.

Jackson, A. (1985) *Catching Both Sides of the Wind: Conversations with Five Black Pastors*, London: British Council of Churches.

Johnson, M.R.D. (1988a) 'Resurrecting the inner city: a new role for the Christian churches', *New Community* 15 (1): 91–101.

Johnson, M.R.D. (1988b) 'The spirit still moves in the inner city: the churches and race', *Ethnic and Racial Studies* 11 (3): 366–73.

Leech, K. (1988a) 'The social gospel', *New Statesman and Society*, 9 December: 34–6.

Leech, K. (1988b) *Struggle in Babylon: Racism in the Cities and Churches of Britain*, London: Sheldon Press.

Longley, C. (1985) 'Church report on inner cities', *The Times*, 2 December 1985: 4.

Marshall, J. (1988) 'Proposal for compiling a feasibility study for a training, employment and enterprise project in the Foleshill and Hillfields areas of Coventry', Evangelical Enterprise/Coventry Youth for Christ (mimeographed)

Maynard, M. (1988) 'We're not divisive', *Voice*, 27 September: 21.

Milwood, R. (1989) 'Billy's message is not for us', *Voice*, 13 June: 2.

Moore, R. (1974) *Pit-Men, Preachers and Politics: The Effects of Methodism in a Durham Mining Community*, Cambridge: Cambridge University Press.

NCVO (National Council for Voluntary Organisations) (1988) *Releasing Enterprise – Voluntary Organisations and the Inner City*, London: National Council for Voluntary Organisations.

O'Brien, R. (1988) *Faith in the City of Birmingham: An Examination of Problems and Opportunities Facing a City*, Exeter: Paternoster Press.

Oldham, J.H. (1924) *Christianity and the Race Problem*, London: SCM Press.

Oliver, J. (1968) *The Church and Social Order: Social Thought in the Church of England 1918–1939*, London: Mowbray.

Onwordi, A. (1988) 'Poor will turn to black church', *Voice*, 1 November: 2.

Parkinson, C. (1988) *Baptists in the Inner City of Birmingham*, Birmingham: Birmingham Baptist Inner City Project.

Patel, R. (1989) 'Prophets amongst us', *Racial Justice* 11: 14–15.

Petre, J. (1988a) 'Black sections in Synod "would break race law"', *Daily Telegraph*, 7 November: 4.

Petre, J. (1988b) 'Synod to recruit 24 blacks', *Daily Telegraph*, 11 November: 1.

Phillips, K. and Haslam, D. (eds) (1988) *Rainbow Gospel: Report of a Churches Conference on 'Challenging Racism in Britain'*, London: British Council of Churches.

Rex, J. and Moore, R. (1967) *Race, Community, and Conflict*, Oxford: Institute of Race Relations/Oxford University Press.

Roberts, J. (1988) 'Pie in the sky? or sharing the cake on the plate? Lessons from evangelical enterprise', *Employment Gazette*, July: 365–71.

Sanders, C. (1989) 'Come on down for Jesus', *New Statesman and Society* 2 (55): 24–5.

Sandford, G. (1989) 'A latter-day turbulent priest', *Independent*, 16 January: 11.

Schwartz, W. (1988a) 'The face of dissent', *Guardian*, 28 March.

Schwartz, W. (1988b) 'In the front line of faith', *Guardian*, 29 March.

Southwark (1986) *Black Anglicans in Southwark Diocese*, London: Southwark Diocese Race Relations Commission.

Synod (1984) 'Schools and multi-cultural education: a discussion paper', Board of Education Memorandum 2/84, London: General Synod of the Church of England.

Turner, H. (1980) 'New religious movements in the Caribbean', in B.E. Gates (ed.) *Afro-Caribbean Religions*, London: Ward Lock.

Tyers, D. (1988) 'The black council worker's daughter who became a Reverend', *Racial Justice* 10: 17-18.

Voice (1988) 'Faith, hope and self-help', *Voice*, 8 November: 21.

Walton, H., Ward, R. and Johnson, M. (1985) *A Tree God Planted: Black People in British Methodism*, London: Methodist Church Division of Social Responsibility.

Werbner, R.P. (1985) 'The argument of images: from Zion to the wilderness in African churches', in W. van Binsbergen and S. Schoffeleers (eds) *Theoretical Explorations in African Religion*, London: Routledge & Kegan Paul.

Werbner, R.P. (1986) 'The political economy of bricolage', *Journal of Southern African Studies* 13 (1): 151–5.

Wilkinson, J., Wilkinson, R. and Evans, J.H. (1985) *Inheritors Together: Black People in the Church of England*, London: Church of England Board for Social Responsibility.

Williams, E. (1966) *British Historians and the West Indies*, London: André Deutsch.

Williams, R.B. (1988) *Religions of Immigrants from India and Pakistan: New Threads in the American Tapestry*, Cambridge: Cambridge University Press.

Chapter eleven

The offence of the West Indian
Political leadership and the communal option

Harry Goulbourne

Introduction

There are several drawbacks in the extensive coverage people of African backgrounds from the Commonwealth Caribbean receive from journalists and academics. They are portrayed almost exclusively as victims of British education, law, unemployment, housing, and so forth. As a result, the efforts at self- and societal improvement this salient fourth estate of the realm engage in are generally ignored by commentators. This has at least two significant consequences. First, whilst the activities of the state, para-statals, and employers are fairly well covered or represented in the extant literature, the willingness of Caribbean people to participate in the nation's institutions, as well as their efforts to utilise traditional British forms of protest in order to challenge their structured subordinate class and racial positions in Britain, remain comparatively hidden from view. Second, despite the evident goodwill and intentions of researchers, the one-sided coverage of contemporary Britain does little to correct a general perception that Afro-West Indians are almost passive net takers or net receivers of state largess rather than active contributors to the general welfare of the country.

There are, of course, some exceptions to this general tendency. Contributions by Gilroy and Hall are exceptional in treating the political discourse of African Caribbean people in Britain seriously (Gilroy 1987; Hall *et al.* 1978). In general, however, there is a persistent misunderstanding of the political action and political discourse which people with a Commonwealth Caribbean background have brought to bear on British society and the values these spring from. There is, in short, a glaring need for a balanced, well-informed, and rigorous analysis of the organisational, ideological, and individual kinds of leadership people from the Caribbean bring to British society and its politics.[1]

In this chapter I wish to offer, in relation to these issues, some general observations about West Indian leadership in Britain and to organise these around two principal propositions. The first of these is that leadership both within and from Caribbean groups has been, in the main, concerned with the twin problems of engagement and participation in the affairs of the nation as a whole and not with *disengagement* and *separation* from either the majority population or other minorities. To one degree or another this is likely to be true with respect to all minorities in Britain. But I would suggest that the willingness to adopt an accommodationist/adaptive posture may be particularly salient in the case of West Indians. Second, whilst their desire to be part of the general stream of society reflects the strong humanistic and democratic socio-political traditions of the West Indies, the aspirations of Afro-Caribbean people in the UK are generally dismissed by decision-makers and academics, because of the group's rejection of the present tendency to embrace what I would call the communal option.

Briefly, the communal option presumes that humanity can be legitimately and properly divided into easily recognisable ethnic or racial categories, and that members of these categories wish to enjoy security within specified enclaves which are exclusively their own. These enclaves are further presumed to constitute the proper boundaries within which individuals should be encouraged to conduct their daily lives. This perception of the human condition is not unique to Britain. Indeed, the communal option in some respects goes back to the French Revolution (Goulbourne 1991; also Goulbourne 1988a). But it is rapidly being promoted both in Britain and elsewhere as the proper and most desirable way in which society may peacefully organise itself. This view of society receives support, intentionally or unintentionally, from a variety of sources in both state and civil society in Britain.

It is my contention that the imperative of the communal option constitutes a very large part of the general context within which questions of leadership, at this pivotal point of British society, must be situated. The offence of the West Indian in Britain, as I shall argue, is that he or she is ill-equipped by tradition and disposition to provide an exclusively 'ethnic' leadership. This is so because, whilst drawing much inspiration from the symbols and history of the ethnic group, West Indians are disinclined to base social and political action on ethnicity. They have instead sought to ground social and political action in one or other universal, rational principle. These propositions are more than likely to be contentious and therefore call for explanation. Before, however, attempting to provide one, it is necessary briefly to consider the rather unsettled concept of political leadership as it may apply to the British racio-ethnic, or what Rex depicts as 'the race-relations', situation (Rex 1979, 1986).

The notion of leadership

Like so many concepts in the social sciences, the highly problematic concept of leadership first made its appearance in the field of political discourse. It is rather surprising, therefore, that throughout the long and distinguished career of this discipline there has been comparatively little discussion of the concept itself. It is, of course, true that in general terms the concept is employed in a largely descriptive way in modern political theory from Machiavelli to today. At another level it is often assumed that both reader and writer share a common-sense understanding of the concept and that it is therefore perfectly acceptable for the writer simply to take the concept as given and proceed to a description of its particular manifestations. For example, the Prince describes what Machiavelli considered laudable qualities and forms of behaviour necessary in a leader who would be forceful enough to establish a unified and strong state out of the chaotic conditions of the Italy of his day. Historians were later to take up this theme of the 'great man' and evaluate the individual actor in the historical evolution or process (e.g. Hook 1943).

In more recent times the political analyst has added to the discussion the problem of the growth or extension of the power of individual political functionaries. For example, a sizeable part of the post-Second World War literature in political science has been about the growth of executive power. Taking a cue from earlier observers of the British constitution such as Walter Bagehot, analysts have sought to show that it has not simply been cabinet, but particularly prime ministerial, power which has grown to hitherto unforeseen heights. This growth is usually measured against the decline of the legislature – the location of constitutional legitimacy – from which both judiciary and executive in turn gain their formal legitimacy (e.g. Crossman 1975). For Marxists this extension or growth of the executive over the legislative forms of collective leadership helps to mark off one phase of capitalist development from another. In this view, whilst liberal democracy and its accompanying parliamentary/legislative strength represented the *laissez-faire* phase of capitalist development, the monopoly phase of capitalist development has been characterised from the late nineteenth century by the growth of executive power (e.g. Poulantzas 1975; Miliband 1973, 1977). There is, of course, good sense in making this periodisation of forms of democratic participation in a world rendered at once more complex and yet more unified through the expansion of the capital, labour, and commodity markets on a world scale.

The emergence and development of sociology from the nineteenth century have forced the traditional political analyst to widen the focus of the discussion over leadership. Whilst, therefore, sociologists are concerned about the ways in which groups of people organise themselves so as to constitute some kind of force in society, the political analyst has been careful to examine the process whereby these groups impact upon decision-makers at the various levels of formulation, decision-making, and implementation of public or corporate policies (Olson 1965; Crenson 1971). But the emergence of the sociological perspective itself may be traced as far back as Alexis de Tocqueville. His acute political and social observations about the workings of democracy in the young American Republic of the 1830s as well as his reflections on his own experiences during the turmoil of revolutionary France of 1848 are relevant here. In this regard Marx's writings on revolutionary France of a generation or so later in his *Civil War in France* and, perhaps more importantly, his *Eighteenth Brumaire* which covers, from a different perspective, much the same historical events as de Tocqueville's *Reflections*, marked the break away from an understanding of ruler–ruled relations to the relationship between leaders and followers, the relationship between the people or elements/classes of the people and those who rule/dominate. Marx's emphasis was upon the dependence of leaders on the behaviour of large groups of people – social classes. For both Marx and de Tocqueville society at large began to have a presence in the narrative, or in the analyst's account or construction of political and social life.

This is not to suggest, of course, that earlier theorists were totally unaware of this relationship. Indeed, social-contract theorists as far apart from each other as Hobbes and Locke in England in the seventeenth century and Rousseau in France in the eighteenth century, hinted at what was later to become the sociological perspective. When they wrote in the singular about the sovereign and the subject, they brought into focus the relationship between the state and what was to become in the last century 'the people', or the 'masses' in our own century.

Admittedly, they saw, like St Paul, through a glass but darkly. It was really the birth of political sociology which gave greater clarity to this relationship. At the turn of the century, the work of Ostrogorsky, Mosca, and Michels revealed different aspects of this complex relationship between leaders and followers. Ostrogorsky and Michels were particularly keen to show how the new kind of political organisation – the political party – which was emerging in Europe, following the birth and development of the modern forms of this institution in Jacksonian America from the late 1820s, resulted in oligarchial rule, contrary to their initial *raison d'être*.

But the concept of, and discussion over, leadership in politics and sociology have, in the main, been cast within the mould of Weber's distinctions between traditional, charismatic, and bureaucratic kinds of authority (Weber 1947). As its name suggests, traditional authority is based on customs whereas charismatic authority is personal, temporal, and informal. In contrast, bureaucratic authority is formal, structured, is exercised by means of established procedures and rules, and is impersonal in application.

A suggestive line of argument may be culled from Weber's distinctions, but in the first instance two general observations are pertinent. The first observation is that, like much else in Weber's thinking, the concept of authority has to be understood in terms of his notion of ideal types: in other words, there are not likely to be real-life situations in which we will see traditional, charismatic, or bureaucratic forms of authority, exclusively or in pure forms (see Giddens 1972; Gerth and Mills 1958). The more likely situation is a mixture of two or all three types of authority, even though one or the other may dominate. It is from this common-sense, or at least arguable, perspective that we often speak of a charismatic leader when, in fact, the person may be far from wielding the personal authority Weber intended to invest in his charismatic leaders.[2] On the other hand, we all understand what is meant when we speak of a person who so stamps his or her personality on an office that its appointive or elective nature seems to assume a subsidiary importance. In some situations traditional, charismatic, and bureaucratic forms of authority/leadership coexist and, as in the case of Britain, happily complement each other as they intertwine through a series of complex webs of social relationships we ordinarily designate as power.

The second observation to be made is that Weber obviously intended that these forms of authority should be viewed progressively. Like the work of all major thinkers (perhaps with the exception of Rousseau and some of the Romantics) from the eighteenth century to the First World War, Weber's work was informed by a progressive view of human history. And whilst he may not have been as convinced as Hegel, or Marx under whose shadow Weber laboured, he shared a common progressive perspective of the human condition with them. In his attempt to understand domination Weber developed a typology of authority which implied a concern with political leadership, and this typology expresses perfectly a progressive view of human society which may be fast disappearing from contemporary discourse about society. There is here an implication that as contemporary society advances both vertically and horizontally the rational, or secular, philosophy which underscores it will undermine traditional and charismatic forms of authority; but the dead weight of bureaucracy may be the price eventually exacted from us for this development or progress.

It is clear from these remarks that *it is not difficult to understand why* it may be easier to discuss authority than it may be to discuss leadership. Whilst it is possible to identify, empirically, structures of authority, it is far from obvious how we may set about identifying leadership or even identifying the qualities which make up what we call leadership. A person may be referred to as a 'born leader' even though he or she does not exercise any legislative, executive, or judicial authority; on the other hand a person may have a great deal of formal authority endowed in his or her office but is not able to exercise it because, as we often hear, that person lacks (Weber's) charisma. No doubt, it is this difficulty in identifying leadership qualities which has led to the situation in political analysis whereby the concept is taken as a given, and therefore carries the implication that there may be no theoretical problem here when, in fact, we are all aware that at a practical level leadership is indeed problematic. The result is that certain forms of behaviour or structures are generally identified as being examples or manifestations of leadership.

But it must be possible to offer a general, even if vague, understanding of the concept. At least for the purpose of this essay the notion or concept of leadership may be taken to indicate situations in which a given group or an individual commands sufficient power to cause other groups or individuals either to change the course of their action or to reaffirm their belief in the correctness of present modes of political behaviour. The exercise of this power may be regarded as leadership, irrespective of whether it is based on authority, force, or influence (see Lukes 1974). The charismatic leader is not accountable to any specific body for his or her power and, therefore, the basis or legitimacy of his or her action may be more intractable than in the other cases. The elected or appointed leader is accountable, to one degree or another, to the electors/constituents and the traditional leader certainly has to respect the traditions and customs which underpin his or her leadership.

Added to these remarks is the fact that leadership is situational in the sense that the qualities which make one person or group a leader or leaders and another person or group a follower or followers are likely to be determined by the specific conditions in which the 'leader' or 'leaders' and the 'follower' or 'followers' are situated. This does not rule out the fact that a given situation is likely to be itself determined by the structural norms of the social system.

Leadership is more than likely to take on characteristics which are markedly ethnic and/or racial in Britain because, in my view, both the state and civil institutions pursue the construction of a society increasingly compartmentalised into ethnic or racial categories and groups. It might be suggested that, from the perspective of society as a whole, the kind of leadership implied here is likely to be either of a traditional or of a charismatic nature. This is because, unlike the situation in many parts of the former British empire, the racial or ethnic group is not – yet? – the normal or formal basis of political representation.

In some minority ethnic groups traditional forms of leadership may predominate even within societies whose values and structures have developed to become mainly rational/secular, and therefore less understanding or empathic to irrational customs. At the same time, however, in certain parts of the majority white society in Britain where traditional leadership has long given way to the bureaucratic/rational form, there has been a reversion to charismatic leadership. Powellism is no doubt the best example of this. Such charismatic and traditional forms of leadership, if forcefully reasserted, would be likely to entail less respect for the values of the wider society based essentially on a rationalist/secular tradition whose antecedents predate western Christianity itself (Patterson 1977).

Both traditional and charismatic kinds of leadership, from a progressive perspective, are forms which, in the main, derive their legitimacy from outside the humanistic tradition. The latter seeks to give primacy to the human capacity to apply reason to our condition/s and therefore places a high premium on tolerance. It is possible, however, for an unsympathetic bureaucraticism to become an obstacle to the value of some other equally human capacity, such as the value of feelings. The last two centuries have witnessed a heated contention between the tradition of reason and that of *faith* in tradition. The growing preference today for *communalism* may, nonetheless, offer us the occasion to grope towards a synthesis of these not completely irreconcilable traditions because the new historicism, upon which this preference is based, is not entirely uninformed by rationalism. In this respect, by a quirk of fate or history, Britain is now one of those few societies which is poised either to provide the example of a new kind of societal order or to point the way to yet another missed opportunity (for a more tolerant and cohesive social order), such as was wasted during the ascendancy and hegemonic dominance of the West. This opportunity lies in the challenge to allow, or provide the context within which, a new culture is permitted to develop freely in a post-imperial/post-colonial context.

This new national culture can no more be the sole determination of the majority white population than it can be simply the sum of the variety of minority cultures: the challenge for both minorities and majority populations consists in the willingness to engage in a conversation towards a new social order.

These general remarks provide a basis for some further comments about the nature of what is mainly but not exclusively Afro-West Indian leadership in Britain. It is not possible here to treat many aspects of social life where leadership is exercised. For example, symbols, style, exemplars, are not treated here. Nor do I intend to discuss the leadership qualities involved in the less visible aspects of day-to-day life amongst people with a Caribbean background in Britain. The 'partnership' system (whereby individuals excluded from access to banking and financial lending facilities establish their own quite informal financial network), the existence of social, sports, music, or recreational clubs which sprang up around families, friends, dominoes, cricket, etc., enthusiasts, are, of course, important aspects of the inner life of the Caribbean communities in Britain (see Pryce 1990, Pearson 1981) but they are not discussed here.

Although the notion of leadership cannot sensibly be restricted to its public political manifestations, the political is, none the less, the clearest expression of leadership. I want, therefore, to direct my comments at three kinds of expressions of leadership likely to be found in any given political situation. These are the organisational, individual, and ideological forms of leadership amongst and from Caribbean people. With respect, then, to the *political*, West Indian groups, and therefore patterns of leadership, have passed through at least three phases during the last four decades of sizeable presence in Britain (Goulbourne 1990). The first phase was characterised by the great expectations with which West Indians came and the shocking disappointment resulting from a rude rejection. The subsequent bitterness initially acted as a brake on West Indian aspirations to participate actively in all areas of national life and their initial enthusiasm for the adventure turned sour. During the second phase, therefore, people with Commonwealth Caribbean backgrounds addressed themselves to specific problems and issues which faced black communities acutely in the late 1960s and the first half of the 1970s. This period was also marked by something of a *disengagement* from mainstream, regular politics as black communities tried to clarify their identities within the changing landscape of post-imperial Britain. This was a time when the frustrations of Britain's black population began to find expression in the Black Power movement (e.g. Egbuna 1971). A shift had occurred from the concerns of homeland and the patient, accommodationist knocking at the door of British society, and West

Indians, a profoundly conservative people, were catapulted into a radical, militant mode of protest.

The third phase began sometime in the late 1970s when black people started to re-enter the Labour and Liberal (now SDLP) Parties as well as the Conservative Party. The new re-engagement with mainstream political institutions such as local councils, Parliament, and the parties has built upon the awareness of community issues which were defined during the second phase of development. Indeed, many of the issues debated over the last decade or more have been significantly contributed to by the community-based groups of the second phase. Admittedly, the issues themselves – such as education, police accountability, employment, housing, the elderly, and so forth – have been changed in the complex processes involved in getting them into the public arena of discussion and onto the political agenda for resolution. But such changes or modifications should not obscure the fact that black groups themselves led in the general effort to have problems developed into issues for the public agenda.

The relative absence of ethnic leadership

In brief, then, the offence of the West Indian consists, I submit, in what leaders and spokespersons of the white majority in Britain see as the *proximity* of the West Indian to mainstream but mainly working-class or popular British culture. The point was well expressed by an official in a London borough whom Fitzgerald interviewed and quoted in a recent paper. Quoth he, 'I'm very *turned on* by the Asian community. *Culturally* I find Afro-Caribbeans much more difficult to get to grips with: they're more like poor whites' (Fitzgerald 1988: 255, emphases added). If we ignore the implied derogation of segments of the population in the statement, I believe we have a terse expression of the offence of the West Indian for many in Britain. There is too much of a similarity with, or proximity to, the majority culture which is claimed to be exclusively *white*.[3] Second, the offence of the West Indian is to be constantly seen in his or her lack of what may be deemed culturally exotic in the eyes of middle- and upper-middle-class decision-makers.

The main cause of the offence, then, is the relative absence of unambiguous ethnic or racial considerations as the *basis* for social and political action amongst West Indians. This is perhaps the single most striking feature of what we may loosely call Caribbean behaviour and leadership in Britain. In the political sphere the offence consists of a difficulty in neatly placing Caribbean organisations, leaders, and particularly the issues they raise, into any specific ethnic or racial category. With respect to the issues raised, these tend to embrace the interests of society as a whole, not simply West Indians. They include questions of police brutality and therefore account-ability to urban communities; better access to housing for all; fair and open competition for jobs, and so forth. From this perspective the riots which occurred between 1981 and 1985 in British cities cannot be described as race riots because they were principally against police oppressive measures, not white people or white society as many would claim.

It may be postulated that to the extent that ethnic or racial groups, leaders, and issues may be racially or ethnically categorised, to that extent most institutions and leaders of the majority white popula-tion, almost irrespective of the place they occupy in the political spectrum, are likely to sympathise with such groups or minorities and their leaders. One important proviso, however, is that the ethnic group and its leaders should not pose a threat to British society.

Obviously, there is no single explanation for the preference for ethnic enclaves and categories. But part of any general explanation must be the deep-rooted racial and/or colour perspective(s) in west-ern civilisation from the time it first came into direct contact with non-European cultures after its age of 'discovery'. Additionally, the attractiveness of easy ethnic identification of people must have something to do with the condition of those doing the identifying. In the context of post-imperial Britain where, I would argue, the majority population is itself uncertain of its fate, such an identifica-tion of the 'other' perhaps adds to a sense of security and well-being. From the perspective of the state there may also be a sense of satis-faction to be derived from an unambiguous identification because it makes for easy control through marginalisation of the 'other' and a strengthening of the 'us'. For a number of reasons it has, therefore, in my view, become necessary for every person in Britain not merely to have an ethnic or racial identity, but to carry this as a kind of passport to be presented before any social intercourse.

These considerations present a number of problems for Carib-bean leadership in Britain. First, the visible forms of leadership developed by people from the Caribbean in Britain do not fit easily and comfortably into the ethnic process. Second, the discomfort is also quite distressful for both the state and some West Indian leaders in Britain who have come to believe that the condition in which West Indians find themselves is in part, if not largely, due to a refusal to behave in a clear ethnic manner, with clear ethnic demands. The aims, therefore, of the state and such leaders are complementary: overall, these are to construct an identifiable ethnic agenda. Part of this project is first to demolish the broadly defined Commonwealth Caribbean or West Indian community which includes people from all 'races' and to construct an exclusive one – the *Afro-Caribbean* community. It may be true that people of African background from the Caribbean would stand to gain something from this finer definition if it were conducted in some Caribbean countries, but in the case of Britain this cannot be taken for granted.

Whilst, however, ease of control may be the main consideration of the state or national leaders, a benign interpretation of the behaviour of some black leaders who have decided against the humanistic Caribbean tradition must be that their principal concern has been to secure the well-being of what is perceived to be a fragile and exposed group on hostile territory. This concern has, of course, arisen largely as a result of the unexpectedly harsh and inhospitable reception experience of West Indians in the years of entry and settlement (which correspond to the first and second phases I identified earlier) and should not therefore be condemned out of hand. It is more relevant to consider briefly some of the main reasons why the effort to construct an exclusively Afro-Caribbean community may be fraught with danger and why it represents a departure from the traditions and practices of African-derived societies in the west, and is therefore of historic importance.

These questions may be looked at from the perspective of those who have found it difficult to have the communal option accepted. For the converts to such an option there are some very real sociohistorical obstacles in the way of constructing a clear ethni-racial perception of society and political leadership in the highly visible but far from easily compartmentalised West Indian minority in Britain.

The first of these considerations is the racial and social composition of Caribbean societies themselves. Although colour continues to be of profound importance in the definition of a person's class in these societies, race and colour do not willingly lend themselves in the culture of the region to the kind of exclusivism which may be necessary for unambiguous ethnic forms of leadership to emerge and develop. In the majority of the seventeen or so English-speaking[4] countries in the region – from the Bahamas to Guyana – the majority population is of African background. But the resultant culture is not exclusively or unambiguously African. Like Africans elsewhere in the west, Africans in the Caribbean have had to struggle to overcome a past of slavery, and part of this struggle entailed countering (Gramscian-like) a narrow and therefore arrogant Anglo-Saxon hegemony. Until recently, this received the full and unqualified support of the state. Not unlike many ostensibly homogenous cultures, West Indian culture has not been the sole 'creation' of the 'racially' defined majority population. This population itself became more mixed with the ending of slavery in 1838, resulting in the importation of indentured labourers from India, China, and the Canary Islands between the 1830s and 1917. The region has also been a refuge, particularly for people from the Middle East, during the present century. The single largest racial group in both Guyana and Trinidad over the last three or four decades has been of East Indian background. But whilst what M.G. Smith calls social and cultural pluralism (M.G. Smith 1965, 1984) may be said to exist in relatively minor forms in these two countries, its widespread prevalence is strongly denied by his fellow anthropologists (e.g. R.T. Smith 1962, 1967). It certainly cannot be maintained that a socially and culturally pluralist society pertains in the majority of English-speaking societies in the region (Braithwaite 1953; Brathwaite 1971).

In brief, then, the socio-racial or ethno-racial composition of the region has been such that different groups of people have come to learn to live together by sharing in a common creole culture derived in the main from West Africa and North West Europe but also contributed to by peoples from India, China, and other parts of Asia. After slavery these groups brought aspects of their languages, cuisine, religions, and so forth to the region (e.g. Dabydeen and Samaroo 1986), but these have all been modified by the dynamism of the creole culture which was and is developing but to which they could contribute. The absence of legal injunctions reinforcing initial cultural and physical differences after slavery also helped in the process of developing a common culture which enables each group to feel that they belong to something called the national community. Even the notable case of Guyana can be pointed to as being the exception that proves the rule (Goulbourne 1991).

Second, there has been a relative absence of traditional forms of leadership in the region itself. The reasons for this are fairly obvious. In the first instance, slaves were not allowed to put together any semblance of the kinds of authority structures they knew in Africa, and what cultural patterns survived from Africa did so despite, not because of, slavery (see Herskovits 1970). In the process, whilst Africans have had an impact on the English language spoken in the region, they were not able to bring into the New World any of their languages intact. Obviously, nor were they able to significantly restructure forms of leadership based on religion, kin, clan, etc., which may have been prevalent in pre-colonial Africa. It is, of course, true that Maroon communities in different Caribbean and South American societies developed resistance and leadership patterns derived from their experience as soldiers in Africa (Hart 1980) but with time this knowledge was no doubt also destroyed or decayed. The slaves' culture was the object of systematic destruction – a fact which is all too frequently ignored or too conveniently shielded by an inexcusable ignorance.

Perhaps, too, the collective memory-lapse of this systematic destruction forms part of an equally majoritarian (white) wish to push it aside from all considerations in confronting the offence of the survival of people of African descent into the modern world. The offence is perhaps greater than that exposed by the contradictions between Christian forgiveness (for the crucifixion of Christ) and Christian intolerance, manifested in the anti-Semitism of western culture.

In terms of leadership, however, there are few regions of the world in which British political institutions and practices have been more successfully implanted and thrived more effectively than in the English-speaking Caribbean. This fact is hardly ever commented upon and there are at least two important reasons for the conspicuous lack of interest in this remarkable situation. First, it stems from the small size of the countries and the region as a whole. Second, and perhaps far more importantly, it stems from the fact that the majority population of the region is of African or non-white descent. Unless the behaviour of non-whites is different from that of Europeans and can establish a claim to be exotic, then, it seems, such behaviour is obviously and demonstrably unremarkable and is therefore generally ignored. But the fact of the Anglophone Caribbean's successful development of democratic institutions and practices is no less remarkable because of the region's size and the race/colour composition of its varied people. Third, the absence of any pre-colonial forms of authority, and therefore pre-colonial forms of leadership (Munroe 1972), seems to have encouraged English-speaking Caribbean leaders to successfully build upon the institutions brought, initially, to the region from Britain and to breathe new life into them – a new life informed by a profound sense of the value of the individual.

Perhaps most relevant to the contemporary British situation, and remarkable to anyone interested in the workings of democratic institutions and practices,[5] has been the refusal by the people of the region to accept that a person's ethnic affinity is all-determinate. And this was achieved despite, not because of, the general policies of the political authorities and those in positions of formal leadership in these societies during the periods of slavery and colonialism.

Of course, the very longevity of these traditions which first grew out of the contacts between Africans and Europeans in the Caribbean has also helped to strengthen these practices and institutions. For example, next to Britain herself Barbados has the oldest national legislature in the world, having been established in 1639 and having continued relatively uninterrupted until today. Most of the islands have established two- or multi-party systems and strong, well-organised trade unions. The professions are organised along British lines and some still deliberately continue to be closely associated with larger professional bodies in the UK.[6] Whilst, therefore, in many parts of the post-colonial world, post-independence regimes have sought to do away with institutions introduced by former imperial powers, in the Anglophone Caribbean leaders have, on the contrary, sought to maintain those institutions worth retaining. And it is not an adequate explanation to say that this is due to the depth of West Indian colonial indoctrination. These institutions and practices have come to be regarded as part of the rightful inheritance of the people by the people themselves, who have actively participated in the construction of what Apter called a two- or multi-party, turnover, pragmatic political system (Apter 1968; Stone 1983). Even traditional forms of authority/leadership such as that provided by the British monarchy have been retained.[7] But, even less than in Britain, the monarch plays no real part in the politics of these countries, represented as she is by a governor-general who is usually a distinguished elder statesman/woman or public figure of national significance and stature.

There is, subsequently, a further relative absence of charismatic forms of leadership in the politics of the region. To be sure, there have been some notable cases of charismatic leaders in some of its countries. One example of this was the late Sir Alexander Bustamante who based his leadership on a national but highly personalistic following. This, however, very quickly gave way to the regular institutionalisation of leadership as the two-party system matured in the 1950s. Another kind of example may be taken from the religious sphere: some of the various messianic sects such as those of Rastafarianism, Pocomaniaism, and so forth variously display a desire for charismatic leadership (Simpson 1955, 1956; Nettleford *et al.* 1960). But these can no more be said to be characteristic of West Indian societies than can hippyism or Druidism be said to be representative of mainstream British society today. Generally, then, West Indian leaders have tended to demonstrate that lack of charisma so evident in the behaviour of leaders in many industrialised countries; there are, of course, significant differences in contents, symbols, assumptions, and style between these politicians.

This kind of rationalist political tradition with which people from the Caribbean came to Britain was to have a lasting influence on their political behaviour as they settled and began to consolidate their presence in what they had come to regard as the mother-country. One noticeable influence of this tradition on West Indian behaviour in Britain has been the emphasis they tend to place upon constitutional practices.

For example, one noticeable feature of English-speaking people from the Caribbean is the use they make of democratic procedures in their associational activity. Invariably, a group commences, after informal discussions, with the formulation of a constitution detailing the procedures for electing officers, the name of the group/organisation, its aims, the powers invested in its officers, how they may be removed, its by-laws, and so forth. Sometimes, indeed, there are not enough persons in the group to fill the number of offices listed in the constitution, but nearly always there will be a constitution of some kind. Procedures, modes of address, and the like are generally adhered to and these obviously include elections, calling of meetings to order, how many members constitute a quorum, and the like. These constitutions clearly reflect a deep respect for democratic norms, and this reflection nearly always mirrors a respect moderated by a cautious suspicion of leaders. A good example of a group's constitution which outlines these features is that of the West Indian Standing Conference (WISC) as revised in 1981. It amounts to a sizeable document of over thirty pages and provides the organisation with guidelines regarding almost every eventuality. Inevitably, the document was the product of a constitutional committee, elected specifically for the purpose.

A second closely related characteristic of these groups is the publication of their aims, the advertisement of their presence, and a general call to all people of goodwill either for their co-operation or for them to join in a common enterprise. The second main aim of the WISC, for example, is to

> work in the United Kingdom towards the elimination of racial discrimination thereby promoting opportunity for all racial groups and to co-operate with all other organisations where common interest coincide with these aims at local or national level both inside and outside of Britain.

(WISC 1981: 1)

Another example of these characteristics of groups founded by people from the Commonwealth Caribbean in Britain may be taken from the first major publication of the Black Unity and Freedom Party (BUFP) in London in 1970. The BUFP boldly stated that 'With the publication of this first issue of *BLACK VOICE*, the BLACK UNITY AND FREEDOM PARTY will be more widely known to black working people as well as other revolutionaries and militants throughout the nation and abroad' (*Black Voice*, August–September 1970: 4). The article went on to speak about the historic importance of the group's founding, its class analysis of British society and the insertion of black people within it, the group's internationalist and non-racialist character, plans to publish the documents from the founding meeting as well as the long- and short-term aims of the group. Although the WISC, founded in 1958 in the aftermath of the Notting Hill riots, is a moderate organisation and the BUFP was a radical marxist group, their members, drawing upon the same broad traditions from the Caribbean, exhibited much the same *organisational* characteristics.

A third characteristic of English-speaking Caribbean leadership, as expressed through group organisation, is the fundamentally multiracial or multi-ethnic composition of group membership.[8] Generally, membership is open to all West Indians irrespective of colour or race, particularly where such groups are formed by people from a specific island.[9] Not only is it usual to find people of different 'racial' groups in these organisations, it would be unusual not to find this to be the case. The important criterion is that members agree with the aims and objectives of the organisation. The criterion for membership tends, therefore, to be politico-ideological; it is likely to be issue-related. Whenever it appears to be exclusively ethno-racial – and it is difficult to find such groups – the group soon falls apart as a result of its own inner contradictions. In this respect, the Notting Hill Carnival, as Cohen shows (this volume), may be a simple example of how the norm in the Commonwealth Caribbean is to include rather than to exclude. Organisations, therefore, reflect the widespread Caribbean belief that a person's views are likely to transcend his or her 'racial' or ethnic grouping or preoccupations. Consistent with this perspective are the ideological underpinnings of groups: the beliefs which inform Caribbean groups are generally egalitarian (perhaps reflecting a retention of African traditions) and rationalistic (the legacy of the European Enlightenment) and much time is devoted to, some would mistakenly say wasted on, debate before, or even instead of, action.

Finally, these characteristics give West Indian leadership in Britain a strong and markedly individualist character and tone. This individualism has many aspects to it. For example, it characterises individuals such as Bill Morris who is, first and foremost, a competent trade unionist; political figures such as Lord Learie Constantine or Lord Pitt, and academics such as M.G. Smith or Stuart Hall. Such personalities stand as individuals and distinctly not as members of an ethnic group. Indeed, sometimes they are hardly recognised as West Indians or blacks at all. And since their names are not distinct from those of the white, native majority, until their faces are seen, the general assumption is that such persons are members of the white majority.

It is also true, of course, to say that in the past, too, some success-ful individual West Indians were not closely associated in the public mind with the majority West Indian population of Britain. This dif-fers from the case in other minority communities, and it may not always be willed by the individuals themselves. For example, whilst we would generally assume that Director Patel of the London School of Economics must at least have something to do with the Indian sub-continent, few would assume that the former Vice-Chancellor of Hull University, the well-known academic lawyer Sir Roy Marshall, or Sir Hugh Springer, former Head of the Foundation of Common-wealth Universities and now governor-general of his country, are Barbadians. Because being West Indian has come today to be synony-mous in Britain with the word *failure*, persons who achieve any degree of professional recognition must by definition either be *excep-tional* or they are simply incorporated into the general cultural majority.

Aspects of this situation have, however, changed quite dramati-cally over the last decade or so. Black trade unionists, such as Bill Morris himself, social workers, such as David Divine, and politicians such as Russell Proffitt in Lewisham or Philip Murphy in Birming-ham, as well as a score of others, have increasingly sought to declare their blackness and make this a large part of their legitimacy to the claim to representation. This may be particularly true for individuals in the more activist or public service occupations which deal directly with clients, many of whom are likely to be black and/or people with a Caribbean background.

The rapid growth in the numbers of councillors among men and women with a Caribbean background during the third phase of Caribbean political experience from the late 1970s into the 1980s, as well as the historic election of four visibly and highly vocal black or non-white Members of Parliament in June 1987, have also assisted in giving Caribbean leadership in Britain a high profile. Two of these MPs, Bernie Grant for Tottenham and Diane Abbott for Hackney, are of Caribbean background, while Paul Boateng for Brent is gener-ally assumed to be Afro-Caribbean, although he is in fact of Ghanaian/English background. The men and women – such as Merle Amory, Bernie Grant earlier, and several others – who have become leaders or mayors of councils in London boroughs, as well as their support for the demand in the Labour Party for a Black Section, have also contributed to a widespread impression that Afro-Caribbean folks in Britain are highly assertive in the political arena.

In the process of creating this political space for itself an exclusive, non-ethnicist form of political leadership appears to prevail in the West Indian community in Britain today, and this calls for some explanation. There were at least two main reasons for the emergence of this form of leadership which can be mentioned briefly here. These were the anger and counter-rejection movement amongst black folks subsequent to their rejection by white majority society and its institutions from the 1940s, and the impact of the Black Power movement of the late 1960s and early 1970s.

In the case of the Black Power movement, it is of course true that in the USA the apparent intolerance of the movement towards the black middle classes and the white liberal establishment was in large part itself a reaction to the black–white coalition against Jim Crowism in the South and the failure of white liberals in the North to effect meaningful change so as to bring about a visible improvement in the life chances of Afro-Americans. In this situation militant black leaders such as Stokeley Carmichael (now Kwame Toure), Bobby Seale, Huey P. Newton, Eldridge Cleaver, and others in the Student Non-violent Co-ordinating Committee (SNCC) and the Black Panther movement sought to develop a leadership for black America which would not include whites. Indeed, at one level the new militant leadership could be viewed as having been simply a replication, or a mirroring, of the majority white ethnic leadership which excluded black people.

This new kind of activism was, and remains, a shock to many (Haskins 1988), because there was a new urgency in black demands which seemed to take little account of the past and was, therefore, in sharp contrast to the racially integrated movements of the earlier part of the 1960s and a tradition of leadership Afro-Americans had developed since slavery in the New World. The break with this aspect of the tradition of leadership was not, however, complete. For example, the Panthers sought to secure the co-operation of white groups and individuals who shared similar political views (Seale 1968). It is clear that post-Panther black leadership in the USA has returned, with Andrew Young, Jesse Jackson, and a score of city mayors, to a longstanding tradition of black leadership which does not exclude but rather seeks to unify as many forces as possible towards attaining justice and democracy for the many. In this sense at least Martin Luther King's vision of black leadership in America has won the day against competing forms of leadership (King 1969; Goulbourne 1989).

The Black Power movement was a more complex phenomenon in the Caribbean. In the first place the political structures were formally controlled by black people as the then Prime Minister of Trinidad and Tobago, the historian Eric Williams, made clear (see, for example, Sutton 1981: 167–72). Another reason was that the word black was, and is, less straightforwardly understood, less obvious, than in North American society where 'black' and 'white' have always been unproblematic ascriptions. In the Caribbean, however, distinctions between black and white take on more subtle shades. In the Britain of the late 1960s and early 1970s, the groups which drew their inspiration from the new militant and radical Afro-American organisations, leaders, and ideology, sought to develop a leadership in Caribbean communities which would be distinctively black. But the pattern they followed bore greater resemblance to the Caribbean expression of black power than to the American.

Irrespective, however, of how groups of people in this country are described or wish to describe themselves there can be little doubt that the British situation combines aspects of both the Caribbean and the American situations. Here are groups of people with different cultural norms and shades of colour spreading along the black–white continuum but with an overwhelming white majority population which, although not itself an entirely self-assured homogeneous whole, does, in the main, determine certain clear ethnic cleavages. For example, we are all slowly coming, through both dicta of state and self-definition, to be regarded as 'white', 'Afro-Caribbean', or 'Asian'. But at present it would probably be a mistake to assume that the new ethnic divisions are simple additions to the list of Jewish-British, Irish-British, and even less to the category of Scots-British or English-British elements of an accepted national community. In the process of this ethnic, racial, colour, or geographical definition a process of *exclusion* is taking place rather than a recognition of *difference* for enrichment within an emerging, new, definition of the British national community. Consequently, a relativism is surfacing in the public realm to fill the space which ought, rightly, to be occupied by a common understanding of citizenship. This should involve the rights, responsibilities, and mutual respect for those values which can help us to strike a balance between the virtues of individualism and collectivism.

The communal option and West Indian leadership

An important part, then, of the task of leadership for West Indians in Britain today is undoubtedly to maintain the universalistic and humanistic stance against mono-ethnic forms of leadership and not be party to the effort to promote racial or ethnic enclaves as ends *in themselves*. The readiness to adopt the communal option, however, in Britain seems to me to present a temptation which may be too strong for would-be leaders in (even) the Caribbean communities to resist. With the passing of time, the kind of non-racial leadership I am speaking of here is likely to become more necessary for mutuality, tolerance, and social peace, but is likely to be less readily acceptable in Britain. This will be because Britain may soon fully achieve what it seems poised to degenerate into – either steadily or rapidly – that is, a social order distinguished in its parts essentially by racial and ethnic characteristics, or, put more brutally, the completion of the construction of what M.G. Smith describes as a socially and culturally pluralist society. Admittedly, the vocal and visible demands from both civil society and the state are restricted to the *culturally* plural, but it is sometimes difficult not to hear also the more muted insistence for consistency that such a scenario demands. Sadly, this perspective of society as necessarily constituted along the lines Hobbes sought to show were intolerable for decent human existence, is, in my view, one of the few elements around which a national consensus appears to exist in Britain.

Consequently, the value of the individual in liberal social thought and the premium socialists have traditionally seen in the group or the collective are today caught in a tension which seems unlikely to be easily contained, let alone resolved.[10] Individuals are not to be treated as individuals nor are they perceived as individual species-beings; the personality of a man or woman can have little or no meaning outside of his or her group, and sometimes the identity of the group is even more imaginary than Anderson's *imagined* community and is, in fact, nothing more than a vague *supposition* – after all, the imagination is (as indeed Anderson argues) firmly based in experience and is very real indeed. The group, on the other hand, is nearly always perceived to be a threat to society, not only majority white society, but society as a whole including members of the very groups themselves which are perceived to be threatening. The groups which are regarded as threatening change from time to time. Sometimes it is the Sikhs, at other times (as presently, due to the Rushdie affair) it is the Muslims. But nearly always – even if it is not at the top of the list – the group is perceived to be West Indian or, more precisely, Afro-Caribbean. Like imported commodity extracts such as orange, rum, or marijuana, people with a Caribbean background have come to be reconstituted in Britain either as carefree and irresponsible or as that super-evil influence which threatens the body politic and social. Dench is therefore correct in pointing to the hypocrisy of the majority and their leaders in open, liberal societies where minorities are encouraged to participate *qua* individuals in society, but their behaviour is judged – notably when one member of the group they ostensibly belong to commits a crime – *collectively* (Dench 1986). Thus, when individuals commit a crime, if they are white people they are portrayed as individuals who assume the responsibility for their actions; if however, they are Afro-Caribbeans, this is not only trumpeted by the media but their individual actions become the *collective* responsibility of all who are designated Afro-Caribbean.

This tension seems likely to create a situation in which the long-term security of most non-white minorities, as well as the comfort derived from the peculiar certainty the majority population appears to enjoy in its relations with minorities, cannot be taken for granted. Such an eventuality places a heavy responsibility on the shoulders of leaders of groups from both the Asian and the Caribbean populations, but especially upon the state and the indigenous society, if only because there are certain moral responsibilities derived from history, and, of course, from the fact of being a physical, demographic, and cultural majority. The chief of these responsibilities is no doubt one of opening the way for groups to be able to transcend the ethnic and racial divisions which have been encouraged between the majority and minority communities, and also between the minority communities themselves. After all, they are constituted as groups which are fundamentally divided through their *differences*.

I would like to suggest that, in the main, the thrust of West Indian leadership in Britain has been to avoid the communal option. This, however, is not always clearly portrayed because, as I have indicated, there is no single, unambiguous line of leadership amongst or from West Indians. But even the Rastafarians, who are sometimes regarded as wishing to withdraw from society, have participated in the creation of innovative, original music and poetry setting the agenda of popular youth culture throughout broad sections of British society. The rejection of West Indian Christians by white congregations during the period of entry and settlement in the 1950s and 1960s resulted in the growth of what is generally referred to as the black-led churches (Howard 1987; Charman 1979). But an important point is often overlooked: the pentecostal movement as a whole has been able to embrace both white and black Christians where the traditional and well-heeled denominations have conspicuously failed to do so. Credit must be given, then, to these churches for not excluding white Christians from their fellowship; if there is any exclusion it is more by way of a boycott by white Christians than any exclusivism on the part of non-white Christians.

There is a danger, however, involved in the mode of political leadership as it has developed in West Indian communities in Britain. And this danger may be said to serve as a bridge between the second and the third phases I have suggested. This danger may be expressed in terms of whether leaders are able to recognise the point at which the protesting mode of political behaviour reaches its limits. It is not militancy itself, however, which will pose the greatest danger for the community; rather, the danger is that West Indians in Britain are now poised to abandon a strong, confident, and humanitarian tradition and to replace it with an alien exclusiveness. It is, of course, easy enough to appreciate the multiple pressures which are forcing many to adopt the exclusivity of the communal option as the only route to salvation. But if it is followed to its logical conclusion, then this exclusivism may become the main obstacle, rather than white racism, to black progress in Britain. The dominated will then have come to accept their subordinated position in society through an apparently voluntarist ideology. This ideology can only be regarded as part of a broader bourgeois ideology according to which society expects individual subjects to accept their condition as a consequence of their own actions and social value. It is also the voluntarism Frantz Fanon sought to dissect with respect to the personality of the colonised subject (Fanon 1969).

Conclusion

Of course, the extent to which people of Commonwealth Caribbean background in Britain have shunned the communal option and proudly borne the scourge for a humanism they have had to fight to win, cannot be fully appreciated until a balanced construction of the history of the years after the Second World War is made. Such an effort must be informed by a close knowledge of the activities, and be perceptive to the perspectives, of the actors themselves. There will, naturally, be several constructions of this history but it will be from these that future historians will be able to better understand the first decade of post-imperial black settlement in Britain. What can, however, be said from the general remarks I have made here is that West Indian leadership cannot be easily fitted into Myrdal's widely used and highly suggestive dichotomy between accommodationist and protest/reform kinds of ethnic leadership. I have argued that this is because West Indians have not generally sought to use ethnicity as the basis for political action. Over the past decade or so, one response to rejection in Britain, however, has been to travel along what appears to be a universally acceptable road, namely the communal cul-de-sac. But there are obvious dangers in this act of desperation. One of these is that West Indians stand to lose that essentially humane disposition with which they came to Britain, by contributing to the construction of a kind of society against which they have always sought to assert and reassert their humanity. They also stand in a

317

position from where they could make a step in a backward rather than a forward direction and this would be to abandon a rich rationalist tradition, from which they have already contributed much and stand to contribute still more, to the construction of a better Britain. Their experiences of slavery, colonialism, and self-emancipation have highlighted the contradictory elements of the raionalist tradition yet strengthened their view that *reason* will prevail.

To paraphrase Dante, it may be said that midway this way of the road we are bound upor. are the choices between communalism and a new national community. Like Dante's hero, if we are not careful we could very well awake to find ourselves in a satanic wood.

© 1991 Harry Goulbourne

Notes

1 There are two closely related reasons for this: first, the relatively absent voice of Caribbean people in academic literature provides preciously little to build upon in a brief discussion of this kind; second, the rewriting of the histories of Britain's non-white groups, particularly the Afro-Caribbean population, has still to be undertaken and, although I have begun gathering the material necessary for this work, I have not commenced the detailed analysis necessary to go beyond the bald statement being offered here.
2 Weber must be credited or condemned for introducing perhaps the most widely used concept in sociological literature which has found its way into everyday vocabulary – charisma – but which is also the most vulgarised.
3 Never mind here the cultural importations and contributions which have been appropriated in much the same way as the wealth of the Caribbean – and other parts of the world – have been appropriated and reconstituted in the forms of lavish homes, galleries, family wealth, libraries, and the like, and designated to be exclusively, or pristine, British.
4 I am deliberately using the term English-speaking instead of Commonwealth here because the former is a larger category than the latter; there are islands, e.g. the Turks and Caicos Islands, which remain under formal British external protection mutually arrived at.
5 The work of Stephens and Stephens is a recent notable exception to this statement (Stephens and Stephens 1986).
6 For example, the slowness of Caribbean governments and educational institutions to establish a regional examining council for their schools is a case in point. The Caribbean Examination Council (CXC) exams were only established in the 1970s, slowly replacing the GCE 'O' levels; the 'A' levels from Britain are still taken in the region.

7 It is interesting that, again, the exceptions to this rule have been Guyana and Trinidad which came relatively late into British possession; both states are formally headed by appointed presidents and both have declared themselves to be republics.

8 My point here is not that there are not likely to be groups whose memberships are entirely of Afro-Caribbean or Indo-Caribbean background. The point, rather, is that a situation such as this was, most likely, unusual for most of the period of sizeable settlement of Caribbean people in Britain in the post-imperial period. Since the late 1960s a multiplicity of groups describing themselves as Afro-Caribbean has emerged. There are also Caribbean-Hindu, etc., groups in existence.

9 There are several island associations which seek to keep certain customs and practices from 'back home' alive as well as to inform members of developments occurring there.

10 It is no doubt for this reason that the Salman Rushdie affair, which is acting as the catalyst for the expression of the opposition of Christian/secular and Islamic/clerical traditions, is fast becoming one of the great *cause célèbres* of all time.

References

Anderson, Benedict (1983) *Imagined Communities: Reflections on the Origin and Spread of Nationalism*, London: Verso.

Apter, D. (1968) *Some Conceptual Approaches to the Study of Modernization*, New Haven, Conn.: Prentice-Hall.

Black Unity and Freedom Party (1970–8) *Black Voice*, passim.

Braithwaite, Lloyd (1953) 'Social stratification in Trinidad: a preliminary analysis', *Social and Economic Studies* 2 (3): 5–175.

Braithwaite, Lloyd (1974) 'Problems of race and colour in the Caribbean', *Caribbean Issues* 1.

Brathwaite, E. (1971) *The Development of Creole Society in Jamaica 1770–1820*, Oxford: Clarendon Press.

Brown, Aggrey (1979) *Colour and Politics in Jamaica*, New Brunswick, NJ: Transaction Books.

Carter, T. (1986) *Shattering Illusions: West Indians in British Politics*, London: Lawrence & Wishart.

Charman, P. (1979) *Reflections: Black and White Christians in the City*, London: Zebra Project.

Constantine, Learie (1954) *Colour Bar*, London: Stanley Paul.

Crenson, M. (1971) *The Un-politics of Air Pollution: A Study of Non-decisionmaking in the Cities*, Baltimore, Md: Johns Hopkins University Press.

Crossman, R. (1975) *Diaries of a Cabinet Minister*, London: Hamish Hamilton and Jonathan Cape.

Dabydeen, D. and Samaroo, B. (eds) (1986) *India in the Caribbean*, London: Hansib/Centre for Caribbean Studies, University of Warwick.

Dench, G. (1986) *Minorities in the Open Society: Prisoners of Ambivalence*, London: Routledge & Kegan Paul.

Department of Education and Science (1988) *Education Reform Act*, London: HMSO.

Egbuna, O. (1971) *Destroy This Temple: The Voice of Black Power in Britain*, London: MacGibbon & Kee.

Fanon, Frantz (1969) [1961] *The Wretched of the Earth*, London: Penguin Books.

Fitzgerald, M. (1988) 'Afro-Caribbean involvement in British politics', in M. Cross and H. Entzinger (eds) *Lost Illusions: Caribbean Minorities in Britain and the Netherlands*, London: Routledge.

Gellner, E. (1983) *Nations and Nationalism*, Oxford: Basil Blackwell.

Gerth, H.H. and Mills, C.Wright (eds) (1958) *From Max Weber: Essays in Sociology*, Oxford: Oxford University Press.

Giddens, A. (1972) *Politics and Sociology in the Thought of Max Weber*, London: Macmillan.

Gilroy, P. (1987) *There Ain't No Black in the Union Jack: The Cultural Politics of Race and Nation*, London: Hutchinson.

Goulbourne, H. (1988a) 'The contribution of Caribbean people to British Society', in Arif Ali (ed.) *Third World Impact*, 8th edn, London: Hansib Publications.

Goulbourne, H. (1988b) *West Indian Political Leadership in Britain*, Occasional Paper No. 4 (The Byfield Memorial Lecture 1987), Coventry: Centre for Research in Ethnic Relations, University of Warwick.

Goulbourne, H. (1989) *Communalism or Community?* (Dr Martin Luther King, Jr. Memorial Lecture 1989), Birmingham: Dr Martin Luther King Memorial Trust.

Goulbourne, H. (1990) 'The contribution of West Indian groups to British politics', in H. Goulbourne (ed.) *Black People and British Politics*, Aldershot: Avebury.

Goulbourne, H. (1991) *The Communal Option: Nationalism and Ethnicity in Post-Imperial Britain*, Cambridge: Cambridge University Press.

Hall, S., Critcher, C., Jefferson, T., Clarke, J. and Roberts, B. (1978) *Policing the Crisis: Mugging, the State and Law and Order*, London: Macmillan Press.

Hart, Richard (1980) *Slaves Who Abolished Slavery*, Mona: Institute of Social and Economic Research.

Haskins, E.W. (1988) *The Crisis in Afro-American Leadership*, New York: Prometheus.

Heineman, B. (1972) *The Politics of the Powerless: A Study of the Campaign Against Racial Discrimination*, London: IRR/Oxford University Press.

Henriques, F. (1969) [1953] *Family and Colour in Jamaica*, London: MacGibbon & Kee.

Herskovits, M. (1970) [1941] *The Myth of the Negro Past*, Gloucester: Peter Smith.

Higham, J. (ed.) (1978) *Ethnic Leadership in America*, Baltimore, Md.: Johns Hopkins University Press.

Hook, S. (1943) *The Hero in History: A Study in Limitation and Possibility*, Boston, Mass.: Beacon Press.

Howard, V. (1987) *A Report of Afro-Caribbean Christianity in Britain*, Department of Theology and Religious Studies, University of Leeds.

Jackson, George L. (1971) *Soledad Brother: The Prison Letters of George Jackson*, London: Jonathan Cape.

Jackson, George L. (1972) *Blood in my Eye*, London: Jonathan Cape.

King, Martin Luther (1969) *Chaos or Community?* London: Pelican.

Lukes, S. (1974) *Power: A Radical View*, London: Macmillan.

Marx, Karl (1969a) [1869] 'The Eighteenth Brumaire of Louis Bonaparte', in *Marx and Engels: Selected Works*, vol. 1, Moscow: Progress Publishers.

Marx, Karl (1969b) [1871] 'The civil war in France', in *Marx and Engels: Selected Works*, vol. 2, Moscow: Progress Publishers.

Michels, R. (1958) [1915] *Political Parties: A Sociological Study of the Oligarchical Tendencies of Modern Democracy*, Glencoe, NY: Free Press.

Miliband, R. (1973) [1969] *The State in Capitalist Society: The Analysis of the Western System of Power*, London: Quartet.

Miliband, R. (1977) *Marxism and Politics*, Oxford: Oxford University Press.

Modood, T. (1988) '"Black", racial equality and Asian identity', *New Community* 14 (3): 397–404.

Moses, W.J. (1978) *The Golden Age of Black Nationalism, 1850–1925*, Oxford: Oxford University Press.

Munroe, T. (1972) *The Politics of Constitutional Decolonization: Jamaica, 1944–62*, Mona: Institute of Social and Economic Research, University of the West Indies.

Nettleford, R., Smith, M.G. and Augier, R. (1960) *The Rastafari Movement in Kingston, Jamaica*, Mona: Institute of Social and Economic Research, University of the West Indies.

Newton, Huey P. (1974) *Revolutionary Suicide*, London: Wildwood House.

Olson, M. (1965) *The Logic of Collective Action*, Cambridge, Mass.: Harvard University Press.

Ostrogorski, M. (1964) [1902] *Democracy and the Organisation of Political Parties*, 2 vols, Chicago, Ill.: Anchor Books.

Patterson, O. (1977) *Ethnic Chauvinism: The Reactionary Impulse*, New York: Stein & Day.

Pearson, D. (1981) *Race, Class and Political Activism: A Study of West Indians in Britain*, Farnborough, Hants.: Gower.

Poulantzas, N. (1975) [1968] *Political Power and Social Classes*, London: New Left Books.

Pryce, E. (1990) 'Culture from below: politics, resistance and leadership in the Notting Hill Gate Carnival 1976–1978', in H. Goulbourne (ed.) *Black People and British Politics*, Aldershot: Avebury.

Rex, J. (1979) 'Black militancy and class conflict' in R. Miles and A. Phizaklea (eds) *Racism and Political Action*, London: Routledge & Kegan Paul.

Rex, J. (1986) *Race and Ethnicity*, Milton Keynes, Bucks.: Open University Press.

Rex, J. and Tomlinson, S. (1979) *Colonial Immigrants in a British City: A Class Analysis*, London: Routledge & Kegan Paul.

Seale, B. (1968) [1970] *Seize the Time*, London: Arrow Books.
Simpson, G.E. (1955) 'Political cultism in West Kingston, Jamaica', *Social and Economic Studies* iv (ii).
Simpson, G.E. (1956) 'Jamaican revivalist cults', *Social and Economic Studies* v (ii)
Sivanandan, A. (1983) 'Challenging racism: strategies for the '80s', *Race and Class* xxv (ii).
Smith, M.G. (1965) *The Plural Society in the British West Indies*, Berkeley, Calif.: University of California Press.
Smith, M.G. (1984) *Culture, Race and Class in the Commonwealth Caribbean*, Mona: University of the West Indies.
Smith, R.T. (1962) *British Guiana*, London: Oxford University Press.
Smith, R.T. (1967) 'Social stratification, cultural pluralism and integration in West Indian societies', in Sybil Lewis and T. G. Matthews (eds) *Caribbean Integration: Papers on Social, Political and Economic Integration*, Rio Piedras: Institute of Caribbean Studies.
Stephens, E.H. and Stephens, J.D. (1986) *Democratic Socialism in Jamaica* London: Macmillan.
Stone, C. (1983) *Democracy and Clientelism in Jamaica*, New Brunswick, NJ: Transaction Books.
Sutton, P. (1981) *Forged from the Love of Liberty: Selected Speeches of Dr. Eric Williams*, Port of Spain: Longman Caribbean.
Tocqueville, Alexis de (1945) [1835] *Democracy in America*, 2 vols, New York: Alfred A. Knopf and Random House.
Tocqueville, Alexis de (1970) [1893] *Recollections*, London: Macdonald.
Weber, Max (1947) *The Theory of Social and Economic Organisation*, New York: Free Press.
WISC (West Indian Standing Conference) (1981) *Constitution*, London: West Indian Standing Conference.
WISC (West Indian Standing Conference) (1987–9) *Team Work*, Journal oɪ the West Indian Standing Conference, passim.

Name index

Abbott, Diane 55, 69, 312
Abrams, Kingsley 73
Adams, B.N. 206
Adams, T.W. 85
Ahluwala, Sardar K.S.N. 54
Alavi, H. 20, 33, 139
Alderman, G. 59
Aldrich, H. 135
Alemoru, O. 290
Ali, Altab 86, 88
Ali, Ashik 96–7
Amory, Merle 312
Anderson, Benedict 24, 33, 161, 315
Anderson, Digby 279
Andrew, Revd Hewie 291
Anwar, A. 8, 10, 11
Anwar, M. 2, 3, 5, 8, 11, 13, 19, 29,
    41, 45, 47, 48, 51, 52, 54, 55, 56,
    57, 59, 82n, 113, 138
Apter, D. 309
Atkin, Sharon 79–80, 81
Aurora, G.S. 138, 257, 260

Bagehot, Walter 298
Bailey, A. 253
Bains, Harwant 147, 152, 155, 157,
    158, 162
Baker, John 178
Ballard, R. 137
Banks, Marcus 16, 17, 21, 22, 32,
    227
Banton, M. 82n
Baptiste, Selwyn 189
Baraka, Amiri 191
Barnett, M. 82n

Barth, F. 141, 253
Barton, J. 32, 59, 119
Ben Tovim, G. 19, 27, 30, 31, 71,
    82n
Benyon, J. 19, 78, 148
Beswick, Pastor Esme 290
Beteille, A. 118
Bhachu, Parminder 205
Bharati 206
Bhindrawala 270
Bhownagree, Sir Mancherjee 54
Blauner, Robert 31
Boateng, Paul 55, 81, 312
Booth, William 284, 285
Brah, Avtar 150–1
Braithwaite, Lloyd 307
Brecht, Bertolt 191
Brennan, John 10
Breton, R. 131
Brown, Colin 8, 9, 10
Bruinvels, Peter 55, 57, 149–50
Bryan, B. 147
Buckman, J. 84, 113
Buddha, Gotama 226
Bustamante, Sir Alexander 309

Calley, M.J.C. 281, 283
Carmichael, Stokely (Kwame
    Toure) 43, 313
Castells, Manuel 15
Cavanagh, T.E. 59
Chaggar, Gurdip Singh 154–5
Charles, Canon Sebstian 291
Charles, Prince of Wales 247
Charman, P. 316

Chase, Louis 189–90
Chaudhary, V. 291
Chima, Babook 256
Chitnis, Lord 54
Clarke, Kenneth 285
Cleaver, Eldridge 313
Cohen, A. 15–16, 16–17, 21–2, 34,
    116, 140, 170–1, 203, 311
Cohen, Gaynor 207
Cohen, P. 148, 151, 161
Constantine, Lord Learie 54, 311
Coupland 278
Crenson, M. 299
Crossman, R. 298
Cuffay, William 147
Cunningham, C. 206

Dabydeen, D. 307
Dahya, Badr 113, 114, 131
Daniel, Revd Rajinder 278, 289
Daniels, R. 59
Davis, Andrew 179
Dench, G. 315–16
Desai, Mrs 147
Desai, R. 253, 254, 256, 257, 260
Dhavan, Rajeev 43
Divine, David 312
Dixon, M. 283
Donnison, David 278
Dumont, L. 30
Dundas, Paul 247
Dunn, Cyril 259

Eade, John 16, 17, 21–2, 25, 26, 29,
    85
Egbuna, O. 303
Epstein, A.L. 118
Esslin, M. 191

Fanon, Frantz 317
Feuchtwang, Stephan 85
Fishman, William 59
Fitzgerald, Marian 58, 82n, 304
Fogarty, M. 279
Forde, Larry 180, 189, 190
Fox, R.G. 203
Frankenberg, R. 170
Fryer, P. 147, 161

Ganatra, R. 57
Gandhi, Indira 262
Garrow, D.J. 280
Garvey, Marcus 185
Geertz, Clifford 24
Gerloff, R. 281, 282
Gerth, H.H. 300
Gibson, A. 284
Giddens, A. 300
Gilroy, Paul 24, 29, 82n, 84, 114,
    117, 119, 147, 148, 158, 296
Glazer, N. 32, 34, 59, 84, 115, 203
Gluckman, M. 27, 170, 192
Goreen, Arthur 59
Goulbourne, H. 16, 19, 21, 28, 280,
    284, 287, 297, 303, 307, 313
Gramsci 161
Granovetter, Mark S. 117
Grant, Bernie 55, 69, 74, 75, 81, 312
Gregory, Chris 244–5

Hall, S. 27, 84, 119, 148, 161, 299, 311
Halloway, H. 59
Handelman, Don 141
Hannan, Abdul 91–3, 98
Harris, Bishop Barbara 290
Hart, Richard 307
Haskins, E.W. 313
Hattersley, Roy 80
Heffer, Eric 72, 81
Hegel, Georg 300
Heineman, B. 18, 19, 22, 29, 32, 43
Helweg, A.W. 128
Hempton, D. 282–3
Henderson, L. 59
Henderson, Russell 173
Herskovits, M. 307
Higgins 18
Higham, J. 21, 22, 23, 42, 117
Hill, Clifford 281, 291, 292
Hill, E. 192
Hiro, D. 254, 256, 257
Hobbes, Thomas 299, 315
Holder, Clare 196
Home Office 3
Hooper, R. 278
Hopkinson, Henry 2
Howard, V. 283, 316

Howe, D. 80, 175, 178, 187, 189, 190
Howe, Irving: *Politics and the Novel*
   191–2
Huggins, N. 18, 134
Hundal, N.S. 265
Huque, Nural 91, 96–7, 100

Islam, Syed Nural 91, 97

Jackson, A. 291, 292
Jackson, Jesse 291, 313
Jacobs, Brian 82n, 149
Jain, Kesu 241, 242–4, 246, 247
Jeffers, S. 16, 17, 19, 25, 29, 30, 53, 60
John, De Witt 56, 253, 254, 256,
   257–8, 259, 264
Johnson, Leonard 286
Johnson, Linton Kwesi 191
Johnson, M.R. 16, 18–19, 32, 288
Johnson, Paul 278
Johnston, Ginger 173
Josephides, Sasha 16, 20, 22, 23, 26,
   32
Joshi, Jagmohan 254–5, 254, 266–7
Jouhal, Avtar 272

Kalilombe, Bishop Patrick 289
Kalka, Iris 16, 21–2, 24–5, 138
Kapferer, Bruce 24
Katznelson, Ira 18, 22, 116
Kaufman, Gerald 80, 135
Keech, W. 59
Kelly, Bill 94
Kennedy, Pastor 292
Keyes, C. 27, 118
Khabra, Piarra 264–5
Khan, Aga 206
Khan, Akbar Ali 256
Khan, Amir 79, 81
King, Martin Luther 42, 280, 290,
   313
Kinnock, Neil 79, 80
Kirp, D.L. 204

Lake, Eileen 290
Laslett, Rhaunee 172–3, 176
Lawrence, D. 18, 28, 78, 116
Layton-Henry, Z. 78, 82n

Le Lohe, Mich 46, 49, 56
Leech, K. 280, 283
Lewin, Kurt 21, 42, 116, 117, 119
Locke, John 299
Lodrick, D.O. 234
Lukes, S. 301

McClean, Bishop Eunice 290
McGlashen, Colin 264
Machiavelli, Niccolo 298
Macmillan, Harold 172
Mahavira 226
Makenji, Narendra 69
Mann, Bashir 54
Marable, Manning 18, 31
Marcuse, Herbert 191
Marley, Bob 182
Marshall, J. 287
Marshall, Sir Roy 312
Marx, Karl 300; *Civil War in France*
   299; *Eighteenth Brumaire* 299
Mauss, Marcel 245
Mayer, Arian C. 245, 253
Maynard 281
Mehmood, T.: *Hand on the Sun* 147
Mehta, Anil 241
Mehta, Natu 241
Mehta, Vipin 241
Mellor, Rosemary 22
Melucci, A. 167
Michaelson, M. 207
Michels, R. 299
Miles, R. 30
Miliband, R. 298
Milwood, Dr Robinson 291
Mitchell, C. 118, 170
Moore, R. 282–3
Morris, Bill 71–2, 81, 311, 312
Morris, H. Stephen 43
Mosca 299
Mukerherjee, Tuku 155, 159, 162
Munroe, T. 308
Murphy, Philip 312
Murray, Leon 288
Myrdal, Gunnar 34, 317; *An*
   American Dilemma 42
Nagata, Judith 117
Nagra, Kartar Singh 256

Naoroji, Dadabhai 54
Narayan, Rudy 291
Nehru, Pandit 257, 259
Nettleford, R. 309
Newton, Huey P. 313
Noel, Lawrence 179–80
Noor, Naranjan 255, 269–70, 271
Novak, M. 203

O'Dwyer, Sir Michael 254
Olson, M. 299
Omi, M. 82n
Onwordi, A. 283
OPCS 4, 5, 7
Osamor, Martha 76, 81
Ostrogorsky, M. 299

Palmer, Leslie 176, 178, 179, 188
Parkinson, C. 289
Parry, J. 118
Patel 81
Patel, Raj 289
Patterson, O. 302
Peacock, J.L. 170
Pearson, D. 22, 303
Pearson, G. 147
Peters, E.L. 170
Petre, J. 289, 291
Phizacklea, Annie 84
Pitt of Hampstead, Lord 54, 60, 311
Poulantzas, N. 298
Powell, Enoch 174
Prem, Dhani 54
Profitt, Russell 69, 312
Pryce, E. 303
Pryce, Ken 22

Ram, Anant 256
Ramdin, Ron 147, 161
Ranger, Chris 10
Ray, Dread 190
Reeves, David 148, 161
Retzlaff, Ralph 262
Rex, J. 21, 24, 27, 31, 32, 41, 42, 74,
  84, 119, 214, 281, 298
Richardson, Jo 69, 80, 81
Roberts, J. 286
Rose, E.J.B. 2

Rousseau, Jean-Jacques 299, 300
Rushdie, Salman 41, 58, 75, 140;
  The Satanic Verses 19, 23, 25

Said, Edward 15, 24
Sailfullah Khan, Verity 113, 114, 116
Saklatvala, Shapurji 54
Sanders, C. 291
Sandford, G. 290
Saunders, P. 106
Scargill, Arthur 149
Scarman, Lord 210
Schwartz, W. 290
Scott, Duncan 137
Seale, Bobby 313
Shah, Hari 241
Shannon, William 59
Sharma, Vishnu 81, 261, 264, 265
Shore, Peter 102
Short, Clare 69
Sills, A. 150, 152
Simpson, G.E. 309
Singh, Udham 254, 255, 256
Singh, Ujagar 256
Sinha of Raipur, Lord 54
Sivanandan, A. 147, 214
Smith, Cyril 56
Smith, David 11
Smith, Io 290
Smith, M.G. 307, 311, 315
Smith, R.T. 307
Smith-Cameron, Canon Ivor 291
Sollors, W. 191
Solomos, J. 115, 117, 119, 159
Springer, Sir Hugh 312
Stone, C. 309
Sutton, P. 314
Swan Committee: *Education for All*
  11

Thomas, Malcolm 178–9, 188
Thomas, William I. 23
Thompson, John L.P. 119
Tocqueville, Alexis de 299;
  Reflections 299
Toor, Tarsem Singh 262
Toure, Kwame (*formerly* Stokely
Carmichael) 313

Toynbee Arnold 280
Trudeau, Pierre 206
Turner, H. 283
Turner, V.W. 26, 170
Tutu, Archbishop Desmond 278, 280
Tyers, D. 290

Uddin, Abbas 90, 91–3, 98

Vaz, Keith 55, 57, 75, 81, 149
Vincent, Joan 141

Wainwright, H. 82n
Walton, H. 288, 291
Walzer, M. 203
Ward, R. 85

Weber, Max 226, 300, 301

Werbner, P. 15, 17, 20, 21, 22, 23, 25, 30, 31, 32, 84, 116, 119, 126, 127, 128, 207, 214, 242, 283, 284
Westwood, S. 16, 17, 21–2, 25, 150
Whitty, Larry 81
Wilberforce, William 278
Wilkinson 288
Williams, Cecil 54
Williams, Eric 278, 280–1, 287, 314
Williams, J. 114
Willis, Carole 12
Wilson, B. 20–1, 30, 59
Wirth, Louis 84
Wood, Bishop Wilfred 288, 289, 291
Wood, D. 192
Wright, Cecil 11

Young, Andrew 313
Young, K. 204

Subject index

accommodation versus radicalism/ protest 31, 34, 42, 60, 134–41, 297, 317–18; *see also* black; leadership; protest

Afro-Caribbeans: attitude to Asians 65; construction of community 306–8; and definition of 'black' 65; development of forms of leadership 307–14; and Gujaratis 215–16; leadership 303–4, 314–17; in mainstream politics 304; nature of culture 306–7; and Pakistanis 215–16; 'partner-ship' system 303; portrayal of 296, 316–15; registration for voting 45–7; seen as threat to society 315–16; stress on democracy 308–11; turn-out at elections 49; voluntary associations 303; voting patterns 50–2; *see also* Notting Hill Carnival; West Indians

Afro–West Indian Council of Churches 284

age structure of ethnic minorities 5–6, 7

Akali Party 270

Amritsar 270; massacre (1940) 254

Anglican Church 277, 278–9

Anglican Church, Committee on Black Anglican Concerns 289; ethnic minorities in 288; Urban Fund 285

Anglo-Asian Conservative Society 53

Anglo-Indian Art Circle 208

Anglo-West Indian Conservative Society 53

Anti-Nazi League 29, 135

anti-racism, and Black Sections 74–5, 77; in churches 288–9; and Greater London Council (GLC) 88; and Indian Workers Association (IWA) 260; movements for 19, 22, 24, 29, 34; Racism Awareness Training 7, 214; and socialism 101–5, 106–7, 315; *see also* racism

Arts Council 185, 191

Asian Herald 102

Asian Youth Movement 154

Asians 4–13; attitudes to leadership 41; in Christian churches 287, 292; corporate property ownership 228–9; and definition of 'black' 65; in Harrow *see* Gujaratis; housing 205; population in Leicester 228; property-ownership 205; registration for voting 45–7; turn-out at elections 48–9; voting patterns 50–2; *see also* Bangladeshis; ethnic minorities; Gujaratis; Indians; Jains; Pakistanis; Punjabis; Sikhs

association alliances 18, 24, 25, 29, 31–2; of Bangladeshis 87, 91, 99; in Harrow 203, 218–19; of IWA 264–5, 267; in Notting Hill 173; of Pakistanis 126–7; West Indian 310–11

associational efflorescence 15, 16, 20–3
'associative empowerment': in social movements 15–16, 33

Bangladesh High Commission 85
Bangladesh Welfare Association (BWA) 96–8, 104–5
Bangladeshi Socialist Society (BSS) 103–4
Bangladeshis: divisions among 96; employment 10; housing 11, 101, 107; organisations 42, 57, 96–7, 100–1; and political situation in Bangladesh 104–5, 107; role of religious leaders 106; settlement in Tower Hamlets 85–7
Barbados 308–9
Birmingham: Christian Festival (1989) 278–9; ethnic minority candidates in 55–6; registration for voting 45
Birmingham Ladywood constituency 44
birth rate 6
black: collective consciousness 186, 196; group loyalty versus class/socialism 30, 63–4, 74–5, 101; identity, incorporating class/ethnic 159, 217; identity recovered 159, 167; militancy 217; solidarity claimed 214; stereotypes of 77, 146, 156; transcendence of ethnic divisions 26, 28, 29, 30, 63, 86, 156–9, 166–7; – white alliance 172–5, 267, 310–11; – white dominant cleavage 27–8, 314; *see also* discourse; ideology
'black': as politically defined 29, 30, 63, 64, 65, 66, 78, 147, 156, 159, 167, 214, 217, 314;
black activists 26, 29, 30; Bangladeshi 85; Carnival leaders as 189, 193; Harrow Gujaratis 210–12, 214, 217, 221–22; in Leicester 147–67, 175; *see also* ethnic elite; leadership/ethnic

black experience 24, 29, 30, 77, 146, 154–6; reconstructed 155–6, 188; *see also* community; ideology
Black Londoners (BBC Radio) 183
Black Panthers 267, 313
Black Parents' Association 186
Black Parliamentary Caucas 60–83
black people: divisions among 93; marginalised 148, 161, 305; *see also* colonialism/ internal; as political agents *see* political; portrayed as victims 296
Black People's Alliance (BPA) 260, 267
Black People's Manifesto Conference 57
Black People's Progressive Association 180–1
Black Power movement 24, 29, 175, 191, 303, 313–14
Black Sections 16, 17, 57, 63–83; and anti-racist movements 74–5, 77; case study 64–74; compared to Carnival 196; distribution of 81–2; future of 71–4; male bias in 70, 74; media coverage of 79–80; National movement 66, 71–5; and power seeking 80; relation to black MPs 79–80; rejection of ethnicity 76–8; relationship to Labour movement 75–80; representatives of 77–8, 80, 196; and Rushdie Affair 75
black separatism 26, 78, 101, 171, 175, 267; dangers of 303, 313–14, 317; *see also* Black Power movement, social movements
Black Solidarity Front 128
Black Unity and Freedom Party (BUFP) 310–11
Black Voice 310–11
black youth 146–74; incorporated into carnival 180–5; and mainstream politics 163–4; racialised 147–8; stereotypes of

146, 156; struggle of 146–67; *see also* political discourse; social movements; violence

black-led churches 316; social role 281–7; white membership 283, 316; *see also* churches, black-led

boundary interaction 141

Bradford 147, 151–2; ethnic minorities and election campaigns 56; and ethnic minority candidates 556; registration for voting 45, 47, 48; religious influence on ethnic politics 82

Bradford Twelve 155

Brent 44, 205, 209

Britain: British Empire 1, 307–9; emigration from 3; immigration into 1–3; as pluralist society 314–17; *see also* colonialism; nation/nationalism

British Campaign to Stop Immigration 3, 56

British democratic traditions undermined 296–317; *see also* class; historical; political discourse; nation; state/local state

British Empire 1, 307–9

British National Party 3

Brixton riots 210

Buddhism 226, 242

'buffer' institutions 18, 22, 31, 78, 79, 116; *see also* state/local state

Calouste Gulbenkian Foundation 43

Campaign Against Racial Discrimination (CARD) 22, 24, 29, 42–3, 260, 264

Campaign Against Racial Laws (CARL) 267

Campaign Against Racism and Fascism (CARF) 267

Campaign for Racial Equality (CRE) 8, 26, 31, 138, 204, 209, 260; Code of Practice 209; recognition of ethnic minority leaders 60; voting research 46, 50–1, 56

Campaign for Racial Justice 53

Canada: Ismaili settlement in 206

Canterbury, Archbishop of, Commission on Urban Poverty Areas 278, 285

Capital Radio 181

CARD *see* Campaign Against Racial Discrimination

Caribbean House, London 284

Caribbean Times 60, 72

Carnival *see* Notting Hill Carnival 170–96

caste association 206–7, 220, 221

caste system 118, 227, 230

Catholic Church: ethnic minorities in 288, 289

centre–periphery: cultural/entrepreneurial 117, 118; in ethnic groups 20, 21, 131; state versus black youth relationship 163; *see also* leadership, ethnic/black

Church Urban Fund 285

churches: affirmative action in 291; and anti-racism 279, 288, 292; and anti-slavery 278, 282; elite 280; failure to incorporate black people 288–9; and leadership formation 279–80, 283; new initiatives 289–91; political activism in 279; political role of black ministers 291; role in race-relations 277–8, 292; tradition of social reform 278–9

churches: black-led 16, 19, 42, 184–5, 186, 280–5, 316; alliance with white churches 285–6; cultural confidence/resistance of 284; growth of 281, 288; internal welfare provisioning 281-2, 285; and leadership formation 283, 292; openness to white membership 316; ordination of black women 290; pastors as community leaders 286–7; self-funding 287; sense of community 282; social role of 280–5; state funded projects in

285–7; *see also* leadership; social movements, American Civil Rights

Churches of God 283

Churches Initiative in Training, Employment and Enterprise 287

class, basis for alliances 186, 266; basis for ethnic internal divisions 17, 20–2, 84, 113, 118, 263; in IWA 262, 263, 271; and caste system 118; discourse of 157; estates 84; and ethnicity 118–19; exploitation opposed 147, 176; fractions 29, 74, 84; middle – Gujaratis 205; ideological divisions within 84; and Labour Party 'statist policy' 63–4, 79, 80; political construction of 84–108, 118; and race 29, 90–1, 100; and socialism 89–90; stress in British politics 25, 78–9, 95–7 *passim*; versus black/ethnic 30, 63–4, 69, 74, 78, 79, 89, 119, 147, 263, 271; working – culture shared by West Indians 304; working – elite 124–5, 126–7, 130; working and business – among Pakistanis 124–31, 136; working – Indians supported by IWA 263; working – solidarity in Carnival 174; *see also* associational alliances; colonialism; discourses; Labour Party

collective consumption *see* state/local state allocation of resources

Co-ordination Committees Against Racial Discrimination (CCARD) 260

colonial: intervention in leadership disputes 142; introduction of democratic institutions in the West Indies 308–9; neo- model 66, 77, 152;

colonialism: battle against 31, 139; and the black experience 24; and black liberation movements 185; class struggle against 266–7; and colonised subject 317; counter-

of Asians 132; cultural protest against 176–7, 192; 'internal' 30–3 *passim*, 102, 114, 135, 140–1, 167, 214; Labour Party accused of 102; and legitimation crises in Britain 148; *see also* historical; slavery; social movements

Commonwealth Immigrants Bill (1962) 2

communal option 28; 'ethnic arena' 287; identity 30; and leadership in Britain 297; rejected 297–318; *see also* community; culturalism; ethnicity; leadership

communalism, growth of 302

Communist Party: and Indian Workers Association (IWA) 255, 257, 258–9, 261

Communist Party of India (CPI): and Indian Workers Association (IWA) 262–3

Communist Party of India–Marxist (CPI–M): and Indian Workers Association (IWA) 262, 266

community: as actively constituted 30, 84–108, 188; appeals to as united 93, 99, 113, 114, 212, 215; black, represented on Council 71; and Carnival 187–8; as culturally bounded 21, 304–6; established hierarchy within 125–6, 134, 228; external definition of 113; as fiction 28, 33, 113–41, 254; ghetto 20–1; 'imagined' 20–3, 26, 161, 315; internal divisions within *see* ethnic groups; internal provisioning 30–3, 125–7, 129, 226–49; 'interpretive' 24–6; and Jain ritual 244; linguistic 27; as localism 89, 161, 212; as locus of cultural resistance 114; as locus of cultural/power/space 114, 161; mediation with Labour Party 70, 147; 'moral' 30–3, 227, 245; as organisationally defined 30, 133; reconstruction of 26, 146, 154,

170–96, 306; religious 27, 226–50; rhetoric of 25; romanticising of 114; and social movement formation 33–4; stressed instead of socialism/anti-racism 90; of 'suffering' 26–30; unity disputed 215; *see also* Bangladeshi; ethnic groups; Gujarati; Jain; Pakistani; West Indian

community centres 230; Gujarati 206–7; for Harrow Asians 215, 216, 218, 221; Jain Centre 229–30, 238; and Pakistani community 124–33; Southall 263

community: concept of 113–14; and state funding 115–16; *see also* state/local state

Community Liaison Working Party (CLWP) 211, 212–17

Community Neighbourhood Service, Notting Hill 172

Community organisations: Bangladeshi 86, 99

Community Relations Commission 43

Community Relations Councils (CRCs) 31, 48, 60; Harrow 204, 208, 211, 216, 217–18; opposition to 267; Manchester 133–4

community relations officers 134

Confederation of Indian Organisations 42, 57

Congress Party, and Indian Workers Association (IWA) 262–3

consciousness *see* black; ethnic; historical; political Conservative Party, anti-worker politics 88–9; and Bangladeshis 87; and ethnic minority candidates 54–6; ethnic minority unit 53; and immigration 2; in Leicestershire 151; radical right in 149; and support of ethnic minorities 16; *see also* Labour Party; voting constituencies 16, 17; ideological 84,

93, 99–107; appeal to different 92–3, 95, 97, 99; *see also* ideological; political discourse

councillors, local: Bangladeshi 87 *passim*; creation of forum 60; from ethnic minorities 16, 55–6, 59; as mayors 59, 312; rapid growth of West Indian 312; *see also* Black Sections; ethnic participation in British politics

councils: hidden agenda of 212–15; and racism 213–14; representation of ethnic minorities 16; *see also* Black Sections

criminalisation: of black community/youth 27; *see also* black youth

cultural, autonomy 15, 25, 34, 114, 132, 140; commodities imported by Asians 132; constitution of the economic 34; discourse 182; forms, in relation to social formations 170, 187; historical trends transcending factionalism 131, 190; identity 15, 30, 175, 178; Indian –heritage praised 207; mastery of dominant culture 137; particularistic/universalistic symbols 116, 131, 314; pluralism 28, 307, 316; and political interaction 171–2, 187; 'politics' 117–18; protest 140, and Carnival 176–8, and Rastafarianism 182; resistance 114, 182; role of Jainism 226; society 123–4; and symbolic field of action 34, 77; vitality 20, 147, 272; *see also* black; churches, black-led; discourse; ethnic; institutional completeness; political discourse; ritual; social movements; symbolic

culture: British, self-ascribed homogeneity 161; Caribbean/creole, constructed, transcending races/origin 306–7;

counter-culture 182, 284; and 'institutional completeness' 132; irreducible 189–93; politicised 24, 29, 118, 187, 188, 191; and politics as mutually constitutive 27, 186–7, 188–93; reified 24, 34, 242; role of community 114; Sikh – and IWA split 269–70; West Indian homogeneity 175; West Indian lack of exotic 304; working class/ popular, shared by West Indians 304; *see also* community

demographic characteristics of ethnic groups 3–13; and voting power 44–5; and Asians in Leicester 149–50; *see also* voting
Des Perdes (Punjabi Newspaper) 259, 268
diaspora 24
discourse: ambiguity in 229; appeal to class/community solidarities 84–107, 118, 151, 208; appeal to different constituencies 92–3, 95, 97–9; appeal to localism 89; 211–12 collective, black 167, 214; cultural in reggae 182; during cross-ethnic meetings 212–15, 218–19; ideological, reflecting historical moments 219, 272; official 116, 213–14; political and cultural 16, 17, 24, 90–100, 155–60; radical 24–6 *passim* 90–1; 214–15; as reconstructing experience 155–6; of socialism and anti-racism 91–105, 147; *see also* ideological; political discourse
discrimination 3, 58, 174; in education 11; in housing 11, 208; in labour market 8–10; and law 12; in National Health Service 11; in political parties 58, 59; redressive action policies 12–13
disengagement 296, 303–4; *see also* racial; racial discrimination

dramatic forms 170
East Africa, expulsion of Asians from 205, 206
economic: Asians as active economic agents 150; domain, as culturally constituted 34; deprivation, as cause of racism 88–9; expansion of British ethnic groups 116, 119; and industrial decline 150, 174; post-war boom, 172; inflation of house prices 195; subordination of ethnic groups; *see also* racial discrimination; racism
education: and black-led churches 281, 285; discrimination 11; multi-cultural 242
educational underachievement 11, 180–1
election campaigns: portrayal of class and race 90–1
electoral process: main parties' response to ethnic minorities 45, 52–6; registration 45–8; turn-out 48–9; voting patterns 49–52; *see also under individual parties*, political; voting
Empire Windrush 1
entrepreneurs 117; Gujarati 207; Jains 239; Pakistanis 119
equal opportunities policies 208–10
Ethiopian Orthodox Church 186, 283
ethnic alliances *see* associational; autonomy, struggle for 15, 25, 114, 132, 175; 'centre' 21, 117, 118, 126; consciousness 203 diversity 156; *see* ethnic groups; 'dual orientation' 25, 116–17, 137–41, 208; enclaves/categories, British preference for 305; interests 117–19, 149, 180, 203; jokes 156; monitoring 25–6, 68, 152, 208–10; particularism rejected 63, 66, 74, 296–319; 'politics of race' rejected 77, 253; polyethnic phase of Carnival 172–4, 186; press, role of 43–4,

132; separatism 137, 175, 303–4;
versus 'black' 26–30, 63, 66, 74,
77, 78; *see also* black; ethnic
groups; politics
ethnic boundaries 133, 141, 245; as
changing 115; crossing 117, 186,
207, 304–5; symbolically
articulated 186
ethnic elite: Bangladeshi 86, 96–7;
Bangladeshi 'old' and 'new' 96,
104; black 80; conflicts within
131; dual orientations of 137–41;
Gujarati, emergence of 221;
leadership drawn from 20, 21,
31, 41, 117–18, 178, 179, 180,
221, 238; middle class in IWA
256, 264; new radical 'salariat'
41–110, 138–9; 178–9, 208;
Pakistani business 126, 130,
133–4, 136; Pakistani working
class 124–25; in West Africa 171;
see also class; leadership; social
movements
ethnic groups: political candidates
from 54–6, 58; political
participation in Britain in
mainstream politics 29–30,
44–61, 95–6, 135; *see also*
Conservative Party; Politics;
Labour Party
ethnic groups/segments: collective
responsibility imputed to 316;
corporate ownership by 22–3;
defined 118; demographic
characteristics of in Britain 3–13;
hegemonic struggles within 114,
141, 245; historical redefinition
of 27, 220; historical
reproduction of 117; increasing
influence in Britain 211; internal
class structure, internal divisions
within 20–1, 60, 84, 91, 96
passim, 113–141, 156, 162,
189–96, 217–18, 227, 228; as
non-marginal 203; regarded as
threatening to British society
315; reification of 21, 304–5;
rivalry/competition between 165,

215–18, 245; sacred values of 20;
segmentary structure of 27, 118,
220, 230; settlement patterns in
Britain 3–5; situational definition
of 23, 28, 84, 217; solidarities
presumed 84–5, 114; *see also*
class; communal community;
historical; leadership; politics
ethnicity: contemporary 203;
'politicised' 218–22; as process
117–18, 131, 219;
'professionalisation' of 152;
rejected as basis for political
action 63, 76–8, 297, 304–5, 308,
311, 317; Sikh 269;
transcendence of 316–17;
upsurge of 203; *see also* class;
communal option; cultural
politics; political ethnicity
ethnic identity: Muslim as against
black 165; multiple 220; West
Indian 178, 179; rejected as basis
for political action 304
Ethnic Minority Project, Lewisham
60
ethnic organisations: attempts to
form 43; 'bridging' 133–6, 207,
260; centralisation of 257;
delegitimised among Jain 246;
division between leadership and
members in 241–2; efflorescence
of 15–16, 20–3; as expressing
symbolic divisions 27, 30, 118,
131, 206, 220; federated/national
23, 42, 57, 71 *passim*, 186,
253–72; and group reproduction
117; Gujarati 206–8; ideological
bases of 15, 20; ideological
divisions within 22–3, 84–5, 131,
162, 189–96, 230, 258–70; *see*
ideological; as informally
articulated 186, 196; Jain
226–47; internal rivalry in 229,
253–70; limited legitimacy of
133–6, 186, 215; local versus
territorial 22, 23; militant versus
moderate 268; as mobilising
funding 32, 125–29, 178, 206,

221, 226 *passim*, 238; numbers of 12–13, 42, 56; representation on multi-ethnic committees 133–8, 203–20; rivalry between Bangladeshi 96–7, 104; role in elections 57; West Indian 186; seeking external recognition 267, 269; territorial 22, 125, 161–6; territorial as hierarchical 22, 32; *see also* associational; community; ethnic groups; ethnicity; leadership; racism; social movements

ethnic organisations: developmental processes in 23, 56; Carnival 170–89; Jain temple 237–8; Pakistani associations 56, 113–44; IWA 253–70

ethnic organisations: West Indian, alliance formation 310–11; openness of membership 311, 316; stress on constitutionalism 310; *see also* Afro-Caribbean; West Indian

ethnic organisations and links to the home country 104, 136, 176, 238; of IWA 256, 262–3, 266, 268

ethnic stereotypes 156; of West Indians as failures 312

Evangelical Christians for Racial Justice 289

Evangelical Enterprise 285–6

exclusion process 314

experience: black *see* black experience; of oppression expressed 178; of colonialism/slavery 318; 'politicised' 155–6; of race/generation/gender 158, 166–7; of unemployment 150; *see also* black experience; racism

Federation of Bangladeshi Organisations 42, 57

Federation of Bangladeshi Youth Organisations (FBYO) 96–7, 101; *Jubo Barta* 100, 101

formal leaders 41, 56, 138

fund raising, among Gujaratis

206–7; for the home country 234; among Jains 226–47; among Pakistanis 125–9; *see also* churches, black-led; ethnic organisation/mobilisation of funding

gender: and Black Sections 70, 73–4; and generation 147; as ideological construction 147; and racism 147, 154, 158; *see also* women

generation: male young–old opposition 147; and racism 147, 154; *see also* black youth; gender gifting, competitive 224–6, 247; 'to god' 245–6, 247; *see also* community fund raising; moral; symbolic

gospel music 284

Greater London Council (GLC) 151; anti-racist policies 88; and ethnic minority candidates 55

Gujaratis 16, 203–22, 226–50; and Afro-Caribbeans 215–16; charitable donations 207–8; emergence of activist elite 221–2; and Pakistanis 215–18; political activity 215, 217–18, 221–2; religious centres 207; settlement in Harrow 205–6; voluntary associations 206–8; *see also* Jains

Guyana 307

Handsworth Connection (community newspaper) 285–6

Harrow: equal opportunities policy 208, 212, 218–19; Gujarati settlement in 205–6; 'hidden agenda' among ethnic minorities 215–18; 'hidden agenda' of council 212–15; schemes for ethnic minorities 204–5; Section 11 funding 216–17

hegemony *see* cultural; ideological; political

hidden agenda: among Harrow Asians 215–18; and Harrow council 212–15

Hindu organisations 42
Hiri Development Corporation 245
historical: development of IWA
    256–70; development of West
    Indian community 303–4;
    dimensions of ethnicity 117, 131,
    161; dramaturgical approach
    192; exclusiveness of Englishness
    161; moments expressed in
    political rhetoric 25; movement,
    Carnival as 17°; reproduction of
    ethnic groups 117; role of
    churches in race relations 277;
    self-redefinition 27, 146, 154,
    180–9; utilitarian ahistorical
    approach rejected 253
history: imposing moral
    responsibility 316; varying
    interpretations of 242
homelessness, among Bangladeshis
    101, 107
host society, accommodation with
    42, 60; and protest 42
household size 5, 7
housing of ethnic minorities *see*
    racial discrimination

identity *see* black; cultural; ethnic
ideological: bases of organisations
    15, 22, 182, 253, 254, 261–70;
    constituencies 85; construction
    of British society 302;
    construction of gender and
    generation 147; convergence in
    social movements 15–17;
    divisions in ethnic groups 29, 34,
    84, 261–70; expansion in
    Carnival 177–85; expansion in
    social movements 33; hegemony
    161; premises disputed 205, 214;
    premises shared 272;
    reconstruction 30, 79, 155–7,
    315; sequence challenged 170;
    terrain shifted 166; *see also*
    discourse; political discourse
ideology: of blackness 78, 175, 214,
    314; fetished 24; humanism 302,
    306, 317; of pluralism versus

individualism 315; as prior to
    power/factionalism 131, 253,
    261; rationalist 309–10, 318; as
    transcending leadership
    squabbles 256, 261–70; of
    voluntarist ethnic separatism
    317; and West Indian
    democratic tradition 302,
    309–10, 318; *see also* black,
    definition of
imagined communities 20–3, 26,
    161, 315
immigrant mobility 117
immigration: of minorities 1–3;
    Bangladeshi chain migration 85;
    demographic characteristics
    3–13; Gujaratis in Harrow
    205–6; and migratory labour
    148; regulations 65, 115; voucher
    system 2
immigration controls, pressure
    towards 2; changed gradually 19;
    as expressions of racism 27, 115,
    174
Independents 97, 105, 107;
    Bangladeshis as 86–7, 88, 91,
    93–5; ethnic minority candidates
    as 52, 55, 57; Muslim candidates
    as 58
India: immigration from 1–3
Indian Workers Association (IWA)
    16, 22, 34, 56, 253–74; aims 273;
    Birmingham 256–7; Bradford
    257; centralisation 257; and
    Communist Party 255, 257, 258,
    261, 262–3; Coventry 257, 259;
    development 256–61; and forged
    passports 257, 259–60; (GB) A.
    Jouhal 267, 268, 271, 273–4;
    (GB) N. Noor 269–70, 271;
    (GB) P. Singh 267, 268, 269,
    270, 271; Gravesend 257;
    Huddersfield 257; and Labour
    Party 268; leadership 253–6;
    Leamington 257; Leeds 257;
    London 257; Nottingham 257;
    Nuneaton 257; political work
    260; relationship with state

270–1; and Sikhism 268, 269–70, 271; social work role 257, 260; South Staffordshire 256, 257, 260; Southall 257, 259, 261–5, 270, 271, 272; split (1967) 266–8; split (1983) 269–70; tensions within 259
individualism: and anti-racism 315–16
Inner Aid Programme 237, 238
Inner Area Programme 152, 153
inner city: black youth of 162; decline 30; concentration of ethnic minorities 58; housing problems 11; riots 19, 78, 148, 151–2, 154, 158, 210, 304–5; sense of identity 20, 162; underprivilege 27, 86, 88, 90
Inner City Partnership Fund 124, 129, 285
institutional racism 11, 214; *see also* racism
institutional completeness 113–14, 130–3
interpretive communities 24–6
Islam: World Islam 24; *see also* Muslim community; Rushdie Affair/*Satanic Verses*
Ismailis 206
IWA *see* Indian Workers Association (IWA)

Jain Bhagini Kendra (Jain ladies' circle) 235, 238
Jain Centre, Leicester 228–47
Jain News/The Jain (magazine) 230, 235
Jain Samaj 227–47; *arti* fund 232–3, 240–2; Building Fund 234–5; donation of temple 236, 238–9; funding 230–42; Happiness Fund 235–6; *jivadaya* donations 233–4; leadership 237, 238–9, 241–4; membership fees 231–2; private donations 236; state aid 236–7
Jain Youth 235, 238
Jainism 32, 226, 231; beliefs 242,

243–4; and competitive bidding (*bolavavun*) 239–42, 244–7; *devdravya* donations 230–1, 233; involvement of laity 226; and patronage 226–7, 232, 246–7; role of leaders 226–7; *sadharana* donations 230–1
Jains: Oswals 227, 228, 244, 245; Srimalis 227–47
Jamaica 1, 182, 187
Janata Party: and Indian Workers Association (IWA) 263
Jang (Urdu newspaper) 132
Jewish Board of Deputies 42
Jewish community 19, 84; external definition of 113; politicisation 59

Khalistan 268, 270, 271, 272

Labour Force Survey 8
labour market: discrimination in 8–10; and ethnic minorities 8–10, 86
Labour Party 28, 60; and anti-racism 87–91; and Bangladeshi activists 85, 86–107; Black and Asian Advisory Committee 53, 69, 77, 81; and Black Sections 57, 60, 63–83; and Campaign Against Racial Discrimination (CARD) 24; in confrontation with black groups 160–7; Ethnic Minorities Groups (EMG) 100–1, 102–3; and ethnic minority candidates 54–6, 57; identified with racism 77, 79, 99, 100; ethnic support for 50–2, 57, 70, 149; failure of 80, 86, 102; labourism 152; left–right divisions within 76, 87, 164; in Leicester 149–52, 160–7; links to Indian Workers Association (IWA) 258, 268; as local brokers of the state, 152, 164–6; male domination of 75; Militant 69–70, 81–2; and Muslim communities 84–107; National Executive Committee 53, 165;

need to change 79; and non-conformist churches 279–80; problems of 75; 'race blind' ideology 71; and Red Star Youth Project 162, 163–7; response to ethnic presence 53, 164–6; in Spitalfields 87–91; 'statist' policy 63–4; support for ethnic minorities 50–2, 53; support of ethnic minorities 59, 72; support for Pakistani Cultural Society 126–7; symbolic aspects of entry into 164; Turkish Section 66, 70, 74; Vauxhall by-election (1989) 291; Women's Sections 65, 67; *see also* class; socialism

Labour Party Race and Action Group (LPRAG) 53

labour movement: shared premises 272

labourism 152

language: and Bangladeshi voters 91–5, 97, 98–100, 105

law: and discrimination 12

leaders, individual: of Carnival 172–3, 175, 176, 178–9, 180, 184, 187–90; of Indian Workers Association 254–6, 261, 264, 268–9; Jain 238–9, 242–4, 246; of Manchester Pakistanis 124, 127–9, 137–8; of Red Star 156–7, 163, 164; West Indian 311–12

leadership: and authority 300–1; bureaucratic versus traditional 300–2; charismatic 300–2; commonsense view of 298, 301; and decision-making 298–9; of Labour Party 79; qualities, elusiveness of 301; as situational 301; sociological perspectives of 299–300; types contrasted 277, 300–1

leadership, Caribbean: absence of charismatic 309; absence of traditional 307; adoption of British institutions 308–9

leadership, ethnic/black: alliance of activists 87–91, 99–127, 157–60,

214, 217; as articulating ideological constituencies 85, 156, 189–93; 'black' as against 'ethnic' 30, 214; brokers, access to patronage 17–18, 31, 86, 106, 116, 133–8, 149, 246–7, 254; buffering role 31, 116, 221; as collective process 189, 192; confrontation with state/police 175; context of 1–13; criticised in IWA by successors 255; dilemmas of 34, 135, 246, 270–1; and electoral candidacy 54–6, 217; 'emblematic' 42, 134; as externally determined 134–5, 254; financial dependency on patrons 227, 246–7; 'formal' and 'traditional'/kinbased 41, 56, 85, 138, 157, 255; from the 'centre' 21, 118, 128–9; from the 'periphery' 22, 42, 116, 128–9, 137, 243; increasing role in politics 43, 58–9, 73, 76, 87, 217; intercalary position 17; internally recognised 23; local and national 19; militant 217; moderate 196, 265; multitude of 18; as non-exemplary 17, 137; as 'non-ethnic' among Afro-Caribbeans 297; and number of local councillors 55–6, 70, 88, 92, 98, 151; and office 253–4; 'organic' 21, 157; 'professionalised' 23, 138, 193; qualities/qualifications cited 254, 255; as qualitatively 'different' 253; radical religious 140; representative legitimacy of 207, 215, 217, 272; rivalry between 91–6, 98–9, 125–6, 133–4, 189–93, 253–6; socialisation into mainstream discourses 95–9, 212–15; strategies 247; strength through alliance 31, 126–7; styles 34, 60, 116, 136–41; suspicion of leaders 17, 56, 106, 114, 272, 310; talents 32, 172–3, 176, 189, 255; types among Afro-Caribbeans 303; weakness of 12,

28, 134–5, 141; young 'salariat' 33, 86, 138–9, 157, 217; *see also* black; ethnic elite; ethnic organisations

leadership, West Indian in Britain: growth of political representatives 311–12; as hidden 311–12; individualistic 310; pressed to abandon humanistic tradition 317–18; rejection of ethnicity 305, 313, 316, 317–18; seen as highly assertive 312; universalistic orientation of 314, 316

Leicester 57, 147, 149–52; and ethnic minority candidates 55–6; Jain community 227–30

Leicester City Council 237, 238

Leicester Link 152

Leicester Mercury 154, 162

Leicester Oswal Association 228

Leicester Survey, The 149–50

Liberal Party: and Bangladeshis 88, 101; Community Relations Panel 53; and ethnic minority candidates 54–6; and support of ethnic minorities 50–2, 53, 56–7

liberation theology 19

Lion Youth (masque group) 184–5, 188

Liverpool: opposition to Labour Party Black Sections 81–2

local authorities: and state resources 203–4; *see also* state/local state resource allocation

Local Government Act (1966) 204

locality: as basis for cross ethnic cooperation 171, 157; defence of 152; and discourse 89, 157; movement beyond 159; territorialism 161

London Collective of Black Governors 291

Manchester: mosque project 125–6; provision for Asian culture 132

Manchester Council for Community Relations (MCCR) 133–4

'Mangrove Restaurant Case' 175, 178

Manpower Services Commission 237, 238; Community Programme 285, 286

marginalisation of black youth 148–9

media: and creation of ethnic leaders 254

Methodist Church: ethnic minorities in 288; historical role 282–3

Metropolitan Police 195, 210; on racial attacks 12

mobilisation of organisations 15, 17

modernism: and ethnicity 203

moral: communities 30–4; confusion as regards donating 241; panic 147; *see also* community

Mosque Association (*Jamiat el Muslemin*) 126, 127, 134, 136

mosque project, Manchester 125–6

mugging: and black youth 147–8

mushairas (poetry reading sessions) 124

Muslim community 23, 105–6, 107, 165, 315; and Labour Party 84–107, 165; radical leadership 140; and religious needs of Bangladeshis 94, 98, 106; and demand for religious schools 129–30, 131, 140; *see also* Rushdie Affair/*Satanic Verses*

nation/nationalism: of Bangladeshis 99–100; black people as part of 161; and British colonialism 148; and citizenship 148, 160–6, 314; English, invoked 164, 161; and ethnicity 34; reconstruction of 149, 161; Sikh 269; *see also* state

National Association of Local Government Officers (NALGO) 67, 68

National Black Section: *Seven Steps to Forming a Black Section* 66

National Front 3, 29, 46, 67, 86, 88, 135–6, 147, 151, 174

National Health Service: and discrimination 8, 10, 11

nationhood 160–1, 163–4, 167; changing ideas of 148; and Sikhism 270

Naxalbari uprising, West Bengal 266

New Commonwealth countries: immigration from 1–3

New Testament Church of God 283, 286

Newham 147, 151–2

Newham Eight 155

Notting Hill 173–4, 195

Notting Hill Carnival 15–16, 17, 22, 25, 170–96, 311; artistic importance 180, 185, 187; Carnival and Arts Committee (CAC) 189–91, 193, 194, 196; Carnival Development Committee 175, 180, 188, 189–91; and crime 181, 194–5; development of 171, 172–85; Development Project 193; financial difficulties 196; local opposition to 195–6; manipulation of 171; masque sections 178–80; and police 171, 190, 194–5; as political event 189–93; (1965–70) polyethnic 172–4; preparation for 171, 176, 179–80, 183, 184–5; and reggae music 182–4, 193–4; social importance of 185–6, 187–8, 196; steel bands 174, 177–9, 183–4, 193; (1971–5) Trinidadian-influence 172, 174–80; (1976–9) youth-dominated 180–5; (1981–90) 193–6;

Notting Hill Carnival (magazine) 193, 194

Notting Hill riots 311

One Nation Forum 53, 57

organisations, aims 15; ideological convergence 16–17; localised associative empowerment 15–16; mobilisation 15, 17; stages 15; West Indians' suspicion of 186; *see also* ethnic organisations

Overseas Doctors Association (ODA) 42

Pakistan: immigration from 1–3

Pakistani community 113–41; and Afro-Caribbeans 215–16; attitude to external funding 126; business leaders 126, 134, 140; commercial services 131–2; divisions in 215; and elections 56–7; existence of 113–14; external definition of 113; and Gujaratis 215–18; and 'institutional completeness' 131–2; and mainstream politics 135; political activity 215–16; power-bases 134–6; Punjabi Sunni majority 126; religious organisations 133; and Sikhs 84; state-provided services 132; Urdu speakers 130; voluntary activities 132–3

Pakistani Cultural Society 119, 124–5, 126–7, 130

Pakistani Welfare Association 56, 133

Pan-Africanism 24

Parliamentary Black Caucus 60

pentecostalist churches 282–3, 316

People's Democratic Alliance (PDA) 97

Poale Zion 72, 81

Pocomaniaism 309

poetry 124; and Indian Workers Association (IWA) leadership 255; *see also* Pakistani Cultural Society

police: attacks on black women 20; bias 115; and black youth 148; 166; and Carnival 194–5; inner-city harassment 27; and inner-city riots 151–2, 305; 'Mangrove Restaurant Case' 175, 178; Metropolitan 195, 210; and Notting Hill Carnival 181, 190; and racism 19; *see also* racial discrimination; racism; state

Police and Community Consultative
Committee (PCCC) 210–11
Police and Criminal Evidence Act 12
Policy Studies Institute (PSI) 10
political: activism of Gujaratis
221–2; agenda 24, 260, 304;
agents, blacks as 149–50, 155,
167, 296; alternative links of
black British to –system, 78;
awareness by British of ethnic
minorities 43, 151; black struggle,
in danger of domestication 146,
196; British institutions in West
Indies 308; collective
consciousness 196; construction
of class and community 84–108;
culture, British 95–9; –cultural
dialectic 187–8, 192; –cultural
movement *see* social movements;
disagreements in IWA 253–71;
'ethnicity' 116–18; identities,
individual and collective 146,
155–6, 196; interests 161, 217;
mobilisation through Carnival
175; rational tradition in West
Indies 308–10; recruitment
through networks 103; strategies
20, 89–90, 155, 193; tokenism
58, 63, 66, 107; *see also* cultural;
black
political action: as complex 155;
detached from ethnicity 304;
linked by cultural forms 172
political discourse: of Afro-
Caribbeans 296; British racial
148, 161, 181; innovative 146;
radicalisation of 24, 84–107, 125;
and rhetoric 24–6, 84–107;
socialisation into 95–9, 212–13;
see also discourse
political participation of ethnic
minorities 41–110; registration
and non-registration 45, 46–9;
response to ethnic vote 44, 52–6;
role of minorities increasing 58,
108–9, 165, 304; turnout 48–9;
see also Conservative Party;
Labour Party

politicisation: of ethnic minorities
12, 24; and Red Star Youth
Project 146, 155–60
politics: anti-racist 76, 77, 154; and
culture 188–93; of (ethnic)
difference 165; of
gender/generation 154 *passim*; of
identity 146, 155–60; machismo
style of 158; progressive 77;
reconstructed 74; and ritual
action 170; of resources, 153; *see
also* cultural; ethnic; black
politics, mainstream: entry of black
activists 29, 41–110, 165–6; and
voting 44–52
population: in Leicester 150;
percentage from ethnic
minorities 1; racial origins 4;
settlement patterns of ethnic
minorities 3–5
Poreporena church scheme 244–5
ports: ethnic minority settlement 1
power, political: base expanded 200;
and Black Sections 80; and
culture 188, 192–6; growth of
executive in modern state 298;
and leadership 301; local 15; and
masculinity 158–9; seeking
among Gujaratis 207–8; struggle
for and ethnicity 203;
protest: and accommodation 34, 42,
60, 137–42; Asian/black 147,
152; Carnival as cultural 176,
178, 190; deflected 116; against
lack of electoral representation
55, 71; limits of 317; militant
140; public 152; as 'ritual
gesture' 71; through social
movement 17; *see also* social
movement; cultural; symbolic
Punjabi community 125, 130, 206;
and Indian Workers Association
(IWA) 256–8
Punjabi Sunni majority 137
purposive groups 141
race and class 29, 100; portrayal of
in election campaigns 90–1; *see
also* class; ethnicity

'race relations' 208–10, 298;
assimilationist philosophy 264;
differing views of in IWA 263–4;
'industry' 217–18; role of
churches 277–8
Race Relations Act (1976) 209
race relations 'industry' 217
race relations professionals 32
Race Today (journal) 175, 190
Race Today Collective 184
Racial Adjustment Action Society 43
racial attacks/ violence 3, 12, 19, 65,
86; in Harrow 211; in Notting
Hill 174–5; by police/courts 12,
115, 147–8, 151, 171, 175, 178,
181; *see also* racial harassment
racial categories as unrecognised in
official discourse 27, 30, 71, 100,
148
racial discrimination 154, 209, 309;
in education 11, 180; in housing
11, 27, 68, 208; in the job
market/unemployment 8–10, 27,
149–50, 174, 181, 193, 209, 210;
and electoral politics 58, 63–83,
148; *see also* ethnic monitoring
racial 'dominant cleavage' 27, 154;
electoral backlash 71;
harassment 3, 12, 65, 67, 88–9,
211
Racial Justice (journal) 289
racial tension 174
racism: anti-racist movements 19,
22, 24, 29; consciousness of 71,
124, 154–5; alleged in
community relations councils
214, 216; constituency of 100; as
constitutive of British way of life
151, 214; crude 19; defined as a
series of violations 27, 87;
experience of 26, 27, 28, 146–7,
154–5; as false consciousness
88–9; fight against 24, 29, 34,
63–83, 87–107, 136–48, 260,
272; and gender 147, 154, 158;
and generation 147, 154;
institutional 11; institutional, in
churches 289; institutional

interpretation of 214, 218; in the
Labour Party 70, 71, 76, 99, 100,
102, 166; and the National Front
see National Front; perceived in
local councils 66, 67–9, 213–14;
reductive view of 77, 79; religion
as protection from 140, 284; role
of churches 19; and the role of
the state 146, 149, 154; and
socialism 89, 101–3; and
unemployment *see* racial
discrimination; unofficial and
disguised 19, 214; *see also* black;
churches; class; leadership;
nation; racial
attacks/harassment; state
Racism Awareness Training 214
radical discourses 24–6; *see*
discourse; political discourse
Rastafarianism 171, 172, 182,
184–5, 186, 191, 283, 309, 316
Red Star Hostel 154, 166
Red Star Youth Project 146–7, 149,
151, 152–67; Afro-Caribbean
membership 153; aims 149; and
Labour Party 162, 163–7; Law
Centre 154, 166; occupation of
school 154, 160, 163; and
politicisation 146, 155–60;
politics 154–5
Redbridge Community Relations
Council 180–1
reggae music and 'counter-culture'
182–4
religious transcendence of divisions:
Jain 243; Muslim 25
riots: inner city 19, 78, 148, 151–2,
154, 158, 210, 304–5
ritual: beliefs and practices 171;
competitive giving 239; drama
170; *see also* symbolic
Rochdale ethnic minorities and
election campaigns 56
Rock Against Racism 29, 147
Rushdie Affair/*Satanic Verses* 19,
20, 23, 25, 41, 58, 75, 140, 315;
see also Muslim community

Salvation Army 284

Second World War 1

Section 11 funding 204, 209–10, 216–17; and 'special needs' 218

segmentary divisions 20; as against 'dominant cleavage' 27; *see also* ethnic groups; ethnic organisations

Seventh Day Adventist Church 281, 283, 292

Sex Discrimination Act (1975) 209

Sikhism: fundamentalist 268; and Indian Workers Association (IWA) 256, 268, 269–70, 271; and Pakistanis 84; seen as threat to society 315

Simon of Cyrene Institute 289–90, 291

slavery 282; abolition of 278; and Caribbean leadership 307–8; fight against 306; *see also* colonialism

social field: unbounded 21; *see* symbolic

social movements: African Messianic 184; American Civil Rights 18, 24, 31, 43, 313; British black 29, 32, 43, 152; in the Caribbean 314; Carnival as 17, 171–4, 185–91; co-existing strategies in 34; cultural versus political 189–93; formation 33–4; growth of Carnival 191; in historical perspective 171–2; internal momentum of 173; Labour, in need of change 79; Pan-Africanism/World Islam/ Black Power 24, 29, 175, 191, 303, 313–314; Rastafarianism 185–6; as requiring funding 32, 152, 191; Southall Youth Movement 154–5, 158, 159, 162; stages in 15–17, 33; as two-dimensional 171–2, 189–93; urban 15–19; youth 29, 147

social transformation 170; *see* discourse, ideology

socialism: and anti-racism 101–5,

106–7, 315; disguised as localism 90; extremism 95; in Manchester 126–7; municipal in Leicester 151–2; *see also* class; Labour Party

Socialist Workers Party 69

Southall 44, 147, 151–2; Punjabi community 206; registration for voting 46

Southall Indian Workers Association 22, 257, 259, 261–5, 270, 271, 272

Southall Youth Movement 154–5, 158, 159, 162

sports organisations 16

Standing Conference of Pakistani Organisations (SCOPO) 42, 57

state/local state: articulation with racism and power 148–9, 160 *passim*; and black leadership 18–19; 'communal option' 28, 297; confrontation with 18, 152, 153–4, 160–6, 171, 213; contradictory role of 115, 141, 152, 195; control/intervention by 22, 29 133–9, 152, 160–6, 193–6, 305–6; control/policing of youth 148, 193; creation of buffer institutions 18, 22, 305; creation of ethnic 'fictions' 26, 28, 33, 113–41, 212–15, 254; dependency upon state welfare 86, 99, 107; dialectical interaction with ethnic groups 141, 219; as dominant society 115; employees 33, 86, 208; and ethnic compartmentalisation 297, 302; and ethnicity 203; evasiveness in multi-ethnic committees 212–15; exclusion process 314; growth of the executive in modern 298; legitimation crisis 148; as major employer 210; manipulation of cultural symbols 189; police/black confrontation 175, 181, 194–5; restructured 148, 152

state/local resource allocation 15, 16, 17, 21, 24, 27, 28, 30–4, 107,

114–17, 119–33, 152, 153–4, 203–4, 216–17, 220, 237; to community organisations 86, 98, 152, 204, 220, 237, 265; competition for in Leicester 228; for cultural purposes 132, 183, 185, 191; dilemmas of working in and against 26, 28, 33, 64, 80, 113, 254; as divisive 152, 220; inadequacy of 221; privileged access to 30, 220; rejected by IWAs 271; Section 11 funding 204; symbolic significance of 31, 161; *see also* ethnic monitoring 'statist' strategy of Labour Party 64, 80
steel-band music 174, 177–9, 183-4, 193
Student Non-violent Co-ordinating Committees (SNCC) 313
styles: of leadership *see* leadership; male street 158, 163
suffering communities 26–30
Sukuya (masque band) 180, 184
Supreme Council of Sikhs 42
symbolic: activities, dramatic processes in 170; aspects of body for young men 158; connotations of state allocations 31, 161; connotations of state recognition 134; constitution of the economic domain 34; dimensions of legal confrontation with state 103; ground of political battle 167; incorporation into the nation 32, 161–6; meaning of Jain ritual giving 230–1, 241; objectification of ethnic segments 27; orientations of ethnic groups 116, 137–41; –political field 77, 167; position of black activists 77, 163; referents of Jain Centre 228; significance of Carnival 176–7; of steel pans 177; value of public defiance 163; *see also* ritual
symbols: ambiguous 192; dominant, containing contradictions 177;

shared 137; of Sikhism 269–70

Task Force 286–7
teachers from ethnic minorities 10
technology: and ethnicity 203
temple project 16
Tower Hamlets: Bangladeshi settlement in 85–7
traditional leaders 41, 56, 138
Trinidad 176–7, 181, 184, 307; Carnival 174, 176–7, 180, 187, 194
Twelve Tribes of Israel (Rastafarian group) 184–5, 186

UK Islamic Mission 42
unemployment 8–10, 30, 150–1; in Harrow 210; in Notting Hill 174, 181, 193; youth 164; *see also* racial discrimination
Union of Muslim Organisations (UMO) 42
United Kingdom Immigrants Advisory Service 138
Universal Coloured People's Organisation 43
Urban Aid 215, 220–1
Urban Programme 285
USA: black leadership in 18; Black Power movement 175, 191, 313–14; black voting patterns 59; civil rights movement 24, 29, 31, 42, 43, 58–9, 280; Congressional Black Caucus 60, 81

violence: Carnival born in 177; as defining feature of racism 27; *see also* racial attacks/harassment; riots; state confrontation
vote, ethnic: as non-deliverable 79
voting: of Asians in Harrow 212; of Asians in Leicester 149; of Bangladeshis in Tower Hamlets 86–107; of black people as active agents 148; in mainstream and local elections 42–54, 70–1; registration for 45–8; response to ethnic– by main parties 45, 52–6;

turn-out 48–9; *see also* political participation
voting patterns 49–52, 59; in the USA 59, 79
voucher system in immigration 2

Welfare Societies 135–6, 137
Wesleyan Holiness 283
West Indian Co-ordinating Committee 22
West Indian Standing Committee (WISC) 42, 57, 186, 310, 311
West Indians: attitudes to leadership 41; churches and politics 280–4; and communal option 297, 314–17; cultural homogenisation 187; cultural identity 175–6; educational underachievement 180–1; immigration to Britain 303–4, 306; leadership 297, 298; and majority culture 297, 304–5; and Notting Hill Carnival 173–4; politicisation 185–93, 196;

portrayal of 312; suspicion of organisation 186; *see also* Afro-Caribbeans

West Indies 4–13; immigration from 1–3
white: authority 158; racist gangs 158; *see also* black; racism
women: black, elected as councillors 70; black ministers 290; comparison with black 63; in immigrant communities 2–3, 5; rejection of male dominance of Carnival 184; Sections in the Labour Party 65, 67, 73; *see also* gender
Working Party on Racial Assaults (WPRA) 211
World Islam 24

youth: Bangladeshi 100, 101, 104–5; black, incorporation into Carnival 180–1; and mainstream politics 56; movements 147; and rebellion against elders 160; significance of rowdiness/violence 159, 162–3, 181, 194; *see also* black youth; social movements/youth

Zulu (steel band) 178–9, 188